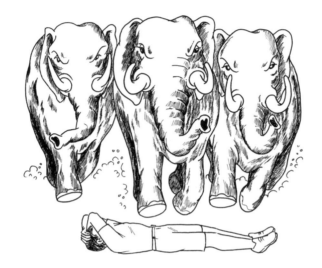

The
ULTIMATE
WORST-CASE SCENARIO
Survival Handbook

The
ULTIMATE
WORST-CASE SCENARIO
Survival Handbook

By David Borgenicht, Joshua Piven & Ben H. Winters

With contributions by Victoria De Silverio, James Grace,
Sarah Jordan, Piers Marchant, Dan and Judy Ramsey,
Sam Stall, and Jennifer Worick

Illustrations by Brenda Brown

CHRONICLE BOOKS
SAN FRANCISCO

Worst-Case Scenario® and The Worst-Case Scenario Survival Handbook™ are trademarks of Quirk Productions, Inc.

Library of Congress Cataloging-in-Publication Data:
Borgenicht, David.
The ultimate worst-case scenario survival handbook / by David Borgenicht, Joshua Piven & Ben H. Winters ; With contributions by Victoria De Silverio ... [et al.] ; illustrated by Brenda Brown.
p. cm.
ISBN 978-1-4521-0828-5
1. Men--Life skills guides--Humor. 2. Survival--Humor. I. Piven, Joshua. II. Winters, Ben H. III. Title.
HQ1090.B673 2012
305.31--dc23
                                                        2012010330

Manufactured in China.

Typseset in Adobe Caslon, Bundesbahn Pi, and Zapf Dingbats.

Designed by Dennis Gallagher and John Sullivan, www.visdesign.com.
Illustrations by Brenda Brown.

Visit www.worstcasescenarios.com

10 9 8 7 6 5 4 3 2 1

Chronicle Books LLC
680 Second Street
San Francisco, California 94107
www.chroniclebooks.com

WARNING

CONTENTS

CHAPTER 2

CRITICAL CONDITIONS: LIFE AND LIMB

CHAPTER 3

SHAKY FOUNDATIONS: HOME AND HEARTH

CHAPTER 4
CAN'T WE ALL JUST GET ALONG?: SOCIAL SCENARIOS

CHAPTER 5

MEAN STREETS: URBAN SURVIVAL

CHAPTER 6

IT'S A JUNGLE OUT THERE: THE NATURAL WORLD

CHAPTER 7

GETTING AROUND: UNSAFE AT ANY SPEED

CHAPTER 8

OH S#&%T!: EXTREME EMERGENCIES

ACKNOWLEDGMENTS

ABOUT THE AUTHORS

First ask yourself:
What is the worst that can happen?

—Dale Carnegie

Failure to prepare is preparing to fail.

—John Wooden

Be brave. Take risks.

—Paul Coelho

INTRODUCTION

It's been more than a dozen years since the first volume of *The Worst-Case Scenario Survival Handbook* was published in 1999. We've sold over 9 million copies worldwide of these handy little life, limb, and sanity-saving guides. We've sold millions more instructional board and video games, and been involved in the creation of two different television series based on our books. Suffice to say, we've taught a lot of folks how to survive some of the worst life holds in store.

And now we have some good news, and some bad news.

Here's the bad news: The world is more dangerous than ever.

From hurricanes to civil unrest, from global warming to shark attacks, from severed limbs to yoga injuries, it seems as if danger lurks around every corner, beneath every surface, behind every Web page. And the fact that we've provided millions of people clear, step-by-step instructions for dealing with life's sudden turns for the worse doesn't seem to have decelerated things. If anything, the speed at which life moves these days, thanks to modern technology, has made things even more dangerous.

We still don't know what's coming our way, and it's heading toward us even faster than ever.

Still, here's the good news: the keys to surviving any of life's sudden turns for the worse are the same as always—Be Prepared. Don't Panic. Have a Plan.

And that's exactly what *The Ultimate Worst-Case Scenario Survival Handbook* aims to give you—tools to use and remember. (In addition to the clearest instructions available for surviving everything from jellyfish and zombies to honeymoons and brake failures.)

Be Prepared. This means thinking through what you'll need to do, take, and learn prior to any adventure or journey you set off on. Heading off into the mountains alone? Be sure to let your friends and family know where you're going and when you'll return, and to take the right equipment and supplies. Heading out for a blind date? Be sure you have an escape plan if it turns out to be a disaster. Heading out on a boat trip? Make sure you know how to make an emergency floatation device out of your pants. You're already tilting the odds in your favor.

Don't Panic. This means just what it says—don't freak out when something happens, expected or unexpected. Panicking means you'll be breathing heavily, which means you'll be expending unnecessary energy and not getting enough oxygen to your brain and muscles, which means you'll almost certainly make a mistake, or lose strength or judgment right when you need it the most (as the rhino starts to charge, or as your Powerpoint falters during the biggest presentation of your career). Take three deep breaths (filling your abdomen first, then your chest, then exhaling fully), then act.

Have a Plan. Or, if you don't have one in advance, formulate one. And quickly. Use your common sense, your instinct, and the information within this book to plan a course of action. And then be ready with Plan B in case Plan A doesn't work.

Conveniently, this book contains not only enough Plan As for your journey through life, but also Plans B, C, D, and far down into the alphabet—all from experts in the subjects at hand, as recorded by accomplished journalists and writers. *The Ultimate Worst-Case Scenario Survival Handbook* presents new scenarios, illustrations, charts, and the most up-to-date survival tips, and also draws on the most useful information from the full range of the series' handbooks, almanacs, pocket guides, and other books.

When the time comes—when you're faced with that act-now-and-get-it-right crisis—we want you to know what to do, and that's why we've written this book. We want you to know all the marine creatures that can kill you without using their teeth, and how you can create a signal fire on a deserted desert island. We want you to be able to find and destroy bedbugs in a hotel room, to be able to bind an alligator's jaws, and to fend off an attacker—whether the attacker is using a fist, knife, chair, or golf club. And we want you to know how to sneak in late to a meeting and many, many other useful skills.

Because even after a dozen years, and after all the advice we've provided, you just never know what life will bring. And we want you to survive!

—The Authors

1
Tooth and Claw

ANIMAL ENCOUNTERS

ALLIGATORS

How to Wrestle Free from an Alligator

1 If you are on land, get on the alligator's back and put downward pressure on its neck.

This will force its head and jaws down.

2 Cover the alligator's eyes.

This will usually make it more sedate.

3 Go for the eyes and nose.

If you are attacked, use any weapon you have, or your fist.

4 If its jaws are closed on something you want to remove (a limb), tap or punch it on the snout.

Alligators often open their mouth when tapped lightly. They may drop whatever it is they have taken hold of and back off.

5 If the alligator gets you in its jaws, you must prevent it from shaking you or from rolling over—these instinctual actions cause severe tissue damage.

Try to keep the mouth clamped shut so the alligator does not begin shaking.

6 Seek medical attention immediately, even for a small cut or bruise, to treat infection.

Alligators have a huge number of pathogens in their mouths.

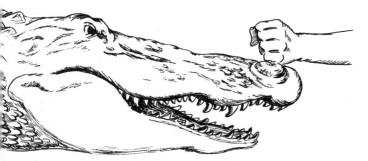

To get an alligator to release something it has in its mouth, tap it on the snout.

> An alligator more than nine feet long is likely to be male, and males tend to be more aggressive.
>
> —*Bill Finger, professional alligator breeder*

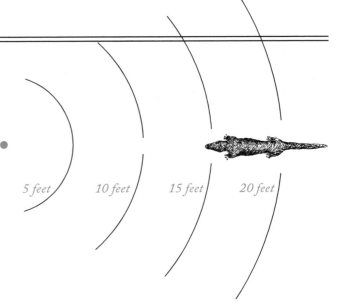

The immediate danger zone is within 15 feet of the alligator.

How to Retrieve an Object near an Alligator

1 Determine the size of the alligator.

Although even small alligators can cause injury, those less than four feet long are not as dangerous to humans. If the alligator is larger than six feet, be especially wary, as a bite can inflict major damage. Alligators larger than nine feet should be considered deadly.

2 Calculate the distance from the alligator to the object.

The immediate danger zone is within 15 feet of an alligator.

3 Try to determine if the alligator sees the object.

Alligators are attracted to objects that appear to be food.

4 Do not stand between the alligator and water.

If disturbed, an alligator on land will seek refuge in water. Make sure the alligator is between you and any nearby water.

5 Make a loud noise.

Alligators are sensitive to loud noises. Yelling or screaming may cause the animal to leave. If the alligator does not move, however, you will have gained its attention.

6 Use a long branch, pole, or golf ball retriever to recover the object.

The alligator may lunge and bite at objects that invade its space.

7 Quickly move away from the alligator's territory.

After retrieving the object, or if you encounter difficulties, run. While alligators can move fast—they rely on surprise when attacking their usual prey—they generally will travel only short distances and probably cannot outrun an adult human.

WARNING!

- Alligators are native only to the United States and China. They are commonly found in the southwestern United States, primarily the Gulf Coast states but as far north as North Carolina.

- You are most likely to be attacked in or at the edge of water.

- The top speed of large alligators is around 10 miles per hour.

- Be especially wary during spring months, when alligators wander in search of mates, and during late summer, when eggs hatch. Mother alligators will respond aggressively to threats to their young, and any adult alligator may come to the aid of any youngster.

- Do not assume any alligator is safe to approach. While some animals may be habituated to the presence of humans, alligators are wild animals and therefore unpredictable: they may attack without provocation.

How to Bind an Alligator's Jaws

1 Approach the alligator from behind.

2 Straddle the creature's back.
Wrap your knees firmly around the midsection of the alligator.

3 Crawl your way up to the head.

4 Cover the alligator's eyes with a cloth.
Use a thick piece of fabric or your own clothing to drape over the eyes of the beast.

5 Push the alligator's snout down to close its mouth.
Lean forward and press firmly down on the snout until the mouth is tightly closed.

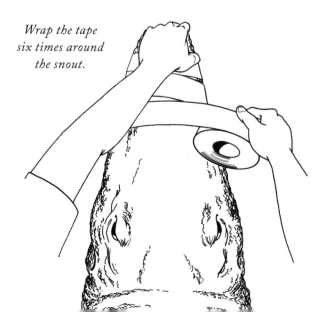

Wrap the tape six times around the snout.

Who Has the Most Bite?

ANIMAL	NUMBER OF TEETH
whale	0
red-bellied piranha	20, in two rows of 10 (the sharpest teeth in the world)
lion	30: four canine, four carnassial, the rest conical
human being	32
sloth bear	40
bear	42, including four canines and 12 incisors
saltwater crocodile	68 to 70
alligator	80 to 88
giant armadillo	up to 100
gavial (fish-eating crocodile)	102
long-spouted spinner dolphin	up to 252
great white shark	up to 3,000 in five rows (the scariest mouth)
snail	10,000 to 30,000 (toothlike structures called radulae)

6 Clamp the jaws.
Press down with your thumbs on the top and hold your fingers tightly underneath. The muscles that alligators use to open their jaws are actually quite weak, so it is possible to hold the mouth shut with bare hands.

7 Take out your binding material.
Maintaining your grip on the gator's snout with one hand, grab your duct tape and tug free a two-foot strip with your teeth.

8 Wind the tape six times around the alligator's snout.

WARNING!

- Lacking duct tape, you should bind the jaws of an alligator with rope, belt, thick cloth (heavy shirt or pants), or any other material that can be tied and knotted.

- Never approach an alligator head-on when its mouth is open.

CHARGING ANIMALS

A charging rhino may avoid a noisy target.

How to Escape from a Charging Rhino

⊘ Climb a tree.

⊘ Run for scrub.

A rhino probably will not follow you into thick scrub brush. Get as far in as possible. Adrenaline will prevent you from noticing the painful thorns until you try to get out.

Average Speed of Charging Animals

ANIMAL	TOP SPEED
Asian elephant	15 mph
hippo	20 mph
African elephant	25 mph
grizzly bear	35 mph
wolf	35 mph
rhino	35 mph
coyote	40 mph
horse	50 mph
moose	50 mph
pronghorn antelope	61 mph
duck and goose	70 mph
cheetah	72 mph
peregrine falcon	200 mph and up in full swoop

⊘ Stand your ground and shout.

If no tree or scrub is available to allow your escape, stand and face the animal (rhinos have poor eyesight but are attracted to movement). As the rhino approaches, scream and shout as loud as you can. A charging rhino may veer away from a noisy target.

⊘ Run in the opposite direction.

A rhino will continue running in the same direction when it is charging and is not likely to turn around and come back for another attack. Once you have evaded the charge and the rhino has veered off, run in the opposite direction.

WARNING!

⚡ A surprised or startled rhino's first instinct is to charge a threat, whether real or imagined.

⚡ A mother rhino will aggressively defend a calf by charging any and all threats.

⚡ Rhinos can climb steep slopes and will also charge into water or mud.

⚡ A rhino will charge and attack a vehicle and may chase one for more than a mile. A large male (5,000 pounds or more) can easily knock over a car.

⚡ African black rhinos are generally considered the most dangerous and likely to charge, though white and Indian rhinos will also charge. Javan and Sumatran rhinos are smaller, shier, forest dwelling, and considered less dangerous to humans.

⚡ A white rhino's anterior (front) horn can be as long as 62 inches.

How to Escape from a Charging Bull

1 Do not antagonize the bull, and do not move.
Bulls will generally leave humans alone unless they become angry.

2 Look around for a safe haven—an escape route, cover, or high ground.
Running away is not likely to help unless you find an open door, a fence to jump, or another safe haven—bulls can easily outrun humans. If you can reach a safe spot, make a run for it.

3 If a safe haven is not available, remove your shirt, hat, or another article of clothing.
Use this to distract the bull. It does not matter what color the clothing is. Despite the colors that bullfighters traditionally use, bulls do not naturally head for red—they react to and move toward movement, not color.

4 If the bull charges, remain still and then throw your shirt or hat away from you.
The bull should head toward the object you've thrown.

If You Encounter a Stampede

If you encounter a stampede of bulls or cattle, do not try to distract them. Try to determine where they are headed, and then get out of the way. If you cannot escape, your only option is to run alongside the stampede to avoid getting trampled. Bulls are not like horses and will not avoid you if you lie down—so keep moving.

If you cannot find safe cover from a charging bull, remove articles of clothing and throw them away from your body.

How to Fend Off a Charging Reindeer

1 Stand your ground.
Most reindeer have been bred to be docile livestock; they are sometimes referred to as "tundra cows." They will run around, rather than over, a standing person, even when charging in a herd.

2 Watch for reindeer in rut.
Reindeer mate from late August to October, when they are in rut, or heat, and much more dangerous. Each male, or bull, will keep a harem of females and will become unpredictable and aggressive with any person who approaches. While both male and female reindeer have antlers, male reindeer are noticeably larger, weighing 400 pounds or more. During rut, necks on males will be large and swollen.

3 Watch for front-leg kicking.
When disturbed, reindeer will rear up on the hind legs and kick out with the front hooves. Females are generally not dangerous except when defending calves. Stay well back and to the side to avoid being kicked. During rut, reindeer bulls will try to gore rather than kick, if antagonized.

4 Watch for antler display.
Before goring, a male will often attempt to intimidate by showing, or "presenting," his antlers, turning his head to the side. Be wary in approaching or cornering a bull reindeer during this display.

5 Back up slowly.
Speak to the reindeer in a soft voice. Do not make any sudden movements.

6 Do not raise your arms over your head.
The bull may take this as a challenge and a sign that you are also displaying antlers.

7 If the reindeer attempts to gore you, grab the antlers.
Grasp one branch with each hand and attempt to steer the head away from you. If the reindeer tries to lunge forward, you may not be able to stop it, but guiding the antlers may allow you to redirect its charge.

8 Move to the side quickly as you release the antlers.
The reindeer will now be beside you and may just move away. Do not run, or you will call attention to yourself. Carefully put distance between yourself and the reindeer.

9 Call for help.
Using a voice and tone that does not further antagonize the reindeer, advise others in the area of your situation. They may be able to distract the reindeer, if it is still in pursuit.

RUNAWAY ANIMALS

Hang on tight and pull the reins to one side to make the camel run in a circle. It will stop on its own.

HOW TO CONTROL A RUNAWAY CAMEL

1 Hang on to the reins—but do not pull them back hard in an attempt to stop the camel.

A camel's head, unlike that of a wayward horse, cannot always be pulled to the side to slow it down. Camels are usually harnessed with a head halter or nose reins, and pulling on the nose reins can tear the camel's nose—or break the reins.

2 If the camel has sturdy reins and a head halter, pull the reins to one side to make the camel run in a circle.

Do not fight the camel; pull the reins in the direction in which the camel attempts to turn its head. The camel may change direction several times—let it do so.

3 If the camel has nose reins, just hang on tight.

Use the reins for balance, and grip with your legs. If there is a saddle, hold on to the horn.

4 Hold on until the camel stops.

Whether the camel is running in circles or in a straight path, it will not run very far. The camel will sit down when it grows tired.

5 When the camel sits, jump off.

Hold on to the reins to keep it from running off.

Ways to Calm a Spooked Horse

- Don't be tense; the horse will be more scared if she thinks you are.
- Hold your hands palms-up.
- Approach slowly, talking in a soft and firm voice.
- Do not reward the skittish behavior with kindness (saying "there, there," etc.).
- Distract the horse.
- Bring a confident, nonspooked horse to stand nearby.
- Be patient; horses can take a long time to recover from being spooked.
- Reward brave behavior, giving a treat and kind words when the horse stops being scared.

Sit up in the saddle as much as you can.
Fight the instinct to lean forward.

How to Stop a Runaway Horse

1 Hold on tight to the saddle with your hands and thighs.
Most injuries occur when the rider is thrown, falls, or jumps off the horse and hits the ground or some immovable object, such as a tree or fence post.

2 Grip the saddle horn or the front of the saddle with one hand and the reins with the other.
If you have lost hold of the reins, hold on to the saddle horn or the horse's mane and wait for the horse to slow or stop.

3 Sit up in the saddle as much as you can.
Fight the instinct to lean forward (it will be especially strong if you are in a wooded area with many trees and branches), since this is not the standard position for a rider when the horse is asked to stop (whoa!), and the horse can feel the difference. Keep a deep seat, with your feet pushed a little forward in the stirrups.

4 Alternately tug and release the reins with a medium pressure.
Never jerk or pull too hard on the reins of a horse running at full speed—you could pull the horse off balance, and it may stumble or fall. There is a very high risk of serious injury or death if the horse falls while running at full speed (25 to 30 mph).

Kicked by a Zebra

Move back: Zebras kick with their hind legs when they are followed too closely, or with the front legs as a defensive measure. The zebra's powerful hindquarters can deliver a kick with force sufficient to break a crocodile's jaw.

How to Dismount from a Rearing and Bucking Horse

Kick your feet out of the stirrups and release the reins. Throw your arms around the neck of the horse as it rears backward. Maintain your grasp and slide around the side of the horse, land on your feet, and push away from the horse to avoid being trampled. This maneuver is known as an emergency dismount.

5 When the horse slows down to a slow lope or a trot, pull one rein to the side with steady pressure so that the horse's head moves to the side, toward your foot in the stirrup.
This maneuver will cause the horse to walk in a circle. The horse will become bored, sense that you are in control again, and slow to a near stop.

6 When the horse is at a walk, pull back with slow, steady pressure on both reins until the horse stops. Dismount the horse immediately, before it has a chance to bolt again. Hold the reins as you get down to keep the horse from moving.

WARNING!

- Long reins dangling in front of a horse may cause it to trip. Inexperienced riders should tie the ends of the reins together so that they cannot fall past the horse's neck and pose added danger.

- Horses bolt when they are frightened or extremely irritated. The key response is to remain in control of the situation without causing the horse greater anxiety. Talk to it reassuringly and rub its neck with one hand. Yelling, screaming, and kicking the horse will only make it more agitated.

DOGS

How to Silence a Barking Addict

✪ **Give your dog more attention.**
Many canines bark out of loneliness. Increased quality time with your pet can help mitigate her tendency to vocalize.

✪ **Give your dog less attention.**
Do not comfort a barking dog. Do not reinforce the idea that making noise reaps benefits.

✪ **Use negative reinforcement techniques.**
Startle the dog in mid-bark by rattling a soft drink can filled with a handful of coins. At the same time, say "Quiet!" in a firm voice. Eventually the dog will respond to the command alone.

✪ **Do not shout at the dog.**
Remain calm. If the dog barks because she believes she is defending her territory, seeing her owner become agitated will only reinforce her view that defense is warranted.

✪ **Introduce your dog to people she finds threatening.**
Dogs will bark at frequent visitors such as mail carriers. Arrange a face-to-face "meet and greet" with such regular strangers. If the canine sees the person as a known quantity, she may respond less aggressively. Closely supervise such meetings.

Introduce your dog to people she finds threatening.

✪ **Reward silence in your absence.**
Walk out the front door as if you are going somewhere. Say "Quiet" to your dog as you leave. When the dog begins to bark, step back in and say "Quiet" again. Leave once more. Only return when the dog is silent—even if she is silent only for a few seconds.

Household Items That Are Toxic to Canines

U.S. pennies	One-cent coins minted since 1982, which contain high concentrations of zinc, can cause anemia and kidney and liver failure.	Macadamia nuts	Can cause depression, weakness, muscular stiffness, vomiting, tremors, elevated heart rate.
Chocolate	The darker the variety, the more dangerous; theobromine, a natural stimulant found in chocolate, can cause arrhythmia, seizures, muscle tremors, and coma.	Raisins and grapes	Can cause renal failure in dogs who eat large amounts.
		Tobacco	Can cause severe vomiting, elevated heart rate, blood pressure drops, seizures, respiratory failure.
Onions	Can cause destruction of red blood cells, triggering severe anemia.	Alcohol	Even small amounts can cause alcohol poisoning; the smaller the dog, the greater the danger.
Garlic	Can also trigger severe anemia.	Mistletoe	Triggers gastrointestinal disorders and cardiovascular collapse.
Antifreeze	Dogs are attracted by its sweet taste; very toxic.		

How to Give a Dog a Pill

1 Sit on the floor in front of your dog.
Place smaller dogs on your lap.

2 Grasp the dog's head using your nondominant hand.
Be firm but not harsh. Place your hand on top of the muzzle, with your thumb on one side and fingers on the other.

3 Raise the dog's nose.
Squeeze firmly behind the canine or "eye" teeth until the jaw opens.

4 Place the pill between the thumb and forefinger of your dominant hand.
Use the hand's other three fingers to open the lower jaw further.

5 Place the pill far back in the dog's mouth.

6 Close the mouth.

7 Tilt up the chin.
Keep the mouth closed and stroke the throat to help with swallowing.

8 Give the dog a treat.

BE AWARE!

- Blowing on the nose may stimulate the dog to swallow.

- Hiding the pill in peanut butter or some other treat the dog covets is the easiest way to administer a pill. However, some canines become quite adept at eating the treat and leaving the pill.

Use your hand to keep the dog's mouth closed after placing the pill in his mouth.

How to Clean Dog Poop Off a Shoe

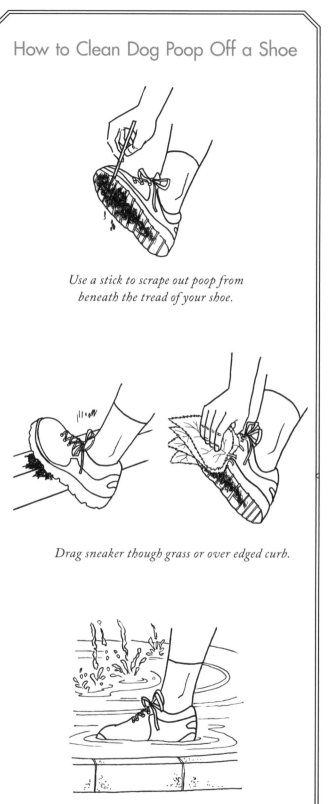

Use a stick to scrape out poop from beneath the tread of your shoe.

Drag sneaker though grass or over edged curb.

Dip shoe bottom into park fountain.

Emergency Rain Gear

Cut or tear holes in a plastic shopping bag for the dog's paws and head. Use a kitchen- or yard-sized bag for larger breeds. Carefully slip the bag over the dog's head, and ease the front and back paws through the holes.

THANK YOU

HAVE A NICE DAY

How to Get Rid of Skunk Odor on Your Dog

1 Keep the dog outside.

2 Flush the dog's eyes with water.

3 Change your clothes and remove jewelry.
The compound used to remove skunk odor can discolor fabric and, in contact with metals, irritate skin.

4 Prepare special odor-removing wash.
Mix 1 quart of 3 percent hydrogen peroxide with ¼ cup of baking soda and 1 teaspoon of liquid dish soap. Ingredients will bubble furiously when combined. This quantity is sufficient for a medium-sized dog. A larger canine may need more.

5 Apply mixture immediately.
Use the odor-removing compound while still foaming, as this is when it is most effective. Place dog in bathtub or outdoor tub and work mixture into fur, avoiding mouth and eyes. Leave for several minutes or until the foaming stops, then rinse thoroughly. Reapply if odor persists.

6 Dry the dog.

7 Repeat washing, if necessary.
This treatment can irritate a dog's skin, so wait at least 48 hours before bathing a second time.

WARNING!

- Skunk spray consists of the ejected contents of the animal's anal glands. A freshly sprayed canine can transfer the scent to carpet, furniture, and anything else he brushes against. The odor can cause nausea and dizziness in humans.

- Discard the dog's collar or harness. It will spread skunk odor to anything it touches and isn't worth the extensive effort it would take to deodorize it.

- Skunks can carry rabies. Examine your pet for bites.

How to Give a Dog CPR

1 Position the dog on her side.
The back is better for barrel-chested breeds. Make sure the dog is on a firm surface.

2 Kneel next to the dog.

3 Compress the chest.
For small dogs, place your palm and fingertips over the ribs at the point where the elbow meets the chest. Compress the chest approximately one inch, twice per second. Alternate every five compressions with one breath. For medium to large dogs, extend your elbows and cup your hands on top of each other. Place hands over the ribs at the point where the dog's elbows meet the chest; then compress it two to three inches, two times per second. Alternate every five compressions with one breath. For dogs that weigh more than 100 pounds, compress the chest two or three inches once per second, alternating every 10 compressions with a breath.

4 Check for a heartbeat.
After one minute, listen for a heartbeat. If none is found, continue with compressions.

To give artificial respiration, tilt the dog's head back, place hand around the muzzle, put your mouth over the nose, and breathe into the dog's nose.

SEA ANIMALS

HOW TO ESCAPE FROM A GIANT OCTOPUS

1 Pull away quickly.

In many cases, a human can escape from the grasp of a small- to medium-sized octopus by just swimming away. Propel yourself forward to create a pulling pressure on the octopus's arms. If you cannot get away, or if you feel yourself being pulled back, continue to the next step.

2 Do not go limp.

Octopi are naturally curious and, if strong enough, will check to see if you are a food item before letting you go. Do not act passively, or you may be bitten or quickly enveloped by the octopus's web, a flexible sheath used to trap prey. Once you are caught in a "web-over," escape will be extremely difficult. However, octopi tire easily, so continue to put pressure on the arms by attempting to swim away. The octopus may decide to let you go rather than bring you in for a closer look.

3 Prevent the octopus's arms from wrapping around your arms.

Initially, the octopus will secure itself to a rock or coral formation and reach out to grab you with just one or two arms. Once it has a firm grip on you, it will move you toward its mouth (called a "beak") by transferring you to the next sucker up the arm. Do not allow the first two octopus arms to pin your own arms to your sides, or you will have little chance of fighting it off.

4 Peel the suckers from your body.

Using your hands, start at the tip of each octopus arm and remove each successive sucker from your body, like peeling up a bath mat. Once you have loosened one of the octopus's arms, give it a spear, raft, surfboard, or other object to latch on to. Work quickly, before the suckers reattach to your body or the octopus's other arms have a chance to grab you.

5 Detach the octopus from its anchor.

Using the sucker removal method described in step 4, separate the octopus from its anchor. Octopi prefer to be anchored to a fixed object and may swim away once dislodged.

6 Turn somersaults in the water.

If you have detached the octopus from its mooring but are still being held, turn your body in circles in the water to irritate it into releasing you.

Peel the suckers starting from the tip of the octopus's arm.

7 Swim toward the surface.

Octopi dislike air intensely and will release you once they break the surface. Continue to peel the octopus's suckers from your body as you swim.

BE AWARE!

- A giant Pacific octopus may be well over 100 pounds, with an arm span of 23 feet.

- Giant octopi are extremely strong but do not constrict prey to kill: they tear victims with their sharp beaks.

- Giant Pacific octopi are not poisonous, though bites may become infected.

- Octopi typically eat crabs and clams, though they may eat fish and birds, and may bite anything.

- Without training or free-diving experience, a swimmer will typically be able to hold his or her breath for only about a minute before losing consciousness.

How to Fend Off a Shark

1 Hit back.

If a shark is coming toward you or attacks you, use anything you have in your possession—a camera, a probe, a harpoon gun, your fist—to hit the shark's eyes or gills, which are the areas most sensitive to pain.

2 Make quick, sharp, repeated jabs in these areas.

Sharks are predators and will usually only follow through on an attack if they have the advantage, so making the shark unsure of its advantage in any way possible will increase your chances of survival. Contrary to popular opinion, the shark's nose is not the area to attack, unless you cannot reach the eyes or gills. Hitting the shark simply tells it that you are not defenseless.

How to Avoid an Attack

✪ Always stay in groups.
Sharks are more likely to attack an individual.

✪ Do not wander too far from shore.
This isolates you and creates the additional danger of being too far from assistance.

✪ Avoid being in the water during darkness or twilight hours.
Sharks are most active and have a competitive sensory advantage in low light.

✪ Do not enter the water if you are bleeding from an open wound or if you are menstruating.
Sharks are drawn to the smell of blood, and their olfactory ability is acute.

✪ Do not to wear shiny jewelry.
The reflected light resembles the sheen of fish scales.

✪ Avoid waters with known effluence or sewage and those being used by sport or commercial fishermen, especially if there are signs of baitfish or feeding activity.
Diving seabirds are good indicators of such activity.

✪ Use extra caution when waters are murky.
Avoid showing any uneven tan lines or wearing brightly colored clothing—sharks see contrast particularly well.

✪ If a shark shows itself to you, it may be curious rather than predatory.
It will probably swim on and leave you alone. If you are under the surface and lucky enough to see an attacking shark, then you do have a good chance of defending yourself if the shark is not too large.

✪ Scuba divers should avoid lying on the surface.
They may look like a piece of prey to a shark, and from there they cannot see a shark approaching.

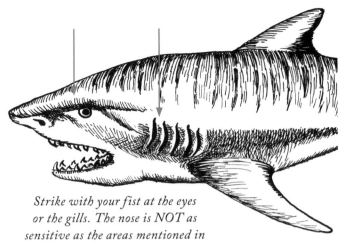

Strike with your fist at the eyes or the gills. The nose is NOT as sensitive as the areas mentioned in step 1, a common misconception.

✪ A shark attack is a potential danger for anyone who frequents marine waters, but it should be kept in perspective. Bees, wasps, and snakes are responsible for far more fatalities each year, and in the United States the annual risk of death from lightning is 30 times greater than from a shark attack.

WARNING!

Most shark attacks occur in nearshore waters, typically inshore of a sandbar or between sandbars, where sharks feed and can become trapped at low tide. Areas with steep drop-offs are also likely attack sites. Sharks congregate in these areas, because their natural prey congregates there.

Three Kinds of Shark Attacks

"Hit and run" attacks are by far the most common. These typically occur in the surf zone, where swimmers and surfers are the targets. The victim seldom sees its attacker, and the shark does not return after inflicting a single bite or slash wound.

"Bump and bite" attacks are characterized by the shark initially circling and often bumping the victim prior to the actual attack. These types of attacks usually involve divers or swimmers in deeper waters, but also occur in nearshore shallows in some areas of the world.

"Sneak" attacks differ: the strike can occur without warning. With both "bump and bite" and "sneak" attacks, repeat attacks are common, and multiple and sustained bites are the norm. Injuries incurred during this type of attack are usually quite severe, frequently resulting in death.

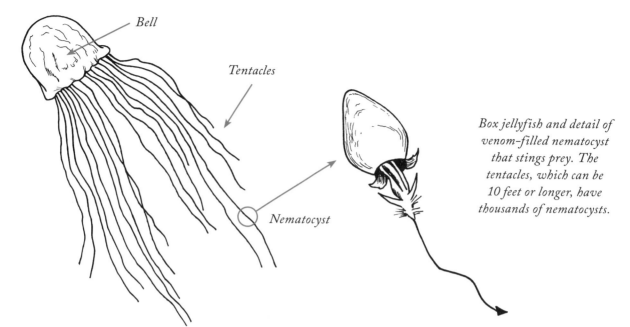

Box jellyfish and detail of venom-filled nematocyst that stings prey. The tentacles, which can be 10 feet or longer, have thousands of nematocysts.

Bell

Tentacles

Nematocyst

How to Survive a Jellyfish Sting

1 Leave the water.

2 Rinse the affected skin with seawater.
Thoroughly flush the affected portions of your body with handfuls or bucketfuls of seawater. Do not rinse with freshwater, rub sand on the skin, or urinate on the stung area, as these actions might cause any nematocysts left behind to fire secondary venom.

3 Pour white vinegar on the affected area.
Vinegar prevents additional toxins from being released.

4 Carefully remove any remaining tentacles.
Lift the tentacles off your skin with a towel or tweezers, or scrape them off with the edge of a credit card or seashell. Do not use your hand or foot, or you risk those areas being stung. Examine your swimwear as well as your flesh for stray tentacles.

5 Do not go back in the water.
Jellyfish often travel in a group, formally called a "bloom" or "smack" of jellyfish, and so it is not uncommon to be stung more than once.

6 Take over-the-counter pain medications such as acetaminophen or aspirin as needed.

WARNING!

⚡ If left on your skin, tentacles will keep stinging until the nematocysts are used up, so rapid removal is important.

⚡ Dispose of tentacles carefully. Don't allow them to get on your clothes, on a beach chair or towel, or anywhere they might be unwittingly stepped on.

Marine Creatures That Can Kill You Without Teeth

ANIMAL	HABITAT	WEAPONRY	CONSEQUENCE
Box jellyfish	Great Barrier Reef and eastern Australia	Dozens of tentacles as long as 10 feet, containing a deadly venom	Poison affects heart and lungs; can kill in minutes.
Surgeonfish	Tropics and coral reefs	Razor-sharp spines in tail	Spines can cause bloody wounds with high chance of infection.
Rabbitfish	Coral reefs in the Indian and Pacific oceans	Venomous spines in fins	Poison can kill even after fish is dead and on butcher's block.
Cone shell snail	Tropics and coral reefs	Harpoon-like barb	Barb injects a paralyzing venom powerful enough to kill a human.
Barracuda	Tropical waters	Ciguatera toxin	Kills humans who eat flesh of infected fish.

BIRDS

How to Survive a Bird Attack

1 Watch for hovering and clacking.
To intimidate predators, many species will hover and clack their beaks before attacking. If you observe this behavior, be ready for a bird attack.

2 Close your eyes and cover your ears.
A bird will swoop down quickly, striking at the head or shoulders with its wings or beak.

3 Run for cover away from nesting and foraging areas.
If on a golf course, run as fast as you can onto the green or fairway and away from the area, most likely in the rough, that the bird is protecting. Many species will attack if their nests or foraging areas are disturbed, even incidentally. If a bird attacks, it will continue to attack until you leave these areas. Continue to cover your ears while running.

WARNING!

⚡ Wearing a hat can offer some protection to your head against attacks.

⚡ Ducks and geese are notorious for going after people. They can approach noisily, heads high. When attacking, they will lower their heads, hiss, and charge, and they can tear exposed flesh with their sharp beaks.

Shield your eyes and face with your arm. With your other hand, grab the bird's feet and legs from behind, pull it from your hair, and lightly toss the bird away from you. Do not attempt to grab the head or beak.

Limit contact with the outside world—especially with birds.

How to Survive a Bird Flu Outbreak

1 Wash your hands frequently.
Hand-washing is your best defense against all strains of virulent influenza, including bird flu. Wash hands, including wrists, in a soapy lather for 20 seconds and dry with a paper towel. In addition, carry an alcohol-based hand sanitizer with you and use it regularly.

2 Get a pneumonia vaccine.
Bird flu victims, especially those who are elderly or have chronic illnesses, often suffer the most serious consequences from a secondary pneumonia infection.

3 Wear glasses or goggles.
Your eyes are the window through which many germs enter your body. When at risk of exposure to bird flu, protect your eyes.

4 Wear a respirator.
When in public places, don a hospital-grade respirator. The commonly worn surgical masks actually have little chance of protecting from the germs that carry bird flu.

5 Do not touch birds.
Do not handle poultry, and if you eat it, cook it to a temperature of at least 165° Fahrenheit.

6 Take recommended antiviral medication.
Prescription medications such as Tamiflu have been successfully used in the prevention and treatment of avian flu.

7 Limit contact with the outside world.
If a bird flu outbreak is spreading quickly, normal human interaction can put you in danger. Work from home, and do not socialize.

8 Consult a doctor if you or someone close to you has symptoms.
Immediate medical treatment is the best way to fight bird flu once the virus has been contracted.

WARNING!

✏ Do not rely on the current seasonal flu vaccine as a safeguard, as newer strains of avian flu are constantly evolving.

CLEANING OFF BIRD POOP

CAR
Spray car with water to wash away loose droppings and to soften the hardened ones. Dribble cleaning fluid—preferably a natural one, such as a citrus-based cleaner—onto the remaining droppings and let dissolve. Apply additional cleaner onto a soft cloth and gently scrub. Spray car with water.

PATIO
Using a high-pressure sprayer attachment, blast the surface with a garden hose to remove dried-on droppings. Add a cup of ammonia to a gallon of hot water and use the solution to wash the cement, scrubbing off any remaining droppings or stains with a strong bristle brush. Scatter kitty litter over the cement to absorb the solution. When the cement has dried, sweep up the litter and dispose of it right away, since potentially toxic dust can rise off the crusted poop and spread illness.

CLOTHING
Pick off individual clots of poop with a paper towel, or remove with a spoon if necessary. Brush off any dried-on bits before scrubbing the remaining stain under cold water. Rub with regular soap and let sit for 20 minutes. Rinse with water.

HAIR
Take a tissue and wipe wet or runny droppings up from the bottom to the top of the affected area, minimizing risk of its spreading further or getting on your clothes. Clean the rest of the poop out of your hair using a damp washcloth or wetted paper towel. Wash the affected area with soap or shampoo and rinse out in a sink.

HOW TO PREVENT SUCKING A GOOSE INTO YOUR JET ENGINE

1 Check in with AHAS.
The online Avian Hazard Advisory System, created by the United States Air Force, provides real-time information on severe flight risk from birds. Adjust your takeoff time based on AHAS information.

2 Do a simple visual scan.
As you taxi your craft, look out the front and to the sides, noting any crowds of birds that might become an airborne hazard to your craft.

3 Scan the skies using NEXRAD.
The Next Generation Weather Radar system, designed to provide information on fast-moving weather systems, has also proved adept at identifying marauding flocks.

4 Engage landing lights.
There is some evidence that the bright lights will scare off geese and other skittish avian species.

5 Flash a "green laser" out the window.
When birds are spotted, use a TOM500 or other automatic laser system to deploy a flashing green light into the air to stun and confuse them.

6 Fly high.
Rapidly ascend to 3,000 feet, past which most birds are unable to fly.

7 Keep flying.
Once a bird has flown into your engine, remain calm and continue to fly the plane. Remember that even if an engine is lost, the other engine will compensate.

8 Assess the damage.
Check engine readings and visually inspect the aircraft.

WARNING!

✏ Bird strikes are estimated to do more than $600 million of damage to the American commercial aviation industry every year, including windshield strikes. More than 200 people have died worldwide from bird strikes since 1980. Birds that fly into planes include geese, turkey vultures, gulls, and starlings.

✏ Bird strikes are known in the aviation business as "bird hits" or by the acronym BASH, for bird/aircraft strike hazard.

✏ Aviation industry bird-strike simulations are performed using a "chicken gun," a compressed air gun that shoots a chicken carcass at the hull or engine of an aircraft.

✏ Most modern engines can easily survive being struck by a single bird; typically problems emerge only when the plane "ingests" an entire flock.

JUNGLE ANIMALS

Identify the oral sucker—the small end.

Place your fingernail next to the oral sucker.

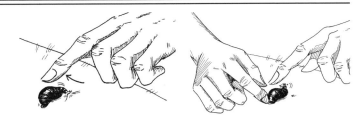

Push the leech sideways to break the seal.

Push or pick at the hind sucker, while continuing to flick at the small end.

HOW TO REMOVE A LEECH

1 Do not attempt to remove a leech by pulling up on its middle section or by using salt, heat, or insect repellent. Dislodging by squeezing, salting, burning, or otherwise annoying the leech while it is feeding will cause it to regurgitate, most likely spreading the bacteria from its digestive system into your open wound, causing infection.

2 Identify the anterior (oral) sucker.
Look for the small end of the leech. A common mistake is to go immediately to the large sucker.

3 Place a fingernail on your skin (not on the leech itself), directly adjacent to the oral sucker.

4 Gently but firmly slide your finger toward where the leech is feeding and push the sucker away sideways.
When the seal made by the oral sucker is broken, the leech will stop feeding. After the oral sucker has been dislodged, the leech's head will seek to reattach, and it may quickly attach to the finger that displaced the head. Even if the oral sucker attaches again, the leech does not begin to feed immediately.

5 Displace the posterior (hind) sucker.
While continuing to flick occasionally at the small end, push at or pick under the large end (hind sucker) with a fingernail to cause it to lose its suction.

6 Dispose of the leech.
At this point, the leech may have securely attached itself to the finger you used to remove it. Flick it off—it should detach easily. Once the leech is detached, you can put salt or insect repellent directly on it to keep it from attaching to anything else.

7 Treat the wound.
After the leech's anticoagulants lose their effect, the wound should heal quickly. Keep the area clean, and cover it with a small bandage if necessary. Avoid scratching the wound. If itching becomes severe, take an antihistamine.

HOW TO ESCAPE FROM AN ANGRY GORILLA

1 Evaluate the gorilla's behavior.
A stressed or angry gorilla is likely to vocalize loudly and pound, jump, or slap the ground before attacking. A gorilla that is just tugging at clothes or grabbing at you may simply be curious.

2 Do not react.
Do not scream, hit, or otherwise antagonize the gorilla. Even if the gorilla grabs you, it may be playful behavior. Scaring or aggravating the gorilla may provoke an angry response.

3 Be submissive.
Do not look directly at the gorilla. Remain quiet. Do not shout or open arms wide to try to appear larger. The gorilla may interpret these acts as hostile.

4 Watch for a bluff charge.
A gorilla may make a "bluff charge" before an attack to scare potential threats. It may scream or "bark," stomp its hands on the ground, and tear at vegetation as it advances toward you. A bluff charge is fast and intimidating and resembles an actual attack.

5 Crouch down and make yourself as small a target as possible.
If the gorilla feels threatened during a bluffing display, it may decide to follow through with an attack.

6 Stay quiet and submissive.
An attack may include severe biting and pounding or tearing with the gorilla's hands. Even if it appears that the gorilla means to harm you, do not actively resist or fight back: it will interpret this behavior as threatening and may attack more severely.

7 Groom.
If the gorilla has gotten hold of you, begin to "groom" its arm while loudly smacking your lips. Primates are fastidious

groomers, and grooming the gorilla in this fashion may distract it in a nonthreatening way. As the gorilla's grip relaxes, slowly move your grooming hand to the gorilla's hand, showing keen interest in any bits of leaf or dirt on the gorilla.

8 Remain quiet and passive until the gorilla loses interest or help arrives.

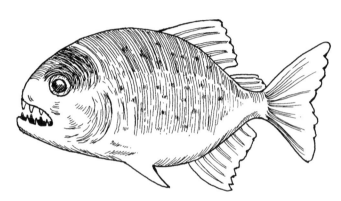

Piranhas are more active (and hungry) during the day, so cross an infested area at night

HOW TO CROSS A PIRANHA-INFESTED RIVER

1 Do not cross if you have an open wound.
Piranhas are attracted to blood.

2 Avoid areas with netted fish, docks where fish are cleaned, and areas around bird rookeries.
Piranhas may become habituated to feeding in these areas and may be more aggressive there.

3 Stay out of the water when piranhas are feeding.
When large numbers of piranhas are attacking prey—a true feeding frenzy—they may snap and bite at anything around them. If you see them feeding, stay away, or well upriver.

4 Cross the river at night.
Virtually every species of piranha rests at night, and when awakened, they will swim away rather than attack. Piranhas are most active at dawn, though some large adults may hunt in the evening.

5 Swim or walk across quickly and quietly.
Try not to create a large disturbance in the water that might awaken piranhas.

Poison Dart Frog Contact

- Poison dart frogs get their poison from the insects and arthropods they eat in the wild; captive-bred dart frogs are not poisonous at all.

- No true and reliable antidote has been discovered for the treatment of batrachotoxin poisoning, the most common cause of death from poison dart frogs.

- Poison dart frogs secrete their poison all over their body. Do not touch.

- Tetrodotoxin, a powerful neurotoxin secreted by the puffer fish, can slow or reverse the chemical effects of batrachotoxin, the most dangerous of the poisons found in dart-frog secretion.

- Digoxin immune fab, typically used to treat overdose of digitalis, the poison secreted by the foxglove plant, may also be helpful.

- Many species of poisonous dart frogs actually secrete very low levels of toxin, so contact may only cause a temporary muscle paralysis, rather than death.

- Deadlier species, such as the golden poison frog (*Phyllobates terriblis*), have such high toxic concentrations that contact can lead to serious muscle contraction and heart failure within a matter of minutes. It secretes sufficient poison to kill 20 men and is considered the most toxic animal in the world. The toxin found in the golden poison frog is being used experimentally in low doses as a painkiller for humans.

- Poison dart frogs are found throughout South and Central America, as well as in Hawaii. A typical poison frog is one or two inches long and bears a camouflage pattern, but there are nearly 200 species, found in a wide variety of often-beautiful colors and patterns.

SNAKES

How to Escape from a Boa Constrictor

1 Act immediately.

Once a boa wraps itself around you, begin taking action to free yourself right away, before the pressure reaches levels sufficient to prevent you from breathing or moving.

2 Make slow, careful movements.

Actively and energetically struggling will cause the boa to tighten its strong grip. Refrain from becoming completely still (i.e., playing dead), as a boa constrictor will typically continue to constrict, even when it thinks its prey is dead.

Hold the head still with one hand and slowly unwrap the boa with your other hand.

3 Splash alcohol in the snake's face.

A small amount of rubbing or grain alcohol in the boa's mouth and eyes will cause it to instinctively loosen its pressure.

4 Grasp the head.

With one hand, hold the head of the snake still.

5 Slowly unwrap.

With your other hand, take hold of the snake's tail and slowly bend it upward. This alone may spur the boa to loosen its grip; if not, slowly uncoil the snake from the tail, ring by ring.

6 Stun the snake.

Should the boa begin to tighten its coils, making it impossible to uncoil further, rap it hard in the center of the head, stunning it and temporarily easing the constriction.

7 Douse the snake with water.

Hot water often makes a boa constrictor's muscles involuntarily relax.

WARNING!

- Boas are not poisonous and a bite will not kill you, although snakebites can and often do result in infection.

- Boa constrictors can grow as long as 14 feet and as heavy as 60 pounds. An adult should not be handled by a single individual.

- Boa constrictors can completely unhinge their jaws, and can eat animals as large as monkeys and wild pigs.

- Do not approach a boa constrictor with the scent of another animal on your body.

Snake in a Sleeping Bag

Pick up the sleeping bag from the bottom and dump the snake outside. If you are in the bag and feel a snake, avoid sudden movements. Very slowly work the bag down toward your feet as you pull your upper body and then legs out. Keep the bag rolled up and tied when you are not using it to prevent snakes from entering, and keep your tent flaps zipped.

How to Survive a Poisonous Snake Attack

Snakes can strike at a distance approximately half their length; half their body does not leave the ground.

How to Treat a Bite

1 Wash the bite with soap and water as soon as you can.

2 Immobilize the bitten area, and keep it lower than the heart.

This will slow the flow of the venom.

3 Immediately wrap a bandage tightly two to four inches above the bite to help slow the venom if you are unable to reach medical care within 30 minutes.

The bandage should not cut off blood flow from a vein or artery. Make the bandage loose enough for a finger to slip underneath.

4 If you have a first aid kit equipped with a suction device, follow the instructions for drawing venom out of the wound without making an incision.

Generally, you will need to place the rubber suction cup over the wound and attempt to draw the venom out from the bite marks.

What Not to Do

✪ Do not place any ice or cooling element on the bite. This will make removing the venom with suction more difficult.

✪ Do not tie a bandage or a tourniquet too tightly. If used incorrectly, a tourniquet can cut blood flow completely and damage the limb.

✪ Do not make any incision on or around the wound in an attempt to remove the venom—there is danger of infection.

✪ Do not attempt to suck out the venom with your mouth, where it might enter your bloodstream.

✪ Do not assume that a snake is nonpoisonous unless you know for certain that it is not.
Venomous snakes have markings very similar to those of nonpoisonous ones.

Venomous Snakes of the Tropics

NAME	APPEARANCE	GEOGRAPHICAL RANGE	HABITAT
bushmaster	light brown body; very wide head	Central and South America	rainforests
cobra	long body; spread hood	South and Southeast Asia, Africa, Middle East	virtually everywhere
death adder	brown/red body, lighter crossbars; triangular head	Australia	bush, rocky areas
Eastern tiger snake	olive or red body with lighter crossbars	Australia	rainforest, grasslands
fer-de-lance	gray/brown/red body with geometrical blotches	Central and South America	rainforests, tree branches
fierce snake	black markings on head; brown/olive body	Australia	grasslands
giant black tiger snake	black body; lighter crossbars	Australia	sand dunes, beaches, grasslands
mamba	uniform dark color; very skinny body; small head	Africa	rainforest
tropical rattlesnake	dark stripes on neck; rattle at tip of tail	Central and South America	dry, hilly terrain
viper	very wide head	Southeast Asia, Africa	rainforest, grasslands

ANIMAL PACKS

How to Escape from Killer Bees

1 If bees begin flying around and/or stinging you, do not freeze.

Run away; swatting at the bees only makes them angrier.

2 Get indoors as fast as you can.

3 If no shelter is available, run through bushes or high weeds.

This will help give you cover.

4 If a bee stings you, it will leave its stinger in your skin.

Remove the stinger by raking your fingernail across it in a sideways motion. Do not pinch or pull the stinger out—this may squeeze more venom from the stinger into your body. Do not let stingers remain in the skin, because venom can continue to pump into the body for up to 10 minutes.

5 Do not jump into a swimming pool or other body of water—the bees are likely to be waiting for you when you surface.

Run away from killer bees. If no shelter is available, run through bushes or high weeds.

How to Outwit a Pack of Wolves

1 Slowly move to solid terrain.

In winter, wolves tend to chase their prey into deep snow or onto frozen lakes, surfaces where the hooves of the victim sink or slide. The wolves' large, padded feet give them a tremendous range-of-movement advantage in these areas. If you see wolves around you, slowly walk toward solid ground. Do not crouch down, and do not run. Even during warmer months, wolves will readily chase prey over solid ground and are capable of bursts of high speed, as fast as 35 mph over short distances. You cannot outrun a wolf.

2 Observe the wolves' posture.

A wolf can attack from any position, but a tail straight up in the air and ears pricked up are a signal of dominance and often indicate that the wolf is preparing to attack.

3 Charge one member of the pack.

Wolves are generally timid around humans and have a strong flight response. Running toward one wolf while yelling may scare it and the other members of the pack away from you.

4 Throw sticks and rocks.

If the wolves continue with an attack, throw sticks and rocks at those closest to you. Wolves tend to attack the lower portions of their victims' bodies in an attempt to hobble and then bring them to the ground. Kick or hit the wolves as they approach your legs until you scare them off.

WARNING!

- Captive wolves are more likely to attack a human than wolves in the wild. Attacks are often a dominance display. Captive wolves may attack and then eat a person.

- Solitary wolves are generally considered more of an attack threat to humans than pack wolves, though a pack of wolves can inflict more damage more quickly.

- Wild wolves habituated to the presence of humans are more likely to attack, since they have lost their fear of people.

- Wolves may hunt at any hour of the day or night.

- The bite pressure of an adult wolf is about 1,500 pounds per square inch. By contrast, the bite pressure of a German shepherd is about 500 pounds per square inch.

- A wolf pack may have 30 members.

How to Survive a Slumber Party

1 Begin the party at around 6 p.m.

Organize strenuous events such as tag, soccer, high-impact aerobics, calisthenics, or wind-sprint drills to exhaust the guests and encourage an early bedtime.

2 Serve carbohydrate-heavy foods.

Pizza, pasta, sandwiches, chili, and other heavy foods help induce sleep. Make certain that these are on the menu, and encourage everyone to go back for seconds.

3 Secure cabinets, rooms, and drawers you want to keep off-limits.

Use travel padlocks and cable ties to protect cabinets and drawers. To keep the children out of rooms that do not lock, place noisy pets inside the rooms, or stack cans behind the door to create an "intruder alert" system.

4 Do not serve caffeinated beverages or dessert.

5 Observe the gathering of guests unobtrusively.

Use small bowls for snacks so that they need to be refilled regularly, providing you with the opportunity to ensure that the herd is well behaved. Listen with a tall glass pressed against a wall or door (holding the closed end to your ear) to eavesdrop. Check in every half hour or so in order to "see if anyone needs or wants anything."

6 Use video games and movies to lower the activity level.

Lower energy levels with nonviolent video games as part of a cooldown phase. Show long, sweeping epic movies around 11 p.m. to get children into sleeping bags and a prone position.

7 Collect mobile phones.

At midnight, offer to recharge phones, and do not return them until morning.

Calisthenics will encourage an early bedtime.

Chased by a Pack of Dogs

Enter a car or nearby building as quickly as possible. Some breeds will tire after a short chase, while others may continue to chase you over long distances. Climb a tree only if you are able to get more than four feet off the ground.

How Many Animals in the Group?

ANIMAL	NAME OF GROUP	HOW MANY ARE IN IT
elephants	herd	6 to 12
bees	swarm	1,500 to 30,000
gorillas	troop	one to four males, a few juvenile males, a few females
sheep	flock	minimum five, can be 1,000 or more
dolphins	pod	12
lions	pride	40
geese	gaggle	minimum five, can be 100 or more
fish	school	hundreds
army ants	colony	thousands

STAMPEDES

How to Survive an Elephant Stampede

⊙ **Take available cover.**
Elephants stampede when they are startled by a loud noise or to escape a perceived threat. If the elephants are running away from a threat but toward you, do not try to outrun them. Elephants can run at a speed in excess of 25 mph. Even while charging, they can make sharp turns and are able to climb steep slopes. Seek a sturdy structure nearby and take cover.

⊙ **Climb a tree.**
The elephants are likely to avoid trees when running. Grab a branch at its base and use your legs to power yourself up the tree, keeping three of your limbs in contact with the tree at all times as you climb. If you cannot climb the tree, stand behind it. Elephants will avoid large obstacles when running.

⊙ **Lie down.**
Unless the elephant is intent on trampling you, because you are hunting or the elephant thinks you are hunting, elephants typically avoid stepping on a prone human being, even while charging.

⊙ **Protect your face.**
Do not get up immediately. After the threat has passed, an elephant may show great interest in the apparently dead bodies of humans and may attempt to "bury" you under tree branches, leaves, and dirt. If you sense an elephant moving above you, lie still and cover your face with your hands. The rough skin on the elephant's trunk may cause severe abrasions if it rubs against you.

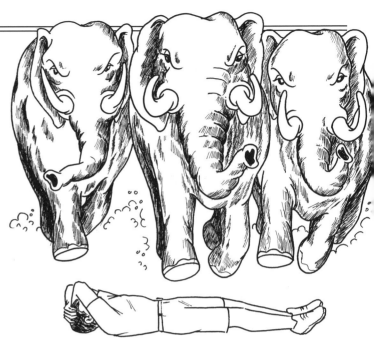

If you cannot find cover, lie down. Elephants typically avoid stepping on a prone human being, even while charging.

WARNING!

⚡ An angry elephant will tuck its ears back and curl its trunk up, away from danger.

⚡ If the elephants are angry at you, they will attempt to spear you with their tusks and then fling your body.

⚡ If the last human the elephant met was a hunter/poacher, it will be more likely to treat you as a threat and attempt to attack.

What Causes Animal Stampedes

Sudden light source (lighting of match).	Single animal panics, panics the rest.	Rabbit jumps.
Sudden loud noise (rattling of pots and pans).	Sudden movement (horse shaking, cowboy stamping).	One steer catches the whiff of a wolf.
Someone jumps off horse.	Whir of a rattlesnake.	Shaking of an empty saddle.
Single animal becomes spooked, spooks the rest.	Cat flicks its tail.	Lightning strike.
		Predator.

How to Evade a Stampede of Shoppers

☺ Stay focused and visualize your goal.
Do not freeze in front of the pack; do not wait for the crowd of shoppers to get close before you make your move. React early and decisively.

☺ Do not attempt to hold your ground.
You risk being trampled if you try to resist the stampede. Turn your body in the direction of the crowd, and let yourself be carried along.

☺ Hold your packages tightly.
Bring your arms in and firmly grasp objects you are carrying. If you drop something, do not stop to pick it up.

☺ Work your way to the outside of the herd.
Move to the edge of the crowd as you move with it. Use the space near the walls to gain a few extra yards of room. Most shoppers will leave at least several feet between themselves and surrounding walls. This will give you room to maneuver and either slow down or escape.

BE AWARE!

- Animals travel in herds because there is safety in numbers, and the safest place is at the center of the pack, insulated from predators. Avoid the temptation to join the middle of the herd—you cannot shop if you cannot see the merchandise.

- When heading into a shopping situation where crowds may be present, wear proper shoes. Open-toed shoes offer minimal protection, and high heels will restrict your mobility. Select shoes with flat heels. Rubber soles provide the best traction.

Brace for an oncoming crowd by wrapping your arms tightly around your packages.

A Stampede of Giraffes

Wade into the nearest body of water. Giraffes typically avoid water, except for drinking. If you cannot reach water, climb a tree or seek available shelter. The giraffe's large hooves pose your most immediate danger.

Surviving Stampedes

- To stop a stampede of longhorn cattle, turn the cattle to the right and get them running in a tight circle. (Longhorns don't like to turn to the left when they are stampeding.)

- Buffalo stampedes are more difficult to stop because buffalo run straight ahead blindly. Buffalo are larger than longhorns, and the stampedes are more dangerous. Buffalo stampedes have knocked trains off the tracks.

- Human stampedes most often occur during religious pilgrimages, professional sporting and music events, and the release of highly-desired consumer products.

CATS

How to Get Your Cat to Cuddle

1 Play soothing classical music.

2 Do aerobic exercise.
Perform jumping jacks, sit-ups, or push-ups until you are lightly perspiring. Elevated skin temperature and a sheen of perspiration are attractive to warm-blooded mammals such as cats.

3 Remove your shirt.

4 Sit down in a large, reclining chair.
Recline the chair by 45 degrees. Move your butt forward so that your lap space is maximized.

5 Call your cat's name in an encouraging voice.
Cats will also respond to any other words.

6 Purr.
Bring your tongue up to the roof of your mouth and gently exhale, blowing air over your tongue and through your front teeth. Alternate between purring and calling your cat's name.

7 Lightly pat your lap.
Establish a slow but insistent rhythm, imitating the pitter-patter of cat feet.

Do aerobic exercise. Perspiration is attractive to cats.

8 Reinforce the cuddling behavior.
When your cat settles in your lap, stroke her gently from the base of the neck, slowly down to the tip of the tail, and then back to the base of the neck. Say "good cat." Give her a treat.

How to Get a Cat Out from Under the Bed

○ Run the can opener.
Go to the kitchen and run an electric can opener.

○ Sweep the cat out from under the bed.
Use a broom or mop to nudge or sweep the cat from his hiding place.

Loudly show affection for another pet.

○ Loudly show affection for another pet.
Sit in an area visible from your cat's position underneath the bed. Hold another cat, dog, or child in your lap and stroke the child or pet gently. Praise the other animal or child in the way you would praise your cat.

○ Sit, roll, or bounce around on the bed.
Move abruptly and make loud noises on top of the bed to try to scare the cat out from under it.

○ Stick your head under the bed.
Make loud hissing noises to scare the cat into running out from under the bed.

○ Make a line of treats.
Create a trail of cat treats starting at the edge of the bed and continuing several feet past it leading out of the room. When the cat follows the treats from under the bed and out the door, shut the door behind him.

How to Toilet Train Your Cat

1 Move the litter box next to the toilet.

2 Incrementally raise the litter box to the level of the toilet. Place telephone books or encyclopedias under the litter box, one at a time, until the box is at the same height level as the toilet. Wait each time until your cat is adjusted and comfortable with the new level before raising the level again.

3 Leave the litter box in this raised, toilet-adjacent position. The box should be positioned so that the cat must step across the toilet to access her litter box. Leave it there until your cat is accustomed to the feel of walking on the toilet seat.

4 Move the litter box on top of the toilet seat. Leave it in this position for several days, so your cat becomes used to doing her business on top of the toilet. When you use the toilet, remove the litter box and then replace it when you're done.

5 Remove the litter box from the top of the toilet seat.

6 Place a mixing bowl in the toilet. Select a bowl that fits snugly in the toilet bowl. Fill it with two to three inches of cat litter. Humans using the toilet should first remove the metal mixing bowl.

Help your cat position herself correctly over the bowl: two paws on the front and two paws in the rear.

Things That Are Toxic to Cats

ITEM	DANGER TO CAT
milk	various stomach problems
poinsettias, lilies, many other houseplants	stomachaches, various forms of poisoning
dog food	vomiting, diarrhea
onions	anemia
garlic	anemia
chocolate	potential kidney failure
cherry tomatoes	various stomach problems
raw salmon	salmon poisoning, death
soy	thyroid malfunction
yeast	allergies, bloating, urinary tract problems
aspirin	gastrointestinal problems, respiratory problems, kidney failure
acetaminophen	severe blood ailments, death
antifreeze	severe kidney damage, death

7 Position the cat's feet. Watch your cat constantly over a period of several days. Every time she goes to the toilet to urinate or defecate, help her set her feet correctly on the lid of the toilet: two paws on the front and two paws in the rear, so that she is squatting over the mixing bowl.

8 Replace the cat litter in the mixing bowl with water. Continue helping your cat position herself correctly over the bowl, and encourage her, so that she becomes used to the sound of doing her business into water. Each time your cat relieves herself successfully in the mixing bowl, empty it into the toilet and flush it while she watches.

9 Remove the mixing bowl from the toilet. Once your cat has become used to relieving herself into water while sitting on the toilet, take the mixing bowl away.

WARNING!

Once your cat is toilet trained, the door to the bathroom and the toilet lid need to be left open, so that the cat enjoys free access to the toilet.

INSECTS

How to Deal with a Tarantula

1 Find something you can use to brush the tarantula off of you or away from you.

A small stick, rolled newspaper or magazine, or glove works well. Most tarantulas are very skittish, and as soon as you poke them, they will leave in great haste. It is safer to remove the tarantula using an implement than using your bare hand.

2 If the tarantula is on you and cannot be brushed off, stand up carefully and bounce up and down gently.

The tarantula should fall off or skitter away.

How to Treat a Bite

1 Do not panic if you are bitten.

The vast majority of tarantulas give "dry" bites (which look like two pinpricks) first, and then a second bite to inject venom. Avoid *Pterinochilus* and *Heteroscodra*, two species of "baboon spiders" in Africa, and *Poecilotheria*, "ornamental tarantulas" in southern Asia, which deliver potent bites.

2 Treat a dry bite like any other small puncture wound: use an antiseptic to clean it out, and bandage the site quickly.

3 Observe the area around the bite carefully.

A few varieties of tarantula may inject venom that can cause swelling and redness in the area around the bite, as well as pain and tenderness lasting 2 to 6 hours. If these symptoms persist for longer than 12 hours, or if other, more serious symptoms develop, seek medical attention. Unless absolutely necessary, do not drive a vehicle.

4 Treat excessive swelling with antihistamines.

The allergic reaction can be eased with antihistamines, although they are usually slow acting. If symptoms such as extreme flushing in the face, blurred vision, dizziness, profuse swelling around the face or eyes, or restricted breathing occur, epinephrine may be necessary.

5 Watch closely for complications.

While the bite itself is probably not life threatening, it can become infected, and this is the greatest danger if you are bitten. Seek immediate medical attention if you see signs of tetanus (muscle stiffness, spasm, fever, convulsions, difficulty swallowing, irregular heartbeat, trouble breathing), tularemia (fever, nausea, swollen lymph nodes, sore throat, vomiting, diarrhea), or septicemia (spiking fever and chills, rapid breathing, shock, disorientation, inability to urinate, swollen limbs, blue lips and fingernails).

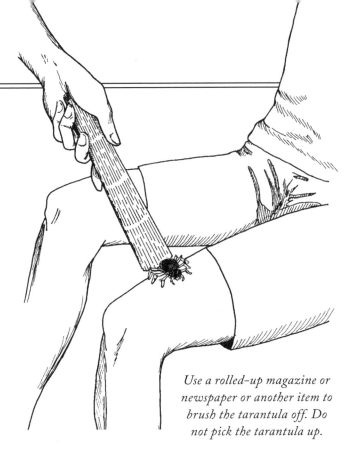

Use a rolled-up magazine or newspaper or another item to brush the tarantula off. Do not pick the tarantula up.

BE AWARE!

- Tarantulas are basically just big spiders. Few will bite you unless you try to pick them up.

- Tarantulas are not carriers of any known disease that affects humans or other vertebrates. Tetanus, tularemia, and other diseases that may follow a tarantula bite are most likely the result of postbite contamination due to unclean environmental conditions. (See step 5.)

- While tarantulas bites are not fatal, they can cause dangerous allergic reactions in some individuals and can be extremely painful.

- Tarantulas are found in North America, west of the Mississippi River; in South America; and in warm climates throughout the world. Their habitats vary, and include deep deserts, grassy plains, scrub forests, and rainforests. Most live in burrows, though a few species prefer trees and areas around the base or under the roof of human dwellings.

- Tarantulas are mostly nocturnal and are difficult to notice unless you are searching for them. Most people encounter adult males, which wander during daylight hours looking for female mates.

- Never try to pick up a tarantula. Tarantulas have tough bristles on the tops of their abdomens, which can irritate the skin. These come loose easily and float freely through the air. They are shaped like small harpoons with barbed tips and may penetrate the skin and cause a rash or hives.

How to Treat a Scorpion Sting

1 Remain calm.

Scorpion venom induces anxiety in victims, so try especially hard to avoid panic. Most species of scorpion have venom of low to moderate toxicity and do not pose a serious health threat to adult humans, other than severe pain.

2 Apply heat or cold packs to the sting site for pain relief.

The most severe pain usually occurs at the site of the sting. Also use an analgesic (painkiller) if available.

3 If an allergic reaction occurs, take an antihistamine.

Scorpion venom contains histamines, which may cause allergic reactions (asthma, rashes) in sensitive persons.

4 Watch for an irregular heartbeat, tingling in extremities, an inability to move limbs or fingers, or trouble breathing.

Most scorpion stings cause only instantaneous pain at the site of the sting; stings feel similar to those of a wasp. The pain of a scorpion sting may radiate over the body several minutes after the initial sting. Pain tends to be felt in joints, especially in the armpits and groin. Systemic symptoms may also occur—possibly numbness in the face, mouth, or throat; muscle twitches; sweating; nausea; vomiting; fever; and restlessness. These symptoms are normal and not life threatening, and usually subside in one to three hours. The

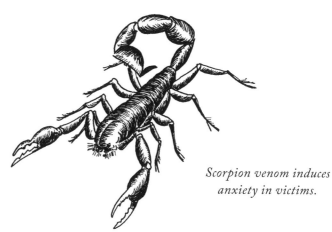

Scorpion venom induces anxiety in victims.

site of the sting may remain sore and/or sensitive to touch, heat, or cold for one to three days.

5 Seek emergency medical care if you exhibit the above symptoms.

Small children who are stung should seek emergency medical care immediately. Adults, however, have much more time—the odds of dying or even becoming seriously ill as a result of a scorpion sting are extremely slim. You will have at least 12 hours to get to a hospital—probably more.

6 Do not apply tourniquets, as the toxins are small and move rapidly away from the site of the sting.

A tourniquet will not help the wound, and could cause more harm if applied incorrectly.

7 Do not attempt to cut the wound and suck out the poison.

This can cause infection or transfer the venom into the bloodstream of the person attempting to remove the poison.

WARNING!

⚡ Scorpions are active at night, when they hunt and search for mates. During the day, scorpions hide in burrows or in any available crack or crevice, depending upon the species. Scorpions are notorious for seeking shelter in objects such as shoes, clothing, bedding, and bath towels. Your presence may surprise the scorpion, and it could sting if disturbed. If you are in an area that has scorpions, shake out these items before using them, and check bedding before sleeping.

⚡ Many species of scorpions will readily enter homes and other buildings, which increases the likelihood of an encounter. Scorpions will sting if surprised or threatened, but generally will not sting if unprovoked.

⚡ Scorpions cannot usually deliver enough venom to kill a healthy adult. While venom toxicity varies among species, some scorpions contain very powerful neurotoxins, which, ounce for ounce, are more toxic to humans than the venom of cobras. However, scorpions inject relatively small amounts of venom (compared with snakes), so the overall dose of toxins per sting is survivable.

Creepy-Crawly Things and How Many Eggs They Lay

CREATURE	HOW MANY EGGS	HOW SMALL
flies	500 at a time (several batches of up to 150)	about 1/20 inch
fleas	50 a day	1/50 inch
termites	2,000 in a day	1/50 inch or smaller
louse	4 in a day, 88 in a lifetime	1/32 of an inch
ant	75–100 a day	larva is 3/16 inch
bedbug	up to 5 a day	1/32 inch
spiders	100 eggs contained in a single sac	1/32 inch
cockroaches	30 to 50 at a time, in a protruding egg case	egg case is 3/8 inch

How to Survive a Cockroach Infestation

1 **Rid your kitchen of any food residue.**
Thoroughly scour the kitchen counters, dining table, stovetops, and any other areas where food is prepared or consumed. Remove all food from the kitchen, and clean inside all cabinets and drawers. Empty, rinse, and scrub every trash can. Clean the refrigerator inside and out, the underside of the microwave, and the crumb tray of the toaster.

2 **Clean the rest of your apartment or house.**
Pull out sofa pillows and vacuum any crumbs using a crack-and-crevice attachment; roll up all carpets and sweep and mop the floor underneath.

3 **Dry out your apartment.**
Look for puddles underneath the sink, around the base of the bathtub, and next to the toilet. At each sink, turn on both taps, and as the water is running, examine the base of the faucet, the tap handle, and the underside of the sink. Tighten the joints and recaulk any areas of seepage. Repeat this procedure with the taps in the bath.

Eat out instead of cooking in your home.

Signs of a Roach Infestation

Roach droppings	Small clusters of black, ridged pellets measuring 1/8 inch.
Gastrointestinal problems	Potential ailments include diarrhea, vomiting, and dysentery. Caused by organisms transferred from the arms and legs of cockroaches onto food and utensils.
Allergic responses	Symptoms include watery eyes, skin rashes, sneezing, and congested nasal passages. Caused by the presence of roach droppings and molted roach skin in the air.
Cockroach sightings	The most common cockroach in New York is the German cockroach, which is a tan or light brown winged insect, measuring from half an inch to an inch, with two dark streaks down its back. You may find roaches in the following places: • The kitchen or any area with abundant food • The bathroom or anywhere there is standing water • In or near the garbage or recycling

4 **Eliminate roach hideouts.**
Get down on all fours and crawl from room to room, carefully examining each pantry, closet, drawer, and cupboard. Destroy any potential roach hiding places, such as bags stuffed with other bags, piles of old magazines, or cardboard boxes waiting to be recycled. Open old boxes, take out their contents, flatten the cardboard, and remove from your apartment.

5 **Place "sticky traps" in 10 sites around your apartment.**
Position "sticky traps" throughout the apartment. Place each trap against a wall or corner, under a sink, or along the baseboards.

6 **Monitor the traps.**
Carefully note the number of dead roaches in each trap to determine where in your apartment the roaches are most prevalent.

7 **Kill the roaches with borax.**
Mix 4 parts borax with 2 parts flour and 1 part cocoa powder. Sprinkle liberally in roach-heavy areas of your apartment.

8 **Maintain a clean, dry apartment.**
After each meal, thoroughly clean the areas where food was cooked and consumed. Store all food in sealed containers. Do all dishes immediately. Take out any garbage

and recycling at least once a day. Make sure to immediately clean up any water spills and repair leaky faucets. Whenever possible, eat out instead of cooking in your home; do not bring home leftovers.

9 Persuade your neighbors to keep equally clean.

How to Escape from Fire Ants

1 Brush the ants off.
Fire ants inject venom from a stinger connected to a poison gland. A single ant will pinch the skin with its jaws and sting numerous times, injecting more venom with each sting. As the venom enters the skin, you will experience the intense, burning sensation that gives fire ants their name. Using your hand or a cloth, make a fast, sharp, brushing motion until their jaws dislodge from the skin and they fall off. Jumping up and down, shaking the affected area, and placing the ants under running water will not prevent the ants from attacking and may cause further injury.

2 Run from the area.
As you remove the ants, flee the area of the attack. When a mound or nest is disturbed, or foraging fire ants are encountered, they immediately climb up any vertical surface and sting. Hundreds of ants may attack within seconds, especially in mild to high temperatures, when ants stay closer to the surface. The ants will continue to attack even after you have left the nest area, however. Continue brushing them as you run.

3 Remove your clothing.
Fire ants will stay in the creases of clothing and may sting later. Once you have reached safety and removed all visible ants, take off your shoes, socks, pants, and any other articles of clothing where the ants were visible. Inspect your clothes carefully, especially the pockets and seams, before putting them back on. If possible, launder the items before wearing them again.

4 Treat the affected area.
After several minutes, the site of each bite will redden and swell into a bump. A topical antihistamine may relieve some itching at bite sites. Several hours to several days later, the bumps will become white, fluid-filled pustules, which will last for several days or, in some cases, weeks. Immediately upon the appearance of pustules, treat the affected areas with a solution of half bleach, half water to lessen pain and reduce itching. Use an over-the-counter pain medication to reduce discomfort. Pustules will form regardless of topical treatment. If pustules break, treat with a topical antibacterial ointment to prevent infection. Pustules may leave scars.

5 Monitor symptoms.
Even a healthy adult may have a severe reaction to hundreds of stings, and people with certain allergies may develop serious complications. Watch for severe chest pain, nausea, severe sweating, loss of breath, severe swelling of limbs, and slurred speech. Seek immediate medical attention if any of these symptoms are present. In highly allergic people, anaphylaxis may occur from fire ant stings. Administer epinephrine immediately.

Dangerous Forest Insects

SPECIES	RANGE	WEAPONRY	PAIN
Bullet ants	Atlantic Coast, South and Central America	One of the most powerful insect venoms on earth	Likened to a three-inch nail in the foot
Jack jumper ants	Australia, Tasmania	Stings that can trigger allergic reactions, sometimes fatally	Pain, local swelling can last for days
Wheel bug	United States, especially Florida	8 to 12 teeth can cause a skin wound lasting one year	Burning and numbness
Killer bees	South and Central America, southern United States	Swarms attack humans with multiple stings, potentially causing death	Localized itching and swelling
Deer ticks	Northeastern United States	Bites can spread Lyme disease	No pain

2

LIFE AND LIMB

AILMENTS

How to Treat Poison Ivy, Poison Oak, and Poison Sumac

1 Wash the exposed area of skin.

Immediately wash the contaminated area with large amounts of running water.

2 Wash shoes, socks, pants, gloves, and golf clubs immediately.

Urushiol oil, which causes the rash, can stay active on objects for up to a year. Dilute the oil by washing equipment with lots of water. Slosh rubbing alcohol over exposed skin (except on the face) and rinse with water. (Carry a jar containing rubbing alcohol and a small cloth.) Rubbing alcohol neutralizes the oil.

3 Do not scratch the rash.

A rash usually develops a few hours to a few days after exposure. It will start with an itch accompanied by a light rash that continually becomes more intense and eventually blisters. Excessive and continual scratching can lead to neural dermatitis (persistent itch) that can continue even after the reaction has stopped. The total reaction usually lasts two weeks or less. If the itch is intolerable, seek medical assistance.

4 To reduce itching, run hot water over the rash or blister area.

Gradually increase the temperature of the water (be careful not to burn yourself). Let the water run hot until you feel bursts of relief from the area, which may take five minutes or more. Hot water helps to release histamines from the

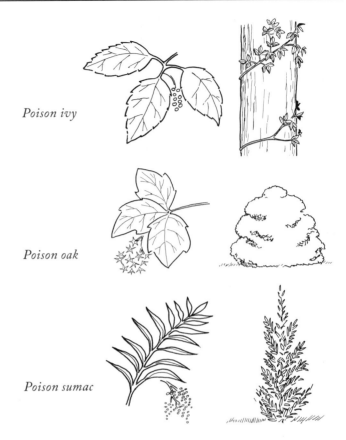

Poison ivy

Poison oak

Poison sumac

skin. This method can relieve itching for eight hours or more. Warm or cold packs and calamine lotion can also reduce itching. Prescription cortisone cream is many times the strength of over-the-counter cortisone cream and can be used for severe itching.

Treating Migraines

The symptoms of a migraine headache can include throbbing in one part of the head, nausea, vomiting, extreme sensitivity to light and sound, and pain lasting up to several days. Migraines can be triggered by alcohol, smoking or exposure to smoke, stress, too much or too little sleep, bright lights, too much or too little caffeine, exercise, odors or perfumes, birth control pills, skipping meals, loud noises, dehydration, allergic reactions, and changes in hormonal levels. Food-related triggers may include, among others, chocolate, dairy products, monosodium glutamate (MSG), baked goods, pickled or marinated foods, fruits (avocado, banana, citrus), nuts, onions, meats containing nitrates (bacon, hot dogs, salami), and peanut butter.

WARNING!

Poison ivy and oak thrive in disturbed ground, such as land molded and shaped for golf courses; be sure to ask if it is present on the course before beginning your round. Size and appearance of poison ivy and oak varies with habitat. Poison sumac is fairly rare and limited to deep swamps. Its leaflets can be two to eight inches long, and the plants can be six inches high, or can vine to the top of a 20-foot-tall tree. All three plants contain urushiol.

Poison ivy and poison oak grow in all areas of the United States except for southwestern deserts and mountain elevations above 4,000 feet.

Even when leaves are not present, the stems, berries, and roots of the plants still contain the oil and should be avoided.

To prevent exposure, wear shoes and socks and long pants, not shorts.

HOW TO TREAT SUNBURN

1 Remove the clothing around the affected area. Do not apply any suntan lotion to the burn.
Clothing irritates the skin, and the lotion will only prevent the skin from getting much-needed exposure to the cooling air.

2 Put a cool compress on the sunburn.
Soak your shirt or another available cloth in cold water and apply it to the affected area. If the burn is especially bad, wrap the shirt around an ice pack and use it as a compress. A bedsheet soaked in ice water is also effective if the burn area is very large.

3 Drink three to six ounces of water.
Drinking water will prevent dehydration and help to cool the skin by promoting sweating.

4 Apply a soothing gel or ointment to the sunburn.
Aloe lotion is ideal. You can refrigerate it first so that it feels cool to the skin.

5 Take a pain pill and lie still.
Ibuprofen will help alleviate the pain around the sunburn. Lie in a position that exposes the affected area to the air.

6 Seek medical attention if your symptoms are serious.
Dizziness, sensitivity to light, quick pulse or rapid breathing, clammy skin, rash, fever, chills, and nausea are all symptoms that could point to something worse than a mild sunburn. If you experience these symptoms, call a doctor.

WARNING!

- Always use sunscreen with an SPF (sun protection factor) of 15 or higher. Apply it approximately three minutes before going out into the sun.

- Avoid exposure in the late morning and early afternoon, when the sun is at its hottest. Bear in mind that the rays of the sun are stronger near the equator and at high altitudes.

- Lengthy exposure to the sun can cause not only sunburn but also heat exhaustion, a fairly mild illness. More serious is heatstroke, which can be fatal. Symptoms of both conditions include fever and sweating, but mental confusion is a sign that the heat exhaustion has progressed to heatstroke.

- A new layer of skin will replace the sunburned skin in as little as two days or as long as two weeks, depending upon the severity of the burn.

HOW TO DEAL WITH INSOMNIA

- Avoid caffeine, nicotine, and alcohol.
- Stretch or do light exercise an hour before bed.
A gentle workout relaxes muscle tension.

- Take a warm bath.

- Eat a bedtime snack.
Drink warm milk or herbal tea.

- Cover illuminated clocks.

- Lie on your back, rub your stomach, flex your toes.

- Think pleasant thoughts.

- Count sheep.

How to Cure Hiccups

Fill a tall glass with water. Holding the glass in front of you, lean forward over the glass so that your mouth is on the rim farthest away from you. Tilt the glass so that the bottom moves toward you and the top away from you; drink the water as it moves toward the front of the glass.

FITNESS

Admit that you have a problem.

HOW TO TREAT A GYM ADDICTION

1 Examine your behavior.

- Do you work out multiple times a day?
- Do you show up at the gym when you know it is not open?
- Do fellow gym-goers think you are an employee of the gym?
- Have you ever lied to family members or friends about the amount of time you spend at the gym?
- Do you have designated equipment that no one else is allowed to use?
- Do you consistently and repeatedly exceed the time limit on the treadmill?
- Does the thought of your gym closing for a holiday terrify you?

2 Admit that you have a problem and that you need help. Realize that you are not responsible for your disease—but you are responsible for your recovery. Make recovery a priority.

3 Admit to one other person that you have a problem. This person will help you wean yourself off the gym. This person should not work at the gym.

4 Reduce the amount of time you spend at the gym. Replace your gym time with other activities to take your mind off the withdrawal you may experience. Make it a point to engage in activities that do not involve exercise. Read a magazine, go to the movies, or take a nap.

5 Watch yourself carefully and be willing to forgive a relapse.
Be prepared to relapse, which is a common occurrence on the road to recovery. If you fall back into your old gym habits, admit it to yourself and seek out others for support.

6 Do not be afraid to ask for help when you need it.
Consult a therapist. Form a support group for other exercise addicts.

7 Remember that no one is perfect.
Seek the ability to change the things you can and to accept the things you cannot change.

WARNING!

Replacing gym habits with workouts at home is a sign of addiction, not a step to recovery.

WORKOUT INJURIES

✪ Trapped under a barbell
Yell "Spot! Spot!" to get the attention of others who can lift the barbell off of you. If you can move, carefully slide your body so the weight is supported by your hands above your chest, rather than over your head, neck, or abdomen.

✪ The R.I.C.E. treatment for shin splints

REST the legs by avoiding jogging.

ICE the shins for 15 minutes several times each day.

COMPRESS the shins with a bandage to reduce swelling.

ELEVATE the legs above the head.

✪ Blister
Sterilize a needle by dipping it in rubbing alcohol or holding it over a match for several seconds, until red-hot.

Out-of-Control Treadmill

Sprint a step faster and lunge for the "kill switch" or yank the red power "key" from its socket on the control panel. If you cannot reach the control panel, keep pace as best you can and call for help.

Holding the needle parallel to the skin, puncture the blister at its edge. Apply gentle pressure to squeeze out the fluid, then cover the blister completely with a bandage.

✪ **Athlete's foot**
Soak your feet in a solution of warm water and 1 tablespoon of tea tree oil three times per day until the condition disappears. Wear absorbent socks made from natural fibers, and change immediately if the socks become damp. Remove shoe insoles and allow them to dry overnight, and dust the insides of shoes with talcum powder.

> Leave all the afternoon for exercise and recreation, which are as necessary as reading. I will rather say more necessary because health is worth more than learning.
>
> —*Thomas Jefferson*

Labels on figure: Deltoid, Chest wall, Pectoralis major, Bicep, Wrist, Gluteus maximus, Adductor muscles, Achilles tendon, Hamstring

Muscles	Injuries
Achilles tendon	calf strain
bicep	partial bicep tendon tear, complete bicep tendon tear
deltoid	posterior deltoid muscle strain
pectoralis major	pec muscle rupture
hamstring	pulled hamstring, chronic hamstring injury
gluteus maximus	gluteal strain
wrist	wrist sprain
chest wall	costochondritis (Tietze's syndrome)
adductor muscles	groin pull

HYGIENE

How to Survive If You Have Excessive Gas

1 Limit your lactose intake.
Many people suffer from an inability to digest milk sugar, or lactose. Colon bacteria ferment the milk sugar, forming a gas that creates a bloated feeling. Keep your intake to less than half a cup at a sitting, and avoid dairy products.

2 Eat a small meal.
Eating a huge dinner is a surefire way to precipitate gas.

3 Avoid gas-forming foods.
Bacteria ferment the indigestible carbohydrates in beans, broccoli, cabbage, and other vegetables and fruits into gases.

4 Drink peppermint tea.
Replace an after-dinner drink with a cup or two of peppermint tea. This herb may give you some relief from the gas discomfort that follows a meal.

5 Emit the gas in private.
As a last resort, head to the bathroom. If you feel bloated but are unable to pass gas easily, you can facilitate the emission of gas as follows:

- Place paper towels on the floor.
- Kneel on the towels.
- Bend forward to the floor.
- Stretch your arms out in front of you.
- Keep your buttocks high in the air
- Form a triangle with your upper body and the floor.

This position will force out the unwanted gas and relieve the pressure.

Kneel on the floor, bend forward, and stretch your arms out in front of you. Keep your buttocks high in the air, forming a triangle with your upper body and the floor.

WARNING!

- On average, humans produce ¾ liter of gas daily, which is released 11 to 14 times a day.
- Men typically produce more gas than women because they consume more food.

Gassy Foods to Avoid

No two digestive systems are alike. Experiment with foods to determine which ones affect you most. In the meantime, exercise caution around the following high-risk items:

- Beans (particularly baked beans)
- Borscht
- Broccoli
- Brussels sprouts
- Cabbage
- Carbonated beverages
- Cauliflower
- Chili
- Cucumbers
- Fatty foods
- Fresh fruit
- Grains and fiber, especially pumpernickel bread
- Gum
- Onions
- Oysters
- Salads (green)

How to Deal with Body Odor

1 Apply cologne or perfume.
If you are out and about and discover a problem with body odor, find a drugstore or department store. Apply the scent liberally.

2 Change your shirt or remove the offending article of clothing.
A simple change of clothing can often eliminate the odor, especially from an undershirt. Purchase a new shirt if you have to.

3 If you are away from home, use one of the following techniques in a bathroom of a restaurant or hotel:
- Wet a stack of paper towels with hot water and a bit of soap. Take a second stack of towels and wet them without adding soap. Wash under your arms and wherever necessary with the soapy towels, then rinse with the remaining towels.
- Obtain chamomile tea bags from your server if you are in a restaurant. Soak them in hot water, then wipe down the offending areas with the bags. If possible, leave them in place for several minutes.
- Obtain a handful of fresh rosemary from the kitchen, wet it slightly, and rub it over the offending areas.
- Apply bathroom soap (powdered works best) to the offending areas to mask the scent.

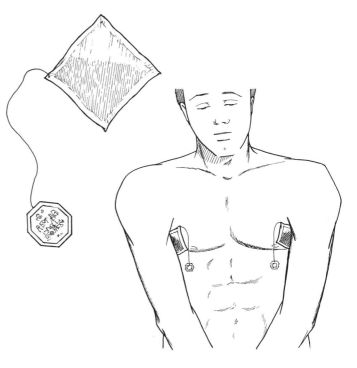

Soak chamomile tea bags in hot water. Wipe the offending areas with the tea bags. If possible, leave the bags in place for several minutes.

WARNING!

⚡ To avoid B.O., try bathing using an antibacterial soap. Prolonged use can cause dryness, however.

⚡ Avoid spicy or garlicky foods—these can cause body odor to worsen.

⚡ Unusual body odor—not the typical "sweaty" smell—may indicate a more serious condition.

⚡ Watch for the warning smells of B.O.:
- Beer smell may indicate a yeast infection.
- Nail polish smell may indicate diabetes.
- Ammonia smell may indicate liver disease.

Excessive Perspiration

Apply antiperspirant containing 2 percent aluminum chloride to armpits, palms, feet, face, back, chest, or other problem areas. Wear loose-fitting, light-colored cotton clothing to help mask visible sweat marks.

How to Deal with Bad Breath

1 Chew gum or mints.
If you are at a restaurant, excuse yourself from the table and head for the host's desk, where there may be a dish of mints. A waiter or busboy may also be able to give you a piece of gum. Go to the restroom and chew the gum for two minutes, then spit it out. This will get your saliva flowing and keep bad breath at bay for an hour or more. Chewing for more than a few minutes is not necessary. Sugar-free gum is best.

2 Chew parsley, mint, or a cinnamon stick.
On the way to the bathroom, pull your waiter aside and ask for one of these common garnishes. Parsley and fresh mint leaves are natural breath fresheners. A cinnamon stick, if chewed, will also clean your breath; do not use ground or powdered cinnamon. Most bartenders will have a stick on hand.

3 Order a salad or some fresh carrots.
If you cannot leave the table, order coarse foods that can help clean the tongue, a major source of bad breath.

WARNING!

⚡ Food odors are generally not as bad as you think, but when possible, avoid onions and garlic.

PERSONAL APPEARANCE

HOW TO TREAT A PIMPLE

1 Apply a warm compress.
Soak a hand towel in hot water, then hold it against the pimple for a minute or more.

2 Apply a topical medication.
Use any over-the-counter benzoyl peroxide product.

3 Do not touch.
Leave the pimple alone for as long as possible.

4 Reassess the situation.
Determine if the pimple has come to a head. If so, proceed to step 5.

5 Pop the pimple.
Place your fingers on either side of the pimple, and gently pull away from it. Do not push inward. The pimple will expel its contents if it is ready to, but no harm will be done if it is not.

6 Apply a cover-up.
Dab the now-empty pimple gently with a tissue to remove any remaining liquid. Apply any cosmetic with a green tint, which will conceal a pimple or the red mark left from a popped pimple (red and green are complementary colors and will negate each other).

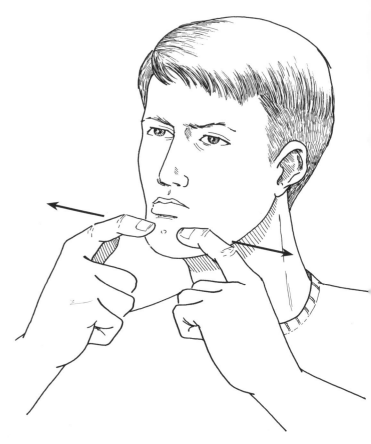

Place your fingers on either side of the pimple and gently pull away from it. Do not push inward.

HOW TO PREVENT WRINKLES

Repeat this sequence of facial expressions for five minutes twice daily to help prevent wrinkles.

To prevent wrinkles in forehead and around eyes

To strengthen mouth muscles and prevent laugh lines

To mold chin and prevent wrinkles around mouth

To relieve tension caused by previous exercise

How to Treat a Shaving Wound

Minor Cut

1 Rinse the cut with clean, cold water.

2 Apply alum salts or talcum powder.
Alum, a mineral sometimes sold as styptic powder or a styptic pencil, stops blood flow. Hold the alum in place for 10 to 20 seconds, depending on the severity of the wound. While effective, this technique can be painful, since it is literally applying "salt to the wound." The quickly dried cut may also form a noticeable scab. Alternatively, apply a liberal coating of talcum powder to the cut. Although slightly messier than alum, talcum is considerably less painful and will conceal the nicks and cuts. If alum or talcum powder is not available, proceed to step 3.

3 Apply toilet paper.
Tear off a tiny piece of toilet paper or tissue and press it onto the cut for at least 15 seconds, until it adheres by itself.

4 Wait a few minutes.

5 Remove the toilet paper.
Moisten the paper before carefully pulling it from the cut. If it is not moistened, the paper may reopen the cut when you peel it off.

Major Laceration

Most serious shaving wounds occur to the neck, underneath the nose, or underneath an earlobe. The steps below focus on a neck laceration but can apply to a major wound anywhere.

1 Apply firm pressure directly over the wound.
Place your fingertips at the point where the bleeding seems to be most severe.

2 If the bleeding stops, continue the pressure for an additional 10 minutes.
Remain still until the bleeding subsides. Then go to an emergency room.

How to Treat Bags Under Eyes

Steep two bags of black tea in warm water for 2 minutes; then soak in ice water to cool. Squeeze out excess liquid. Place a tea bag over each eye for 15 minutes. The tannic acid in the tea will reduce the swelling.

3 If the bleeding does not stop, do not panic.
You probably have slowed the flow enough to have time for the next steps.

4 Pinch and hold the bleeding area.
Use your dominant thumb and index finger to pinch the skin where the blood flow is coming from. This will most likely close the vessel even if you cannot see it and will stop the serious bleeding.

5 Locate the bleeding vessel.
If the bleeding continues despite the steps above, use a piece of cloth or tissue to help you find the exact location of the cut vessel. Carefully ease off the finger pressure while wiping blood away from the wound with the cloth. This should make it easier to see the end of the cut vessel, or to pinpoint its location even if it is deep under the skin. When you see it, try pinching it again.

6 Apply pressure directly above and below the bleeding site.
If bleeding is still profuse, maintain finger pressure over the wound while pushing immediately above and below the bleeding site. This will seal the areas where blood vessels enter the wound.

7 Get to an emergency room.
If you are being driven to the emergency room, recline with your head raised slightly. Keep firm pressure on the wound even if the bleeding seems to slow.

WARNING!

If the blood flows in a steady stream, you have hit a vein and can block the blood flow by pressing above the wound. If the blood is spurting, you have lacerated an artery and can block the blood flow by pressing (hard) below the wound. (See step 6.)

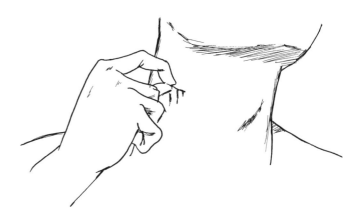

Pushing above or below the site will help seal the area where blood vessels enter the wound.

INNER PEACE

What to Do If You Forget Your Mantra

1 Remain calm.
If you cannot remember your mantra, let it go.

2 Be here now.
Be present in mind and place. Survey the contents of the room, and note three items or people.

3 Create a new mantra.
Combine the first syllable of the name of each item or person in the order you noticed them. This is your new mantra.

4 Recite the mantra.
Repeat your new mantra over and over until it loses its "meaning value" and transcends conscious thought.

5 After yoga class is over, write down your new mantra.

WARNING!

⚡ Common yoga injuries involve the neck, hip flexors, and lower back. Rarer and more serious injuries include herniated discs and fractures, which can be caused by poses such as plow and shoulder stand.

⚡ Do not attempt more challenging versions, such as "power yoga," without the guidance of an experienced teacher.

How to Treat Yoga Mishaps

Get Unstuck from Lotus Position

1 Take a calming breath.
Breathe in for a count of four, and then out for a count of four. Use your heartbeat to time the breaths.

2 Wedge your right hand beneath your left foot and your right thigh.
As you are removing the foot off the thigh, use your left hand to cradle the left knee.

3 Gently shift your left leg forward off the right thigh.
Fully extend your left leg and stretch your calf muscle. Rotate your ankle and wiggle your toes until you are sure your leg has not fallen asleep.

4 Use your hands to lift and move the right leg.
Stretch out the right leg as you did the left.

5 Allow your muscles to relax before standing.

Muscle Cramp

1 Get out of the position.
Stop doing whatever pose has caused you to cramp, and carefully reverse the movements that resulted in the cramp position.

2 Massage the cramped area.
Rub your hands in a gentle, circular motion over the cramp for one minute.

3 Stretch.
Extend the cramped area to its full length by pushing out your heel to stretch the calf muscle (if suffering a leg cramp) or fully extending your arm (if suffering an arm cramp).

4 Apply ice.
Wrap six chunks of ice in a headband and press against the cramping area. Rub the ice pack into the cramp for 10 to 15 minutes. Repeat steps 2 and 3.

5 Drink water.
Drink eight ounces of water within a half hour of the onset of the cramp, and remain hydrated until the cramp subsides.

Wedge your right hand beneath your left foot and your right thigh and gently lift your leg.

Focus your thoughts on your mind, body, and swing.

HOW TO TEE OFF IN FRONT OF A CROWD

1 Relax.

Try to see the first tee as any other shot in the round. Do not make significant changes in your tempo. Try not to rush any aspect of your pre-shot routine or swing. Ignore comments from the crowd waiting to play or pressure from the starter to speed up.

2 Warm up.

Thoroughly stretch in whatever way increases blood flow to your body and feels good. Take as many practice swings as you need.

3 Release the tension in your body.

Identify where the tension is, consciously tighten that area of your body, and then consciously relax that area while noticing the difference. Take a deep breath—in through your nose and out through your mouth—before you hit.

4 Be mindful.

Tune in to your feelings prior to your first swing. Are you nervous? Anxious? Steeped in self-judgment? Be aware of these negative feelings and the consequences of them on your body. Recognize that these feelings often get in the way of your true golf swing and game. Replace those feelings with positive energy. Choose to feel competent and content. Remember a time when you played your best. Generate these thoughts until you are ready to hit the ball.

5 Be confident about your abilities and expectations.

If you hit the ball 200 yards 80 percent of the time, you will most likely hit the ball 200 yards this time. This does not mean that you should not strive for your personal best throughout the game. Recognize that the first tee is a starting point on which you are building a solid foundation for your day's golf game.

6 Select the club with which you feel most comfortable.

This may not be your driver. Use a long iron or three wood if your driver is not your best club off the tee.

7 Follow a routine for addressing the ball.

Keep to an established pattern of how you walk up to the tee, how many practice swings you take, how you set your stance, and at what moment you start your swing. This routine is especially important on the first tee.

8 Do not overanalyze your swing.

Your muscle memory will complete the swing for you if you cease to over-think it. Do not over-swing in an effort to hit the ball farther.

9 Focus.

Choose a single location on the fairway and aim at that spot.

BE AWARE!

🖊 Spend time on the practice tee prior to hitting off the first tee. Go through six to eight clubs in your bag—start with wedges (they are easy to swing) and work your way up to woods. Visualize hitting off the first tee on your last 10 to 12 practice drives.

ILLNESS

HOW TO SURVIVE THE FLU PANDEMIC

⊙ **Wear a surgical mask in public.**
Influenza is a virus that enters the body through contact with mucous membranes, so you must protect your nose and mouth. If you cannot get a mask, keep a bandanna tied securely over your nose and mouth. Do not touch or rub your eyes, nose, or mouth.

⊙ **Restrict and ration towel usage.**
Each member of the household should have an assigned towel, washcloth, dishcloth, and pillow. (All household members should sleep in separate bedrooms, if possible.) Label towels with masking tape to avoid mix-ups. Wash all towels with bleach.

⊙ **Sneeze and cough into your elbow.**
Sneezing and coughing into your elbow will prevent germs from reaching your hands and being spread through contact. Recommend that others follow suit.

⊙ **Keep your hands clean.**
When washing hands in a public restroom, first pull the lever on the towel dispenser to lower a towel, then wash your hands. Rip off the dispensed towel, then use it to pull the dispenser lever again and to turn off the water faucet. Discard the first towel. Tear off the second towel and use it to dry your hands and open the bathroom door, then discard.

⊙ **Sanitize before touching areas with high germ potential.**
Disinfect light switches, doorknobs, keyboards and mice, telephone receivers, refrigerator door handles, sink faucets, and the flush handle on the toilet. Do not use public telephones.

⊙ **Empty the trash often.**
Do not let used tissues pile up in wastebaskets; they may carry the flu. Wear rubber gloves when emptying trash. Wash the gloves frequently, or throw them out after each use and get a new pair.

⊙ **Avoid areas with recirculated air systems.**
Do not get on an airplane. Avoid entering buildings that use recirculation systems designed to reduce fuel consumption. (In the United States, many such structures were erected during the 1970s energy crisis.)

⊙ **Do not enter areas where people congregate.**
Hospitals, prisons, day care centers, college dorms, movie theaters, checkout lines, and other places where large numbers of people cohabitate or group closely together should be avoided during the pandemic.

Limit Exposure

Cough into elbow.

Use only your own towel.

Avoid places where children gather.

Avoid recirculated air

Disinfect everyday objects.

Light switches

Doorknobs

Faucets

WARNING!

✓ Get a flu shot as soon as they become available.

✓ Wash hands frequently and immediately upon returning home from being outdoors.

✓ Not all masks are equally effective. For best protection, use an N95 "respirator" mask that completely covers the nose, mouth, and chin.

The Common Cold

Rest. Drink plenty of fluids. Gargle with warm salt water for scratchy throat. Chicken soup may help fight infection through intake of salt, heat, and fluid. Zinc interferes with cold-virus replication in lab settings—zinc nasal sprays may reduce symptoms if used at first sign of cold. There is no clear evidence of colds being prevented or eased by echinacea or vitamin C, or being caused by overheating or chills.

How to Survive Food Poisoning

1 Stay hydrated.
The symptoms of food poisoning vary depending on the type of microorganism or toxin ingested, but it can generally cause severe stomach cramping, fever, vomiting, and diarrhea, leading to dehydration. Drink lots of water.

2 Replenish mineral salts.
Eat bland foods, in moderation, as soon as you are able. Diarrhea depletes the body of salts, and drinking water alone will not replace them; sports rehydration drinks are effective. Nibble on dry salted crackers or plain rice to replenish salts, too.

3 Do not induce vomiting.
Depending on the microorganism or toxin involved, food poisoning may cause vomiting, which does not clear the bacteria from the body but will cause further dehydration.

4 Do not take anti-peristaltic medication.
Some anti-diarrhea medications work by slowing the movement of waste in the gut, causing the toxins to remain in the body for a longer period of time.

5 Avoid alcohol, spicy foods, and milk products.
These drinks and foods may aggravate the gut and cause additional gas and cramping. Never follow a suspect meal with a drink of alcohol to "kill" the germs; this is not effective.

6 Be prepared for several days of discomfort.
Food poisoning may induce a severe headache and sweating. Keep the body cool: never try to sweat out the germs. The symptoms of food poisoning are usually short-lived. If the symptoms persist for more than a week, or if you detect bleeding, consult a health care professional.

WARNING!

- Food poisoning is caused by a range of microorganisms or their by-products. Each bug has its own properties and set of symptoms: Some must be alive and present in large quantities to cause harm, while others, such as *E. coli* 0157, can inflict a lethal dose from just a few bacteria.

- To avoid botulinium toxin, do not eat food from dented cans.

- Oysters should be eaten cooked. Poultry should be fully cooked, with no traces of pink or red, to an internal temperature of 165°F. Beef and game should be cooked to at least 140°F.

- To prevent bacteria growth, keep hot foods piping hot and cold foods chilled; do not allow hot foods to cool to room temperature before storing them.

- Wash hands before handling food.

- Do not use the same knife on meat and vegetables unless they will both be cooked.

- Shigellosis, a foodborne illness, may be in the body for seven days before symptoms appear, including diarrhea, fever, abdominal cramps, and vomiting.

- If you get food poisoning from a restaurant, alert your local health department to prevent an outbreak.

Common Diseases and Means of Transmission*

strep throat	direct contact with saliva or nasal fluid; less easily from crowded environment
measles	travels very easily, from droplets expelled into the air by sick person coughing and sneezing
chicken pox	direct contact with infected person, or through coughing and sneezing
herpes	direct skin-to-skin contact only
malaria	bite of an infected mosquito
lice	most often direct hair-to-hair contact, or through a shared brush or hat
flu	through coughing and sneezing, to persons up to six feet away

* The most reliable means of stopping all contagious diseases is thorough and consistent hand-washing.

FIRST AID

How to Stitch a Gaping Wound

You will need three clean, dry hand towels or other cloths, clean water, tweezers, small pliers, scissors, a high-proof liquor (preferably vodka or gin), diphenhydramine (a liquid antihistimine), a sewing needle, unused fishing line or dental floss, and tissues.

1 Stop the bleeding.
Hold one of the hand towels over the wound for 15 minutes, using firm pressure. Do not use a tourniquet because you will cut off the blood supply and may force an amputation. Raise the affected limb above the level of the heart to slow bleeding. Do not attempt to stitch the wound until bleeding is under control.

2 Clean the wound.
Soak the injured body part in warm water. Gently scrub the wound, taking care not to dislodge any obvious blood clots. Irrigate by running cool water over the wound for five minutes.

3 Inspect the wound carefully for foreign material.
Use tweezers to remove any foreign objects, then irrigate again. (Remember the phrase, "The solution to pollution is dilution.")

4 Sterilize your equipment.
Wash the needle, tweezers, pliers, and scissors in hot, soapy water. Rinse once with warm water, then again with alcohol. Lay the tools to dry on one of the towels.

5 Wash your hands.
Lather for at least five minutes.

6 Prepare the victim.
Instruct the victim to lie down on a table or the floor, preferably on his back. Do not allow the victim to sit or stand. Rinse the wound again with warm water and pat it dry. Splash lightly with alcohol and wait three minutes. Pour several capfuls of the diphenhydramine directly into the wound to provide some anesthesia.

7 Prepare a clean work space.
Cut a hole in the center of the third towel. Place this "smock" over the wound, making sure the complete wound is visible through the hole.

8 Prepare the needle and thread.
Using the pliers, bend the needle into a "C" shape. Measure out 10 times the length of the wound in fishing line or dental floss. Cut. Run the "thread" through the eye of the

Grip the needle with the pliers so that the needle's point curves upward.

Enter the skin ¼ inch from the wound's edge. Pull the needle through the skin using the pliers.

Wrap two loops of thread from the "needle" side of the thread around the nose of your pliers. Grab the two-inch tail of the thread with your pliers, and gently pull it through the looped thread to create the knot.

needle so the needle rests one-quarter of the way down the thread. Rewash your hands.

9 Make the first stitch.
You should "throw" the first stitch at the midpoint of the wound. First, grip the needle with the pliers, clamping over the needle's hole. Next, hold the pliers so that the needle's point curves upward. Turn your wrist and aim the point directly down at the skin. Use your other hand to hold up the wound edge with the tweezers. Finally, enter the skin

one-quarter inch from the wound's edge, come through the wound, enter the other side of the wound's edge, and come out one-quarter inch from the other edge of the wound.

10 Knot each stitch.
Pull the needle through the skin using the pliers, then pull the thread with your hand until two inches are left on the side where the needle entered the skin. Loosely wrap two loops of thread from the "needle side" of the thread around the nose of your pliers. Grab the two-inch tail with your pliers, then apply gentle upward pressure to bring both edges of the wound together. Pull your pliers back through the looped floss to create the knot, pulling gently in opposite directions so that the knot lies flat on the skin.

11 Lock the knot.
Quickly arc your pliers-hand toward the needle side of the thread, and pull both ends of the thread down onto the skin. Doing so "locks" the knot and moves the knot onto the skin rather than over the wound.

12 Secure the knot.
Repeat the looping and knotting five times, alternating the direction of the looping; this will avoid "granny" knots that will not hold. If you notice that your hands are alternating back and forth in a rhythmic pattern as you tie each knot, you are tying correctly. Double-check that the knot is pulled to the side so that it lays over the skin, not on the wound itself.

13 Cut the thread.
Cut both ends of thread. Leave a ¼ inch tail of thread so that the stitching can be removed later.

14 Continue stitching.
Choose the midpoint between the first stitch and one end of the wound, and repeat steps 9 through 13. Continue to bisect the wound between stitches, throwing additional stitches and tying knots until the wound is closed.

Tourniquets

- Use a tourniquet to temporarily stop severe bleeding from a limb.

- Apply tourniquet (a band, cloth, etc.) tightly between the wound and the heart, close to the wound and above the elbow or knee.

- Tourniquets stop all blood flow and can kill the tissues in the limb, eventually necessitating the loss of the limb.

How to Make a Splint or Sling

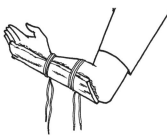

Immobilize the injury site with a splint extending to a joint above and below the break. Wrap the fracture in soft material (cloth, cotton, moss). Bind with firm material (branches, poles, boards, magazines) and tie with shoelaces to secure.

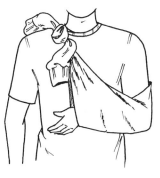

For fractures below the elbow, make a sling by securely tying together the sleeves of a buttoned-up shirt or jacket and slipping it over your head and around the back of your neck. Tuck the injured arm in the bulk of the shirt or jacket.

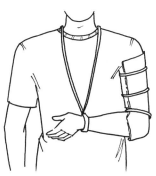

For fractures above the elbow, make a sling by running string or shoelaces around the back of your neck and tying them to the wrist of the injured arm. Place a pad of soft cloth material into the armpit.

How to Treat a Leg Fracture

1 If skin is broken, do not touch or put anything on the wound.

You must avoid infection. If the wound is bleeding severely, try to stop the flow of blood by applying steady pressure to the affected area with sterile bandages or clean clothes.

2 Do not move the injured leg—you need to splint the wound to stabilize the injured area.

3 Find two stiff objects of the same length—wood, plastic, or folded cardboard—for the splints.

4 Put the splints above and below the injured area—under the leg (or on the side if moving the leg is too painful).

5 Tie the splints with string, rope, or belts—whatever is available.
Alternatively, use clothing torn into strips. Make sure the splint extends beyond the injured area.

6 Do not tie the splints too tightly; this may cut off circulation.
You should be able to slip a finger under the rope or fabric. If the splinted area becomes pale or white, loosen the ties.

7 Have the injured person lie flat on his back.
This helps blood continue to circulate and may prevent shock.

WARNING!

- Do not push at, probe, or attempt to clean an injury; this can cause infection.
- Do not move the injured person unless absolutely necessary. Treat the fracture and then go get help.
- If the person must be moved, be sure the injured part is completely immobilized first.
- Do not elevate an injured leg.
- Do not attempt to move or reset a broken bone; this will cause severe pain and may complicate the injury.

Do not move the injured leg.

Find two stiff objects of the same length— wood, plastic, or folded cardboard.

Place the splints above and below the injured area.

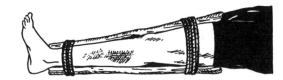

Tie the splints with string, rope, or belts—whatever is available.

Do not tie the splints too tightly— you should be able to slip one finger under the rope, belt, or fabric.

Symptoms of a Fracture, Sprain, or Dislocation

- Difficult or limited movement
- Swelling
- Bruising of the affected area
- Severe pain
- Numbness
- Severe bleeding
- A visible break of bone through the skin

EMERGENCY MEDICINE

How to Treat a Severed Limb

1 Locate any individual bleeding arteries on the stump. The arteries will bleed in pulsating spurts.

2 Pinch off the large arteries that are bleeding the most. The brachial artery in the arm and femoral artery in the leg carry blood into the limb, and are the major vessels you should find. Someone (the victim or another person) should continue pinching while you proceed to the next step.

3 Apply a tourniquet.
Choose a strip of material at least an inch wide, and tie it around the stump as close to the end as possible so that the tourniquet will not fall off when it is tightened. Tie the tourniquet moderately tight, but do not immediately cinch it as tight as possible or you may crush and destroy viable tissue. Tighten the tourniquet just enough to stop most of the remaining bleeding. Keep pinching the arteries.

4 Tie off the ends of any blood vessels being pinched.
Use fishing line, dental floss, or heavy thread (in that order of preference) along with a sewing needle if available to carefully tie off the arteries. Pass the line completely around the blood vessel being pinched, as far up as possible. Tighten the first knot down hard, then place several securing knots on top of the first one. You may want to tie the vessel down in two places, in case one of the stitches comes apart later.

5 Clean the stump thoroughly.
Preventing infection is very important:

- Pick out foreign material lodged in the wound.
- Cut off crushed tissue remnants still attached to the stump. Use a sharp knife or scissors.
- Wash the wound, vigorously irrigating it with a stream of water.

6 Optional: Cauterize remaining bleeding sites.
Using an iron or piece of heated metal, identify the vessels that are still oozing blood. This is simpler during irrigation, when debris and clotted blood are washed away. Dab at each vessel lightly with cloth or gauze to allow yourself to see exactly where its end appears in the wound, then apply cautery at that point. Do not worry about completely eliminating bleeding. If rapid bleeding is well controlled, oozing will be controllable once the dressings are applied.

7 Loosen the tourniquet.
As the pressure from the tourniquet decreases, you will be

To preserve the limb, wash it gently; wrap it in a clean, moist cloth; pack it in a watertight material; and keep it cool.

able to check your ties and ensure that more ties (or cautery) are not needed. If bleeding is just a moderate ooze, you have been successful and the tourniquet can be removed. To preserve tissue at the stump, do not leave a tourniquet applied for more than 90 minutes.

8 Dress the stump.
Coat the end of the stump with any type of available antibiotic ointment (examples include bacitracin, polymyxin, and mupirocin). Then tightly cover the end of the stump with clean cloth or gauze. Elastic strapping works well to hold the dressing onto the stump end. The tighter the dressing, the less the chance of sustained bleeding.

9 Elevate the stump end as high as possible to allow gravity to assist in slowing further bleeding.

10 Put an ice pack over the dressing.

11 Be prepared to apply and tighten a tourniquet again, should heavy bleeding resume.

12 Treat pain and shock from blood loss.
Use any available pain medication to treat pain from the injury. To treat shock, give the victim animal meat or a liquid containing salt (such as chicken soup). These will help to restore plasma and hemoglobin.

How to Preserve the Severed Limb

1 Gently wash the severed limb with water.

2 Wrap the limb in a moist, clean cloth.

3 Wrap the limb again in watertight material (such as a plastic bag).

4 Keep the limb cold.
Do not freeze the limb. Freezing will destroy tissue. Use a cooler full of ice or a refrigerator.

5 Get to a hospital immediately.
A limb saved in this manner can remain viable for reattachment for up to six hours.

WARNING!

Traumatic amputation of a limb is not necessarily a fatal injury. In order of severity, the immediate problems that you must deal with are rapid severe arterial bleeding; slower bleeding from cut veins; pain; and infection. Only severe bleeding carries an immediate, life-threatening risk, with the possibility of death in minutes.

Submerging a severed limb in water may cause damage that could hinder its reattachment. You can, however, place it in a watertight container and then submerge that in a river or lake to keep the limb cool.

HOW TO PERFORM A TRACHEOTOMY

What You Will Need

- A first aid kit, if available.

- A razor blade or very sharp knife.

- A straw (two would be better) or a ballpoint pen with the inside (ink-filled tube) removed. If neither a straw nor a pen is available, use stiff paper or cardboard rolled into a tube. Good first aid kits may contain "trache" tubes.

There will not be time for sterilization of your tools, so do not bother; infection is the least of your worries at this point.

How to Proceed

1 Find the person's Adam's apple (thyroid cartilage).

2 Move your finger about one inch down the neck until you feel another bulge.
This is the cricoid cartilage. The indentation between the two is the cricothyroid membrane, where the incision will be made.

3 Take the razor blade or knife and make a half-inch horizontal incision.
The cut should be about half an inch deep. There should not be too much blood.

4 Pinch the incision open or place your finger inside the slit to open it.

5 Insert your tube in the incision, roughly one-half to one inch deep.

6 Breathe into the tube with two quick breaths.
Pause five seconds, then give one breath every five seconds.

7 You will see the chest rise, and the person should regain consciousness if you have performed the procedure correctly.
The person should be able to breathe on his own, albeit with some difficulty, until help arrives.

WARNING!

This procedure, technically called a cricothyroidotomy, should be undertaken only when a person with a throat obstruction is not able to breathe at all—no gasping sounds, no coughing—and only after you have attempted to perform the Heimlich maneuver three times without dislodging the obstruction. If possible, someone should call for paramedics while you proceed.

Find the indentation between the Adam's apple and the cricoid cartilage.

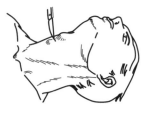

Make a half-inch horizontal incision about one-half inch deep.

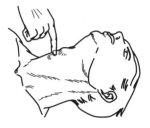

Pinch the incision or insert your finger inside the slit to open it.

Insert your tube into the incision, roughly one-half to one inch deep.

How to Save Yourself If You Are Having a Heart Attack

1 Chew aspirin.

As soon as you suspect a heart attack, thoroughly chew and swallow one 325-mg aspirin tablet or four 81-mg baby aspirins. For best effect, do not swallow the aspirin whole. Heart attacks occur when the blood vessels supplying oxygen to the heart muscle become clogged. Aspirin will not stop the heart attack or remove the blockage, but it will prevent blood-clotting cells (platelets) from adding to the blockage.

2 Alert others.

If possible, tell people around you that you are having a heart attack. Instruct them to call emergency services.

3 Decrease the heart's oxygen consumption.

Stop all activity. The faster your heart pumps, the more oxygen it uses up. Think calming thoughts about bringing your heart rate down to one beat per second. If you have a watch with a second hand, focus on the second hand. For each second, think or say quietly "heartbeat." Repeat.

4 Increase oxygen delivery to the heart.

Lie down on the ground. Elevate your legs to keep as much blood pooled around your heart as possible; this will decrease the work your heart must do to pump blood. Open the windows to increase the room's oxygen level. If you have access to an oxygen tank, place the nasal cannula under your nose, turn the knob to four liters (or until you feel air coming through the nasal prongs), and take deep, slow breaths through your nose and out your mouth.

5 Perform cough CPR.

Breathe, then cough every three seconds. Take a breath in through your nose, think "heartbeat, heartbeat, heartbeat," then cough. Repeat. Coughing will deter fainting and help you stay conscious until conventional CPR can be administered.

WARNING!

Do not consume food or water. You may need a hospital procedure to "unclog" your arteries, and food or liquids in your system complicate treatment.

How to Use a Defibrillator to Restore a Heartbeat

1 Turn on the defibrillator by pressing the green button. Most machines will provide both visual and voice prompts.

2 First, remove the person's shirt and jewelry, then apply the pads to the chest as shown in the diagram displayed on the machine's LED panel.

One pad should be placed on the upper right side of the chest, one on the lower left.

3 Plug the pads into the connector.

The defibrillator will analyze the patient and determine if he needs a shock. Do not touch the patient at this time.

4 If the machine determines that a shock is needed, it will direct you—both audibly and with visual prompts—to press the orange button to deliver a shock.

Do not touch the patient after pressing the button. The machine will automatically check to see whether or not the patient needs a second shock, and if so, it will direct you to press the orange button again.

5 Check the patient's airway, breathing, and pulse.

If there is a pulse but the patient is not breathing, begin mouth-to-mouth resuscitation. If there is no pulse, repeat the defibrillation process.

Apply one pad to the upper right of the patient's chest, the other pad to the lower left.

WARNING!

A defibrillator should be used for a person experiencing sudden cardiac arrest (SCA), a condition where the heart's electrical signals become confused and the heart ceases to function. A person experiencing SCA will stop breathing, the pulse will slow or stop, and consciousness will be lost.

Defibrillation is the delivery of a powerful electrical shock to the heart. (The defibrillator is the device used in movies and TV shows: two handheld pads are placed on the victim's chest while an actor yells "Clear!") In the past, defibrillators were very heavy and expensive, needed regular maintenance, and were mostly found only in hospitals. Now more portable units are available.

CHOKING

Pull your fist in and up, quickly and with strength.

Strike your date between the shoulder blades with the heel of your open hand.

HOW TO SAVE YOUR DATE FROM CHOKING

1 Speak firmly.
Keep your voice low and your sentences short. All communications should be in the imperative. Explain that you are going to perform the Heimlich maneuver.

2 Tell your date to stand up and stay put.

3 Hug your date from behind.
Put your arms around your date and make one hand into a fist.

4 Place your fist in your date's solar plexus.
The solar plexus is the first soft spot in the center of the body just below the ribs.

5 Place your other hand, palm open, over your fist.

6 Tell your date to bend forward slightly.
If your date does not respond, push on the upper back and say, "Lean forward."

7 Pull your fist in and up.
Use force and a quick motion. This will push out the residual lung gas under pressure, clearing any obstructions from the trachea.

8 Repeat steps 3 through 7 several times if choking persists.

9 After several unsuccessful attempts, instruct your date to bend over the back of a chair.
The top of the chair should be at the level of your date's hips.

10 Strike your date between the shoulder blades with the heel of your open hand.
The blow generates gaseous pressure in a blocked airway and, with a head-down position, sometimes works when the Heimlich does not.

WARNING!

↯ If the choking is noiseless—or if your date raises her hands to her throat—then the air passage may be completely blocked and you must proceed quickly.

↯ If your date is coughing or gagging, you simply need to be polite, smile sympathetically, and offer water when the choking is over. Water does nothing for choking, but it gives the choker some time to regain dignity.

↯ In most cases, the first thrust of the Heimlich maneuver will dislodge the choked item from the trachea. Once the choking is over and the blockage has been removed, there is usually no need to go to the emergency room.

HOW TO GIVE A DOG THE HEIMLICH MANEUVER

1 Check for throat obstructions.
Open the dog's mouth and inspect the back of the throat, looking for the object causing the obstruction. If you see it, carefully remove it. If the dog is unconscious, pull the tongue forward for a better view.

2 Shake the obstruction free.
If the dog is small, pick him up and hold him by the hips with his head hanging down. For larger dogs, hold the hind legs so that the head hangs down. If this fails to dislodge the obstruction, place the dog back on the ground and proceed to the next step.

3 Place your arms around the dog's waist.
With the dog standing or lying down, clasp your hands together around the stomach, placing them just below the last rib.

4 Compress the stomach.
Push up five times rapidly.

5 Check for an obstruction.
Sweep the dog's mouth with your fingers to see if the object was dislodged.

6 Repeat.
If the object has not come free, strike the dog firmly between the shoulder blades with the flat side of one hand, and then do another five abdominal compressions. Alternate the back-slapping and compressions until the object is knocked free.

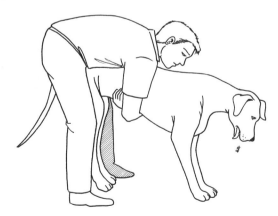

Place your arms around the dog's waist below the last rib and compress the stomach.

WARNING!

⚡ An unconscious dog may still bite reflexively. Be careful when sweeping the mouth. When jarring the obstruction free by striking the dog, do not hit him so hard as to injure him.

How to Perform the Heimlich Maneuver on Your Cat

Kneel and hold the cat in front of you, close to your chest. Place one forearm under the cat's front legs and hold him up and out-stretched, facing away from you. Place the fist of your other hand just below the bottom rib. Give two or three quick, firm pushes inward to force the air out of the lungs and dislodge the object.

HOW TO SAVE YOURSELF FROM CHOKING

1 Try to talk.
If you can talk or are able to vocalize in any way, or if you make a sound when coughing, your airway is not completely blocked and you are not in imminent danger of death. Keep coughing to dislodge the stuck material. If you cannot make any sounds, you will need to perform the one-person Heimlich maneuver.

2 Quickly locate a blunt object at waist level.
If you are indoors, find a chair, table, counter, or other piece of furniture; if you are outside, look for a tall tree stump, fence, ledge, or large rock.

3 Face the object.

4 Bend over the object.
Lean so that the object touches your body six inches above your navel.

5 Fall.
Let yourself drop forward hard and fast onto the object. This movement should force the air up your windpipe and eject the item that is blocking your airway.

3
Shaky Foundations

HOME AND HEARTH

WEDDINGS

How to Raise Money for the Wedding

○ **Ask family members to pay for specific expenses.**
Have numbers ready to justify costs. If you sense resistance, threaten to elope or to have the reception at a seedy nightclub. For grandparents, offer upgrades at the reception in exchange for funding, such as seating at a table far from the band, their food served first, or wider, cushioned seats.

○ **Register for wedding ceremony and reception components.**
Instead of a bridal registry for china, crystal, and silver, register for floral arrangements, the band, limousine service, liquor for the reception, and each course of the meal.

○ **Hold a raffle.**
Offer the guests a chance to buy tickets to win the wedding dress, a ride in the limo, or a chance to join the honeymoon.

○ **Wash guests' cars.**
Hire a student at a low hourly rate to sell expensive car washes to the guests as they attend the ceremony and reception.

○ **Sell your belongings on Internet auction sites.**
Check to see which items you've registered for have been bought, or estimate which items you are sure to receive, and sell them online. The buyer will send payment, and, after the wedding, you send the sold item.

○ **Procure sponsors.**
Strike a deal with a local company. Agree to place its logo on the invitation, wedding dress, tuxedo, or cake. Have the bandleader announce each song with, "This song has been brought to you by the good people at [*name of company*]." Hang company banners around the altar and behind the bandstand. Allow the company to set up a kiosk at the ceremony and reception site to dispense information, key chains, and other swag.

○ **Sell incentive packages to investors.**
Offer a percentage of wedding gifts, naming rights to kids, occasional dinners at your home, an invitation to the wedding (with preferred seating), the first dance with the bride/groom, and, for enough money, the opportunity to give away the bride.

Procure sponsors to help defray costs.

How to Treat a Panic Attack

1 Realize that you're panicking.
Panic begets panic. Do not panic about panicking. Tell yourself that you are not dying or going crazy, but experiencing an anxiety attack. This awareness will prevent the attack from escalating.

2 Loosen your clothes.
Do not tear off your dress or jacket. Open a few buttons; lower a zipper.

3 Control your breathing.
Prevent hyperventilation by slowing your breathing.

Breathe into a paper bag to restore a balance of oxygen and carbon dioxide in your lungs.

4 Distract yourself.
Focus on a physical object in the room. While breathing into the bag, close your eyes and try to recall the location and colors of all the objects in the room.

5 Act natural.
Open your eyes. Stop using the bag. Refasten zippers and buttons. Walk. Try to smile. Tell yourself it's over and everything is fine.

6 Resume your activities.

BE AWARE!

✎ An attack usually lasts between 15 and 30 minutes. Symptoms include pounding heart, sweating, dilated pupils, trembling, dry mouth, shortness of breath or sensation of being smothered, feelings of being choked, chest pain, nausea, dizziness, sense of being detached from oneself, and fear of losing control or going crazy.

✎ Knowing that you can conquer the attacks will sharply reduce their occurrence. Conversely, knowing that you are prey to attacks and cannot control them may sharply increase their occurrence.

Control your breathing.

HOW TO AVOID A NERVOUS BREAKDOWN BEFORE THE WEDDING

☺ Ignore minor irritations.
Avoid driving at rush hour, upgrading your computer software, dealing with a governmental agency, thinking about your job, rooting for any sports team, undertaking a plumbing project, or listening to the local news.

☺ Imagine yourself in a relaxing situation.
As you visualize, hold on to something tactile—a lucky rabbit's foot or your grandmother's favorite handkerchief. Hold it again later to restore your sense of calm. If you do not have a soothing object when the panic begins, conjure up safe and peaceful images.

☺ Practice yoga.
Find a quiet room and close the door. Dim the lights.

- **Tree pose.** Stand with your feet together. Draw your left foot up your right leg until it rests on your inner thigh. Put the palms of your hands together and raise them over your head. Balance and remain still. Lower your leg and repeat with the other side.

- **Child's pose.** Get on your hands and knees and sit back so that your bottom touches your heels; lower your chest so that it is resting on your thighs. Keep your arms alongside your body with your fingers close to your ankles and your cheek on the floor. Rest.

- **Corpse pose.** Remain on the floor. Turn over on your back. Rest your arms and legs flat on the floor. Close your eyes and relax every muscle. Do this for as long as it takes, but for at least five minutes. Do not fall asleep. Get up slowly when you feel calm or when it is time to walk down the aisle.

☺ Laugh.
Rent videos of musicals from the 1930s, 1940s, and 1950s, especially those with Gene Kelly and Fred Astaire.

☺ Go to sleep early the night before the wedding.
Even if you cannot sleep, at least your body will be resting. Do not plan the bachelor or bachelorette party for the night before the ceremony.

☺ Eat and drink.
Make sure you eat on the big day, even if you do not feel hungry. Avoid caffeine, alcohol, and gassy, bloating foods. Remain hydrated. If you are prone to fainting, drink some juice, sugary soda, or a shot of grappa (for courage) before walking down the aisle.

☺ Elope.

How to Deal With Lost Rings

○ **Use cigar bands.**
The best man or groomsmen may have cigars in their pockets. Slip the paper band off the cigar and give one to the bride and one to the groom to use in place of wedding bands. Large cigars with wide ring gauges have bands that are most likely to fit.

○ **Borrow from guests.**
Send the best man to collect rings from guests. Ask him to bring back an assortment of sizes so that one is sure to fit. The style of the ring does not matter.

○ **Use a ponytail holder.**
Twist the elastic in figure eights until it is small enough to fit on a finger.

○ **Bend paper clips.**
Straighten and then bend the paper clips into a ring. Watch for sharp ends.

○ **Braid rubber bands.**
Braid three rubber bands, then tie loose ends together to form a ring.

How to Make an Emergency Ring

You will need the foil wrapper from a stick of chewing gum and a piece of tape. For a man's ring, use an entire wrapper; for a woman's ring, use a wrapper that has been cut in half lengthwise.

1 Remove the gum from the foil wrapper.
Discard or chew the gum.

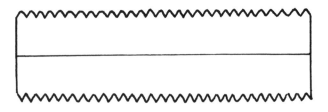

2 Smooth the foil on a flat surface.
Flatten all wrinkles and folds.

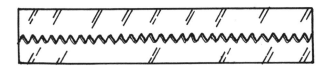

3 Refold the wrapper lengthwise.
Follow the existing crease lines and fold each of the longer sides up to meet in the middle, leaving the short ends unfolded.

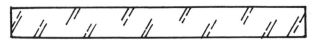

4 Fold the wrapper in half lengthwise if making a woman's ring.
The seams will be hidden in the middle.

5 Fold one end into a point.

6 Insert the point into the fold.

7 Fit the strip around your finger in the shape of a ring.
Size the ring to a comfortable fit.

8 Secure the ring with a small piece of tape.

WARNING!

⚡ If a gum wrapper is not available, or if you prefer a different color ring, you can use paper money. Select foreign currencies for a more dramatic palette. Other options (cut to fit) include candy bar wrappers, aluminum foil, writing paper, or bank checks.

Thank-You Note Generator

Use the following equation and score chart to assess the actual value (AV) of any wedding gift; then select the appropriate thank-you note.

V/GI x (TQ + AQ) = AV

V = Estimated retail value
(in dollars)

GI = Estimated gross annual income of giver
(in thousands of dollars)

TQ = Tastefulness quotient (from tacky to attractive to classy, on a scale of 1–10)

tacky   attractive   classy
| 1 | 2 | 3 | 4 | 5 | 6 | 7 | 8 | 9 | 10 |

AQ = Appropriateness quotient (from dumb to useful to cool, on a scale of 1–10)

dumb   useful   cool
| 1 | 2 | 3 | 4 | 5 | 6 | 7 | 8 | 9 | 10 |

AV = actual value

Score Chart

Below 10
A very bad gift—
no note

10–20
A bad gift—
use Note A

21–40
A good gift—
use Note B

41+
A great gift—
use Note C

Example:

You are given a blender with a retail value around $100 by a college friend with a gross annual income of around $40,000. It is quite tasteful in design (you'd rate it a 9 in TQ as blenders go) and will be quite useful (a 9 as well, since you don't have a blender). Thus, this gift receives a score of: 100/40 x (9 + 9) = 45, a high score. If you received the same gift from a wealthy family friend, however, with a gross annual income around $140,000, the gift would receive a score of 100/140 x (9 + 9) = 12.86, a low score.

You are given a doormat with a retail value around $35 by a neighbor with a gross annual income of around $100,000. It's hideously ugly (a TQ rating of 2), and you already have a doormat (AQ rating of 3, as there would be some pleasure in wiping your feet on it).

35/100 x (2 + 3) = 1.75, a score below the scale.

NOTE A

Dear _____,

Thank you so much for the [*name of gift here*]. We can't believe you thought of it for us! We will put it in a special place. Know that whenever we look at it, we'll think of you.

Sincerely,

[*your names here*]

NOTE B

Dear _____,

Thank you so much for the [*name of gift here*]. We genuinely appreciate your thoughtfulness in seeking out such a practical gift. Just know that whenever we use it, we'll think of you.

Sincerely,

[*your names here*]

NOTE C

Dear _____,

Thank you so much for the [*name of gift here*]. We can't believe you thought of it for us! We can't believe your generosity and creativity. It's a fabulous gift. You must come over and enjoy it with us soon. We'll think of you always.

Sincerely,

[*your names here*]

MARRIAGE

Extreme sunburn

Tongue injury

How to Survive a Honeymoon Disaster

Extreme Sunburn

1 **Expose damaged skin to air.**
Remove all clothing around the burn area: Clothing will irritate the burn site and may cause increased pain.

2 **Drink water.**
Drink at least 32 ounces of water to help promote sweating, which cools the skin.

3 **Apply a cold compress.**
Put ice in a plastic bag, wrap in a cotton T-shirt or other fabric, and apply to the burn area. If the burn area is very large, soak a bedsheet in ice water and apply it instead of a compress. Let the skin cool under the compress for 15 minutes to help reduce pain.

4 **Apply a soothing gel or ointment to the burn area.**
Carefully rub a cooling aloe lotion into the burned area. This is especially soothing if the aloe has been chilled in a refrigerator or a bucket of ice. Do not apply suntan lotion, baby oil, petroleum jelly, or any other foreign substance to the burn.

5 **Take pain medication.**
Ibuprofen will help reduce pain at the burn site.

6 **Lie still.**
Lie in a position that best exposes your sunburn to the air without coming into contact with the bed, your clothing, or another person. Do not bend sunburned joints.

7 **Continue with your honeymoon.**
Take advantage of loose-fitting island fashions as your sunburn heals.

WARNING!

⚡ Depending on the severity of the sunburn, a new layer of skin will replace the burned area in two days to two weeks.

Acute Tongue Injury

1 **Prepare a tea bag.**
Soak a tea bag in warm water for two minutes. Let it stand one minute at room temperature, then wrap it in gauze or a clean cloth napkin.

2 **Apply tea bag to tongue.**
Place the moist tea bag on the injury site and press steadily. The tannic acid in the tea is a natural coagulant and should

stop the bleeding. The tongue has a large number of blood vessels near the surface and will bleed profusely until the blood coagulates.

3 Rinse.
Swish and spit using an anesthetic mouthwash, if available.

4 Apply a numbing agent.
Apply ice to the wound to numb and reduce pain.

5 Avoid acidic and salty foods and liquids.
Acidic substances, such as citrus fruits and vinegar, and those high in salt, such as nuts and potato chips, may aggravate the injury.

6 Keep the tongue still.
The tongue will heal more quickly if it is inactive.

7 Protect the tongue.
Wear an athletic mouth guard to protect the tongue until the injury heals.

How to Apologize When You Don't Know What You've Done Wrong

1 Evaluate the threat level.
Examine your partner's pupils and nostrils. Pupils dilated and nostrils flared means that you are in extreme amount of trouble. If the pupils are not dilated and nostrils are not flared, make a small silly joke or offer a nonsexual compliment and see if a smile is offered. An apology may not be required.

2 Do not guess.
Do not panic and start apologizing for things that your partner may not in fact be aware of. By saying, "I am sorry I was late paying your mortgage," when she may not have known that, may put you in twice as much trouble as before.

3 Offer a nonspecific apology.
"I'm sorry for what I did. What I did was bad. It was a dumb thing to do."

4 Offer a nonspecific excuse.
"I had a lot on my mind when I did that, which was dumb and bad."

5 Solicit information.
Trick your partner into filling you in on what you have done wrong by feigning interest in learning how to do it better next time. "Why don't you tell me exactly what it was that bothered you so much, so I never do it again." Once it is clear what you did, offer an event-specific apology and/or excuse.

6 Offer a guarantee of universally improved performance in future.
Promise that you will do better in all aspects, in all ways, from now on.

How to Prevent Snoring

✪ Change sleep positions.
Snoring is often caused by lying on your back. Train yourself to sleep on your side or stomach.

✪ Sew a tennis ball to the back of your pajamas.
Prevent yourself from turning over onto your back in the middle of the night by attaching a tennis ball to your back. This will force you to lie on your side, effectively ridding you of the habit.

✪ Avoid alcohol.
Alcohol and other sedatives increase muscle relaxation, which increases snoring.

✪ Change your diet.
Reduce the amount of refined carbohydrates and dairy products that you consume. Both increase mucus production, which can cause snoring. Also avoid eating large meals at night right before bed.

✪ Exercise.
Extra body fat, especially bulky neck tissue, can cause snoring. Losing just 10 percent of your body weight can improve your overall breathing.

✪ Apply nasal strips.
Open nasal passages with adhesive nose strips.

✪ Use a throat spray.
Lubricate your throat with a spray that will relax the throat muscles.

✪ Practice aromatherapy.
Reduce nasal congestion with essential oils. Leave a jar of marjoram oil open on your nightstand while you sleep. Add a few drops of eucalyptus oil to a water-filled humidifier. Breathe in the steam just prior to going to bed.

✪ Use a neti pot.
Reduce allergens in your sinuses by washing out your nasal passages with a neti pot. Fill the pot with water and ¼ teaspoon of salt. Hold your head over a sink at an angle so your chin is parallel with your forehead. Tilt the pot so the tip of the arm enters one nostril. Allow the water to flow in one nostril and out the other. Repeat in the other nostril.

✪ Prop up your mattress.
Put a dictionary, encyclopedia, or phone book under your mattress to raise your head and change the angle of your neck.

How to Survive If You Forget Your Anniversary

○ **Order an emergency bouquet.**
Many florists can assemble arrangements with little notice. If you have just minutes to prepare, scour your neighborhood flowerbeds for daisies. Wrap them in colorful ribbon and present them as your initial gift.

○ **Buy chocolates.**
Most supermarkets and drugstores carry chocolate assortments. Choose a tasteful boxed set rather than several loose candy bars tied with ribbon.

○ **Create a voucher card.**
Prepare a card or piece of paper that shows the wonderful gift you're giving but can't give now because it isn't ready yet. Draw a picture of the gift on the card or paper.

○ **Apologize, apologize, apologize.**
If you're caught with nothing, making excuses will not help your case. Your level of contrition should be so extreme that your spouse begins to feel bad because you feel so terrible.

○ **Give an intangible present.**
Give her a homemade certificate for a weekend spa getaway. It could be for her only, or for a romantic weekend for both of you—a "second honeymoon" (but don't push your luck). A week free of household chores, a weekend of breakfasts in bed, or getting her car detailed are other possibilities.

First anniversary

Tenth anniversary

How to Sleep on the Couch

1 Remove the back cushions.
If the couch has loose back cushions, take them off to add more width to the sleeping surface.

2 Remove the arm cushions.
Side cushions take up previous head and leg room, and will just end up on the floor in the middle of the night anyway.

3 Fluff and flip.
If the sofa design permits, remove the seat cushions, fluff them, then flip them so the side that was down is now the top. This will provide a more even sleeping surface.

4 Cover the seat cushions with a sheet.
The sheet will protect your face from odors trapped in the cushions and will protect the seating area from saliva.

5 Use your usual pillow.
You will sleep better with your head resting on a familiar pillow. Get yours from the bedroom, if the bedroom is still accessible to you.

6 Depending on the temperature of the room and your comfort level, get a sheet, blanket, comforter, or large towel to put on top of you.

7 Relax.
Do not go to bed angry.

WARNING!

⚡ If you are an active sleeper, lay the sofa cushions next to the sofa to break your fall should you roll off during the night.

BABIES

How to Deliver a Baby in a Taxicab

1 Time the uterine contractions.

For first-time mothers, when contractions are about three to five minutes apart and last 40 to 90 seconds—and increase in strength and frequency—for at least an hour, the labor is most likely real and not false (though it can be). Babies basically deliver themselves, and they will not come out of the womb until they are ready. Have clean, dry towels, a clean shirt, or something similar on hand.

2 As the baby moves out of the womb, its head—the biggest part of its body—will open the cervix so the rest of it can pass through.

(If feet are coming out first, see "Warning!") As the baby moves through the birth canal and out of the mother's body, guide it out by supporting the head and then the body.

3 When the baby is out of the mother, dry it off and keep it warm.

Do not slap its behind to make it cry; the baby will breathe on its own. If necessary, clear any fluid out of the baby's mouth with your fingers.

4 Tie off the umbilical cord.

Take a piece of string—a shoelace works well—and tie off the cord several inches from the baby.

5 It is not necessary to cut the umbilical cord unless you are hours away from the hospital.

In that event, you can safely cut the cord by tying it in another place a few inches closer to the mother and cutting it between the knots. Leave the cord alone until you get to a hospital. The piece of the cord attached to the baby will fall off by itself. The placenta will follow the baby in as few as 3 or as many as 30 minutes.

WARNING!

Before you attempt to deliver a baby, use your best efforts to get to a hospital first. There really is no way to know exactly when the baby is ready to emerge, so even if you think you may not have time to get to the hospital, you probably do. Even the "water breaking" is not a sure sign that birth will happen immediately. The water is actually the amniotic fluid and the membrane that the baby floats in; birth can occur many hours after the mother's water breaks. However, if you leave too late or get stuck in crosstown traffic and you must deliver the baby on your own, these are the basic concepts.

The most common complication during labor is a breech delivery, when the baby is positioned so the feet, and not the head, will come out of the uterus first. Since the head is the largest part of the baby, the danger is that if the feet come out first, the cervix may not be dilated enough to get the head out afterward. Today, most breech babies are delivered through cesarean section, a surgical procedure that you will not be able to perform. If you have absolutely no alternatives (no hospital or doctors or midwives are available) when the baby begins to emerge, you can try to deliver the baby feet first. A breech birth does not necessarily mean that the head won't be able to get through the cervix; there is simply a higher possibility that this will occur. Deliver the baby as you would in the manner prescribed above.

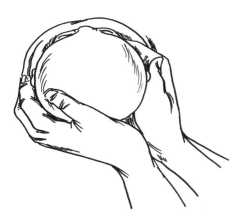

As the baby moves through the birth canal, guide it out by supporting the head.

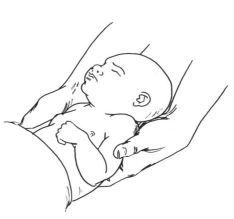

Support the body as it moves out. Do not slap its behind to make it cry; the baby will breathe on its own.

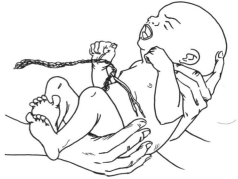

After you have dried off the baby, tie the umbilical cord with a shoelace or a piece of string several inches from the body. Leave the cord alone until the baby gets to the hospital.

Show equal affection to your cat and the new baby.

How to Deal with a Cat Who Is Jealous of a New Baby

1 Rub baby lotion and baby powder on your skin.
Prior to the baby's arrival in the home, acclimate your cat to baby smells by wearing baby-scented products around the house.

2 Fill your house with the sound of a baby.
Purchase a recording of "baby sounds," such as crying, laughing, and gurgling, or begin making such sounds yourself. Play or make the sounds constantly while your cat is at home.

3 Reward a positive response to the smells and noises.
When your cat reacts calmly to the crying baby sounds and smells, pet her and give her treats, or praise her.

4 Elevate your cat.
Before the new baby arrives, move the cat's sleeping place and litter box to a raised location. Cats feel most comfortable when they are high up and can monitor an unfamiliar situation.

5 Keep the baby away from the cat's playing areas, litter box, and feeding area.
As the child ages, instruct him on how to properly treat a cat.

6 Show as much affection to your cat as you do to the new baby.

How to Get Your Baby to Sleep

✪ Swaddle the baby.
Fold down one corner of a receiving blanket, and place the baby on top of the blanket with his head above the fold. Pull one side of the blanket securely across the baby's chest, and tuck it underneath his body. Then pull up the bottom, folding the edge back, and finish by pulling the remaining side of the blanket across the baby's chest and underneath the body. The baby should fit snugly inside the blanket.

✪ Sway.
Hold the swaddled baby close to your chest. Shift your weight from one foot to the other. This rhythmic stimulation will induce a sleepy state in the baby. Position the child so that his ear is over your heart. The beating will soothe him.

✪ Generate soothing white noise near the baby.
Sound produced by a clothes dryer, dishwasher, blender, coffee grinder, hair dryer, vacuum cleaner, lawn mower, leaf blower, or air conditioner has a lulling potency that many babies cannot resist. Metronomes and ticking clocks can also soothe a baby to sleep by reminding a child of his mother's heartbeat.

✪ Put the baby on a washing machine or dryer.
Turn on the machine and set to normal cycle. The vibrations and noise are sleep-inducing. Do not leave the baby unattended.

✪ Go for a drive.
The steady vibration of the car will have most infants asleep quickly. Open the window a crack, and the air will keep you awake while the sound of the wind functions as soothing white noise for the baby. Do not get behind the wheel if you are exhausted and cannot operate heavy machinery.

HOW TO SURVIVE BABY GEAR OVERLOAD

1 Wear cargo pants.

Fill the pockets with soft items: burp cloth, bibs, change of clothes (for you and for baby).

2 Dress the baby in cargo pants.

Fill the pockets with small necessities: baby's cap, small board book for entertainment, teething ring.

3 Wear a photographer's or fisherman's vest.

Fill the pockets with necessities: crib toy, baby manual, hand sanitizer, bowl and spoon, changing pad, shampoo, bath soap, fever-reducing medicine, teething gel, anti-itch cream, saline drops, nasal bulb syringe, thermometer, tissues, antibiotic ointment, plastic bag for soiled diapers, plastic bag for wet/dirty clothes.

4 Wear a fanny pack.

Fill with adult necessities: keys, wallet, headache medicine, sunglasses, makeup, cell phone, shopping list, pen.

5 Circle your waist with a web belt.

Attach a canteen (for you) and a bottle or sippy cup (for baby).

6 Clip a pacifier to the baby.

7 Sling a messenger bag across your back.

Fill with remaining necessities: umbrella, toys, diapers, diaper wipes, cotton balls, sunscreen, diaper cream, juice, crackers, baby blanket.

8 Wear a baby carrier or sling.

Place the baby in the carrier and go. Remember where you are going, and why, and be sure to take your house keys with you.

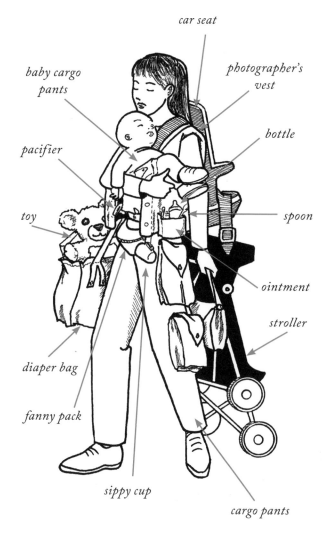

car seat
baby cargo pants
photographer's vest
pacifier
bottle
toy
spoon
ointment
stroller
diaper bag
fanny pack
sippy cup
cargo pants

Remember where you are going, and why.
Be sure to take your house keys.

Means of Soothing Colicky Babies

Offer the breast or bottle to the baby.	Carry the baby around in her car seat.	Put on loud music.
Give a pacifier to the baby.	Go to a different room.	Turn off music.
Rock the baby.	Sit down with baby in your lap.	Give the baby a warm bath.
Swaddle the baby.	Stand up with baby in your arms.	Take off all the baby's clothes.
Put the baby in a vibrating chair.	Go outside.	Lie baby down under a ceiling fan.
Put the baby in a swing.	Go inside.	Put baby in crib, collapse into sleep at the foot of the crib, wake up an hour later and begin again.
Carry the baby around in a sling.	Put on soft music.	

CHILDREN

HOW TO PREVENT BACKPACK OVERLOAD

⊙ **Clean out the backpack.**
Remove extra pairs of running shoes, soda bottles, dead batteries, and obsolete chargers.

⊙ **Pack only the necessary books.**
All books do not need to go to and from school every day.

⊙ **Buy a second set of books.**
Keep a set of textbooks, usually the heaviest books, at home, so the books don't need to be transported. Alternatively, photocopy the entire book at the beginning of the year and instruct your child to take home only those pages necessary for each day's assignment.

⊙ **Hire a neighborhood sherpa.**
Pay a sibling, larger neighborhood child, or teamster to carry the load.

⊙ **Affix saddlebags to your dog.**
Bike stores usually sell a variety of different-sized bags that can be slung across a dog's back. Use only large dogs and watch for overload.

⊙ **Ship the books overnight directly to school.**
As long as your child completes his homework by 8 p.m., you should be able to ship the books for next-day delivery at a courier's local drop box. Specify that the books should arrive for "early delivery" to ensure that they make it to school before your child's first class of the day.

WARNING!

⚐ A backpack should never rest more than four inches below the waistline or be wider than the shoulders.

⚐ Symptoms of backpack overload include pain or numbness in the arms, shoulders, and mid- to lower back; jaw pain; neck pain; and headache. If the child reports any of these symptoms, consult a health care professional.

Explain to your child that both he and his imaginary friend are responsible for their bad behavior.

HOW TO DISCIPLINE IMAGINARY FRIENDS

1 Outline responsibility.
Explain to your child and the imaginary friend that when they play together, they both need to be on good behavior and are both responsible for any broken vases, stolen cookies, or messes.

2 Assign consequences to the child and imaginary friend together.
Tell your child that he and his imaginary friend must wash dishes or take out the trash "together."

3 Ask your child to suggest ways to make his friend behave.
Explain that you need his help in making his friend understand and behave.

Pack only necessary books.

4 Create activities to keep the imaginary friend out of trouble.

If the imaginary friend is a continuing source of mischief, enroll him in (imaginary) music lessons, (imaginary) summer camp, or (imaginary) boarding school to keep him occupied.

How to Get Children to Eat Vegetables

⊙ **Eat vegetables yourself.**
Be enthusiastic about vegetables. "Broccoli is awesome!" "Peas rule!" "Rutabagas rock!"

⊙ **Talk in euphemisms.**
Encourage your child by calling the vegetable a "growing food" or "brain food" or "run-fast food" or "beauty food."

⊙ **Require one bite.**
Even if she does not like it, with the "one-bite rule" the child should eventually grow accustomed to the taste, though it may take years.

⊙ **Let the child select the vegetable.**
Take your child to the grocery store to pick out one vegetable. Invite her into the kitchen to help you prepare it for dinner. She will become emotionally invested in the vegetable and proud of it. She may not only eat the vegetable but also urge others to do so.

⊙ **Sneak vegetables into other dishes.**
Camouflage vegetables in stews, lasagna, potpies, pizza toppings, casseroles, or soups.

⊙ **Change presentation.**
Arrange vegetables in a happy face. Use unnaturally colored ketchup (pink, green, blue) to jazz up a pile of vegetables. Make trees with broccoli and asparagus, boats from endive, and a lake out of guacamole.

⊙ **Prepare the vegetable in different ways.**
If she rejected the steamed broccoli, next time serve it raw with a dip. If the asparagus in cream sauce was not popular, try it with butter and lemon. Use a blender or a juicer to transform the vegetable into a purée or a smoothie.

Arrange vegetables in unusual ways.

⊙ **Make vegetables the only option.**
Designate "vegetarian night" and serve nothing but vegetables. Your child will eat them if she is hungry and there is no other food available. When the meal is over, declare the kitchen closed, and do not allow snacks or dessert.

⊙ **Do not make food into a battle of wills.**
Be matter-of-fact about whether your child does or does not eat her vegetables. Do not force a vegetable on your child or bribe her to eat. Do not say, "If you eat your brussels sprouts, you can have dessert." This will interfere with her developing a genuine affection for the vegetable and will reinforce sweets as the truly desirable food.

How to Get Rid of Bedroom Monsters

1 Turn on the lights.
Show your child that there are no monsters in the room.

2 Explain that you are making sure there will be no monsters in the future.

3 Spray infested areas with water.
Monsters are afraid of water. Fill a spray bottle with water and lightly mist problem areas, including under the bed, around the door, and in the closet.

4 Place sentries outside of closets and by windows.
Monsters will avoid friendly-looking stuffed animals, dolls, clowns, and puppets. Assemble a battalion of these around all likely points of entry.

5 Use the color green.
Many monsters are afraid of the color green. Use a green night-light, or encourage your child to wear pajamas with some green on them. A bandage, a washable tattoo, nail polish, or a sticker with the color green is also effective.

IN THE KITCHEN

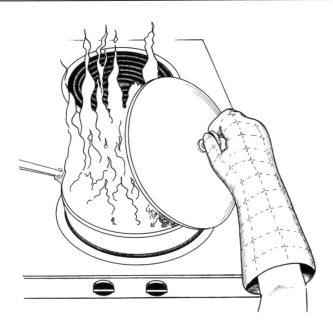

Slide lid over flames to cover pan completely.
Wear a barbecue or oven mitt for protection.

How to Put Out a Grease Fire

1 Do not douse with water.
Oil and water do not mix: water will cause the burning oil to spatter and spread the fire. Do not move the burning pan to the sink.

2 Turn off the stove.

3 Put on an oven mitt.
Large mitts are the safest option. If barbecue mitts—those that cover the forearm—are available, use for added protection.

4 Find a lid that fits the pan.
A lid that is slightly larger than the pan will also work.

5 Hold the lid at an angle toward the fire.
Do not try to lower the lid directly onto the pan or you risk burning your arms. Keep your face and chest as far from the flames as possible.

6 Slide the lid on the pan and hold it in place until the pan cools.
The pressure from the heat and flame can force a lid off the pan. Hold it securely in place.

7 Do not lift the lid.
Lifting the lid will add oxygen and feed the fire. Take the lid off only when the pan has bcome noticeably cooler.

8 If no lid is available, use baking soda.
Dump a large amount of baking soda on the grease fire to extinguish it quickly. Avoid using baking powder, which can cause the fire to flare.

WARNING!

⚡ Do not use a dry chemical extinguisher to try to put out a grease fire. It is not effective, and the force of the compressed chemical agent can spatter burning material and spread flames.

⚡ Never leave cooking oil on the stove unattended: flames may develop quickly.

How to Treat a Grease Burn

1 Cool the burned area.
Immediately run cold water over the burned area for several minutes or until the injury site is cool.

2 Dry the burned area gently.
Blot the injury site using a clean, dry towel or sheet.

3 Check for blistering.
If the blisters are small, pop them with a sterilized pin and remove dead skin using scissors. (Wiping the tip of a pin in alcohol or heating it in the flame from a match will adequately sterilize the pin.) If there are no blisters and the burn is less than one inch across, apply burn cream and a sterile dressing.

4 Cover severe burns.
If the burn is larger than one inch across or is very blistered, cover it with a clean, dry sheet or towel, and seek medical attention promptly.

WARNING!

⚡ Infection is the main risk. Signs of infection include fever or local warmth, increased redness around the burned area, increased soreness, red streaks, swelling, or drainage of pus.

⚡ Do not apply oily or greasy substances such as petroleum jelly or butter to the wound. These popular but misguided burn remedies are detrimental to the healing process.

Emergency Substitutions/Out of Ingredients

OUT OF INGREDIENT	INGREDIENT AMOUNT	SUBSTITUTION
Baking powder	1 teaspoon	¼ teaspoon baking soda plus ⅝ teaspoon cream of tartar
Butter, melted	Any amount	Equal portion of oil
Butter, solid	1 cup	1 cup margarine or 1 cup vegetable shortening for baking
Buttermilk	1 cup	1 tablespoon lemon juice or vinegar plus enough whole milk to make 1 cup (allow to stand 5 minutes)
Cocoa powder	¼ cup	1 ounce unsweetened chocolate (decrease fat in recipe by 1½ teaspoons)
Cornstarch	1 tablespoon	2 tablespoons all-purpose flour
Cream	1 cup	⅞ cup whole milk plus ½ tablespoon half and half, butter, or margarine
Cream, heavy	1 cup	¾ cup milk plus ⅓ cup butter or (40% fat) margarine (for use in cooking and baking)
Cream of tartar	½ teaspoon	1½ teaspoons lemon juice or vinegar
Garlic	1 clove	⅛ teaspoon garlic powder
Honey	1 cup	1¼ cups sugar plus ¼ cup additional liquid called for in recipe
Lemon juice, fresh	1 teaspoon	½ teaspoon vinegar
Mayonnaise	1 cup	1 cup yogurt or 1 cup sour cream
Molasses	1 cup	¾ cup sugar plus 1¼ teaspoons cream of tartar (increase liquid in recipe by 5 tablespoons)
Shortening	1 cup	1⅛ cups butter or margarine (decrease salt called for in recipe by ½ teaspoon)
Sugar, brown	1 cup, firmly packed	1 cup granulated sugar
Sugar, granulated	1 cup	1¾ cups confectioners' sugar or 1 cup firmly packed light brown sugar
Vinegar	1 teaspoon	2 teaspoons lemon juice
Yogurt	1 cup	1 cup whole milk plus 1 tablespoon lemon juice

JAR WON'T OPEN

Rap on counter.

Pry lid with butter knife.

Hold under hot running water.

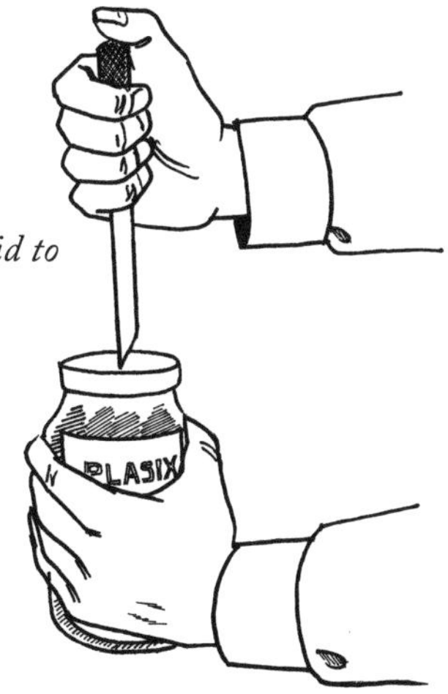

Puncture lid to break seal.

Try these techniques individually or together to loosen a stuck jar lid.

HOLIDAYS

HOW TO MAKE AN EMERGENCY MENORAH

If Hanukkah arrives and you are without a menorah or candles, you will have to make your own.

Baked Menorah

You will need 2 cups flour, 1 cup salt, 1 cup water, 9 nuts or washers (at least ½ inch in diameter), a large mixing bowl, and at least three hours.

1 Preheat the oven to 200°F.

2 Mix the flour and salt together in the large bowl.

3 Add water.
Slowly pour water into the mixture and stir until it becomes the consistency of dough. If it is too dry, add more water; if it is too wet, add more flour.

4 Roll the dough into a strip about 12 inches long, 1 to 2 inches wide, and 2 inches thick.

5 Cut a 1-inch piece off of one end and press it into the center of the strip.
The center area will be raised slightly: it will hold the Shamos candle, which is used to light the other candles.

6 Add the nuts to the dough.
Press the nuts into the dough, four spaced evenly on each side of the Shamos holder. Place the ninth nut in the raised center portion. The nuts should be pushed in so that part of the nut sticks up above the top of the dough. The nuts are the candle holders.

7 Bake.
Place the menorah on a baking sheet, and place in the oven. Bake for about two hours. The menorah is ready when the dough becomes hard. (You can air-dry the menorah instead of baking it; allow two to three days for hardening.)

8 Let cool.
The menorah should be completely cool before use.

Baked menorah: Press nuts into the dough before baking. Let menorah cool completely before use.

Bowl and Dirt Menorah

You will need a baking dish or bowl and sand, dirt, rice, or gravel.

✪ **Fill a 2-inch-deep (or deeper) bowl with sand, dirt, rice, gravel, or other nonflammable material.**
Stick the appropriate number of candles in the dish each night (placing the Shamos on a slightly elevated mound) to create a makeshift menorah.

Bowl and dirt menorah: The Shamos candle should be set on a raised mound in the center of the bowl.

WARNING!

Do not make a menorah out of wood. Hanukkah candles must be allowed to burn down completely, and wood presents the risk of fire.

HOW TO EXTINGUISH A CHRISTMAS TREE FIRE

1 Assess the size and nature of the fire.
Quickly determine if the source of the fire is electrical, and observe how large an area of the tree is burning. A fire larger than the size of a small wastebasket cannot usually be contained, even with a home extinguisher. If the fire is that large, evacuate the building and call the fire department from a cellular phone or a neighbor's house.

2 If the fire is small and not electrical, douse it or smother it.
Extinguish the fire with a bucket of water or a multipurpose (Class ABC) fire extinguisher, or smother it with a wet blanket.

3 If the fire is electrical, use a fire extinguisher.
Do not throw water on an electrical fire. Use a multipurpose (Class ABC) fire extinguisher.

4 When using a fire extinguisher, stand with your back toward an exit, six to eight feet from the fire, and Pull, Aim, Squeeze, Sweep (PASS).
Pull the release tab, aim at the base of the fire, squeeze the lever to release the pressurized chemicals, and sweep from side to side as you slowly move closer to the fire.

5 If the fire is still spreading, exit the house.
Evacuate the building quickly. Do not attempt to save ornaments, Christmas presents, or other valuables.

How to Prevent a Christmas Tree Fire

1 Select a fresh tree.
A dry tree is a major fire hazard; to get the freshest tree, cut it yourself. If you purchase a cut tree, run your hand down a branch to make sure it is not dry and shedding needles. Test the tree by bending a needle: if it snaps, the tree is too dry.

2 Leave the tree in a bucket of water overnight.
Place the tree in the stand the next day. Water it daily.

3 Place the tree at least three feet away from a fireplace, radiator, or other heat source.

4 Unplug tree lights when not in use.
Do not leave the lights on during the day, when you go to bed, or when you leave the house.

5 Do not place lit candles on or near a tree.
If tradition requires candles, use specially weighted sconces that do not tip over. Do not add electric tree lights or other electrical equipment to or around the tree (such as a train set), in the event that water must be thrown onto the tree. Do not leave the tree unattended.

If the fire is larger than the size of a small wastebasket or is spreading quickly, get out of the house.

The "There Is No Santa Claus" Speech

Son/Daughter,

Please sit down over here by me. There's something I've been meaning to tell you for a long time, and I think you're old enough now.

I know you believe with all your heart that there is a person called Santa Claus who brings you presents every year if you are good. But the truth is that there is no Santa Claus. "Santa Claus" is really all the parents in the world, who love their children very much and buy them presents to show how much they love them.

Your presents are not made by elves in a toy shop at the North Pole. There is no such thing as an elf; and the North Pole is actually one of the loneliest and most desolate places on earth. The truth is that Mom and Dad buy all your presents at the mall or online, and we're the ones who eat Santa's cookies and drink Santa's milk. Reindeer can't fly, either.

But don't cry. This doesn't mean that the spirit of Santa Claus isn't real. "Santa Claus" is inside all of us, whenever we give presents to those that we love or to those who are less fortunate. When you grow up, you can be Santa, too. Or the Easter Bunny. Or the Tooth Fairy.

Signs of danger: anchor vehicles moving toward curb, handlers reining in the ropes.

How to Escape from a Runaway Parade Balloon

1 Watch for sudden changes in wind speed.

Parade balloons are deployed only if sustained winds are 23 mph or less, with gusts no more than 34 mph. If the winds exceed these levels during the parade, controlling the balloons becomes much more difficult. If you detect a significant change in wind speed or direction, look for other indications of danger.

2 Watch the anchor vehicles.

Large balloons (5,000 cubic feet and bigger) will be tethered to two anchor vehicles that look like oversized golf carts. These vehicles weigh 2½ tons each and act as failsafes, keeping a balloon from moving uncontrollably in case of emergency. In calm winds, the vehicles will be directly under the balloon and in the center of the street. If the anchor vehicles begin to move outward, toward the sidewalks, the wind is increasing substantially.

3 Watch the height of the balloon.

In calm winds, balloons will float at a maximum height of 50 feet. If the balloons are lower than this, winds may be dangerously high. In very strong winds, balloons may be almost at ground level.

4 Observe balloon handlers.

Each balloon has at least one handler; the largest balloons may have 50. Each handler holds a rope, and each rope is marked in foot-long increments. As winds increase, handlers will pull in their ropes and move into the wind for better control of the balloon in a headwind. If you see handlers reining in lots of rope, they are dealing with a clear and present danger.

5 Do not try to rescue a balloon.

It is difficult for an observer to gauge the hugeness of a parade balloon, the tension in the ropes, and the amount of energy required to control a balloon in high winds. Lending a helping hand may seem easy, but the situation may be more out of control than it looks. Stay clear of the street and the balloon operators. Balloons and their handlers need lots of space to maneuver. Never attempt to pull on any ropes, and do not poke or prod any balloon.

6 Avoid lampposts and traffic lights.

The most immediate risk is that a runaway balloon may knock over a traffic light or lamppost, which will strike those standing below. Often, traffic lights are either removed or repositioned before the parade; if any remain, stay away from them.

7 Do not panic.

A stampeding crowd is a greater threat than a renegade balloon. If you have detected the early signs of danger and have responded, you will be moving ahead of the crowd.

8 Evacuate the area.

Seek safety away from the parade route, if you have time. You may take immediate shelter in a building or subway station.

How to Survive If You Have No One to Kiss on New Year's Eve

If You Are with Others

1 Keep a glass in your hand.
If others think you are being festive and uninhibited, you are much more likely to receive a kiss. Even if you are not drinking, always hold a partly full glass of champagne.

2 Hug people.
As the clock strikes midnight, begin hugging everyone around you.

3 Select a desirable person.
As you are hugging, look for an attractive person who you would enjoy kissing and who might kiss you. If a person is not randomly kissing others, he or she may be less likely to kiss you.

4 Begin your approach.
Act casual, but keep your destination in view. Slowly move toward your chosen one, hugging everyone on the way.

5 Time your arrival.
Do not appear to be "lining up" to kiss this person. Time your arrival precisely as the person releases the previous reveler.

6 Yell first, then hug.
Yell "Happy New Year!" as you move in. Hug, embrace, then pull away slightly.

7 Kiss.
Keep your mouth closed, pucker slightly, and plant the kiss.

If You Are Alone

☉ Kiss a pet.
Dogs are generally agreeable and have relatively clean mouths. Cats are usually well groomed but are more passive and tend to get rather than give. Keep your mouth closed.

☉ Kiss yourself.
Find a mirror, pucker up, lean close, and kiss. Keep the lips slightly parted. Do not attempt to use your tongue. Wipe the mirror clean after you have completed your kiss. You may also try kissing the back of your hand.

☉ Kiss a celebrity.
Watch a favorite movie or show on television and kiss the screen when an appealing star has a close-up. Wipe the screen first to remove dust and static electricity, and wipe the screen after to remove any evidence.

☉ Hug a pillow.
Full-body pillows are more satisfying.

☉ Call a friend on the phone.
After you wish your friend a happy New Year, give the telephone mouthpiece loud, smacking kisses. (This works less well with cellular phones.)

If no humans are available to kiss at midnight, try kissing a pet. Keep your mouth closed.

TEENAGERS

How to Tell If Your Child Was Switched at Birth

1 Compare a photograph of yourself or your spouse as a teenager with a photograph of your child.

Look particularly at facial features—eyes, nose, mouth—and at body shape. If there are absolutely no similarities and your child was not adopted, you might be right: this strangely behaved person may not be your biological child. Proceed to step 2.

2 Compare personality traits.

Look for common tendencies and habits that are signs of a genetic connection. Allow for generation-specific differences, such as musical taste and fashion sense.

3 Examine what happened immediately after your child's birth.

- Did you actually see the doctor place the ID band on your child's arm or leg in the hospital room?

- Was your child out of your immediate view for more than a few seconds?

- Did you notice any marked similarities between yourself and any other children in the nursery? If the answer to any of the above questions is "Yes" or "I don't know," look for further evidence of a long-ago error.

WARNING!

⚡ Your child's difficult and dissimilar traits might be attributable to your spouse.

⚡ DNA testing can be expensive, and by now you're a family anyway.

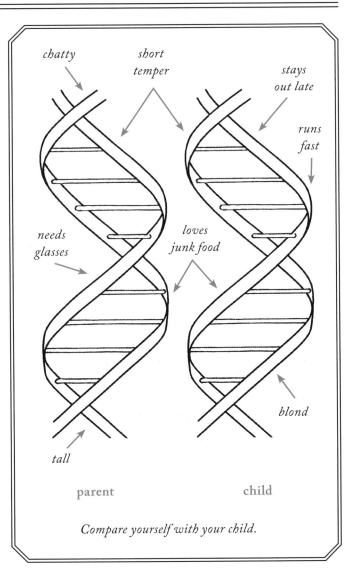

Compare yourself with your child.

How to Deal with Provocative Clothing

1 In a firm and calm voice, tell your teen to change into something more suitable.

Do not yield to a tantrum. Remain neutral and impervious to eye rolling and heavy sighs.

2 In a calm and firm voice, tell your teen to change into something more suitable.

Do not yield to a tantrum. Remain neutral and impervious to eye rolling and heavy sighs.

3 In a firm and calm voice, tell your teen to change into something more suitable.

Do not yield to a tantrum. Remain neutral and impervious to eye rolling and heavy sighs.

4 In a calm and firm voice, tell your teen to change into something more suitable.

Do not yield to a tantrum. Remain neutral and impervious to eye rolling and heavy sighs.

5 Employ reverse psychology.

Wear the same outfit as your teen. The anarchy T-shirt, hoodie sweatshirt with silk-screened profanity, or teeny-tiny skirt and ripped fishnet stockings will not look as cool when you are wearing them, too.

How to Survive Your Child's First Driving Lesson

1 Dress casually.

Do not wear a helmet or extra padding.

2 Check safety devices.

Make sure that seat belts are securely fastened and mirrors are properly adjusted.

3 Breathe in deeply and exhale slowly.

Continue to breathe.

4 Relax.

Do not tense your muscles.

5 Keep your hands folded in front of you.

6 Avoid sudden movements.

Do not clench the dashboard, grab for the emergency brake handle, or make other movements that may surprise the teen and cause him to lose control. Do not smoke, eat, read, sing, play the radio, finger worry beads, or talk on the telephone.

7 Compliment the driving.

Avoid the urge to comment negatively on your child's performance. Do not say things like "You're going to get us both killed!" Speak positively and in a calm voice.

8 Do not grab the steering wheel, gearshift, or hand brake.

Trust the driver.

9 Stay relaxed.

It will be fine.

How to Reattach a Damaged Bumper

1 Assess the damage.

Examine the bumper and bumper cover. Many vehicles have a plastic or rubber bumper cover over a steel bumper. The lightweight cover, rather than the steel bumper, is likely to be the damaged portion.

2 Remove the bumper cover.

If the cover is completely separated from the bumper, reattachment is not advisable. Place bumper cover in the trunk or backseat and seek professional repair. If the cover is only partially separated from the car, proceed to step 3.

3 Check bumper cover bolts.

Bumper covers on passenger cars are attached in four to six places, generally with plastic screws or metal bolts through the bumper cover and into the plastic or metal bumper itself. Examine the screw or bolt holes to determine if they have been ripped or are still usable.

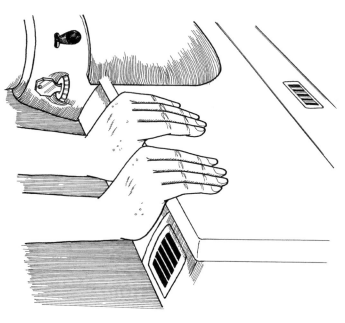

Relax. It will be fine.

4 Reattach the bumper cover with wire.

If the holes are still intact, tie bumper back on the bumper frame with wire, string, rope, or yarn. Feed the wire through the holes where the bumper cover has come loose. Make several passes through the holes for security. Tie with square knots.

5 Reattach bumper cover with duct tape.

If the mounting holes have been ripped or are inaccessible, apply duct tape completely around the bumper and cover. If necessary, tape the bumper cover to the hood of the car to prevent slippage.

WHAT PARENTS WANT TEENAGERS TO DO	WHAT TEENAGERS DO
talk to parents	text friends
read	check social networks
household chores	download videos
homework	upload videos
watch movie with family	play video game in room
answer phone calls	send unintelligible text
say where they really are	send vague text
turn off the phone at the table	send and receive texts
get some sleep at night	text friends/check social networks

COLLEGE

Compare the number of books in the library with *the number of seats in the stadium.*

How to Avoid Going to the Wrong College

1 Visit the college during the school year on a day with a regular class schedule.

Visiting during holidays, homecoming, or other times when students are away or not in their normal routine will not give you an accurate picture of everyday life at the school.

2 Observe the students.

- Are the students walking energetically to class while talking animatedly, or are the few students in sight wandering aimlessly?

- Are the students bright-eyed, with glowing complexions, or are they red-eyed, with a pasty pallor?

- Are the students carrying armfuls of books and notebooks, or are they carrying surfboards and coolers?

- Are the students eagerly seeking out professors after class and in the cafeteria, or are the students ducking into doorways and under tables to avoid professors?

- Are students in class paying attention and taking notes, or are they wearing headphones, reading the newspaper, or dozing?

3 Evaluate the facilities and surroundings.

- Compare the number of books in the library with the number of seats in the stadium.

- Compare the number of flyers promoting free lectures with the number of flyers promoting spring break getaways.

- Compare the number of nearby art galleries with the number of nearby hair salons.

- Compare the number of nearby bookstores with the number of nearby bars.

- Compare the number of students wearing T-shirts featuring the school logo with the number of students not wearing any shirt.

- Compare the number of ads in the school newspaper offering "Students Available to Tutor" with the number of ads offering "Research Papers Written—Any Topic."

- Compare the number of times you hear chamber music with the number of times you hear sirens from emergency vehicles.

4 Select your school accordingly.

How to Identify a Party School

⊕ **Assess the school's location.**

Party schools are often those farthest from urban centers: Such a location necessitates that all social activities occur on campus or in campus-adjacent locations, and therefore there are parties daily due to the lack of other entertainment opportunities. Cities with a warm climate and good beaches are also home to party schools, as many students opt for surfing, sunbathing, and pitchers of margaritas over class.

⊕ **Count the number of bars, liquor stores, fraternities, and sororities on or near campus.**

The more plentiful the watering holes and Greek organizations, the more likely the students are to party.

⊕ **Look for schools with successful sports teams.**

Schools with particularly winning sports programs are likely to offer many months of pre- and post-game victory parties. Avoid schools with losing records or sparsely attended games, and those with teams that usually lose the homecoming alumni game.

⊕ **Interview the school's administrators and alumni.**

Talk to the school's local boosters (ask the admissions office for names) about their memories of social activities at the school. If more than three of them recount stories of drinking at 6 a.m. or have no memory of college at all, the school is most likely a party school.

Interview the school's administrators.

⊕ **Visit the school on a Thursday.**

A good party school will have multiple parties raging on this night. Walk the campus and listen carefully for whoops, yells, and loud music. Look for students staggering, talking loudly, or vomiting in the bushes, all of which are signs of raucous social activity. Enter a fraternity or sorority party. Gatherings without alcohol and centered around a knitting circle or a discussion of 19th-century English poetry indicate a college that does not measure up.

A warm climate often encourages a party atmosphere.

How to Deal with a Nightmare Roommate

✪ Cover foul odors.
Burn incense or spray air freshener to mask your roommate's scent. To better circulate the incense, place it in front of an open window or oscillating fan.

✪ Secure your possessions in locked storage containers.
To discourage theft or misuse of your belongings, lock as much as possible in safes, military-issue foot lockers, trunks, and other lockable storage containers. Long, flat containers can be placed under your bed for further protection.

✪ Divide the room in half.
Draw a line down the center of the room to designate your own private space. Remember that you'll have to share the door.

✪ Wear noise-reduction headphones.
Don the headphones anytime your roommate is in the room with you.

✪ Leave a bar of soap on his pillow.

✪ Put neglected dirty dishes in your roommate's bed.

✪ Gather long-unwashed clothes into a pile.
If the pile of dirty clothes isn't remedied after a week, transfer the pile to trash bags and seal tightly to eliminate odors. If the bags remain after several weeks, put them in the trash.

✪ Misalign the satellite dish.
Disrupt the constant blare of sporting events by redirecting your roommate's satellite dish.

✪ Buy your roommate concert tickets.
If your roommate never leaves the room, buy him a ticket to an all-day concert, a movie, or a sporting event. Do not ask your roommate if he wants to go; just purchase the ticket—the farther away the event, the better.

WARNING!

⚠ If you notice any of the following in your room, you may have a nightmare roommate:

- Giant speakers
- Lack of toiletries
- Machete
- More than 15 stuffed animals

How to Hook Up in the Library

1 Scout out a suitable make-out location.
Look for dim lighting and empty aisles in the stacks on a higher floor. Avoid areas near doors, entrances, main aisles, and passenger elevators. Library carrels, stairwells, and freight elevators in out-of-the-way locations are also good options. The oversized book collection features large tables and big, bulky volumes that allow for privacy. Determine less-traveled areas by reviewing the Dewey decimal system. Sections that begin with the call numbers below are most likely to be quiet:

- **090** Manuscripts and book rarities
- **110** Metaphysics
- **170** Ethics (moral philosophy)
- **210** Natural religion
- **480** Hellenic; Classic Greek
- **510** Mathematics
- **670** Manufacturing
- **707** Antiques and collectibles
- **930** General history of the ancient world

Sections with the following call numbers offer more risky locations but may provide some inspiration and atmosphere for the hook-up:

- **440** Romance languages, French
- **577** Pure science: General nature of life
- **618** Gynecology and other medical specialties
- **757** Painting: Human figures and their parts
- **770** Photography and photographs
- **811** Poetry

2 Time your rendezvous.
Select a time when your designated location will be deserted.

3 Meet at a predetermined location.
Pass a note to your hook-up target with a time and location. Indicate a specific Dewey decimal section for the rendezvous.

WARNING!

⚠ Be respectful of the books. Do not damage or misuse them.

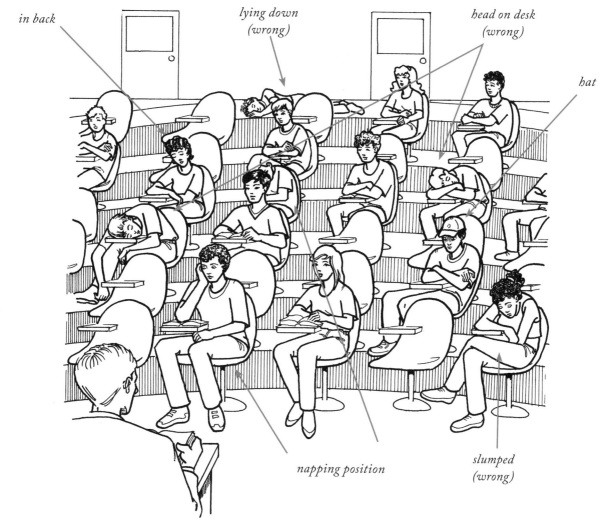

in back

lying down (wrong)

head on desk (wrong)

hat

napping position

slumped (wrong)

HOW TO SLEEP IN CLASS

1 **Wear a hat.**

Sharply bend the brim of a baseball cap, and pull the visor low over your face to hide your eyes in the shadow. Do not wear a wool ski hat, beanie, or yarmulke, as none of these casts a shadow.

2 **Sit in the rear of the class.**

Choose a seat in the back of the classroom or at least far enough from your professor that he will not notice your heavy breathing.

3 **Sit behind a tall person.**

Position yourself behind a member of the basketball or volleyball team to interrupt your professor's line of vision. Sitting behind an obese person can also block your professor's sight line.

4 **Sit on the opposite side of the class from known class participants.**

5 **Pad the desktop in front of you.**

Fold a scarf, sweater, or sweatshirt on your desk. Bend one arm and place your elbow on the folded item.

6 **Assume the napping position.**

- Place your thumb under your chin, supporting your jaw.
- Rest your four fingers on the side of your face.
- Balance your head on your hand, keeping it upright.
- Place your notebook open and in front of you; hold a pen in your other hand, to look as if you are ready to take notes.

WARNING!

⚠ Avoid wearing dark sunglasses in class. While they may serve to shade your eyes, they also attract attention.

⚠ Do not let your head slump down to your chest.

⚠ Do not rest your head on your desk.

⚠ Do not lie down.

SUBURBS

HOW TO FIND YOUR CONDO IN A CONDO DEVELOPMENT

✪ **Check the mailbox.**
Open the box and look at the name on the bills and letters.

✪ **Ask people on the street.**
Inquire at the management office. Ask neighbors for directions. Check with the mail carrier.

✪ **Study the driveways in your development.**
Look for your car or other recognizable cars with identifying characteristics such as bumper stickers, roof racks, or flags. Locate your neighbor's fire-red Mustang convertible.

✪ **Inspect the lawn.**
Look for identifying lawn features such as garden gnomes, lawn jockeys, benches, or distinct flowers or shrubs.

✪ **Use your garage door opener.**
Roam the streets activating your remote garage door opener until it opens a garage door, which will most likely be yours.

How to Distinguish Your Condo from the Rest

✪ Paint your front door purple or orange.
Place a skull-and-bones or other distinctive lawn flag in front of your place.

✪ Paint an arrow or hopscotch pattern on the sidewalk leading to your door.
Put a nameplate with your last name on it beside your front door.

✪ Hang your child's artwork in your front window.
Create a flower or vegetable garden in your front yard.

✪ Get a dog that will bark at the door until you return.
Get a cat that will sit in the window.

Look for recognizable features such as flags, lawn ornaments, or bumper stickers on your car.

How to Tell Whether a Black Widow Spider Is Dangerous

Only female black widow spiders, which have an hourglass marking (two triangles facing each other) on their abdomen, are dangerous. Though the color may be yellowish, orange, or red, the presence of an hourglass always indicates a female. Males are much smaller than females, generally half the size, and have different markings: red spots and white bars or lines radiating out to the sides of the abdomen. The female's bite contains the neurotoxin latrotoxin, which can cause severe muscle pain, cramping, headaches and dizziness, shock, coma, and (very rarely) death.

Garage Hazards

PERIL	RESPONSE
Bats living in garage	Leave a bright light on all night, several nights in a row.
Box avalanche	Duck and cover your head with arms; curl into a ball on the floor; wait.
Carbon monoxide buildup	Open garage door from the outside with remote opener; open side doors from outside; wait 10 minutes before entering garage. Turn off car engine.
Oil stains on garage floor	Cover with kitty litter; stomp with sturdy shoes; sweep up. OR: Wet area; cover with baking soda; pour on hot water; let cool; scrub with stiff brush; rinse.

How to Put Out a Grill Fire

1 If you can safely reach the knobs, turn off the burners on a gas or propane grill.
If a propane tank itself is involved in the fire, evacuate the vicinity and call emergency services immediately.

2 Smother the fire.
Never spray water onto a grease fire. It will intensify the flames and spread the burning grease to a wider area. Throw salt, baking soda, or sand onto the fire to smother the flames.

3 Close the lid.
Make sure all the grill vents are closed to further starve the fire of oxygen.

4 If the fire is still burning after 30 seconds, douse the grill with a fire extinguisher.

WARNING!

Flare-ups are usually caused by excess fat and grease dripping from meat through the grates. To prevent a flare-up from getting out of control, quickly move food to a warming rack with a pair of long-handled tongs. Return each piece to the center of the grill one by one, let the excess fat burn off, and remove it to the warming rack again. When every piece has been treated in this fashion, return all the food to the grill and continue cooking.

Douse the flames with any available water or nonflammable beverages.

How to Extinguish a Lawn Fire

1 Locate fire-suppression tools.
Instruct others nearby to quickly gather a bucket of water, shovel, and rake.

2 Smother the flames.
Apply water liberally, or if none is available, use a shovel to dig soil or sand and cover the fire. A long-handled shovel with a wide blade can be used to swat or tamp out errant flames. Stand well back from blazing grass as you attempt to put out the fire.

3 Clear the area of fuel.
As you dig or tamp, push flammable items, such as leaves or brush, away from the path of the fire.

4 If you are unable to extinguish the fire, use the rake or shovel to clear a path to safety.

5 Call emergency services.

AROUND THE HOUSE

How to Make Household Chores Fun

⊕ **Raise the stakes.**
Pretend you are a secret agent. Imagine that if you do not finish washing, drying, and folding laundry within one hour, a large city will be destroyed.

⊕ **Make it a drinking game.**
Award yourself a beer or shot for every dish washed, toilet cleaned, etc.

⊕ **Do a play-by-play.**
Offer an ongoing description of your actions as you perform them. "And he's reaching for the cord of the lawn mower—he's pulling it, and pulling it, and—he's got it! The mower is on!"

⊕ **Do the chores in the middle of the night.**
Pretend you are a ninja or a burglar, and you must complete the chores in total silence or risk discovery.

Broken Lightbulb in Socket

Cut potato in half.

Shut off power to the light, then place half of the potato over the broken bulb and firmly press down.

Turn the potato to remove the broken bulb.

How to Remove Stains from Carpet

Red Wine

Blot wine with an absorbent cloth. Saturate the stain with club soda or cold water, blotting until no more wine transfers to the cloth. If the stain remains, apply a paste of borax or baking soda and water (at a ratio of three to one). Smear paste onto stain with an old toothbrush and let dry. Vacuum, then repeat until no more stain can be removed.

Bleach

Sponge the stain immediately with cold water to remove as much bleach as possible. Mix baking soda and water to make a paste (at a ratio of three to one), and rub onto the stain. Scrub into carpet with an old toothbrush, then let dry. Vacuum, then repeat until no more stain can be removed.

Grease, Motor Oil

Use a dull knife or spoon to remove as much as possible. Blot remaining liquid with an absorbent cloth. Work shaving cream into the carpet with an old toothbrush. Wipe it off with a damp cloth, then sponge with cold water. If the stain remains, apply dry-cleaning fluid (be careful not to wet the carpet backing), then sponge the stain with a damp cloth.

Blood

Use a dull knife or spoon to remove as much as possible. Blot remaining liquid with an absorbent cloth. Sponge the stain with a sudsy mixture of liquid laundry enzyme detergent and cold water, then sponge with cold, clean water. If the stain remains, sponge with a mild bleaching agent such as lemon juice or hydrogen peroxide (do not let it saturate the carpet), then sponge with clean cold water. Repeat as needed.

Removing Wasp Nests

Put on protective gear. Layer clothing to include a long-sleeved shirt and zippered jacket, two pairs of long pants (jeans under sweatpants) tucked into two pairs of socks, leather shoes or boots, thick work gloves, and an insect veil. Spray the nest with a commercial aerosol containing pyrethrin and rotenone to paralyze the insects. When wasps are not flying from the nest, dislodge it from the house with a rake handle or dig it up from the ground (making sure to get all larvae). Burn the nest on a grill, or place it in a large sealable freezer bag and freeze overnight, then dispose.

How to Thaw Frozen Pipes

1 Locate the frozen pipe.

Turn on the water at each tap. If no water comes out or it comes out only in a trickle, the frozen section is connected to that tap. The most likely pipes are those running through exterior walls.

2 Turn off the water supply where it enters the house.

If the pipe cracks while you are thawing it, having turned off the water will prevent a flood.

3 Apply heat to the frozen section.

Use a hair dryer, wrap a heating pad around the pipe, or position an electric space heater near the pipe. Do not use a blowtorch, a propane heater, or an open flame device.

4 Open the tap to see if water flows.

When the frozen area begins to melt, the water will begin to flow.

5 Turn on the water supply to the house.

To Prevent Pipes from Freezing

- Both hot and cold water pipes should be insulated. Use a pipe sleeve, heat tape, or newspapers (¼ inch thick).

- Let the cold water drip from a faucet connected to the most vulnerable pipes.

- Keep the thermostat set to the same temperature day and night.

- Keep the garage door closed in cold weather.

Falling Through the Floor

Spread your arms wide to distribute your weight across unbroken flooring. Place your palms down, and push your body up and back, away from the hole. If you are in the hole up to your waist or farther, lean forward onto your forearms and push to raise as much of your body mass as possible above the hole. Repeat until free. Do not grasp at furniture legs above the hole or kick with your legs below.

How to Avoid Doing Laundry

Gather.

Indent.

Cover.

RETIREMENT

Use your grandchildren as golf caddies.

How to Incorporate the Grandkids into Daily Activities

○ **Use them as golf caddies.**
Divide the clubs equally among all the grandkids.

○ **Ask them to be your ball boy or girl when playing tennis.**
The smaller ones should work the net.

○ **Go running with them.**
Push a stroller while jogging for increased resistance. Have older children set your pace by riding their bikes beside you while you are jogging. The bikes can carry drinking water, towels, or snacks.

○ **Let them play waiter/waitress.**
Teach them how to serve and clear the table, open wine, and pour beverages. Let them dress up as a waiter or waitress when you entertain friends.

○ **Show them how to do the dishes.**
The taller ones can put the dishes in the high cabinets.

○ **Let them set you up on the Internet.**
Have your grandchildren teach you how to sell an item online, join a social networking site, or start a blog.

○ **Have them sort and roll your spare change.**
Pay them a percentage of the value of the coins.

○ **Show them how to garden.**
Teach them how to mow, weed, water, and plant.

○ **Teach them how to play card games.**
Sharpen your bridge, poker, or rummy skills by playing against your grandchildren. Avoid War, Go Fish, and 52-Card Pickup.

How to Take a Nap Anywhere

○ **In the park . . .**
Select a desirable spot in the shade. Avoid areas with ant-hills or dog poop. Clear any debris. Spread a blanket on the lawn.

○ **In the pool . . .**
Wear a swimsuit or other light clothing. Lather yourself with high-SPF sunscreen. Lie flat on a float with your legs dangling in the water.

○ **On a bus, train, or plane . . .**
Take off your jacket or request a blanket to use as a pillow. Turn away from your seatmate(s) to discourage conversation and hide drooling. Put on sunglasses or an eyeshade. Insert earplugs or earphones.

BE AWARE!

✎ A power nap is a timed nap, typically for 20 to 45 minutes, that terminates before a deep sleep or slow-wave sleep.

✎ A catnap is for an undetermined time, often used as a break from activity.

✎ If you cannot fall asleep within 10 to 15 minutes, simply rest. A power rest can be nearly as refreshing as a power nap.

Places Not to Take a 4 p.m. Nap

- In the steam room
- At the grocery store
- In the car, while driving
- On the tennis court
- In the shower
- At the blackjack table
- On the ski slopes
- In a public restroom
- On the sidewalk
- At the bank
- On a surfboard
- At a car wash
- On a safari
- In the kitchen, while baking
- On the treadmill

Take an entry-level job to show you're willing to work.

How to Get Your Old Job Back

○ Schedule a casual lunch with your former boss to "catch up."

○ Sell yourself.
Present your boss with a list of reasons why you should be rehired: you are experienced, you work well with other employees, you have many industry contacts. Mention that hiring you back will eliminate the need for training a young, inexperienced worker. Remind him that you were a hard worker; refer to specific accomplishments, awards, or achievements.

○ Bargain.
Offer to work part-time or to jobshare without health benefits.

○ Grovel.
Show your boss pictures of your wife, children, and pets. Explain their needs.

○ Offer a bribe.
Promise your boss use of your boat for long weekends, expense-paid trips, or a cash payment.

○ Threaten.
Casually mention your familiarity with anti-age discrimination laws.

○ Compromise.
If your old job is not available, offer to work an entry-level position for a while to prove your dedication. Work on call or fill in for vacations and sick leave.

Labor-Expanding Tips to Fill the Day

IN THE KITCHEN	IN THE BACKYARD	IN THE BASEMENT
Grind your own coffee beans by hand.	Start a compost pile.	Label and scrapbook all photographs.
Squeeze oranges for fresh orange juice.	Mow crop circles.	Reorganize all your books by genre or color.
Make homemade spaghetti sauce.	Build a patio.	Construct a wine cellar.
Brew your own beer.	Practice topiary.	Paint a mural.

Clever Ways to Take Your Medicine

• Hide medicine in a mixed drink, such as an Old Russian (Ensure and Kahlua) or a 5 a.m. Sunrise (Metamucil and tequila).

• Grind your meds and add them to your mashed potatoes. Pour on gravy to mask the flavor.

• Alternate each pill with an M&M or a spice drop.

• Put pills in a bowl of cereal.

• Replace the chocolate chips in an already baked cookie with your pills.

• Mix pills in trail mix or mixed nuts.

• Hold your nose, pop in the pill(s), and swallow quickly. Chase with water.

4

Can't We All Just Get Along?

SOCIAL SCENARIOS

FAKING IT

How to Fake a Presentation

1 Speak clearly.

Do not mumble or raise your voice. Speak slowly and evenly. Act as if you are overexplaining very difficult material that the audience might not understand.

2 Stand up straight.

Project confidence with your body language. Smile and make frequent eye contact with your listeners.

3 Make up statistics.

Pepper your presentation with facts and figures. Bombard the listeners with numbers. Glance down at notes in your hand so it appears that you are being careful to get the statistics right.

4 Scrawl.

Use a messy scrawl when writing statistics or other imaginary information on an easel or dry-erase board. Erase each number or flip the page immediately to make room for new fictional information.

5 Ask the audience questions.

Broad questions such as "What are the results we're looking for here?" or "Who are our competitors?" or "What are the greatest risks?" will provoke numerous and varied responses. Use your presentation time to write them on the board or flip chart.

6 Use entertaining props.

Make a puppet out of a coworker's tie. Pour water from a pitcher into a glass to illustrate how capital flows into the market. Remove your blazer and wave it in front of you as if you are a toreador, taking on the bull-like challenges of a changing economy.

7 Give nonanswers to all questions.

Praise the questioner ("That's a really good question. Thank you for asking that."), insult the questioner ("I don't think we need to waste time explaining that."), or say you'd like to answer but want to keep going ("That falls outside the scope of this presentation.").

8 Conclude with a personal anecdote.

Change the subject from business to a story your father used to tell you. When finished, smile and raise your eyebrows enigmatically.

9 Exit the room.

Say thank you and leave immediately.

Make up statistics. Use entertaining props.

How to Fake an Orgasm

1 Begin your vocal and physical ascent.

During sexual activity, start to make noise and move rhythmically.

2 Moan and cry out, building in volume and intensity.

You may say your partner's name over and over. Many people, in the thralls of ecstasy, will blurt out sentences or requests that are utterly incomprehensible: try this occasionally.

3 Move faster rhythmically and then increasingly "out of control."

As you approach "climax," increase the tempo of your movements, particularly of the hips. Add jerky movements. If you have not moved or vocalized much before you start to fake the orgasm, it will seem all the more fake, so you might need to fake enjoyment all the way through. (Note: If you do not usually move your hips during sex, try it. You may find it affects your arousal enough that you will need less faking.)

4 Contract your muscles.

For many people, this is an involuntary side effect of an orgasm; the classic examples are toe-curling or fingers clutching the sheets. You might also arch your back, scrunch your facial muscles, or open your mouth wide.

5 Ratchet up the moaning and writhing in volume and intensity.

6 Culminate in a loud moan or cry.

7 Slow down immediately, tensing your body.

8 Relax, as if exhausted or spent.

9 Smile with enjoyment.

How to Detect a Real Orgasm

Real orgasms are not always as theatrical and loud as fake ones. Some people are silent comers and do not exhibit many visible signs. Real orgasms tend to have some or all of the following elements:

- changes in breathing
- increased vocalizations
- intensified movements
- involuntary muscle contractions
- a pink or reddish flush on the face and chest
- sweat on the shoulders
- pelvic muscle contractions

WARNING!

Be sure that you want to fake the orgasm. You will be sending your partner a message that you are enjoying the sex more than you really are. If your partner is an ongoing lover or spouse, think hard before giving him or her the impression that he or she is doing everything right when that is not the case. If you are enjoying a one-night encounter, consider why it should make a difference to you if your partner thinks you have had an orgasm or not.

Men can fake orgasms too, particularly if a condom is being used.

Do not accuse your partner of faking an orgasm if they are not demonstrative, spasmodic, and loud. Conversely, do not accuse your partner of faking if they display all the characteristics of a faked orgasm.

Orgasms are often accompanied by vocalizing and involuntary muscle contractions, including clutched sheets and curled toes.

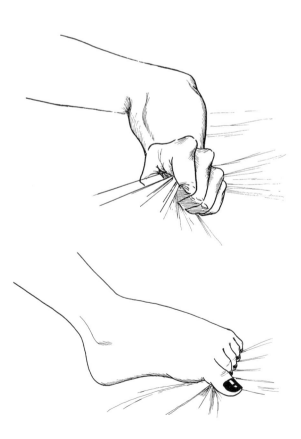

How to Take a Test When You Haven't Studied

Essay

⊕ Find a pocket of related knowledge.

Pull in details from a subject you know well. If you are passionate about abstract expressionism, bring in details of the art movement to answer a question in a 20th-century history exam.

⊕ Use a few key words.

Employ short, less common words, such as wan, fey, nay, and cur. Add a few French bons mots. If you cannot spell the words, write sloppily. You will impress your professor with your linguistic erudition, which is better than not impressing him at all.

⊕ Write something.

Do not leave a question unanswered. You may not receive full credit for the answer, but displaying some knowledge about something will prevent you from taking a zero.

⊕ Scribble an outline.

On the inside cover of your blue book, illegibly write what appears to be an outline of an answer to show that you thoughtfully planned your answer.

⊕ Do not complete the last sentence.

No matter when you finish the essay exam, do not write the last sentence. Instead, write "TIME" across the bottom of your exam. This indicates that you would have written much more if you had more time.

Multiple Choice

⊕ Eliminate the wrong answers immediately.

When there are four choices, two answers are usually completely wrong. Cross them out. If you can discount any other answer, cross it out. "None of the above" and "All of the above" are often the correct answer. Do not discount these right away if you are unsure of the answer.

⊕ Trust your instincts.

Do not talk yourself out of your gut reaction. If you think a particular choice is the right answer, there is a reason. You may vaguely recall a lecture, something you read in passing, or even relevant information from an episode of your favorite television show.

⊕ Look for a pattern on your answer sheet.

Watch for some order, be it ABCDABCDABCD or BADDABBADDAB. Be wary if your answers are AAAA AAAAAAA.

⊕ Do not labor over one question.

All questions are worth the same amount on multiple-choice exams, so do not get overly involved in any one question. Move on and return to unanswered questions as you have time.

⊕ Answer every question.

Very seldom are wrong answers weighted more heavily against you than an unanswered question. Depending on the number of choices, you have a 20 to 25 percent chance of answering a question correctly. Guess every time.

Job Description Euphemism Chart

WHAT YOU DID:	WHAT YOU LIST:
Worked the deep fryer	Acted as sous chef in popular lunch venue
Bagged groceries	Coordinated order fulfillment
Answered phones	Interfaced with clients
Mowed lawns	Landscaped for private clients
Made beds	Arranged accommodations for a hotel
Dug ditches	Industrial waste facilitator
Waited tables	Managed client relations
Babysat child	Development consultant
Folded clothes in department store	Sales associate in the garment industry
Gas station/ convenience store clerk	Auto mechanic's assistant
Lifeguard	Health and safety supervisor
Washed dishes	Restaurant critic
Lifted boxes	Inventory manager in a warehouse
Centerfold	Centerfold

WARNING!

- Take a class pass-fail if it is not in your concentration, if you have an overloaded schedule, or if you are concerned about your grade point average.
- There are usually more "true" answers than "false" answers on a true-false exam because false answers are harder to write.
- Determine what part of the test counts for the most points. Spend a proportionate amount of your time on this section.
- When possible, reuse facts and information from the multiple-choice portion of an exam in an essay question.

POLITICS

How to Survive a Sex Scandal

1 Circle the family.

Gather your spouse, children, and any other available family members for a photo op showing them standing around you looking proud and trusting. Invite the press to film you at a family picnic or volleyball game. Present yourself as a solid family person whose family members continue to support you.

2 Respond quickly.

If the allegations of sexual impropriety are true and can be proved, apologize and say you have asked your family for forgiveness and they have granted it. Then ask voters for forgiveness. If charges against you are false—or true but cannot be proved—vigorously deny them in front of media cameras and urge reporters to respect you and your family's privacy.

3 Do not lie.

Providing inaccurate accounts of your activities may create a whole new avenue for problems.

4 Move on.

When pressed about the scandal by reporters, say you want to focus on issues that affect the everyday lives of your constituents rather than your personal life. Invite the press along to film you engaging in job-related activities such as talking to voters or signing legislation. Present yourself as someone who is too dedicated to his work to let a personal crisis keep him from going forward with more important matters.

5 Leave town.

If the scandal persists, arrange travel on official business. Do not allow reporters to go along, and do not give a press conference when you arrive. Be visible and untroubled, but not quotable. If you cut off reporters' access to you, the story may die down.

6 Take refuge in rehab.

If the furor over the scandal does not dissipate, declare that you have an alcohol or prescription drug dependency that drove you to the impropriety. Then check into a secure and secluded rehabilitation clinic.

7 Ask for forgiveness.

Upon checking out of the rehab clinic, declare that you are cured and now a far better person who can't wait to get back to working for voters. Ask again for forgiveness and vow to work even harder on important issues.

Only appear in wholesome family situations.

8 Declare war.

If the scandal refuses to die down, announce a bold new initiative, such as a war against crime, or if you are in a position to do so, declare war on a small country.

BE AWARE!

- Outside of England and the United States, sexual dalliances are more casually considered by the public.

How to Pretend You Care

Act Like You're Actually Listening

✪ **Lean toward the speaker.**
Lean closer when a voter talks to you, as though you want to hear every word she says. If appropriate, emphasize your undivided attention through physical contact by grasping the voter's arm or putting your hand on her shoulder.

✪ **Mirror the voter's body language.**
If you are face to face with the voter, mirror her posture and body language. This common sales technique makes it appear as if you are listening intently.

✪ **Pause before responding.**
After the voter has finished speaking, act as though you are digesting what you have just heard and are thinking about an answer, even if you already know exactly what you are going to say.

✪ **Address the speaker by name.**
Establish a friendly rapport by using her first name. Ask her to remind you if you forgot her name or if she failed to tell you. If the voter holds an office or honorary title, use that instead of the first name. If the voter is a senior, call him or her by the last name prefaced by "Mr." or "Mrs." as a sign of respect.

✪ **Mimic the voter's emotion.**
If you appear to share the feelings of the voter, she will be more likely to believe that you have heard and appreciated what she has said to you. She will also be much more likely to believe what you say to her.

✪ **Integrate the voter's own words into your response.**
The voter will hear familiar language and believe that you are engaged and on point.

✪ **Ask a question.**
Pick out a key phrase from what the speaker just said, and use it to construct a simple question to seem further interested. The voter's "Taxes are too high" becomes your question, "Have taxes become too much of a worry for you?"

✪ **Do not yawn, sigh, or roll your eyes.**

Appear to Agree

✪ **Nod.**
If a voter is expressing an opinion or telling you something positive, nod along as he speaks. Alternate between smiling and tightening your lips while nodding to avoid looking as though you are nodding on autopilot.

✪ **Accentuate the positive.**
If a voter expresses an opinion that you only partially agree with, focus on the part of his statement that you do agree with. Reiterate your support without discussing other aspects of the voter's statement.

✪ **Sidestep confrontation.**
If a voter has staked out a position that you vigorously disagree with, respond with a noncommittal acknowledgment like "I hear what you're saying" or "That's interesting. I'm glad you shared that." Clap the voter on the back and smile, then move on.

✪ **If the voter insists on arguing, bring up a common belief or value that no one can dispute.**
Relate your statement to the political process or patriotism. For example, "You and I are both patriots who want to do what's best for our country. That means we have to hear each other out and respect each other's opinions, then work together to solve the problem."

✪ **Do not scowl, grimace, or curse.**

How to Simplify a Complicated Message

✪ **Be emotional.**
Effective and memorable political messages depend on inspiring emotional responses from voters that drive them to polls. Invigorate your material with emotion suggestive of deep engagement in the issue or situation. Most voters vote with their hearts first.

✪ **Draw a picture.**
Reduce the issue or situation to a single image or pair of opposing images in which it is clear what is good and what is bad. A criminal walking through a revolving prison door and a child holding a flower pointed at a soldier with a rifle are strong images. The direct connection between the images and the issue is less important than the positive or negative emotional reactions that they stir in support of your campaign or against your opponent's campaign.

✪ **Use an analogy.**
In circumstances where visuals cannot be readily used, describe the situation or issue in terms of a familiar, folksy saying in which it is obvious what is preferable, in a way that even the least sophisticated of voters can understand and appreciate. Associate your opponent with the negative aspect or outcome.

✪ **Remove all doubt.**
Remove all shading, nuance, or equivocation from your statements about the issue. State that any acknowledgment of complication surrounding the issue by your opponent is a sign of weakness or being "soft" on the matter at hand.

✪ **Compare and contrast.**
Paint the issue as a conflict in the broadest possible terms, between right and wrong, or good and evil. Point out that your side is right and good, while the opposition is wrong and evil.

Accept.

Observe.

Kiss.

Return.

HOW TO KISS A DROOLING BABY

1 Take the baby from the parent.

Place your feet about hip distance apart to increase balance. Fully extend your arms away from your body, locking your elbows to help maintain maximum distance. Grasp the baby firmly beneath the arms so she is facing you.

2 Get a good look.

Raise your arms so the baby's head is about six inches above your own. Smile broadly and look admiringly at her. Maintain visual contact with the baby's drool streams. Hold this position long enough to allow any high-flow drool to drip off her face and into the space between the two of you.

3 Kiss the baby.

Aim for a dry area of the baby's cheeks or chin. If all these areas are drooled on, kiss her on the forehead. Hold the position long enough to let your staff photographer and any nearby photojournalists snap a picture.

4 Return the baby to the parent.

As you hand the baby back to the parent, offer a compliment about the baby or ask the parent a friendly question about her to make it appear that she has made a deep and positive impression on you. Thank the parent for having such a wonderful child and move on.

SPORTS

How to Ski Off a 100-Foot Drop

1 Look for danger below.
Just before you ski off the edge of the cliff, look down and out over the slope. If your projected path takes you toward rocks, trees, or another cliff, change your takeoff angle by jumping to the left or right so that you will head toward safer, wide-open terrain.

2 Jump up and off the ledge.
Just as you are leaving the ground, hop up and slightly forward to help you clear any rocks or other obstructions that may be hidden just below the ledge and that could knock you off balance.

3 Pull your legs and skis up and tuck them under your rear end.
This compressed "ball" position will help you to maintain balance while airborne and help you to land safely.

4 Thrust both arms out in front of you, elbows slightly bent.
Avoid the "cat out the window" position, where your arms and hands are splayed out above your head. That position will put you off balance when you land.

5 Look out, not down.
Looking down at the ground will lead to a "door hinge" landing, where you bend forward at the waist and plant your face in the slope. Look out over the mountain.

6 Focus on a suitable landing site.
Land on very steep terrain. Avoid a low-angled slope or, worse, a flat section of the mountain. As long as the snow is powder and at least one foot deep, you should be able to land without serious injury.

7 Bend your knees as you land.
As you approach the side of the mountain, keep your knees bent to absorb the force of the impact with the ground. Avoid leaning back, which will cause a "tail first" landing and probable back injury. If you cannot ski away from a landing, land on your hip. Do not lean too far forward or you will fall on your face.

8 Extend your feet, bend your knees, and turn across (or "into") the mountain to slow down.
Because of your extreme speed while airborne, you must minimize acceleration by turning as soon as you land, or you risk hurtling down the mountain out of control. Modern skis should stay on top of deep powder instead of sinking, giving you a reasonable amount of control.

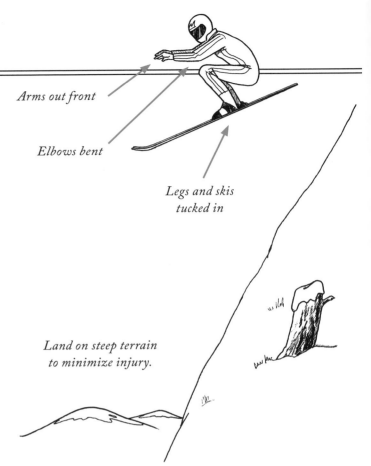

Arms out front

Elbows bent

Legs and skis tucked in

Land on steep terrain to minimize injury.

9 Continue making turns to keep control and reduce speed as you ski away.

WARNING!

- If you feel yourself falling backward while airborne, move your hands farther in front of you and make fast circular motions, forward and back. This balancing maneuver is called "rolling down the windows."

- In any jump greater than 15 feet, avoid landing in the same spot where a previous jumper landed; the snow will already be compacted and will not provide sufficient cushioning.

How to Survive a Stadium Riot

1 Scan the crowd.
Quickly determine the focus of the rioting: mascot, goalpost, star player, referee, fans, band members, coaches, or cheerleaders. Physically distance yourself as quickly as possible.

2 Hide any obvious team affiliation.
If the mob appears to be attacking your team's fans, remove any clothing items with team colors, letters, or emblems. If you can stuff these items into a nondescript bag or plastic bag, do so and take them with you. If not, leave them behind.

3 Create a protective helmet.

Stuff crumpled-up newspaper or cardboard inside your hat for cushioning (if your hat bears a logo, turn it inside out). If you do not have a hat, place an empty popcorn tub or other container over your head.

4 Move away from the mascots.

Regardless of whether they are the focus of the riot, both teams' mascots are especially vulnerable to attack. Stay well clear of either mascot.

5 Observe movement patterns.

Most rioters move en masse in a single direction toward a particular object. Determine which way the mob is headed.

6 Watch for projectiles.

Bend your knees and keep your head low to avoid flying cans, bottles, pennants, water balloons, rocks, pipes, benches, people, or other objects.

7 Move sideways through the crowd to the nearest exit.

Avoid moving forward (toward the center of the riot) or backward (against the surging mob).

WARNING!

⚡ If you are the cause of the riot due to your actions as a fan, player, or mascot, ditch your uniform or suit and run.

HOW TO SURVIVE A TWO-WAVE HOLD-DOWN

1 Bail your board.

If you are in the impact zone (the area where the lip of the wave meets the trough), dive off your board.

2 Avoid the "washing machine."

The washing machine, the white water that occurs as the wave crashes, is turbulent, full of air, and difficult to pierce and swim in. Attempting to surface through it will extend your hold-down.

3 Do not struggle.

Fighting a very big (or "rogue") wave will quickly exhaust you and increases your risk of drowning. Remember to "think before you sink."

4 Dive.

Swim as deep as you can. Big-wave leashes (the rope that connects you to your floating board) may be 20 feet long, allowing you to go very deep.

5 Allow the first wave to pass over you.

6 Locate the board's leash.

If you are disoriented and unable to determine which way is up, grab your ankle and "follow your leash." Since the leash is attached to your floating surfboard, it will lead you to the surface.

7 Swim toward the surface.

As you approach the surface, place your hands above your head. Your surfboard may be "tombstoning," with its tail submerged and its nose pointing to the sky. Positioning your arms above your head will protect you from hitting your surfboard, a Jet Ski, or another wiped-out surfer as you come up for air.

8 Wait out the set of waves by diving underneath them.

Waves typically come in sets of three to five, depending on the day and surf conditions. Count the waves as they break so that you'll know when the water will calm. Swim as deep as you can and curl your body into a defensive ball as the waves pass overhead. Come up for a quick breath between each wave, if possible, as you wait for the set to subside.

9 Paddle to calmer water.

When the set has passed, swim to the surface. Climb on your surfboard and paddle as fast as you can farther out to sea, beyond the impact zone, or into the "channel," the blue water that is sometimes to the left or right of the white water.

WARNING!

⚡ Never position your surfboard between your body and a big wave: it will smash into you.

⚡ Never put your back to the waves unless you are paddling to catch a wave and ride it.

⚡ A big wave may hold you down for more than 30 seconds.

Leash

Stay down to wait out the wave set.

Grab here.

Grab the club of the irate golfer as it starts to descend or at the top of the swing.

Tuck the club under your armpit, and wrench it away by rotating away from the irate golfer.

How to Disarm an Irate Golfer

1 Determine the level of danger.

If a golfer is waving a club around angrily or drunkenly, or is exhibiting undue hostility, it may be necessary to act quickly to restore order and safety.

2 Try to talk him down.

Speak calmly, keeping your tone even and your voice low. Do not make sudden gestures or movements. Remind him that it's only a game. Tell him to take a few deep breaths.

3 If he threatens to strike, quickly move into the center of the potential swing.

As he draws the club back to swing at you, approach him at an angle that will bring you to the center of the club. Try to remain close to his body. You are much more likely to be injured by the outer end of the club.

4 Grab the club.

At the top of his swing, or just as the club starts to descend, step close to him and, using one or both hands, clutch the club tightly near the grip. Pull down, staying close to him, until you can wrap your arm around the club. Hold the shaft with your armpit while keeping a firm grasp on the club's grip.

5 Wrench the club away.

Maintaining your hold, rotate your body around, away from the golfer's face. This maneuver should give you the leverage you need to wrench the club out of his grip. Pull with just enough force to free the club from his grasp.

6 Step back quickly, and be prepared for him to continue to be angry and to flail.

If necessary, use the club to keep him away from his bag, where he might obtain a second weapon.

7 If necessary, call for help.

Seek the assistance of your fellow golfers to help defuse the situation.

8 Continue to talk to him until he calms down.

WARNING!

It is always advisable to make all possible attempts to avoid physical confrontation. Your first choice should be to ignore and walk away from an irate golfer. Your next choice should be to use verbal skills to calm the golfer by speaking in low tones and showing understanding. Become physical only as a last resort, to avoid greater injury to yourself or others.

ALCOHOL

Turn the key of the wire cage six clockwise half-turns while keeping constant pressure on the cage and cork.

Cover the cork and neck of the bottle with a cloth napkin. Carefully turn the bottle clockwise until the cork pops.

HOW TO AVOID SHOOTING A CHAMPAGNE CORK

1 Hold the thumb of your nondominant hand over the cage and cork.

The cork may fly out of the bottle as soon as the wire mesh (known as the "cage") is loosened. Keep pressure on the cork, and point the bottle away from yourself and anyone nearby.

2 Turn the key of the wire cage.

All cages on champagne and sparkling wine open after six clockwise half-turns. Remove the cage.

3 Place an opened cloth napkin over the cork and neck of the bottle.

Hold the bottle in your nondominant hand and the napkin over the cork in your other hand. Keep the bottle angled away from people.

4 Hold the cork tightly and slowly turn the bottle clockwise.

Do not turn the cork or you risk breaking it.

5 As the cork begins to come out, apply downward pressure on it.

The pressure will prevent the cork from shooting away from the bottle.

6 Hold the cork at the mouth of the bottle for five seconds.

If champagne begins to bubble up and out, it will react with the end of the cork and flow back into the bottle.

7 Slowly pour the champagne.

Pour the champagne slowly until the froth (called "mousse") reaches about 2/3 up the glass, then pause. When the mousse has receded, continue filling until the glass is approximately 2/3 full.

WARNING!

↗ The quieter the pop, the better the opening. A poor opening will cause champagne to spurt out of the bottle, resulting in lost champagne and carbonation.

↗ An uncontrolled opening may result in the cork's leaving the champagne bottle with enough force to cause injury to someone nearby.

↗ Crystal flutes will improve the champagne experience: The slender shape makes the long streams of bubbles more visually appealing and concentrates the aroma. The finest leaded crystal (with a lead content of about 25 percent) has the smoothest surface and allows the champagne to maintain maximum carbonation.

↗ Never chill champagne flutes.

↗ Avoid champagne "saucers": their larger surface area releases more carbonation.

↗ The smaller the bubbles, the better the champagne.

How to Open a Bottle of Wine with a Broken Cork

1 Examine the cork.
If the cork has broken due to improper corkscrew use, treat the broken cork as if it were whole. If the cork is pushed too far into the bottle, push it all the way in using any long, thin implement and proceed to "With a Very Dry Cork," step 5, below.

2 Reinsert the corkscrew.
Six half-turns of the corkscrew will usually be enough to allow you to remove a full cork, but you may need fewer for a partial cork. Turn the corkscrew slowly to prevent further cork breakage.

3 Pull the cork out.
Pull up steadily on the corkscrew, being careful not to jerk the cork out of the bottle. If the cork remains in the bottle, go to "With a Very Dry Cork," step 2, below.

With a Very Dry Cork

1 Check for crumbling.
If the cork is soft and powdery, it will not offer the corkscrew enough resistance. It may also be stuck to the sides of the bottle, making intact removal impossible.

2 Bore a hole through the center of the cork.
Use the corkscrew as a drill.

3 Widen the hole.
Wiggle the corkscrew from side to side to increase the diameter of the hole.

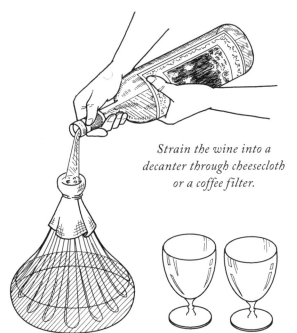

Strain the wine into a decanter through cheesecloth or a coffee filter.

4 Try to pour.
If the wine will not pour, continue to enlarge the diameter of the hole as above, or force the remainder of the cork into the bottle.

5 Make a filter.
Place a piece of clean, unwaxed, unbleached cheesecloth over the mouth of a decanter and secure it tightly with a rubber band. If no cheesecloth is available, use a coffee filter (preferably unbleached). Do not use a T-shirt or any article of clothing you have washed in detergent—the detergent can affect the taste of the wine.

6 Strain the wine.
Carefully pour the wine through the filter into the decanter. When the bottle is empty, remove the filter containing the pieces of cork from the mouth of the decanter and serve the wine.

How to Deal with the "Spins"

1 Focus your gaze on a stationary object in the room.
Keep your eyes open. Avoid looking at ceiling fans. Stare at the object for one minute.

2 Close your eyes.

3 Picture the object you were looking at.
Imagine that the object is imprinted on the inside of your eyelids.

4 Open your eyes.
If the spinning returns, stare at your object for one minute.

5 Close your eyes.
Repeat steps 3 and 4.

6 Repeat steps 3, 4, and 5 until the spinning stops or you pass out.

WARNING!

⚡ The spins usually occur when your eyes are closed. Watch television, go out for some air, or eat a meal—anything to stay awake and keep your eyes open until you sober up.

⚡ Eating reduces drinking-related sickness by reducing the speed at which alcohol in the stomach is absorbed into the bloodstream. Eat before drinking: once you have the spins, it is too late.

⚡ Alcohol is a diuretic and dehydrates. After drinking, replace lost fluid, vitamins, and electrolytes by consuming sports drinks. Avoid drinking excessive amounts of plain water, which will dilute the sodium concentration in the body.

How to Win a Bar Bet

Make bets that you know you will win, or perform a sure-fire bar trick for drinks. Select a mark, preferably someone who has been drinking heavily.

Brandy Snifter and Cherry

1 Place the snifter upside down over the cherry.

2 Wager a free drink that you can get the cherry into the empty glass without touching the cherry or the empty glass.

The cherry can only touch the snifter, which must remain upside down. Squashing the cherry onto the rim is prohibited.

3 Use centrifugal force.

When your mark bets, show him the power of centrifugal force. Hold the base of the snifter and rotate it quickly on the bar top. When the cherry starts spinning inside the glass, lift the snifter off the table. Keep rotating the snifter and hold it over the glass. When you slow your rotation, the cherry will drop into the glass. Collect your free drink.

A Race to the Finish

1 Identify your mark.

At the bar, find a small group of men drinking together who seem tipsy, but not so drunk that they will try to kill you when played for fools.

2 Make your proposition.

Sit down next to the group, and casually say, "You guys want to see something cool?" State the proposed bet simply and clearly: "Anyone want to bet I can drink three beers before you can drink a single shot?"

3 Let them decide who will take the bet.

Faced with a challenge, a group of men will naturally jockey for supremacy by mocking or goading each other into taking the best.

4 Let the mark determine the stakes.

Allow the other person to set the stakes, especially if his friends are suggesting he will lose. Offer gentle reassurance such as, "It's totally up to you. Whatever you want to make it." And then whatever he proposes, up the ante by saying, "Oh, okay. Or we could make it a real bet. Whatever you want."

5 State the rules.

Clearly say what the bet is and how it works. "I will drink three beers before you drink a single shot. You will give me a one-beer head start, and neither of us can touch the other's glasses.

Rotate snifter. Lift snifter off of the table as the cherry spins. Drop the cherry into the target glass.

6 Hear the mark repeat it back.

Have the mark repeat the rules back to you, and make sure that all his friends and anyone else present can hear, so there are plenty of witnesses.

7 Put the money on the bar.

Illustrate your commitment to the wager by suggesting that both you and the mark place your money directly on the bar in front of you. This will also allow you to collect the money more easily once you win.

8 Feign second thoughts.

As the bartender brings the drinks, suddenly look anxious and say things such as, "Oh wait, did I get that right?" Try to back out: "You know what? Forget the whole thing." When the mark presses you, relent and agree to go through with it. He may try to raise the stakes of the wager; if so, reluctantly agree.

9 Win the bet.

After you drink your head-start beer, place the empty glass upside down over his shot glass. This way he cannot drink his drink, because he's not allowed to touch your glass, per the rules of the bet. Finish your other two beers.

10 Be gracious.

If the mark seems upset, offer to buy him a beer (with his own money) from the winnings on the bar. You've still come out several beers ahead.

HOW TO OPEN A BEER BOTTLE WITHOUT A BOTTLE OPENER

Another Bottle

1 Hold the bottle you wish to open upright in your nondominant hand.
Grip the neck of the target bottle, placing your index finger over the back edge of the cap.

2 Hold the second bottle horizontally around the label.
Grip this bottle, the opener, as though shaking hands with the bottle.

3 Fit the shallow ridge found at midcap of the opener bottle under the bottom edge of the cap of the bottle you wish to open.
By using this ridge, and not the bottom of the cap, you will not risk opening the second bottle in step 4.

4 Using the opener bottle as a lever, press down and pry the cap off the target beer bottle.

5 Enjoy.

Alternate Method

Hold both bottles end to end parallel to the ground, with the crimped edges of the caps together, locking them in place. Pull. Be careful, however, as either or both bottle caps could come off.

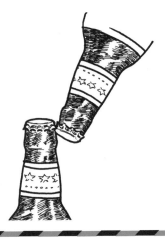

Lighter

1 Grip the bottle in your nondominant hand.
Make a fist around the top of the bottle so that your thumb overlaps your index finger and the web between your thumb and index finger sits in the groove under the cap.

2 Fit the bottom of the lighter under the teeth of the cap.
Position the lighter so that it rests on the middle knuckle of your index finger.

3 Press the top of the lighter down and toward the bottle.
Use the index finger on your dominant hand to provide resistance.

4 Pry off the cap.
If necessary, turn the bottle and repeat.

Screwdriver, Spoon, Fork, or Knife

1 Place the implement under the bottle cap, as high as it will go.

2 Pry off the cap.
Slowly go around the cap and lift up each crimped area with the tool, similar to opening a can of paint.

3 When the cap starts to move, fit the tool higher up under the cap and remove it.

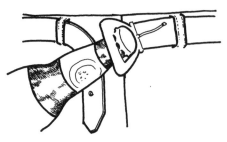

Belt Buckle

1 Unfasten your belt buckle.
If your pants are in danger of falling down, sit.

2 Pull the "tooth" of the buckle to one side.

3 Fit the cap into the buckle so that one edge is wedged against the buckle.

4 Pry off.
Pull the bottle slowly. A quick tug may result in a spill.

5 Refasten your belt.

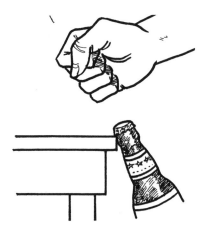

Table Edge

1 Put the teeth of the bottle cap against the edge of a table.
The cap should be on top of the table edge; the bottle should be below the table. Do not attempt on a soft wood or antique table.

2 Use your fist to hit the bottle.
The bottle will take a downward trajectory, and the cap will pop off.

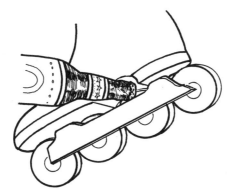

Vending Machine

1 Locate a newspaper, snack, or soda vending machine.
An older soda machine might actually have a bottle opener.

2 Place the cap in the coin return.
Wedge the cap against the top of the opening.

3 Press down slowly until the cap is removed.

Deadbolt Lock

1 Fit your bottle into the lock.
Place the head of the bottle into the recessed part of a doorframe, so that the cap fits against the notch where the deadbolt slips.

2 Pull up slowly.
The bottle cap should pop right off.

Fire Hydrant

1 Look for an arrow on top of the hydrant labeled "open."

2 At the end of the arrow, locate the recess between the screw and the nut.

3 Insert the cap into the recess.

4 Press down slowly on the bottle until the cap comes off.

In-Line Skate

1 Place the cap between the shoe and the blade.
Hold on to the bottle with your dominant hand. If you are wearing the skate, use the hand opposite the skate to open the bottle.

2 Pull up slowly on the bottle and pry off.
Quickly right the bottle to avoid spilling.

Metal Pool Bridge

1 Hold the stick of the bridge in one hand and a beer bottle in the other.
Do not attempt to open over the pool table.

2 Position the cap inside the opening of the bridge.
Fit the cap snugly against the edge.

3 Press down on the bottle.
Slowly increase the pressure until the cap loosens. Right the bottle immediately to prevent spillage.

COIN RETURN

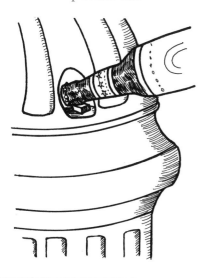

WARNING!

⚡ Never drink from a bottle with broken or chipped glass.

GAMES AND HOBBIES

Watch for facial expressions, body language, or other nonverbal cues that can be used to signal another player.

HOW TO SPOT A CARD CHEAT

○ **Examine the cards.**
Before play begins, look for irregularities in the cards that might help a cheater identify a particular card. Marks in a round design, like marks on a clockface, may indicate the value of a card; an ace is marked at one o'clock, an eight at eight o'clock. Nicks, nail marks, stains, and crimps may also be marks. Beware if a player bends cards during play.

○ **Watch for false shuffling.**
Confirm that the dealer actually shuffles the deck; a cheat may have brought in a prestacked deck. An overhand shuffle can stack a deck right in front of your eyes. Insist on a reshuffle if you are suspicious. Require that the deck be cut by someone other than the dealer.

○ **Watch for team cheating.**
Shufflers who first bend the deck can be sending a signal to the cutter where to cut the deck; the bent half of the deck should be easy to spot when the deck is placed on the table for the cutter. A cheater can also leave a slight jog in the deck indicating to the accomplice where to make the cut.

○ **Listen for verbal cues between partners.**
Repeated phrases may have hidden meanings. Be suspicious of players (or nonplayers) who wander the room, then interact with another player. Signals can also include nonverbal cues such as facial expressions, body language, gestures, and subtle indicators such as sighs or sneezes.

○ **Watch the banker.**
Keep an eye on the tender of the pot, the banker, or other special task holders. Cheaters can palm a chip when distributing winnings, skim off bank winnings, shortchange a player, or otherwise sweeten their own winnings.

WARNING!

⚡ Mirrors, windows, and sunglasses can reflect a player's hand.

⚡ Draw cards to determine seating to decrease cooperative cheating.

⚡ Make a rule that someone other than the dealer shuffles the cards.

⚡ Require that players keep cards on the table at all times.

⚡ A cheat may deal you a good hand, but his will be better.

⚡ Use a position or joker on the bottom of the deck so that no one can see the bottom card and the dealer cannot deal from the bottom of the deck.

HOW TO DEAL WITH A DART INJURY

1 If the dart is embedded in the head, neck, chest, or back, leave it in place.
Rinse a small, clean towel in cold water, wring it out, and wrap the towel around the base of the dart to stabilize it and prevent further penetrating or shearing injury. Take the person to the hospital, or call for an ambulance.

2 Remove the dart.
If the dart is embedded in an arm or leg, remove it from the victim using a fast, pulling motion. Put the dart in a safe location where it will not cause further injury.

3 Place the victim in a sitting position.

4 Examine the wound.
If blood is spurting from the wound, apply a clean cloth to the injury site. If there is bleeding but no spurting, skip to step 8.

5 Apply pressure.
Elevate the affected area above the level of the heart. Hold the cloth firmly in place for five minutes.

Locate the dart.

6 Remove the cloth and check the wound.
If blood continues to spurt, apply a new, clean cloth, elevate, and apply pressure for 15 additional minutes. Change the cloth as needed. For persistent oozing, apply pressure for 30 minutes.

7 Examine the wound.
Once the wound has stopped spurting, check the injury site, wiping away any seeping blood.

8 Rinse.
When the bleeding has stopped or slowed, gently rinse the wound under cool tap water.

9 Bandage.
Cover with a large, sterile dressing.

10 Clean the dart.
Rinse the dart under hot tap water, then wipe thoroughly with rubbing (isopropyl) alcohol.

11 Remove the victim from the field of play.

HOW TO SURVIVE A BUNGEE CORD BREAK

The bungee cord is under maximum stress at the very bottom of your jump, before you rebound; it is at this point that a break is most likely. If you are over water and the cord breaks or comes loose, you will be falling headfirst and have about two seconds to prepare for impact.

1 Straighten your legs and body.
Put your feet and legs together, and point your toes.

2 Tuck your chin into your chest as far as it will go.
Avoid the urge to look down: it will result in black eyes, whiplash, or severe spinal trauma.

3 Point your arms below your head in a diving position. Ball your fists.

4 Enter the water fists-first.
Your hands will break the surface tension of the water, putting less stress on your head. If the bungee cord was attached and broke at your rebound point, it will have slowed you almost to a stop, making for a relatively safe entry. If the cord was not attached or came loose during your fall, the impact will be more severe.

5 Spread your arms and legs.
On entering the water, spread your arms and legs to slow your momentum and reduce the chance of hitting the bottom.

6 Swim to the surface.
Signal to the crew above that you are okay.

WARNING!

Bungee cords are weight-specific, and you should always jump on a cord designed for your weight. Always overestimate, not underestimate, your weight.

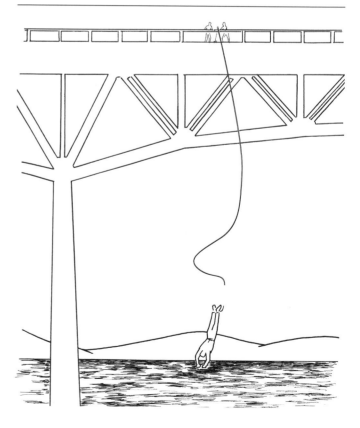

Enter the water fists-first.

DIFFICULT RELATIONSHIPS

Laugh at your boss's jokes.

How to Flatter an Insecure Boss

○ Sit next to your boss.

○ Loudly agree with your boss's statements.

Enthusiastically say "yes" to each of her suggestions and ideas. Vary your expressions of agreement to include: "I agree," "I totally agree," "I completely agree," and "I couldn't agree more." After your boss completes a declarative statement, add the word "obviously."

○ Silently affirm your boss's statements.

Constantly nod as your boss speaks. Smile and chuckle quietly to yourself to express how much you completely agree with what is being said. Write down everything your boss says.

○ Duplicate your boss's food order.

When someone is taking sandwich orders, wait until after your boss has made her order, and then say "Ditto," "The same," or "Sounds good."

○ Laugh at your boss's jokes.

Watch your boss's body language for signs that what she is saying is meant to be humorous, such as raised eyebrows and teeth showing. Only laugh if you are sure that what your boss is saying is meant to be a joke.

○ Take your boss's side in arguments.

When other people continue to disagree with her, roll your eyes and shush them.

○ Ask your boss for advice.

During breaks in the meeting, ask her for counsel on work issues. Write down each piece of advice and thank her profusely. During subsequent conversations, ask for advice on nonwork issues, such as romance, fashion, and family relationships.

○ Offhandedly compliment your boss as you exit the meeting.

As the meeting breaks up, position yourself near the doorway as your boss passes by. Remark to a coworker how enlightening/exciting you found the meeting to be. Place your compliments within a larger pattern. Make statements such as "Wow! Another great meeting from [*boss's name*]."

How to Deal with Meddling Parents

1 Prepare yourself mentally.

Try to maintain a positive attitude no matter what your parents may say.

2 If your parents give unwanted or annoying advice, be polite and attempt to change the subject.

Thank them for their concern. Say "I appreciate your advice, but I'd really rather talk about [*insert new subject here*]."

3 Avoid confrontation.

Never respond to a meddling parent with phrases that include "you always," "you never," or "leave it alone." Suggest discussing the issue at another time. If you are a guest in someone else's home, confrontation should be avoided at all costs.

4 Smother the conversation with kindness.

Always counter a negative remark with a positive one. If your parent says, "Your house really needs painting," counter with, "This house is in such a great neighborhood. Isn't that great for the kids!" If your parent says, "When are you going to get a real job?" counter with, "I'm making great progress on my novel!"

5 Do not discuss money in public.

How much things cost and financial success are attractive topics for a meddling parent. These are inappropriate subjects for group conversation, however. Do not get angry;

deflect the inquiry. If a question about money is asked, say, "I can't remember what we paid" or "We're just thankful for what we have."

6 Avoid taking the bait.

If a meddling parent keeps mentioning how well other people are doing compared with you—how important a job, how many children, how big a house—or makes other implicitly critical comparisons, just say, "That's wonderful."

7 Ask for their advice about a less irritating topic.

Meddling parents often simply want to be asked for their opinions. Seeking their thoughts on a less important subject or even on a made-up problem may placate them or distract them from sensitive issues (ask for their input on remodeling the kitchen, for example, even if you are not intending to do so).

8 If the meddling parent will not relent, excuse yourself from the conversation.

Casually excuse yourself (do not say, "I can't listen to this anymore!") and move to another room. For example, finish your drink and say, "I need to get a refill" (do not offer to get your parent one); or say, "Excuse me, I have to go to the bathroom" or "I have to make a phone call" or "I promised I would help in the kitchen." Do not make any promises to come right back.

WARNING!

⚡ It is best to preempt meddling parents by announcing lots of news before their arrival. Phone or e-mail the week before with updates, keeping the news positive and upbeat.

⚡ Remember that you do not have to answer every question. Practice nonresponses or evasive responses, such as "Do you really think so?" or "That's an interesting question. Let me think about it." In front of a mirror, practice the blank stare.

HOW TO DATE THREE PEOPLE AT ONCE

⊙ **Assign them the same nickname.**
Call them all "honey" or "sweetie" or "pumpkin" so that you do not accidentally use the wrong name with the wrong person. It also helps if you discuss the same topics and pick the same song as "our song."

⊙ **Keep to a schedule.**
See them only on their assigned day—Mary every Thursday, Emily every Friday, and Jenny every Saturday. They will see you as highly disciplined and will not expect to monopolize your time.

Most Stressful Relationships

1. With spouse/partner
2. With boss/manager
3. With food
4. With money

⊙ **Select three different favorite bars, activities, or restaurants.**
A special place for each reduces your chances of running into another date. Look for dimly lit locations.

⊙ **Be vague.**
Provide few details to each date about your whereabouts during nondate evenings. Offer ambiguous responses like "I wish I had time to see you more often, too."

⊙ **Keep your cell phone out of other people's hands.**
For additional protection, use initials, not names or nicknames, to identify your contacts. Erase text messages as soon as you read or send them.

⊙ **Advise your roommate to say as little as possible.**
Explain your situation and ask for cooperation. Tell your roommate to say only "Nice to see you" when he sees one of your dates. He should avoid "Nice to meet you" or "Nice to see you again," since he may be easily confused about whom he is talking to.

⊙ **Do not place photographs around your room.**
The fewer things and people to explain, the better. Also remove stuffed animals, flowers, cards, mix CDs, or anything that might look like a romantic gift.

⊙ **Tell everyone that you have a large family.**
Prepare for the time when you will be spotted with another date. If asked later whom you were with, you can say she was your cousin.

⊙ **Refer to several part-time jobs.**
Say that you are sorry to be so unavailable because you are always working. Mention that you are saving all the money you are earning so that you don't build expectations about gifts or expensive dates.

⊙ **Do not boast.**
Aside from your roommate, keep any mention of the simultaneous relationships to yourself. The more people you tell about your multiple assignations, the more likely it is that you will be discovered.

How to Deal with Nightmare Customers

Irate Retail Customer

1 Watch for warning signs.
A customer will usually display several "buildup" physical cues before becoming irate. Look for clenching of the hands, locking of the knees, crossing of the arms, rolling of the eyes, and leaning in toward you to reduce the amount of personal space between you.

2 Listen, listen, listen.
The customer will raise his voice and become demanding, and may begin assessing blame, claiming victimhood, threatening to report you, and insisting on satisfaction. Let him rant—interrupting or defending your actions during the rant will only exacerbate the problem.

3 Do not mimic the posture or volume of the irate patron.
Avoid leaning in, but do not lean away, either: moving away indicates that you are becoming defensive. Maintain a placid, neutral position.

4 Stay loose.
Keep your weight evenly distributed on both feet. Breathe deeply and exhale slowly.

5 Speak softly.
Wait until the customer is finished speaking, then speak calmly. Never state that the customer is angry or upset. Instead, say, "I recognize that you are raising your voice. What is it you need me to do? What is it you need the store to do?" Anger results from unmet needs, so try your best to solve the problem.

6 Send a clear message and offer a clear resolution.
Say, "My commitment is to a quick, successful resolution of this problem." Offer an exchange, a return, or a new item according to your company's policies. If you are unable to provide a satisfactory solution, ask a manager for help.

7 Apologize.
Before you find a manager, say, "I am sorry we were unable to help you today. I do hope that you will come back to shop at our store again."

Abusive Restaurant Patron

1 Listen.
Allow the customer to explain what is wrong. If he begins yelling or using foul language, do not respond in kind.

2 Do not argue.
If the customer complains that the food is a funny color,

Remain calm.

that the bread is stale, or that the coffee tastes of detergent, do not respond by saying, "It looks/tastes okay to me!" Never taste a customer's food.

3 Observe the customer.
If the customer stands up angrily, moves in close, or begins gesticulating wildly, move away and quietly ask him to lower his voice. If he refuses, or if he starts poking or grabbing the food, ask him to leave.

4 Observe the room.
Quickly check the room to see if other diners are being disturbed. If you notice turned heads or whispering, contact the manager immediately to deal with the other customers or to back you up with yours.

5 Placate.
Keep your tone even and your volume low. If a dish is unsatisfactory, offer to take it back and provide the customer with another selection. If his dinner arrived late or cold, offer to remove it from the bill.

6 Check back.
Once the problem is resolved, check back with the customer to make certain that everything is acceptable. Do not check more than once. Consider offering a dessert or after-dinner drink "on the house."

WARNING!

↗ Watch for a setup. A customer may eat and complain in hopes of getting a complimentary meal. If a customer returns to the restaurant to dine and complains again, alert the manager, and consider asking the customer to leave and not return.

↗ Avoid physical confrontation with customers, particularly if the tables in the restaurant are close together.

DATING

HOW TO SURVIVE IF YOU WAKE UP NEXT TO SOMEONE AND DON'T REMEMBER THEIR NAME

At Their Place

1 Do not panic.
Evidence of your partner's name exists somewhere nearby. Your task will be to find it before she awakens, or before she starts any sort of meaningful conversation.

2 Get up and go to the bathroom.
The bathroom is a normal place to visit first thing in the morning, and it is also a place where you might discover her name.

3 Look through the medicine cabinet for prescription medicines with her name on the label.

4 Sort through magazines, looking for subscription labels with her name and address.

5 Go through a wastebasket to find discarded junk mail addressed to her.

6 Return to the bedroom.
If she is awake, ask her to make coffee for you. Use the time alone to search the bedroom for evidence. Look for: wallet, checkbook, ID or name bracelet, photo album, scrapbook, business cards (a stack of cards, not just one), or luggage labels. If she is sleeping, look for these and other items throughout the house.

WARNING!

Try to find at least two items with the same name to be certain that you have identified her, unless the name on one item rings a bell.

At Your Place

1 Use terms of endearment when addressing her.
Do not guess at her name. Acceptable terms of endearment are

- Honey/Sweetie/Cutie
- Darling/Baby/Sugar
- Beautiful/Handsome/Gorgeous

2 Unless you are certain that you have ample time, do not go through her belongings.
If your partner is showering, you can count on having

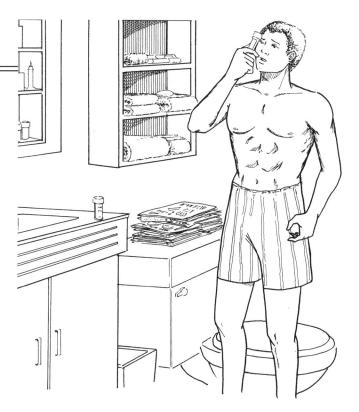

Look through medicine cabinets for prescription medicines with your date's name on the label.

at least a few minutes of privacy to search through her belongings. Otherwise, do not risk it—it would be far more embarrassing to be caught searching through her possessions than to admit that you cannot remember her name. (She may be in the same predicament.)

3 Ask leading questions while making small talk.
Fishing for information is risky and can backfire by calling attention to what you are trying to do. However, if you feel you can pull it off, try to trick her into revealing her name:

- While getting dressed, pull out your own ID and ask her if she thinks that your hair is better now or in the picture. Laugh about how silly you used to look. Ask her if she likes the picture on her license. (She may think that you are checking her age.)

- Ask her if she ever had a nickname. She might say, "No, just [*Name*]."

- Ask her how she got her name.

4 As she is leaving, give her your business card and ask for hers.
If she does not have a business card, ask her to write her vital information on yours. Tell her you may want to send her a little surprise. Do not forget to send something later in the week, and make sure that you spell her name correctly.

How to Spot a Fake

Breast Implants

1 Remember: if they look too good to be true, they probably are.

If a woman is over 30 and her breasts defy gravity without a bra, or she has a strikingly full and firm upper cleavage and bosom, chances are her breasts are not fully natural. You should also be suspicious of breasts that sit very high on a woman's chest; this is another good sign of implants.

2 Assess breast size as compared with frame size.

Most, though not all, petite women have naturally small breasts.

3 Be suspicious of baseball-shaped breasts or strangely arranged breasts.

In cases of a poor augmentation, the outline of the implant may be noticeable, or the breast may have a very firm, round, baseball-like appearance. Poorly placed implants can often be seen through tight tops. While a good augmentation procedure can be difficult to detect by visual inspection alone, a bad one is quite noticeable.

If a woman is over 30 and has strikingly full breasts that sit very high on her chest, you have reason to be suspicious.

4 Check cleavage for rippling of the skin.

Implants may ripple in the cleavage or on top of the breasts; look for a wave pattern across the surface. Natural breasts, even very large breasts, although soft, will never have a rippled appearance.

5 If appropriate, brush up against or hug someone with suspected breast implants.

If her breasts feel firmer than normal, implants may be in use.

6 Check under and around the breast for scarring.

In an intimate situation, the opportunity may arise for a closer visual and tactile inspection. Look for scarring under the breasts, around the nipple, and in the armpit area.

Toupees

1 Look for uneven hair texture.

Since toupees do not cover the entire scalp the way a wig does, there will always be a place where the real hair meets the purchased hairpiece. Generally, men who wear toupees have thinning hair, so look for a patch of thick hair surrounded by areas with thinner coverage.

2 Beware of an abnormally thick patch of hair on the top of the scalp.

Toupees are very thick in order to effectively cover the nylon or fabric cap that is attached to the scalp.

3 Watch for inconsistent coloring.

Toupees generally do not perfectly match the color of the hair surrounding them. A very dark area of hair surrounded by thinner, lighter hair may indicate a toupee.

4 Note any shifting of hair on the scalp.

Toupees are usually attached to the scalp with wig tape or special adhesive, which can come loose, especially during high winds or excessive perspiration. A patch of hair that has moved or is out of place is a sure sign of a toupee.

5 Test your theory.

Reach for your date's head, saying, "You've got something in your hair." If he reacts quickly to stop you from touching his hair, you may have found a toupee.

BE AWARE!

↗ Many men with thinning hair choose hair plugs, which are hair follicles that have been surgically implanted in the scalp. Lots of small bumps that resemble knots at the base of the hair shafts are a good indicator of hair plugs.

Assume the "pickup screen" position by wedging yourself between the suitor and your date, with your back to the suitor. Try to block the suitor's path of vision.

How to Fend Off Competitors

1 Evaluate the situation.

Is your date paying more attention to the interloper than to you? Do you want to continue dating this person? How big is the interloper?

2 Determine the seriousness of the offense.

Is it a passing rude drunk, a persistent boor, or someone seriously interested in leaving with your date?

3 Stand your ground.

Put your arms around your date, whisper in her ear, and kiss and caress her. Show the suitor that your date is enamored with you, and you with her.

4 Place yourself in the "pickup screen" position.

Wedge yourself between the suitor and your date, with your back to the suitor. Try to block the suitor's path of vision.

5 Ask the interloper to stop.

Politely but firmly explain that you are trying to have a conversation with your date and that you would both prefer to be left alone. If the suitor persists, use humor or sarcasm to diffuse the situation. Tell him that you can offer him a few phone numbers, or tell him that tonight she's taken, but you will let him know when she's available.

6 Ask your date to tell the suitor to back off.

Your date should tell him that she's flattered but not interested.

7 Try to leave.

If given the choice, choose flight over fight. Suggest to your date that you both move to a table or go to a new establishment. A fight generally doesn't make the evening go any better.

Good Signs/Bad Signs Body Language

GOOD SIGNS	WHAT THEY MEAN
Leans in	receptiveness
Legs slightly apart	attraction
Makes good eye contact	sincerity
Matches your breathing	a meeting of the minds
Moves when you do	a good match
Holds palms open	receptiveness, an invitation
Parts lips	desire
Smiles with crow's-feet	genuine amusement, attraction
Touches face, cheek	interest, attraction
Touches you	desire, attraction
Twirls hair	attraction, flirtation
Unbuttons jacket or shirt	comfort, interest
BAD SIGNS	**WHAT THEY MEAN**
Clenches jaw	impatience, anger
Crosses legs or arms	defensiveness
Holds finger to chin or lips	evaluation, criticism
Looks around	disinterest, boredom
Looks away	insincerity
Nods too much	disinterest, short attention span
Rubs neck or head	impatience, frustration
Rubs nose or eyes	dismissal, readiness to move on
Shifts weight	uncertainty, nervousness
Shoves hands in pockets	feelings of inadequacy or insecurity, disinterest
Slouches	boredom, disinterest
Smiles without crow's-feet	an attempt to look happy

BREAKING UP

How to Live with an Ex Until One of You Moves Out

○ **Divide the apartment.**
Affix tape to the floor. Move all belongings to the appropriate side. Hang drapes or sheets around your space to create the feeling of separate rooms.

○ **Arrange a board in the center of the bed.**
Divide pillows evenly.

○ **Label food.**
Declare certain cabinets off-limits. Claim sides of the refrigerator.

○ **Cut your couple pictures in half.**
Return to appropriate parties.

○ **Divvy up antidepressants in the medicine cabinet.**

○ **Schedule custody of the shared pet.**
Draw up a timetable that clearly outlines when each of you is allotted time with Spot.

○ **Arrange for two entrances.**
Take turns entering and exiting the apartment through the fire escape.

○ **Communicate via sticky notes or texts.**

How to Fend Off an Obsessive Ex

1 Make your rejection final and firm.
Do not give your ex a chance to manipulate or negotiate. Refuse all offers for dates, favors, and "friendly meetings." Express your wish to be left alone. Make sure your body language sends the same message. Do not touch during the rejection, but look your ex firmly in the eyes.

2 Do not discuss the past.
Never mention the good times you had together. Instead, speak enthusiastically about how happy you are now, and make it clear that you have moved on with your life.

3 Immediately sever all ties.
Return all of your ex's belongings (including any gifts to you) in one shipment. Do not prolong the process. If your ex continues to call, get a new, unlisted phone number. Do not call or send cards, letters, or e-mails; these will result in a mixed message and may give your ex hope of reconciliation.

Divide the apartment to create the feeling of separate rooms.

4 If your ex will not leave you alone, sound a warning.
At the first sign that your ex is not listening to you, announce that if the unwanted behavior persists, you will take action. Threaten to contact the authorities, and be prepared to do so. Do not give in to any threats that may come your way. Be ready to secure a restraining order or civil protection order if it becomes necessary for your peace of mind.

5 Inform your family, friends, and coworkers about the situation.
Having larger, stronger friends around may serve as a deterrent.

6 Keep a paper trail.
You may need evidence later. Save any relevant letters, notes, e-mails, and voicemails—anything that can prove unwanted attention. Maintain a log or diary of your ex's actions, and report any unlawful behavior to the police immediately. Report phone calls from your ex to both the phone company and the police. Write down your caller ID log, if you have one.

7 Inform the authorities.
Do not let fear of retribution stop you from taking action. If

your ex persists in contacting you, becomes easily enraged by your rejections, is overly interested in your private life, or shows up in unexpected locations, he or she has become a stalker. Take legal action immediately and obtain a restraining order.

8 Move.

Make sure that your new address is unlisted. Contact the department of motor vehicles and the voter registration bureau to have them block your address. Forward your mail to a P.O. box, and do not accept any packages unless you are certain who sent them.

How to Survive If You Run into Your Ex

Running into your ex at a party can be problematic for many reasons: lingering affection, pain over being dumped, unresolved emotions, passionate memories, or poor selection of your current date.

1 Do not avert your gaze.

Look him in the eye and smile. Shying away from eye contact only diminishes your power. Keep someone's gaze and you keep control.

2 Be nice.

3 Do not sit.

Do not let yourself get stuck in a corner or on a couch with your ex. Remain standing and be ready to move.

4 Take charge of the conversation.

Start by mentioning something that you noticed earlier in the day. This keeps the dialogue fresh and superficial and in your control, and helps you to avoid complimenting or talking about the ex. Be upbeat—enthusiasm is a handy tool. Breezing by someone indicates that you are not fazed or upset.

5 Introduce your date, and send clear signals that this is who you are with now.

Touch your date as you converse with your ex, making it clear that you have moved on.

Breakup Texts

4GET IT	H8 U	NO LUV U
TTYN	MOVD ON	NO MO
C U NVR	UR DUMPT	BEAT IT
ITS OVR	U & I R DUN	U SUK
		U R NOW EX

6 Keep your conversation short and sweet.

Tell your ex that you are "meeting friends" but that it was nice to see him. Or tug your date's arm and say, "Oh look, there's Sally. I want you to meet her."

7 Move on.

How to Regain Your Confidence

◐ Hang a small mirror in a location you walk past often.

Post affirmations such as "I am special," "I am unique," or "I am the best me I can be" around the mirror. Every time you walk past the mirror, smile at your reflection and recite the affirmations out loud.

◐ Write down compliments you receive.

Place them in a jar. The next time you are feeling worthless, take out a compliment and read it aloud.

◐ Call your mother.

Tell her you are feeling down in the dumps.

◐ Adopt a mantra.

Recite a positive mantra to yourself every morning before you begin your day.

◐ Strut past a construction site.

Put on a skirt or dress and high heels. Apply red lipstick. Style your hair. Choose a heavily trafficked construction site to walk past. Sway your hips. Smile. Stop and ask the workers for directions.

◐ Make a list of all the people who have ever had a crush on you.

◐ Exercise.

Release endorphins and boost your mood by exercising for at least 20 minutes every day.

◐ Eat spicy food.

Hot foods also release endorphins.

◐ Join a group or club.

Surround yourself with positive people who enjoy doing similar activities. Open yourself up to meeting new people.

◐ Volunteer.

Helping out others who may be in difficult situations themselves will provide perspective on your situation. It can be reassuring to see people worse off than you are.

◐ Try a new hobby.

Plant a garden, learn a new language, go skydiving, or learn how to play the guitar.

◐ Get glamorous.

Have your hair, makeup, and nails done. Accentuate a favorite feature. Have professional photographs taken.

FIGHTS

How to Win a Sword Fight

How to Deflect and Counter a Blow

1 Step up and into the blow, with your arms held against your body.
React quickly and against your instincts, which will tell you to move back and away. By moving closer, you can cut off a blow's power. Avoid extending your arms, which would make your own counterblow less powerful.

2 Push or "punch" at the blow instead of simply trying to absorb it with your own sword.
If a blow is aimed at your head, move your sword completely parallel to the ground and above your head. Block with the center of your sword, not the end. Always move out toward your opponent, even if you are defending and not attacking.

How to Attack

1 Move the sword in steady, quick blows up and down and to the left and right.
Assuming you must disable your attacker, do not try to stab with your sword. A stabbing motion will put you off balance and will leave your sword far out in front of you, making you vulnerable to a counterblow.

2 Do not raise the sword up behind your head to attempt a huge blow—you will end up with a sword in your gut.

3 Hold your position, punch out to defend, and strike quickly.

4 Wait for your attacker to make a mistake.
Stepping into a blow or deflecting it to the side will put her off balance. Once your opponent is off balance, you can take advantage of her moment of weakness by landing a disabling blow, remembering not to jab with your sword but to strike up and down or from side to side.

WARNING!

Always keep your sword in the "ready" position—held in front of you with both hands and perpendicular to the ground. With this method, you can move the sword side to side and up and down easily, blocking and landing blows in all directions by moving your arms. Hold the tip of the sword at a bit of an angle, with the tip pointed slightly toward your opponent. Picture a doorway—you should be able to move your sword in any direction and quickly hit any edge of the door frame.

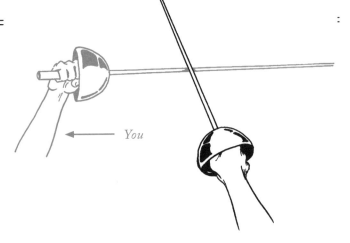

If a blow is aimed at your head, move your sword parallel to the ground and above you.

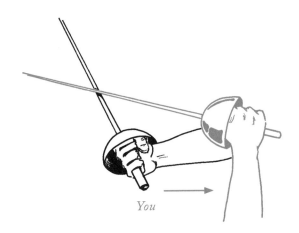

Wait for your attacker to make a mistake. Deflecting a blow to the side will throw your opponent off.

How to Take a Punch

A Blow to the Body

1 Tighten your stomach muscles.
A body blow to the gut (solar plexus) can damage organs and kill. This sort of punch is one of the best and easiest ways to knock someone out. (Harry Houdini died from an unexpected blow to the abdomen.)

2 Do not suck in your stomach if you expect that a punch is imminent.

3 If possible, shift slightly so that the blow hits your side, but do not flinch or move away from the punch.
Try to absorb the blow with your obliques: this is the set of

muscles on your side that wraps around your ribs. While a blow to this area may crack a rib, it is less likely to do damage to internal organs.

A Roundhouse Punch

1 Clench your jaw.
A punch to the ear causes great pain and can break your jaw.

2 Move in close to your attacker.
Try to make the punch land harmlessly behind your head.

3 (optional) Hit back with an uppercut.

A Straight Punch

1 The straight punch—one that comes straight at your face—should be countered by moving toward the blow.
This will take force from the blow.

2 A punch can be absorbed most effectively and with the least injury by the forehead.
Avoid taking the punch in the nose, which is extremely painful.

3 Attempt to deflect the blow with an arm.
Moving into the punch may result in your attacker's missing the mark wide to either side.

4 (optional) Hit back with an uppercut or roundhouse.

An Uppercut

1 Clench your neck and jaw.
An uppercut can cause much damage, whipping your head back, easily breaking your jaw or your nose.

2 Use your arm to absorb some of the impact or deflect the blow to the side—anything to minimize the impact of a straight punch to the jaw.

3 Do not step into this punch.
If possible, move your head to the side.

4 (optional) Hit back with a straight punch to the face or with an uppercut of your own.

A Blow to the Head

1 Move toward the blow, not away from it.
Getting punched while moving backward will result in the head taking the punch at full force. A punch to the face can cause head whipping, where the brain moves suddenly inside the skull, and may result in severe injury or death.

2 Tighten your neck muscles and clench your jaw to avoid scraping of the upper and lower palates.

HOW TO BREAK UP A CAT FIGHT

1 Identify the aggressor.
Look for the cat that is on top of the other one. This is the aggressor.

2 Scold the aggressor.
In a loud voice, yell "NO!" "STOP!" or "THAT'S ENOUGH!" and the aggressor's name.

3 Make loud noises.
Clap your hands, stomp your feet, or bang two pot lids together.

4 Physically separate the cats.
Use a long-handled implement such as a mop or broom, to nudge the cats apart. If the fight is happening outside, throw water or turn a hose on them.

5 Scruff the aggressor cat.
Grasp the aggressor cat by the loose skin at the back of his neck. Remove him from the other cat and push him toward the floor with firm but gentle pressure. Hiss loudly. While the aggressor is being scruffed, allow the victim cat to flee the area.

6 Keep the cats apart.
Separate the aggressor and victim cat for one hour. If aggressive behavior resumes, establish a "safe room" for the aggressor and reintroduce the cats to each other over a weeklong period.

WARNING!

⚠ Do not get in the middle of a cat fight and try to pry the cats apart with your hands. The cats will instinctively treat you as another combatant.

⚠ Play fighting is a part of a healthy cat's social life and needn't be discouraged. If the cats are frequently switching roles (one chasing, the other being chased; one pouncing, the other acting as "prey") and neither cat is hissing or showing teeth, do not intervene.

Use a long-handled broom to nudge the cats apart. Throw water or turn a hose on them.

Have one person make fresh snowballs while another keeps an eye on the enemy.

How to Win a Snowball Fight

1 Test the snow.

Stick a twig, chopstick, or thin utensil in the snow and pull it out quickly to determine the packing consistency. It should go in and come out smoothly, not hitting icy or solid patches. Snowball snow should not be frozen, nor should it be too dry ("powder") or too wet ("granular" or "corn"). The snow needs just enough moisture to hold together as you shape it.

2 Doctor the snow.

The best air temperature for snowball making is above 5°F and below 32°F. If the air temperature is below 5°F, warm the snow in your hands before attempting to make a snowball.

3 Establish a base camp.

Find a suitable location with good sight lines and plenty of fresh snow. Consider keeping a wall at your back to thwart flanking maneuvers.

4 Begin preparations.

Make as many snowballs as you can in advance of the battle. A good snowball should be larger than a golf ball but smaller than a cantaloupe and should hold its shape when others are stacked on top of it.

5 Build a snowball sled.

Secure a wooden produce crate or waxed cardboard box to a sled's rope. Fill the box with snowballs. Use the snowball sled to transport ammunition or a fresh supply of snow.

6 Use shields.

Maintain a supply of garbage-can lids with handles; use these for shields during battle.

7 Aim low and throw straight.

Snowball fight rules dictate that hitting in the face is forbidden. Aim for the chest or lower body. Ice balls or snowballs containing foreign material are also considered unfair.

8 Secure prisoners.

Snowball fight rules provide for the taking of prisoners: An enemy hit three times is considered captured. Captives may not be forced to fight their comrades but may be pressed into service as snowball makers.

Thrust your hand in attacker's face.

HOW TO DEAL WITH SOMEONE WIELDING A CHAIR

1 Thrust your hand toward the attacker's face.
If the attacker is close to you and the chair is raised, rapidly stick your hand close to his eyes to distract him and slow the attack.

2 Duck and grab his closest ankle.
Latch firmly onto the ankle with your hand. Moving close to him makes it harder for him to strike you with the chair.

3 Yank upward on his ankle.
Reaching down to grab the ankle and pulling up abruptly should be one continuous and swift motion.

4 Smash downward on his thigh with your other forearm.
As you sharply lift his ankle, strike the blow to the upper thigh of his same leg. You are pulling his feet out from under him and are knocking him backward.

5 Watch for the falling chair.
As he loses his balance and tumbles down, he will release the chair.

BE AWARE!

↗ If you are able to keep your distance from the attacker, throw objects at him to slow his approach and cause him to defend himself while you look for an opportunity to flee.

Duck and grab attacker's ankle.

Yank ankle upward and hit downward on thigh.

REALITY TV

Surround yourself with things that you like and make sure your facial expressions are visible.

How to Make a Successful Audition Video for a Reality Show

1 Make it look good but not too good.

Record the video with your smartphone or digital camera, so that the video quality is solid but it looks handheld and charmingly amateurish, rather than fancy and overproduced. It's okay if the video starts with a blank wall and then you appear in the shot, because you are filming it yourself.

2 Show your living environment.

Producers like to see where you live. It gives an insight into who you are. Place characteristic items such as posters, dolls, and books, in the background.

3 Get to the point.

Make your case immediately. Many video applications will

be viewed for only a few seconds, so that the casting director can see what you look and sound like.

4 Stand close to the camera so your features can be seen.

The producers are basing their decisions on a gut reaction to you, and so it is critical that your eyes and facial expression are clearly visible. Wear makeup to cover blemishes if necessary.

5 Speak loudly.

Don't record your video in a noisy environment.

6 Keep it simple.

Remember, you are sending this to people who are professionals in the craft of making television, so don't try to wow anyone with fancy postproduction effects.

7 Don't use copyrighted background music.

If you are selected for the show, the producers will not be able to use your audition tape for a best-of "clips" show without permission.

8 Review the video before you submit it.

This is especially important if you made the video while intoxicated.

How to Talk Without Being Caught on Mic

1 Get wet.

Remove your microphone and jump into the hot tub or the ocean. The audio department will try to record you with a boom mic, so stay away from the shore or hot-tub edge and splash while you're speaking.

2 Play music.

Have private conversations while music is playing loudly. This is even more effective with copyrighted music. In extreme cases, ask a friend to loudly sing a copyrighted song while you quickly convey information.

3 Remove the microphone battery.

Turning off your body mic is an easy way to stop recording, but the audio department will immediately note and fix the problem. To foil them, take out the battery from the mic's transmitter and throw it away.

4 Put the mic in your pocket.

When no one is looking, transfer your body mic from your shirt front to your rear pocket. Anything you then say in whispers will not be heard.

How to Extend Your 15 Minutes of Fame

- Move to New York or Los Angeles.
- Star in the next installment of the reality show in which you just participated.
- Guest star as a judge or walk-on on the next installment of the reality show.
- Write a book.
- Do a cameo in a sitcom or TV commercial.
- Guest star on another reality show of a different genre; if you were on a dating show, appear on a competitive-dance show.
- Announce the breakup of your reality-show relationship.
- Run for public office.
- Pose nude.
- Appear on a cast reunion special.
- Get a daytime talk show.
- Allow a network to film your wedding.
- Dramatically alter your appearance by losing a significant amount of weight, getting breast implants, or having cosmetic surgery.
- Participate in a celebrity boxing match.
- Be interviewed on morning-show radio.
- Become a morning-show radio DJ.
- Start your own line of clothing or fragrance.
- Become the national spokesperson for a nonprofit organization.
- Provide on-screen testimonials for infomercial products.
- Sign things at the mall.

5 Use inappropriate language.

Use such foul language that anything you say can never be shown on broadcast television.

WARNING!

⚡ Having a conversation near a running sink or shower seems like it will distort your words, but they will still be discernible, and the producers will subtitle you on-screen.

⚡ Even if you take off your mic, stash it away somewhere, or toss the battery, your conversation partner's mic will still record what you're saying.

HOW TO FAKE INTENSE EMOTION

1 Apply salt water or sand to the corners of your eyes to make them water.

Carry a small amount of salt water or sand at all times, just in case.

2 Breathe faster and more shallowly.

Off camera, vigorously run in place to make yourself take raspy, ragged gasps and to give yourself a blotchy and flushed complexion.

3 Constrict your vocal cords and stutter as you speak.

4 Make a show of being overwhelmed.

Cover your face with your hands, look away, bite your lip, and put your head down on a table or tree stump to appear as if you are trying to compose yourself.

5 Fake a faint.

Take a deep breath, gasp for air, roll your eyes back, buckle your knees, and reach out to the other person as you fall forward.

To fake fainting, roll your eyes back, buckle your knees, and reach out as you fall forward.

SOCIAL MEDIA

How to Make an Online Dating Profile More Alluring

⊕ **Post a flattering photograph.**
Pose with children or animals if you are male. Look like you are having the time of your life if you are female.

⊕ **Use euphemisms.**
For instance, avoid the word "unemployed" by saying that you are currently enjoying a sweat-free lifestyle while you search for a new challenge.

⊕ **Seem rich.**
Refer to signs of affluence such as luxury brands, cruises, extended vacations, resorts in exotic locales, and tax shelters.

⊕ **Seem interesting.**
Discuss a variety of interesting hobbies such as rock climbing, photography, and wine.

⊕ **Seem cultured.**
List "favorites" that present you as educated and sophisticated, yet not pretentious. Mention highbrow and mainstream books, movies, TV shows, and musicians to create the impression that you have eclectic and wide-ranging taste.

⊕ **Keep it positive.**
Avoid mention of your breakup.

Social Networking Etiquette

⊕ **When rejecting a friend request, provide an explanation.**
If you know the requester but don't want to be connected, explain that you have an only-close-friends policy.

⊕ **When requesting a friend, provide a refresher.**

Post a flattering photograph. Pose with children or animals if you are male.

Remind the potential new friend who you are and how you've met.

⊕ **Request friends using a real picture of yourself.**
People may not recognize who is friending them if your identifying picture is of your child or dog, or a cartoon version of you.

⊕ **You are not obligated to friend/follow anyone.**

⊕ **Unfriend quietly.**
When unfriending or unfollowing someone, do not make an effort to apologize or explain why. Just go.

⊕ **Comment back sparingly.**
You don't need to write "Thanks" or "I agree" in response to every comment on your post. Only comment in response if you have something substantive to say.

⊕ **When forging a connection, explain to both parties.**
If you tell one friend to friend another friend, alert the second friend that you have done so, so that they know who this person is and where they've come from.

⊕ **Respect preferred communication modes.**
When someone makes clear that they prefer to communicate via e-mail rather than on a social-networking site, don't persist in messaging them that way.

Social Media at Work

If you're using an office computer to get online, you most likely have no privacy or right to privacy. The information technology department of your employer probably has the ability to monitor and capture every screen you view and every Web site you visit; every e-mail you send both on work e-mail accounts and personal Web-based accounts; and even every keystroke you make. The folks in IT might be doing this for fun, even if it is not company policy, but that would be hard to complain about, since you're supposed to be working, too.

✪ Don't pick fights.

Avoid making controversial or argumentative responses in comment threads on a friend's page, even if you think that person wouldn't mind; his or her other friends may be insulted, which could cause stress for your friend.

How to Avoid Sending Employers the Wrong Message with Your Social Media Bio

1 Do not include too much information.

Long-ago kindergarten awards and school football awards are not that impressive, and it's not helpful to mention everyone you've ever met, studied with, or worked for. Do not embellish and overdescribe your accomplishments. Selectivity and directness is the key.

2 Do not include too little information.

3 Avoid spelling mistakes and sloppiness.
Get the prospective employer's name right.

4 Keep out romantic experiences and preferences.
No tales of memorable (or not remembered) feats at parties. Don't boast, and don't confess about personal matters.

5 Keep yourself clothed in the photograph.
No matter how good you look with your shirt off, use a head shot for your profile photo.

6 Use words, not emoticons.
No smiley faces.

7 Be yourself.
Show them who you really are, and don't try to be who you think they want you to be, at least at the beginning of your job search.

WARNING!

⚡ Before applying for a job, search for your name online, as your potential employer probably will, to see how you are perceived. Also check social networks for photos and postings that might not work in your favor. Try to clean up your image.

How to Expand Your Online Friend Network

1 Friend your real friends.

2 Friend your family members.

3 Friend your friends from high school, college, and graduate school.

4 Friend your friends from elementary school, summer camp, and religious or language school.

5 Friend your work friends.
Acknowledge in your friend request that it's a little weird to be friending them.

6 Examine your e-mail contacts.
Make sure that you are now friends with everyone with whom you have ever communicated.

7 Friend the friends of all the friends you've friended from the above categories.

8 Friend the friends of all the friends-of-friends you've now friended.

9 Join groups.
"Like" all the bands, TV shows, authors, movies, and political figures you actually like, sort of like, or have heard of.

10 Friend the group members.
Engage in conversations and arguments on the pages of the groups you've joined, and then friend the strangers with whom you've engaged.

11 Friend their friends.

WARNING!

⚡ Based on the size of the neocortex in the human brain, a person can handle between 100 and 200 social contacts, according to a study by British anthropologist Robin Dunbar. The standard "Dunbar's number" of 150 real contacts has been confirmed by a recent study of three million Twitter users.

Personal Ad Photo Decoder

PHOTO POSTED FOR ONLINE PERSONAL AD	WHAT IT SAYS ABOUT YOU
Photos with an ex-boyfriend or ex-girlfriend	I have been on a date before.
High school yearbook photos	I am 20 pounds heavier than this.
Party photos	I am drunk right now.
Baby photo	I was cute a long time ago.
Mug shots	I will stalk you if we break up.
You with stuffed animals	I will stalk you if we break up.
Altered pictures of you with celebrities	I live in my parents' basement.
Wedding photos	I am married.
Nude photos	I am desperate.

5

Mean Streets

URBAN
SURVIVAL

HOW TO ESCAPE A SWARM OF PIGEONS

1 Run in a zigzag pattern.

2 Pull your shirt over your head.
Crouching forward at a 30- to 45-degree angle, reach behind your head with one hand and grab the collar of your shirt. Pull your shirt up over your head. Stretch it far enough forward that it covers your entire scalp and your eyes.

3 Scatter food.
Use your free hand to remove any food from your pockets and bag and throw it in every direction. Employ vigorous flinging motions to draw the pigeons' attention away from you and toward the food. Toss the food as quickly and as far away as possible.

4 Flap your arms like a falcon.
Extend your arms completely, and flap them up and down vigorously.

5 Make loud noises.
Jump up and down and clap your hands repeatedly. Bang trash-can lids, set off car alarms, scream, or make other loud noises that will scare away the pigeons.

WARNING!

⚡ Pigeons cluster around partially eaten and discarded food, especially starchy items such as soft pretzels and hot dog rolls. Avoid people sitting on park benches distributing handfuls of popcorn, grain, or seeds.

⚡ Pigeons are highly unlikely to peck at your neck and eyes, but depending on the season, they may try to claim strands of hair for their nest. Defecation is frequent.

⚡ A pigeon peck is not strong enough to break human skin. The primary health hazards associated with pigeons stem from the three illnesses caused by pigeon droppings: histoplasmosis, cryptococcosis, and psittacosis. All attack the respiratory system and pose the greatest danger to anyone with a compromised immune system.

⚡ If you come into contact with pigeon droppings, wash the affected area immediately and as thoroughly as possible. Be on the lookout for flulike symptoms over a 14-day period after the initial contact.

*Use a swimming stroke to move in cement.
Keep your eyes and mouth closed.*

HOW TO SURVIVE A FALL INTO A POOL OF WET CEMENT

1 Keep your body upright.
The high density of the cement will prevent you from sinking very far down into the pool. If your head is under the cement, use your legs and arms to push yourself above the surface as you would if you were underwater.

2 Yell for help.
Shout until the workers pouring the cement have cut off the flow.

3 Keep your eyes and mouth closed.
Cement contains lime and other alkaline compounds that will burn skin with prolonged contact. Sensitive tissue, such as the eyes, nasal passages, and mouth, is especially vulnerable. If opening your eyes may put cement in direct

contact with your eyeballs, keep at least one eye closed at all times, and open the other only to determine in which direction you should move to get to safety.

4 Use a freestyle swimming stroke to move toward safety.
If the cement is wet and deeper than you are tall, keep your head above the surface and push the cement away from you as though you are swimming.

5 If you are unable to move, instruct bystanders to pour sugar into the cement.
Sugar slows the chemical reaction that causes cement to harden. Adding sugar to the cement will buy time and make it safer for rescue personnel to extract you.

6 Remove cement-covered clothing.
As soon as possible, take off all clothes that contacted cement, including socks, underwear, and hats. Prolonged contact with the skin can result in third-degree burns or skin ulcers, necessitating hospitalization and skin grafts. Cement burns can happen painlessly, so you may not even know you've been hurt until severe skin damage has occurred.

7 Wash thoroughly.
Vigorously wash the burn with soap and water. Rinse all skin that came in contact with cement for at least 30 minutes.

8 Seek professional medical attention.
Cement burns can be worse than they first appear. Visit a doctor to see if additional treatment is required.

HOW TO ESCAPE A WILD TAXI RIDE

1 Claim that you have no money.
Tell the cabbie that you forgot your wallet. The ride should end immediately.

2 Light a cigarette.
Tell the cabbie that his driving is making you nervous and light a cigarette (or a cigar, for better results). Smoking in cabs is usually illegal, and your driver may stop the car.

3 Threaten to vomit.
Inform the cabbie that his driving is making you sick. There are few things cabbies like less than a passenger who vomits in the backseat. The driver may ask you to exit the cab.

4 Use your cell phone.
Make a loud show of pretending to call police (or the local taxi commission) and reporting the driver's name and license/medallion number. The driver will want to get rid of you as soon as possible.

How to Walk on Sidewalks

Getting Through a Large Approaching Group. Aim for the middle. Divide the two most vulnerable people. Do not make eye contact. Do not break stride.

5 Run.
If the cab stops at a light, open the door and take off.

6 Jump.
If the driver will not stop, wait until the cab approaches a turn or slows for a light. As the driver brakes, open the door on the side of the cab facing the sidewalk. Do not bail out into traffic. Tuck your chin to your chest, cover your head with your hands, and jump out of the car. Roll away from the taxi in a somersault position, protecting your head with your arms. If you have a bag or leather briefcase, hold it on top of your head for added protection. Make sure that your path takes you away from the rear wheels. The cab's forward momentum will cause you to roll for several yards before coming to a stop.

UNDERGROUND

How to Survive Being Trapped in a Sewer

1 Find a light source.

Sewers are usually pitch-black over long stretches, and navigation will be impossible without some type of light. Use a flashlight, a penlight, an LED from a cell phone or car key, matches, or a lighter to see. If you have no light source, look upward for daylight reaching the sewer main through storm drain inlets, gratings in the street, or the small holes in (or around the rims of) manhole covers. Head to the light source: generally it will lead to a way out or a place where you can communicate with the surface.

2 Stand straight and tall.

Bacteria breaking down organic material create hydrogen sulfide (H_2S), which is responsible for the "rotten egg" odor in sewers. While the foul smell is distasteful, in small concentrations the gas is not deadly; in high concentrations it can be fatal. Since hydrogen sulfide is slightly heavier than air, it will be in higher concentrations lower in the sewer pipe. Keep your head as high as possible, near the top (or "crown") of the pipe. Covering your nose and mouth with a handkerchief may provide minimal relief.

3 Wait until late at night to move.

Large, combined sewer systems—those that aggregate household wastewater and storm water—generally have their highest flows after breakfast and after dinner, when toilets are flushed and dishes are washed, and during or just after rainstorms. Flows will be lowest, and navigation and movement easiest, in the middle of the night. Wait until 2 or 3 a.m. to begin your escape, unless it is raining and the system is filling with storm runoff. Expect a sewage depth of 12 to 18 inches in the middle of the night, and up to 36 inches during busier periods. The deeper the flow, the greater the forces acting on you will be, making it harder for you to maintain balance.

4 Check the direction of the flow.

Sewers move wastewater downhill, using gravity. Smaller-diameter pipes enter the system upstream and connect to larger and larger mains as you move downstream in the system. Locate a larger main (72 or 92 inches in diameter) and establish the directional flow of the sewage.

5 Move upstream.

Though it seems counterintuitive, move upstream toward smaller pipes. Larger mains downstream will contain older

Rats will indicate that the air is safe to breathe.

sewage, which has been broken down by bacteria over a longer period of time. These downstream pipes will have much higher levels of hydrogen sulfide, which may be deadly. Instead, move upstream to areas with fresher sewage and lower concentrations of gas.

6 Watch your step.

The floor and walls of the sewer will be coated with slime and will be extremely slippery. There may also be a channel in the center of the pipe to accelerate the flow of sanitary sewage. Walking in this channel will be difficult, so keep to the sides of the main.

7 Observe the behavior of rats and cockroaches.

Though both rats and cockroaches can swim, they prefer dry land and are likely to be on ledges above the sewage flow, on walls (for roaches), and in your path. As you walk, check the concentration of rats and especially roaches: both serve as your early-warning system of danger in the sewer. The presence of rats in large numbers can be a good sign. Rats indicate that the air is safe to breathe, even near the bottom of the sewer main. If you notice a sharp increase in the number of rats and roaches, or see them heading past you upstream, dangerous conditions exist downstream—a broken pipe or a full siphon may be causing sewage to back up toward your position. If they begin scurrying past you, be ready to move upstream quickly, away from the problem.

8 Locate a lateral storm sewer.
Look for a relatively dry main entering the combined main; this is a storm sewer "lateral" and should be easier to walk in, with lower levels of gas and odor. The lateral pipe may be smaller in diameter (48 inches, perhaps less), so be prepared to kneel or crawl. Look up for an overhead storm sewer grate or inlet. Push it up and to the side; then slide it over and climb out or yell for help.

WARNING!

🔪 Although sewer gases are generally not combustible in the concentrations found in mains, use an open-flame light source as a last resort.

🔪 In general, rats will shy away from human contact. However, a hungry group of rats (a pack may include 60 members) may attack even a large mammal.

🔪 Rats are very good swimmers and may swim for a mile or more.

HOW TO SURVIVE A RAT BITE

1 Wait for the rat to let go.
Rat bites typically last only a few seconds, and it is preferable to withstand the pain of the bite rather than to attempt to fling the rat away, which will create a messier wound.

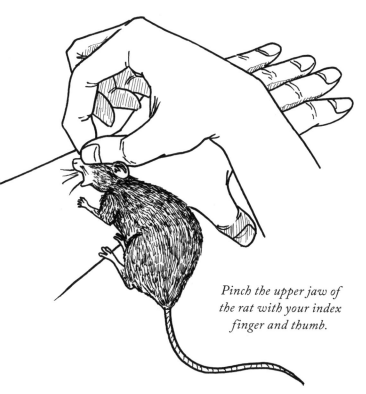

Pinch the upper jaw of the rat with your index finger and thumb.

Rat Bites

- Rat-bite fever (*Streptobacillus moniliformis*) can appear up to 10 days after a bite, even after the initial wound has healed. Symptoms include back and joint pain, vomiting, headache, fever, and a rash, usually on the hands and feet.

- The upper incisors of rats are approximately 4 millimeters long and 15 millimeters wide. Their lower incisors are 7 millimeters long and 12 millimeters wide.

- Rabies has never been passed to a human from a rat in the United States. Rats do, however, carry a host of other diseases, including hantavirus, salmonella, and hepatitis E. They can also carry parasites such as maggots, botflies, lice, and ticks. All of these things are more likely to be passed by skin-to-skin contact with the rat than through a bite.

2 Remove the rat.
If after several seconds the rat has not let go, pinch the upper jaw of the rat with your index finger and thumb and gently pry its incisors out of your flesh. Place the rat on the ground.

3 Stanch the bleeding.
Hold a dry, clean handkerchief or other small piece of cloth against the bite until bleeding subsides, which should only take a few seconds. In the event of persistent bleeding, tear a piece of cloth off of your shirt and tie it tightly around the wound, pulling the piece of cloth closed.

4 Dress the wound.
Clean the bite mark, and any other parts of your body that came in contact with the rat, with soap and water. Flush the soap fully out of the wound with water to prevent irritation.

5 Remove jewelry.
Take off any rings or other constricting jewelry, as swelling of the extremities may occur.

6 Bandage the wound.
Use a bandage or gauze and adhesive strip, applied loosely enough so that air can circulate to the wound.

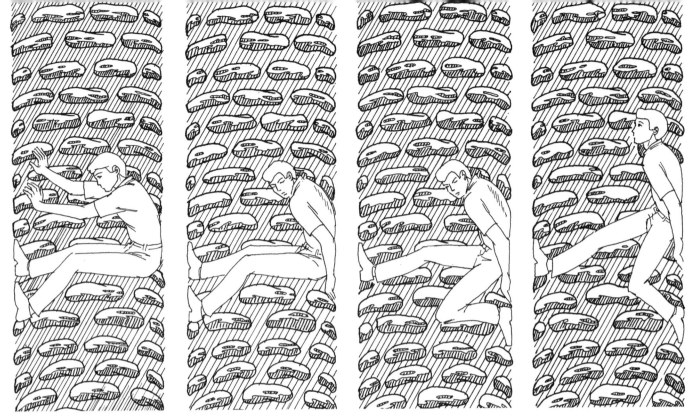

To climb out of a well with a narrow opening: Place your back against one wall and your hands and feet against the other. Using even pressure to maintain traction, place your hands below your rear. Take one foot off the wall and place it under your rear. Push up with your hands. Repeat.

HOW TO SURVIVE FALLING DOWN A WELL

With a Narrow Opening

Use the "chimney climbing" technique if the opening is narrow enough to keep your back against one wall and your feet against the opposite side, holding yourself off the ground.

1 Place your back against one wall and your hands and feet against the other wall.

Your body will be in an L shape, with your back straight and your legs sticking out—the soles of your feet pressing against the opposite wall. If the well is not completely vertical but is tilted in one direction, place your back on the lower wall.

2 Use even, steady pressure from your thighs to maintain traction on the feet and friction on your back, and to hold yourself off the ground.

3 Place the palms of your hands against the wall behind you, below your buttocks.

4 Take your left foot off the opposite wall and place it under your backside.

Bend your leg under you so that your right foot is on one wall and your left is on the other.

5 While pressing your back away from the wall with your hands, push up with your hands and your feet.

Move only about 6 to 10 inches.

6 Place your back on the wall again and move your left foot back onto the opposite wall, now a bit higher than your right foot.

Rest.

7 Repeat the procedure, beginning with your right foot. Alternate feet, slowly working your way to the lip of the well.

8 When you approach the lip of the well, reach up with your hand overhead and perform a "mantle move."

Pull yourself halfway up from a chin-up hang position, then roll (shift) your weight onto your forearms as they clear the lip of the well. Shift your body weight to your hands, and press up. Use your feet against the wall to assist in pulling yourself up out of the well.

With a Wide Opening

Use the "spread eagle" or "stemming" technique for an opening that is too wide to use the chimney climbing technique but narrow enough that you can touch opposite walls with your hands.

1 Place your right hand and right foot on one wall and your left hand and left foot on the opposite wall.
Your hands should be lower than your shoulders, and your fingers should point down.

2 Keep the pressure on your feet by assuming a somewhat scissored leg stance, with your body facing slightly to your right.

3 Brace yourself by pushing out with your hands.

4 Move one foot quickly up a few inches, followed quickly by the other.

5 Continue until you reach the top, where you will have to grab something sturdy and swing up over the edge.
If nothing is available to grab on to, keep going until your upper body is out of the well; then flop over forward and use leverage to climb out.

How to Survive a Fall onto Subway Tracks

1 Do not attempt to climb back onto the platform unless you are certain that you have enough time to do so.
If a train is approaching, you will need to act quickly.

2 Avoid areas of the ground near the track and the wall that are marked with a strip of tape or with red and white painted stripes.
Such markings indicate that the train passes extremely close to these areas, and you will not have enough clearance. In areas with these markings, there should be alcoves every few yards. These alcoves are safe to stand in if you can fit within them.

3 If the tracks are near a wall, check to see if there is enough space to stand between the train and the wall.
Clearance of 1½ to 2 feet should be enough. Remove any articles of clothing or bags that could catch on the train. Stand straight, still, and tall facing the train, which will pass just inches in front of you.

4 If the tracks are located between the platform and another set of tracks, you may be able to move to the other track instead.
Be mindful of trains approaching on the other side. Cross the third rail (which carries the electric current) by stepping completely over it—do not step on the wooden guard, since it may not hold you.

5 If a line of columns separates the tracks from other tracks, stand between the columns.
Remove any articles of clothing or bags that could catch on the train, and stand straight, still, and tall.

6 Check to see if there is enough space for you to crawl under the lip of the concrete platform and avoid the train.
Use this only as a last resort—this strategy is not recommended, since all platforms are different.

WARNING!

If none of these options are feasible, you have two other more dangerous alternatives:

- Run past the leading end of the platform, beyond where the front car will stop. Since trains running on the track closest to the platform are likely to stop at a station (as opposed to express trains, which usually run on center tracks), you can clear the train by running well past the leading end of the platform and thus the front car. (Note: This method will not work for express trains that only stop at some stations, so you are taking your chances.)

- If there is a depression in the concrete between the rails, lie down into it—there will be enough room for a train to pass over you. (Use this method only in desperation—the train may be dragging something, or there may not be enough clearance.)

Lie down in the depression between the rails if the train starts moving behind you.

ROOFTOPS

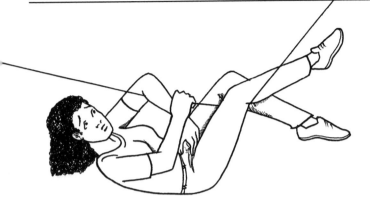

Keep your body as close to the wire as possible.

HOW TO CROSS BUILDINGS ON A WIRE

1 Test the wire.
The wire should be at least one inch thick and fully secured on both sides, preferably bolted or clamped (with steel) to stationary objects. Place your foot on the wire and apply hard downward pressure. The wire should flex slightly. If the wire remains taut, your weight will put too much stress on the side anchors.

2 Check the wire's angle.
The wire should be basically level, parallel to the ground. If slightly angled, the departure side should be a bit higher than the arrival side, so you are traveling "downhill" rather than "uphill" for at least the first half of the trip. (Because of the flex of the wire, you will be climbing "uphill" once you reach the midpoint of your journey.)

3 Protect your hands.
If you do not have gloves, tear out your pants pockets and use them as mittens, put your socks on your hands, or hold two squares of thick cardboard. Gloves will protect your hands, absorb sweat, reduce friction and "rope burn," and allow your hands to slide more easily along the wire.

4 Hold the wire.
Stand on the edge of the building, facing the wire. Grab the wire with your hands, approximately two feet beyond the edge of the building. (Crouch down if the wire is at your feet.)

5 Position your legs.
Holding the wire tightly, bend at the waist and swing one leg up and over the wire. This leg should be on top of the wire, with the wire running under your knee. Swing your other leg up and cross your legs at your calves. The leg sitting on the wire should be "locked down" by your other leg.

6 Position your arms.
Holding on to the wire with your dominant hand, let go with your other hand and place your free arm up and over the wire. Bend this arm so the wire runs under your elbow, similar to the position of your leg. Your other arm should be gripping the wire a few inches beyond your bent elbow.

7 Check your position.
You should be hanging upside down, stomach toward the wire, head facing your direction of travel. Your body should be slightly bent at the elbows, knees, and waist.

8 Begin moving.
Slightly extend the arm that is gripping the wire. Pull your lower body after you, keeping one leg locked over the other. Your face should be as close to the wire as possible, with your hand not too far beyond your head. You will have moved about a foot.

9 Continue to face the wire, keeping your body as close to it as possible.
Do not look down.

10 Repeat.
Continue to travel in this fashion, resting between moves as necessary. Once you reach the midpoint of the wire, you will be traveling "uphill," and progress will be slower and more exhausting.

WARNING!

⚡ Do not attempt to cross an electrical wire. Follow the path of the wire visually. If it appears to run from a pole into a building, the wire may be electrified and should not be crossed.

⚡ A wire with too much flex will be extremely difficult to climb up once you reach its midpoint.

HOW TO JUMP FROM ROOFTOP TO ROOFTOP

1 Look for any obstructions, if you have time.
You may have to clear short walls, gutters, or other obstacles as well as the space between buildings.

2 Check your target building.
Make certain that you have enough space to land and roll. If the target building is lower than your building, assess

Jump with your arms outstretched, ready to grab the ledge if you undershoot your mark.

how much lower it is. You risk broken ankles or legs if there is more than a one-story differential in the buildings. If there are two stories or more, you risk a broken back.

3 Check the distance between the buildings.
Most people cannot jump farther than 10 feet, even at a full run. If the buildings are farther apart than this distance, you risk catastrophic injury or death. You must clear the distance and land on the other roof, or be able to grab on to a ledge on the other side. If the target building is lower, your forward momentum will continue to carry you even as you fall, so you may be able to leap a greater distance—though probably not more than about 12 feet. You could successfully leap a span across an alley, but not a two-lane road.

4 Pick a spot for takeoff and a spot for landing.

5 Run at full speed toward the edge.
You must be running as fast as possible to attempt a leap of a distance of more than a few feet. You will need 40 to 60 feet of running room to develop enough speed to clear about 10 feet.

6 Leap.
Make sure your center of gravity is over the edge of your target building in case your whole body doesn't clear the span and you have to grab hold. Jump with your arms and hands extended and ready to grab the ledge.

7 Try to land on your feet, then immediately tuck your head and tumble sideways onto your shoulders.
Because you will not be moving fast, it is safe to roll diagonally head over heels, unlike jumping from a moving vehicle.

HOW TO JUMP FROM A BUILDING INTO A DUMPSTER

1 Jump straight down.
If you leap off and away from the building at an angle, your trajectory will make you miss the Dumpster. Resist your natural tendency to push off.

2 Tuck your head and bring your legs around.
To do this during the fall, execute a three-quarter revolution—basically, a not-quite-full somersault. This is the only method that will allow a proper landing, with your back facing down.

3 Aim for the center of the Dumpster or large box of debris.

4 Land flat on your back so that when your body folds, your feet and hands meet.
When your body hits any surface from a significant height, the body folds into a V. This means that landing on your stomach can result in a broken back.

WARNING!

☑ If the building has fire escapes or other protrusions, your leap will have to be far enough out so that you miss them on your way down. The landing target needs to be far enough from the building for you to hit it.

☑ The Dumpster may be filled with bricks or other unfriendly materials. It is entirely possible to survive a high fall (five stories or more) into a Dumpster, provided it is filled with the right type of trash (cardboard boxes are best) and you land correctly.

Aim for the center of the Dumpster, and land flat on your back.

HOTELS

How to Survive a High-Rise Hotel Fire

Always treat a hotel fire alarm seriously, and exit following hotel procedure. If the fire is nearby, use the following procedure.

1 Feel your hotel room doorknob with the back of your hand.

If the doorknob is hot to the touch, go to step 2 and then skip to step 5. If it is not hot, follow the steps in order.

2 Partially fill the bathtub with cold water.

Soak towels, washcloths, bedsheets, and blankets in the water. If the water is off, use water from the toilet tank. Put a wet washcloth over your mouth and nose and a wet sheet or towel over your head.

3 Open the door.

4 If the hallway is smoke-filled, get as low as possible— one to two feet above the floor.

Make your way to an emergency exit. Never use the elevator.

5 If the door or doorknob is hot, do not open the door.

Wedge wet towels in the crack under the door to keep smoke out.

6 Try calling the front desk or rooms on other floors to check on conditions in other areas.

7 Turn off fans and air-conditioners that could draw smoke into the room, and open the window slightly.

If the fire is on a floor below you, smoke may enter the room through the window, so keep the opening narrow. If the fire is not below you, open the window a third or halfway.

8 Make a tent of wet towels and sheets at the window.

Do not build the tent if smoke is billowing into the room. Hold or attach one side of the towel or sheet to the window and allow the other side to fall behind you, so that you are protected from smoke and are breathing outside air. The towels should help to cool the air and make it easier to breathe.

9 Signal rescue personnel with a white towel or a flashlight.

Wait for rescue.

10 If the air in the room is getting worse, breathing becomes difficult, and no rescue is forthcoming, try to kick through the wall into the adjacent room.

Closets are the best locations to try to break through. Sit on the floor of the closet, and knock on the wall until you hear a hollow sound. (Wall studs are normally spaced 16 inches apart.) Use both feet to kick through both surfaces of drywall. You may survive by using this as a breathing hole, or you may need to continue breaching the wall until you can escape into the next room.

11 If you cannot breach the wall, go to a window and look at the outside of the building.

If the rooms have balconies that are close together, consider climbing to another balcony on the same floor. If there are no neighboring balconies, you can tie bedsheets together and climb to a balcony directly beneath yours. Use square knots (the first step in tying your shoes, done twice) and lower yourself one floor only. Consider this option only as a last resort, and only do it if you are attempting to escape an immediate danger or to reach rescue personnel.

WARNING!

- Ladders on fire trucks usually reach only to the seventh floor of a high-rise building. Consider booking a room below this level.

- Poolside or courtyard rooms are likely to be inaccessible to ladder trucks, even if they are below the seventh floor. Consider staying in a street-side room.

- Upon check-in, make sure the hotel has smoke detectors and fire sprinklers.

- Count the doors between your room and the nearest fire exit. This will help you to get out safely if smoke reduces visibility.

- Keep your room key where it can be found in the dark.

- Never jump from a height of more than two floors.

How to Scour a Room for Bedbugs

1 Leave luggage in the car.

Do not bring your things into the hotel room until you have checked for bugs.

2 Shine a light.

Turn on a powerful flashlight and run it up and down the walls of the room, focusing on corners, cracks, and seams. Run the flashlight along the baseboards and into the closets. Look for oval, reddish-brown bugs about the size of a pinhead. Eggs, when they can be seen at all, resemble a minutely small translucent dot or a flake of dust. You are

hatchling

Bedbug (enlarged) and actual size hatchling.

Sort through the accumulated dust and carpet fibers for dead bugs or cast shells.

8 Watch for bites.
The best way to detect the presence of bedbugs is the redness, swelling, and itching resulting from a bite.

9 Set traps.
Surround the bed with sticky tape to catch bedbugs on the move.

WARNING!

⚡ Online and printed directories listing the names of bedbug-infested hotels and motels have proliferated in recent years. Before you make your reservation, check to see if your intended hotel is listed as having a problem.

⚡ Do not place your luggage on the bed, since you might be bringing in bedbugs. Use the folding-rack luggage stand.

⚡ Hang clothing far from the bed.

⚡ Bedbugs can live for one year without feeding (on your blood).

looking for live bedbugs, dead bedbugs, cast shells, or bedbug eggs. Adult bedbugs can be ¼ inch in length.

3 Strip the bed.
Pull back the sheets, shake the pillows out of their cases, and perform a careful visual inspection of the sheets, the pillows and pillowcases, and the mattress itself. Look for live bugs, dead bugs, or dark brown smears of blood.

4 Disassemble the headboard.
Using a handheld Phillips-head screwdriver, remove the headboard from the bed and shine your flashlight into the crevices in the wood of each piece. Examine the joints where the headboard connects to the bed.

5 Check the drawers.
Open every drawer and cupboard in the room one by one, shining your flashlight into the corners. Look under the telephone, the TV, and in any other dark, hidden places.

6 Check the bathroom.
Get down on all fours and crawl the length of the bathroom, peering under the toilet, under the sink, and in the bathtub.

7 Vacuum.
Run a small portable vacuum cleaner over the carpeting of the room; then shake the vacuum bag out into the sink.

What to Avoid in a Filthy Hotel Room

Do not touch the following (unless your hand is covered with your sleeve or another washable object):

- Light switch
- Air-conditioning/ heating controls
- Bedspread
- Blanket
- Sheets
- TV remote control

- Bathroom sink
- Toilet seat
- Handle on toilet
- Room telephone (if any)
- Window handle (if any)

Do not do the following:

- Take a bath
- Take a shower without footwear
- Drink the tap water
- Swallow water from the shower

- Reach under the bed
- Eat food in the room
- Pick up unknown objects

SMALL SPACES

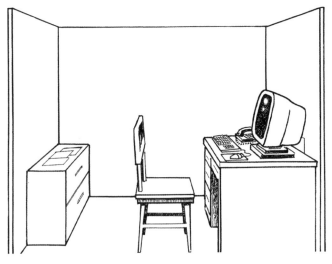

Too little.

Too much.

How to Survive in a Tiny Workspace

Cubicle

1 Select a good location.
Opt for a cube away from main hallways, bathrooms, supply rooms, and other high-traffic areas, if you have the choice. Avoid cubes within the boss's line of sight.

2 Use comfort devices.
Requisition a more comfortable chair, or select one from an empty cubicle or office (some styles of chairs may be assigned to employees above a certain level, so be careful about what you borrow). Alternatively, obtain a doctor's note stating that you require a comfortable chair for medical reasons—your employer will be obligated to provide you with one. A back pillow and footrest will also make cube life more comfortable and relaxed. Do not attempt to fit in recliners, love seats, or hammocks.

3 Install convenience items.
A wireless telephone headset will give you increased freedom of movement. Noise-canceling stereo headphones (with an extra-long cord) will eliminate outside distractions. A small fan is effective in filtering out annoying noises such as typing and phone conversations. (The fan will also make it more difficult for coworkers to eavesdrop on your conversations.) Small refrigerators, hair dryers, televisions, VCRs, and blenders should not be easily visible.

4 Personalize your space.
Decorate your cubicle with your family photographs and drawings, as well as other pictures and cartoons you like, giving your cube a homey touch. Avoid hanging too many items, or you risk a cubicle that looks like a dorm room or refrigerator door.

5 Build upward.
There is usually no limit to the amount of vertical space you can occupy. Stack in/out trays high atop elevated surfaces for additional room. Staplers, tape dispensers, card files, and other items that traditionally occupy valuable space on top of a desk can be suspended from the ceiling to create a more spacious environment below.

6 Use mirrors.
Hang a large mirror on the cubicle wall to create the illusion of spaciousness.

WARNING!

- Health and safety codes dictate that cubes may not have roofs. Do not attempt to construct a fully enclosed cubicle for privacy.

- Adding a small, stick-on, wide-angle mirror to the edge of your monitor allows you to see if someone is peering into your cubicle from behind.

- Notify your supervisor that you would like to sit in a "double-wide" cubicle if one becomes available. Standard cubes are eight by eight feet and four to six feet high—double-wides offer twice the floor space of standard units, plus an L- or U-shaped desk. The double-wide cubicle does carry some risk: if office space gets tight, you may find yourself with a cube-mate, a particularly undesirable situation.

How to Have Sex in a Small Space

Airplane Lavatory

1 Pick a rendezvous time.

Select a time when you are least likely to have to wait in line and when you will not be disturbed. The best times are just before the plane reaches cruising altitude or during the in-flight entertainment.

2 As the plane is ascending, listen for a beep from the in-flight messaging system.

The first beep comes without a subsequent announcement and indicates to the flight attendants that cruising altitude has almost been reached and that it is safe to begin their preparations. The Fasten Your Seatbelt sign will still be illuminated, but the flight attendants will get up. As soon as the flight attendants clear the aisle, head for the lavatory. Try to select one that is not visible from the galleys. Have your date wait at least a minute, then meet you in the lavatory. You should hear the beverage carts roll by. After a few minutes, the flight attendants will begin to serve drinks, blocking the aisle from passenger access. Alternatively, or in addition, proceed to step 3.

3 Meet during the movie.

Plan your rendezvous for the beginning of the film, preferably when the film is at least 15 minutes under way. Most passengers and flight attendants stay out of the aisles and galley areas during the entertainment portion of the flight, so you will have more privacy. You should proceed to the lavatory first, to be followed a minute later by your date.

4 Put down the toilet seat lid and clean it.

Wipe the seat with Sani-Wipes if they are available, or use a wet paper towel with soap. Place paper towels or a sanitary toilet seat cover on top for extra protection.

5 Be quiet and be quick.

You will not have a lot of time before people are lining up to get into the restroom.

6 Be ready for turbulence.

The safest positions involve one partner sitting on the closed toilet seat. Then, in the event of bumpy air, neither partner will be too close to the ceiling, risking a concussion.

7 If you do encounter turbulence, hold on.

Brace yourself against the sink and do not try to stand up or move. Stay where you are and ride it out.

8 Exit the lavatory together, feigning illness.

It is illegal to have sex in an airplane bathroom—so deny it in the unlikely event that you are asked. Tell the flight attendant or other passengers that one of you was ill and the other was offering assistance.

Elevator

1 Find a building with an older elevator.

Many older elevators have an emergency Stop button that will allow you to halt the elevator. On other units, flipping the switch from Run to Stop will cause an alarm bell to sound. You will still have plenty of time, at least 10 or 15 minutes, possibly as long as an hour, before firefighters or other emergency personnel are able to access the elevator cabin.

2 Alternatively, look for a freight elevator with padding on the walls.

Freight elevators will be less likely to have an alarm that sounds when the Stop switch is thrown. The padding may also muffle sound and provide comfort.

3 Look for a camera.

Virtually all new elevators have security cameras, as do some older ones, including freight elevators. If a camera is present, cover the camera lens—it will probably be in a rear corner—with a piece of tape or with several postage stamps. The security system may include audio as well, however.

4 Stop the elevator between floors.

Elevator doors house a mechanical clutch that opens the corridor (outer) doors. If the elevator is not level with a floor, the corridor doors cannot open, and someone from the outside will not easily be able to open the inner doors.

5 Release the Stop button or flip the switch to Run when you are ready to leave.

Exit the elevator normally. If emergency personnel are present, tell them that there was a malfunction but you are okay.

WARNING!

If the elevator is stopped level with a floor, an elevator technician will be able to open both the outer (corridor) doors and the inner (elevator) doors from the outside.

Dressing Room

1 Look for a dressing room that has a door and walls that extend to the floor.

If all the dressing rooms have a gap between the floor and the walls, look for one with a secure door, rather than a curtain. If you are in a store that has several dressing rooms, look for the least-trafficked or least-monitored areas. Some dressing rooms have very-hard-to-detect security systems—including two-way mirrors—so you cannot guarantee that you will not be seen.

2 Carry clothes as if you are going to try them on.

Trail after a demanding customer who is requiring the attentions of the sales associate on duty. When the employee is occupied, make your move and duck into the dressing room.

3 Have your partner follow behind a few minutes later.

4 Be quiet.

The walls to dressing rooms are thin.

5 Be quick.

Speed is important, especially if your legs are visible beneath the walls.

6 Depart from the dressing room one person at a time.

Check your appearance in the mirror, and leave the store's clothes in the dressing room. If you are in the women's section of a department store, the woman should leave first and make sure the coast is clear. If you are in the men's department, the man should leave first.

BE AWARE!

✔ For speed and efficiency in airplanes, elevators, and dressing rooms, be sure to wear loose, baggy clothing. Do not wear underwear.

How to Share a Studio Apartment with Three Roommates

○ Put everything in writing.

Before all roommates move in, create a "roommates contract."

○ Label all possessions.

Put your name on your food, books, CDs, portable electronic devices, and clothing. Nothing, including food, should be considered "communal property," unless explicitly agreed upon by all roommates in the contract.

○ Utilize feng shui.

Minimize clutter, decorate with bright colors, and hang numerous mirrors to maximize the feeling of openness and harmony. Store or throw away any possessions that are unnecessary. As many furniture items as possible should be designated multiuse: futon pulls out into bed, ottoman turns into night table, bathtub with plank of wood across it becomes desk.

○ Subdivide.

Place a bookcase in the middle of the space to give the illusion of multiple rooms; repeat several times until the apartment is divided into several tiny mini-apartments.

Subdivide the room into several tiny mini-apartments.

Hang framed signs at the entrance to each "room," with titles such as Bob's Room, Allison's Room, and the parlor. Put tape on the floor to demarcate various territories and provide directions.

○ Communicate.

Convene weekly roommate meetings to maintain an ongoing dialogue. Each roommate should keep a notebook to write down things that are bothering him. Share complaints and positive support at the weekly meeting. Encourage all roommates to use "I" statements to express their feelings in a calm, nonconfrontational manner.

SURVEILLANCE

How to Lose Someone Following You

If You Are in a Car

1 Determine if you are actually being followed.

If you suspect a tail, observe the car as you continue to drive. If the car remains behind you, make three to four turns in a row to see if it continues to follow you. Then signal a turn in one direction but turn quickly in the other direction. See if the other car turns as well.

2 Once you are certain that you are being followed, get on a highway, or drive to a populous and active area.

Do not drive home, to a deserted place, or down an alley. You are more likely to shake your tail in a crowd than in a deserted area.

3 Drive at the speed limit, or a bit slower.

Soon, another car (not that of your pursuer) will attempt to pass you. Speed up slightly so that the car pulls in behind you. Repeat, but don't go so slowly that an innocent car behind you is able to pass you.

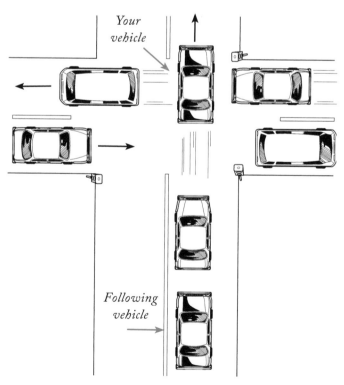

Your vehicle

Following vehicle

If you think it is safe, accelerate through the intersection just after the light changes against you.

4 Slow down at a busy intersection with a traffic light, then accelerate through the intersection just after the light changes.

The car following you may get stuck at the red light. If you attract the attention of the police for running a red light, your pursuer will most likely leave the scene.

5 When you have several cars around you, speed up, get off the highway (if you are on one), and make several quick turns to further elude your pursuer.

Your pursuer should be too far back to follow closely.

6 Once you are out of sight of your pursuer, pull into a parking lot, a garage, or a shopping center with lots of other cars.

7 If you still have not lost your tail at this point, drive to a police station and get help.

If You Are on Foot

1 Determine if you are being followed.

Take a random path: make unexpected changes in direction at intersections and retrace your steps, effectively making a U-turn. Do not, however, get yourself disoriented or lost. Note any identifying characteristics of your tail (dress, gait, height, and weight).

2 Keep an eye on your pursuer, but do not look back at him.

Use reflective surfaces such as shopwindows to see behind you. If you have a makeup case with a mirror, use that.

3 Stay in a crowd.

Do not head for home, to a deserted place, or down alleys.

4 Once you are certain that you are being followed, use these methods to shake your tail:

- Enter the front of a store, shop, or restaurant and go out through the back entrance—most restaurants have exits in the kitchen.

- Buy a ticket for a movie, enter after it has started, and leave through an emergency exit before your pursuer enters the theater.

- Use mass transit, and exit or enter the train or bus just before the doors close.

5 If you have not shaken your tail, walk to a police station or call the police from a public place.

Never head for home unless you are certain that you are no longer being followed.

How to See If Your Car Has Been Tampered With

1 Examine the ground around your car.
Get down on all fours and crawl along the ground around your car up to a distance of 25 feet away, looking for small bits of wire or wire insulation, discarded scraps of tape, or puttylike lumps.

2 Examine the locks and windows.
Run a flashlight along the cracks between the doors and the door frames, looking for small wires. Using a magnifying glass, examine the door locks and windows, and the area directly surrounding them, for scrapes or scratches indicating forced entry. Check the seam around the trunk; open the trunk and make sure the mats have not been moved, and there are no unfamiliar objects or bits of wire or wire insulation.

3 Examine the gas tank.
Run your hands over the crack between the gas tank cover and the tank to make sure that the cover is flush and shows no signs of prying. Use a magnifying glass to look for scuff marks or scratches. Open the gas tank cover and sniff the tank for strong, nongas odors.

4 Open the hood.
Shine your flashlight around the engine block, particularly the wiring, to see if anything is disconnected or if there are any new wires present. Run the light along the firewall (the back wall of the engine, separating the fuel tank from the passenger compartment) to make sure it has not been sabotaged.

5 Use a mirror to examine the underside of the car.
Slide a small handheld mirror under the chassis and slowly move it clockwise around the underside of the car, examining the reflected image for foreign objects attached to the vehicle. Use a flashlight if necessary.

6 Check your brakes.
Lie down a foot away from the front of the car and sweep your flashlight underneath it, looking for a puddle of greasy liquid, which may be brake fluid that has been drained from your vehicle. Run one finger slowly along the brake lines, from each brake pad back to the master cylinder, feeling for pinholes or cuts.

7 Look into the exhaust pipe.
Shine a flashlight into the pipe to look for foreign objects.

8 Inspect your wheels and tires.
Run your hands all the way around each tire to feel for minor punctures or small slashes. Feel each lug nut to make sure it is still properly tightened. Check the air pressure of

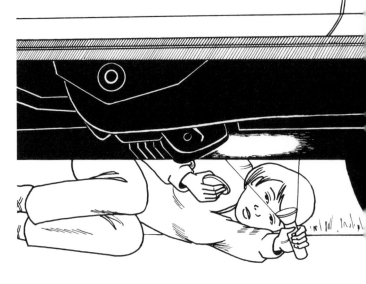

Use a mirror and flashlight to examine the underside of your car.

each tire with a tire pressure gauge to make sure no one has let the air out of your tires.

9 Examine the front seats for signs of intrusion.
Before opening the car door, look through the window for signs that someone has been in the car. Note whether the angle of the seats has been altered, if the rearview mirror has been redirected, or if the floor mats have been moved or disturbed.

10 Take a deep breath.
Once settled in the driver's seat, sniff the air. The odor of gasoline within the vehicle can indicate that the gas tank has been tampered with or punctured.

11 Look for a planted device.
Run your fingers along the underside of the passenger and driver's seats in search of foreign objects. Check under the brake and acceleration pedals. Do not apply pressure to the seats until you are satisfied that there is nothing beneath them that may be pressure-triggered.

BE AWARE!

⚡ The best way to notice any tampering is to know your vehicle well under normal circumstances. Carry a photograph of the inside of your engine so you can check the arrangement of wires against the picture before starting your car each time.

⚡ Always leave objects on your front seat, such as newspapers or tissue boxes, so you can gauge whether someone has moved them when you return to the car.

How to Tell If Your Cell Phone Has Been Tapped

✪ Requires frequent charging.
A cell phone that has been tapped is always using battery life, even when you are not on it. Check frequently to see if the battery life is running down with unexpected frequency, even when you are not using it that often.

✪ Elevated battery temperature.
A tapped phone may remain warm even when it has not been used for a while or has been powered down.

✪ Frequent general background noise.
The frequent intrusion of strange echoing noises, voices, or pings may indicate a surreptitious listener; note, however, that these sounds can result from simple nonmalicious line interference.

✪ Pulsating-static background noise.
A pulsing, staticky hiss is a surer sign of a tap, especially if you hear it on every call.

✪ Affecting other devices.
Bring your phone close to other electronics, such as televisions and computers, and note whether their performance is negatively affected, possibly indicating the presence of surveillance hardware installed on your phone.

✪ Random new stuff.
Another sign of being tapped is the sudden appearance of new software, or that the phone suddenly lights up or powers down on its own.

How to Tell If You're Under Surveillance

* Pieces of mail missing from mailbox.
* Same car parked near yours, or in front of your house, day after day.
* Unexplained viruses or hardware malfunctions on your computer.
* Strange behavior or static from radio or cell phone.
* E-mails disappearing and reappearing, or showing up as "read" when you have not yet read them.
* Furniture shifted when you return home.
* A pattern of overly friendly strangers asking personal questions.
* Persistent clicks and hisses on the telephone line.
* An abundance of wrong-number telephone calls or survey/census/newspaper subscription "junk" phone calls.
* Visits from deliverymen with packages you didn't order or packages they've mistakenly brought to the wrong address.
* Workmen doing construction projects, coincidentally, across from your home and your workplace.

How to Rig a Room to Tell If Someone Has Been There

1 Arrange a few small hairs in the shape of a plus sign.
Place the hairs carefully in a drawer where you suspect someone might snoop. These hairs are certain to be disrupted if someone rifles through the drawer.

2 Plant a crumpled $20 bill in a corner or similar spot where it appears to have been mistakenly dropped.
A greedy intruder will have a hard time resisting the temptation to take money that appears lost.

3 Insert a small strip of paper between the doors of a cabinet.
When the cabinet door is opened, the strip will fall out. Make sure it's large enough that you can lodge it between the doors but small enough that it appears inconsequential to your intruder.

4 Leave various inside doors ajar and drawers slightly open.
Note their exact placement, and when you return, you will be able to see if they have been moved.

5 Lightly dust the entry area to your home with baby powder or laundry detergent.
When you return, check the area to see if you spot footprints or smudges in the powder.

6 Stick a toothpick in the edge of the front door.
If you see it fall when you later open the door, you'll know that no one has been there.

7 Carefully apply a piece of tape on the underside of your front door knob.
Be certain to only touch the edges of the piece as you stick it to the knob. If someone tries to open your door, her fingerprints are likely to get on the tape. Peel it off the knob (again taking care not to get your own fingers on it) and hold it up to the light to see if there are fingerprints on it.

BE AWARE!

⚡ Write down the exact placement of your "traps" and measurements, where applicable, for your reference when you return.

TECHNOLOGY

Remove the phone from the toilet.

HOW TO SURVIVE DROPPING A CELL PHONE IN THE TOILET

1 Get the phone out of the toilet.

2 Turn off the phone.

3 Take off the case.
Unclip the protective case and remove the screen shield. Place these accessories on paper towels to dry out.

4 Shake it out.
Vigorously shake the phone up and down, removing all excess droplets.

5 Remove the battery and SIM card.
Place the phone face down on dry paper towels or tissue. Open the back cover and remove the battery and SIM card, drying each thoroughly with tissue or paper towels.

6 Clean the phone.
Using a clean cloth towel, gently blot the USB slot, the headphone jack, and other open-air areas of the phone.

7 Stick the phone in a bowl of rice.
Fill a jar or mixing bowl with dry uncooked rice and drop the phone, battery, and SIM card in, completely submerging them in the rice.

8 Wait 24 hours.
Leave the phone in the bowl of rice for 24 hours.

9 Repeat.
If the phone won't turn on after you put the battery back in, leave it in the rice for one more night.

WARNING!

⚡ One in five cell-phone customers will at some point drop their phone in the toilet.

HOW TO CURE A VIDEO GAME ADDICTION

1 Find equivalent pleasures in other areas of life.
Addiction is a neurochemical phenomenon, in which the favored substance or activity activates pleasure centers in the brain. While weaning yourself from video games, approximate gaming sensations by pretending that your daily life is a video game, and that small accomplishments such as "getting dressed" and "eating breakfast" count as "winning a level."

2 Calculate the amount of time you spend on gaming.
Be honest with yourself. Include time you spend thinking about gaming, shopping for games, talking about gaming, texting about gaming, and e-mailing about gaming.

3 Slowly reduce gaming time.
In one week, cut the amount of daily gaming time from 22 hours a day to 20. After one week, cut it to 15. Continue to cut down until you are gaming less than one hour every day.

4 Have a funeral for your avatar.
Eulogize your avatar: "CaptainWizardFeather147 was a kind and smart pretend person with massive forearms and a gleaming dragon-slaying sword. He will be missed."

5 Find new, nongaming friends.
Look for friends whose thumbs do not twitch involuntarily when they are not holding controllers.

6 Find healthy activities to replace gaming in your life.
Seek out pursuits to replace the role of gaming, such as sports and social relationships. Experiment with reading books and magazines. Do not read books and magazines about gaming.

WARNING!

⚡ Signs of video-game addiction include gaming to escape from anxiety or depression, irritability when unable to game, thinking about gaming when pursuing other activities, and lying to others about the amount of gaming you do.

HOW TO SURVIVE TECH INJURIES

How to Treat Carpal Tunnel Syndrome

1 Stop typing.
As soon as symptoms appear, severely limit the amount of typing you are doing day-to-day.

2 Rest hands for two weeks.

Be careful to avoid any closed-fist motions, such as punching your boss in the face when he says you can't have sick days for carpal tunnel.

3 Wear a splint.

Construct a rigid splint out of a ruler, gauze, and masking tape. Wear the splint on the wrist of the affected hand to keep the wrist straight during sleep and while doing any necessary typing.

4 Apply cold packs.

If the hand or wrist swells, wrap ice in a plastic baggie and strap it to the affected area for an hour at a time, several times a week.

5 Take over-the-counter pain medication.

6 Do hand yoga.

Several times a day, slowly uncurl the fingers of the affected hand, one by one, and then recurl them one by one into a loose fist.

WARNING!

⚡ Symptoms include burning, tingling, and numbness in the hands; note that these symptoms often first appear at night.

⚡ Stop using the scroll wheel on your computer mouse. Frequent usage might not cause carpal tunnel, but it will hurt.

How to Treat Eyestrain

1 Limit direct glare.

Light can come from numerous sources: overhead lights, computer screens, and bright light shining through the window.

2 Limit contrast.

Many cases of eyestrain are caused not by glare but by contrast, when you are staring at a dimly lit screen set against a brightly lit background. Dim the lights in the room surrounding your computer.

3 Get elevated.

Position your chair higher up, or stand, so that you are looking down at your computer instead of straight on or from below.

4 Experiment with light settings.

Some people's eyes function better in bright lights, some in dim. Adjust the lights in your workplace to try out different levels of brightness. Warn your coworkers before you do this.

5 Experiment with viewing distance.

Your goal should be to sit as far away as you can while still being able to read the words on the screen.

How to Avoid Being Hacked

- Install a firewall, a trojan scanner, and antivirus software.
- Use a less-popular email program—i.e., one that does not come bundled with your computer.
- Avoid accessing open Wi-Fi connections, especially in public places.
- Don't open files that you don't recognize or that are sent from people you don't know.
- Use a different password for every login or account.
- Change your passwords frequently.
- Turn off "file sharing" and "print sharing" options on your networked computer.

6 Employ the 20=20=20 rule.

Every 20 minutes, stop working and look at a point 20 feet away for 20 seconds.

WARNING!

⚡ Shifting physical position to avoid glare often leads to new ergonomic problems caused by the new, uncomfortable seating position.

How to Treat Texting or SMS Thumb

1 Rest your thumbs.

Only send messages when there is an emergency that cannot be communicated by a phone call, e-mail, letter, or actual in-person speech.

2 Do thumb exercises.

Hold your right thumb between your left forefinger and index finger; gently pull back on the thumb and hold it for 10 seconds; switch hands and repeat.

3 Soak your thumbs

Dunk each thumb in ice water for 10 minutes at one-hour intervals throughout the day.

4 Splint your thumbs.

At night, keep your thumbs still by making each of them a splint out of half a popsicle stick and some masking tape.

5 Switch digits.

Use your other fingers to type messages.

WARNING!

⚡ 38 million people report some kind of text-related pain every year.

⚡ Ten percent of SMS or text-message users send more than 100 messages a day.

LAW AND ORDER

How to Survive a Night in Jail

1 Request a single.

If you notice an empty cell, ask to be housed there. Do not offer special reasons for wanting a private cell—those factors may work against you if you are later placed in a group cell.

2 Do not show fear.

Fear means weakness in jail. If you cannot stop shaking, pretend you are psychologically unsound: wave your arms around, babble nonsense, and yell at no one in particular.

3 Stay within sight of the guard.

The cell may be monitored in person by a guard or via closed-circuit television. Make sure you remain visible.

4 Do not sleep.

Lying down on a bench or cot gives other inmates the opportunity to claim that you are lying on "their" bunk. Sit on the floor with your back to the wall, preferably in a corner of the cell. Do not remove any clothing to use as a blanket or pillow, or you will risk losing the item to other inmates.

5 Keep to yourself.

Do not start a conversation with anyone, but do not be rude. Answer any questions you are asked, and keep your responses short. Do not talk about the reason for your arrest, as there may be police informants in the cell. Do not make eye contact with other inmates, but do not avert your eyes.

6 Do not accept favors.

Other inmates may offer to help you in various ways, then claim that you "owe" them. Resist the temptation to ask for or accept help.

7 Do not try to escape.

How to Tail a Thief

1 Before attempting to follow someone who you believe has stolen from you, try to alter your appearance.

Remove your jacket; remove your shirt, if you are wearing a T-shirt underneath; put on or remove a hat or sunglasses. You do not want the thief to recognize you.

2 Never stare directly at the person you are following.

You can observe the person without being obvious. Never make eye contact.

3 Note the thief's identifying characteristics (dress, gait, height, and weight).

You will be able to keep track of the thief in a crowd (or after losing sight of him or her) if you are looking for particular details.

4 Stay well behind the person you are following.

Never tail a person by walking right behind him or her. Follow from a distance of at least 40 feet, or from across the street.

5 If the thief goes into a store, do not follow.

Remain outside, looking in the store window, or wait a few doors down for the thief to come out. If the thief does not emerge quickly, check for a back exit.

6 Once you have determined that the thief has arrived at his or her destination, call the authorities.

Confronting thieves alone is risky. Use a phone or ask a store owner to call the police. Describe your target and his or her location.

WARNING!

✎ Wallet thieves and pickpockets often follow a similar pattern: They pass the wallet to another person immediately following the theft in order to throw you off the trail, and that person passes it to another. If you can, follow the initial thief: the thief may no longer be carrying your wallet but might lead you to those who are.

Relax hand and roll finger to make a clean print.

Attack vulnerable areas.

How to Survive a Mugging

1 Do not resist.

Remain calm and follow the mugger's instructions. Answer questions slowly, with an even tone of voice. Avoid any hints of sarcasm, irony, or aggression. Do not look directly at the mugger's face.

2 Attack vulnerable areas.

If you are certain that the mugger means to do you harm, take swift aggressive action.

- Thrust your fingers into the mugger's eyes.

- Hold your hand flat and chop sharply at the mugger's Adam's apple.

- Grab his crotch and squeeze.

- Thrust your knee up into his groin.

- Swiftly sweep your left foot into his right ankle. At the same time, grasp his left elbow and pull sharply downward. As the mugger begins to totter, lunge forward into his midsection, pushing your attacker to the ground.

3 Use an object as a weapon.

Clench a car key between two fingers and use it to poke or stab. Wield a glass bottle to use as a bludgeon or, if broken, as a knife. Break off a car antenna and use it as a weapon.

4 Flee.

Run as quickly as possible to the closest well-lit area, such as a store or a crowded sidewalk.

WARNING!

- Most street criminals want to get what they can and make a quick getaway. There is no possession worth losing your life over.

- Do not call attention to any mobile technological device you may be carrying.

- Walk in small groups and avoid dim, isolated areas.

How to Survive Identity Theft

1 Get your cash.

As soon as you realize your identity has been stolen, go to the bank and withdraw as much money as you feel comfortable having in cash. Request that they disallow your accounts ATM access, as identity thieves will work quickly to drain your accounts.

2 Cancel everything.

Call every organization, financial or otherwise, that someone with your identification could access, inform them that your identity has been stolen, and cancel the account. This includes credit card accounts, subscriptions, savings and retirement accounts, library cards, and gym or other memberships.

3 Freeze your credit.

Call the three major credit bureaus and follow the instructions they give you to put a "fraud hold" on your credit. This will make it impossible for anyone to open new credit accounts in your name until you unfreeze it.

4 E-mail everyone you know.

Someone holding baseline identifiers such as driver's license and Social Security number (or National Insurance number in the UK) has a wide range of access to your online identity. Open a new e-mail account, and e-mail all your friends and business contacts, explaining what happened and instructing them to ignore any e-mails from your old e-mail accounts, especially if they come with requests for money.

5 Monitor your credit.

Request that the credit bureaus send you monthly credit statements, and monitor the statements for any new activity that you did not initiate. Each time a new account appears, contact the issuing organization and formally dispute it. Be alert for any unfamiliar address on your credit statement, which indicates that someone has made large purchases for delivery.

6 Monitor your mailbox.

One sign that a new account has been opened in your name is that your mail suddenly stops coming or dwindles to a trickle. Someone may have placed a phony change-of-address order at the post office.

7 Get a new Social Security number.

By telephone, contact the federal Social Security Administration in the United States for a new Social Security number, or if in the UK, contact the Department for Work and Pensions for a new National Insurance number. Explain your situation, and request a new number. This is a long and time-consuming process, because of strict laws relating to illegal immigration and, ironically, identity theft.

GETTING IN

How to Break Down a Door

Interior Doors

⊙ Give the door a well-placed kick or two to the lock area to break it down.

Running at the door and slamming against it with your shoulder or body is not usually as effective as kicking with your foot. Your foot exerts more force than your shoulder, and you will be able to direct this force toward the area of the locking mechanism more succinctly with your foot.

Alternate Method (if you have a screwdriver)

Look on the front of the doorknob for a small hole or keyhole. Most interior doors have what are called privacy sets. These locks are usually installed in bedroom and bathroom doors and can be locked from the inside when the door is shut, but they have an emergency access hole in the center of the door handle that allows entry to the locking mechanism inside. Insert the screwdriver or probe into the handle and push the locking mechanism, or turn the mechanism to open the lock.

Exterior Doors

If you are trying to break down an exterior door, you will need more force. Exterior doors are of sturdier construction and are designed with security in mind, for obvious reasons. In general, you can expect to see two kinds of latches on outside doors: a passage- or entry-lock set for latching and a deadbolt lock for security. The passage set is used for keeping the door from swinging open and does not lock. The entry-lock set utilizes a dead latch and can be locked before closing the door.

⊙ Give the door several well-placed kicks at the point where the lock is mounted.

An exterior door usually takes several tries to break down this way, so keep at it.

Alternate Method (if you have a sturdy piece of steel)

Wrench or pry the lock off the door by inserting the tool between the lock and the door and prying back and forth.

Alternate Method (if you have a screwdriver, hammer, and awl)

Remove the pins from the hinges (if the door opens toward you) and then force the door open from the hinge side.

Get a screwdriver or an awl and a hammer. Place the awl

Exterior doors are of sturdier construction. Kick at the point where the lock is mounted.

or screwdriver underneath the hinge, with the pointy end touching the end of the bolt or screw. Using the hammer, strike the other end of the awl or screwdriver until the hinge comes out.

Assessing Amount of Force Required

Interior doors in general are of a lighter construction than exterior doors and usually are thinner—$1^{3}/_{8}$ inches thick to $1^{5}/_{8}$ inches thick—than exterior doors, which generally are $1^{3}/_{4}$ inches thick. In general, older homes will be more likely to have solid wood doors, while newer ones will have the cheaper, hollow core models. Knowing what type of door you are dealing with will help you determine how to break it down. You can usually determine the construction and solidity of a door by tapping on it.

Hollow core. This type is generally used for interior doors, since it provides no insulation or security, and requires minimal force. These doors can often be opened with a screwdriver.

Solid wood. These are usually oak or some other hardwood, and require an average amount of force and a crowbar or other similar tool.

Solid core. These have a softwood inner frame with a laminate on each side and a chipped or shaved wood core, and require an average amount of force and a screwdriver.

Metal clad. These are usually softwood with a thin metal covering, and require average or above-average force and a crowbar.

Hollow metal. These doors are of a heavier-gauge metal that usually has a reinforcing channel around the edges and the lock-mounting area, and are sometimes filled with some type of insulating material. These require maximum force and a crowbar.

How to Sneak In Late to Meetings

○ Enter quietly.
Remove your shoes outside the door to the conference room. Crack the door and scan the room for an open seat closest to the door. When someone dims the lights to make a multimedia presentation, walk on your toes into the room and hurriedly take your seat. Put your shoes back on before the meeting is over.

○ Enter tapping your watch.
Hold your watch to your ear to hear if it's still ticking. Shrug ruefully as you sit down.

○ Bring snacks.
Enter the meeting with doughnuts and coffee, chips and dips, or bagels.

○ Hover outside the meeting room talking on your phone.
Pace back and forth within sight and, if possible, hearing of people at the meeting. Loudly say "terrific" even if you are faking a call. Then walk confidently and smiling into the meeting.

○ Lower expectations.
When running 20 minutes late, call the office and have a message relayed to the meeting that you are running 45 minutes late. When you arrive, accept thanks for rushing.

○ Enter "commando style."

Crawl into the room on your stomach, below your coworkers' line of sight.

Lie down on your stomach just outside the entrance to the conference room, clutching your laptop to your chest. When a colleague opens the door to go to the restroom, wriggle into the room on your stomach, remaining below eye level with those inside. Climb up on and into a chair.

○ Enter wheeling a cart full of files and materials.
Create the impression that you have been gathering vital information and just could not stop.

○ Give yourself a handicap.
Enter the meeting wearing an arm sling or tourniquet, in a wheelchair with a full-leg cast, or pushing an IV tube on a cart. Do not offer any explanation for your condition.

○ Create a diversion outside the meeting room.
Set fire to a wastepaper basket, turn chickens loose in the hall, or otherwise cause people to leave the meeting room. When they return, slip in with them.

How to Break in to a Car

How to Break in to a Car with a Hanger

1 Take a wire hanger and bend it into a long J.

2 Square off the bottom of the J so that the square is 1½ to 2 inches wide (see illustration).

3 Slide the hanger into the door, between the window and the weather stripping.
Open the door by feel and by trial and error. Feel for the end of the button rod and, when you have it, pull it up to open the lock.

How to Break in to a Car with a Slim Jim

A slim jim is a thin piece of spring steel with a notch in one side, which makes it easy to pull the lock rod up. It can be purchased at most automotive supply stores.

1 Slide the tool gently between the window and the weather stripping.
Some cars will give you only a ¼ inch of access to the lock linkage, so go slowly and be patient.

2 Do not jerk the tool trying to find the lock rod.
This can break the lock linkage, and on autolocks it can easily rip the wires in the door.

3 Move the tool back and forth until it grabs the lock rod, and then gently move it until the lock flips up.

How to Pick a Car Lock

1 You will need two tools—one to manipulate the pins or wafers inside the lock core and one to turn the cylinder. You can use a small Allen wrench to turn the lock and a long bobby pin to move the pins and wafers. Keep in mind that many car locks are harder to pick than door locks. They often have a small shutter that covers and protects the lock, and this can make the process more difficult.

2 While the bobby pin is in the lock, exert constant and light turning pressure with the wrench.
This is the only way to discern if the pins or wafers—which line up with the notches and grooves in a key—are lined up correctly. Most locks have five pins.

3 Move the bobby pin to manipulate the pins or wafers until you feel the lock turn smoothly.

Alternate Method

○ Use a key that will unlock a different car from the same manufacturer.

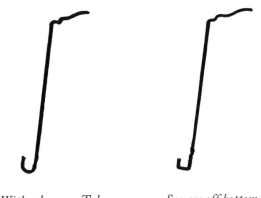

With a hanger. Take a wire hanger and bend it into a long J.

Square off bottom.

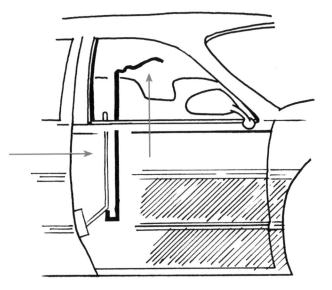

Slide hanger in door between glass and weather stripping. Feel for the end of the button rod and lift up.

There are surprisingly few lock variations, and the alien key may just work.

BE AWARE!

⚡ Most cars that are more than 20 years old have vertical, push-button locks. These are locks that come straight out of the top of the car door and have rods that are set vertically inside the door. These locks can be easily opened with a wire hanger or a slim jim, or picked, as described at left. Newer cars have horizontal locks, which emerge from the side of the car door and are attached to horizontal lock rods. These are more difficult to manipulate without a special tool but can also be picked.

⚡ Only seek to enter your own car.

GETTING A JOB

How to Survive the Interview

If You Are Late

1 Call ahead.
If you are stuck in traffic or otherwise running late, call as soon as you know you will be substantially late. Ask to reschedule, either later in the day or on another day.

2 Clean yourself up.
Use a bathroom before meeting your interviewer if you are sweaty and disheveled when you arrive. Wash your face with cold water and blot it dry with paper towels. Gargle. Check your teeth for pieces of food.

3 Apologize.
Tell the interviewer you are sorry for your tardiness, but do not overdo the apology. Do not fabricate an explanation that can easily be verified. The following are acceptable excuses, if true.

- The traffic was terrible.
- There was an accident on the bridge.
- My car caught on fire.
- I was stuck in the elevator.
- I had to take my mother/daughter/pet to the emergency room.

Do not say:

- My alarm clock is broken.
- I lost track of the time.
- I couldn't find my belt.
- I was out so late last night . . .

If You Are Asked a Difficult or Leading Question

1 Always respond with a positive.
If the interviewer says, "I see you don't have experience," counter with, "That's true, but I've always wanted to learn and I'm a quick study!"

2 Use personal experiences to demonstrate strengths in areas that are professionally weak.
If the interviewer asks about project management experience and you don't have any, talk about planning your wedding or organizing a large family function (hiring vendors, designing a database, and creating seating charts based on the interests of guests).

Résumé Euphemisms	
WHAT YOU DID	**WHAT YOU CALL IT**
Worked for a company with a Web site	Internet pioneer
Ran failed businesses	Experienced entrepreneur
Filed for bankruptcy	Fiscal realist
Grew backyard tomatoes	Small farm owner
Had children	Child advocate
Got fired	Friend of the working people
Dropped out of college	Learned by experience
Took inconsistent positions on issues	Maverick

3 Answer confidently.
It isn't always what you say, but how you say it. Often, questions are designed to assess your professional attitude and maturity level more than your knowledge base. Be sincere in your responses, and act professionally—even if you don't have a good answer. Be straightforward, even when your answer is "I don't know."

4 Memorize the following good answers to these standard, hard-to-address questions:

Q: **Where do you see yourself in five years?**

A: At a good job in this industry, at a good company, learning and contributing to the company's growth.

Q: **Why should I hire you?**

A: I've got the right experience, I understand your needs, and I'm a good team player—both in the office and on the softball field.

Q: **Why did you quit your last job?**

A: I simply wasn't able to contribute to the company's future in the way I wanted. I'm looking for more opportunities for myself, and for a company that can fully utilize my abilities.

5 Prepare a last-resort response.
If you are asked the one question you dreaded, take a page from the politicians' playbook: Acknowledge the question, then move on. Say, "I'm very glad you asked that, and I'd like to give it some thought. But I'd really like to discuss . . ."

Combine items of clothing to cover tattoos.

How to Disguise a Tattoo

1 **Wear long sleeves.**
Long-sleeved shirts can cover arm and shoulder tattoos. The garment should be a dark, medium-weight fabric, not sheer or ultrathin; lightweight white shirts and blouses will not effectively cover upper-body tattoos in bright light.

2 **Wear a scarf and hat.**
A tasteful scarf (for women) or ascot (for men) can be used to hide neck tattoos. A wide-brimmed hat is effective for concealing forehead tattoos.

3 **Wear boots.**
Cover ankle tattoos with ankle boots, but they should be worn to an interview only if accompanied by a pantsuit or a long skirt. Do not wear cowboy boots or high-top, lace-up shoes to a job interview.

4 **Wear pants or dark stockings.**
For leg tattoos, wear pants, or use cosmetics (see step 5) and wear black or off-black medium-sheer hosiery; ultra-sheer hosiery will not hide a tattoo. (Colored tattoos may be noticeable even through opaque stockings without the preliminary application of makeup.)

5 **Apply a layer of eye shadow over the tattoo.**
Use matte shadow without sparkle. Depending on the tattoo's colors and complexity, you may need to apply multiple colors of eye shadow:

- Dark tattoo colors (black, blue, purple): Use yellow eye shadow to cover.
- Red: Use light green eye shadow to cover.
- Yellow: Use light to medium pink eye shadow to cover. If no eye shadow is available, use colored makeup.

6 **Apply full-coverage makeup.**
Use a layer of thick, full-coverage foundation that matches your skin tone. Cover with a dusting of translucent powder to set the coverage. Allow the makeup to dry.

How to Clean Up Your Online Reputation

1 Take down your own postings.
The vast majority of embarrassing material about people online are things they posted themselves. Remove all such material from your Facebook page, MySpace page, Classmates page, and anywhere else it appears. When evaluating whether material is unacceptable, imagine that you are your grandmother or a potential employer.

2 Block outsiders.
Reset the "settings" on your social networking profiles to limit access to people you have approved.

3 Search for your name.
Find your entire online presence by searching for yourself in all the various search engines. Dig in to all the result pages and open every link. Look for pictures from your past in which you are doing embarrassing or questionable activities.

4 Search smarter.
Redo your search, this time searching for just your last name, in combination with your hometown, college, or any institution you've been a member of.

5 Politely request removal.
E-mail the administrator of any site that includes dubious material relating to you, and ask him politely to remove it.

6 Litigiously request removal.
Draft a threatening e-mail and send to the site owner, with a cc: to your local prosecutor's office. Generally it is impossible to force removal of noncopyrighted personal photographs, but the threat of a lawsuit can be enough to intimidate nonexperts.

7 Clarify photographs.
For those unremovable photos that show you intoxicated or in a compromising position, add photo "tags" or captions that condemn your identical twin's behavior, or express regret over your decade lost to amnesia.

8 Counterpost
Flood the Internet with attractive, nonincriminating photographs of yourself, and launch a blog detailing your charity work. The more positive material you post, the further the negative material is exiled to the end of the search results.

Slouching and pouting.   *Staff leaves promptly at quitting time.*

How to Identify a Nightmare Workplace

1 Interview at the beginning or end of the day.

Arrive early for your morning interview and observe the workers as they arrive. Slouching, pouting, and dejected expressions indicate low morale. Note whether workers acknowledge the receptionist with a smile and a greeting or are oblivious to the receptionist. With an interview at the end of the day, observe if large numbers of workers leave promptly at quitting time, which may indicate a bored, clock-watching staff. Large numbers of people working late, however, may indicate that employees are overworked and deadlines are unrealistic.

2 Examine the bathrooms.

Are the bathrooms clean? Is there enough toilet paper? Are paper towels strewn about the floor? Lack of attention to these small details may indicate a lack of respect for the workplace and lack of attention to larger details.

3 Monitor the air quality.

Does the work area have natural light and outside air? Is the environment quiet? Is the air too hot or too cold? Are there any rancid or chemical smells? Is smoke billowing from any vents or machinery? Are workers sniffing or sneezing frequently? All of these are indicators of poor air quality or a "sick" workplace.

4 Look for signs of a troubled workplace.

- Lack of personal photos on desks—only motivational images of rowers and bears catching salmon

- Droopy eyelids obscuring the whites of the workers' eyes
- Multiple sandwiches (partially eaten) and cans of soda at workstations
- Employees sleeping, doodling, or fistfighting at meetings
- Employees with their foreheads on their desks, fists pounding the desktops
- Outdated or no-longer-manufactured candy in the vending machine
- Brown water in the cooler
- Flickering or humming fluorescent lights
- Music playing through speakers in the ceiling
- Warning: Hazardous Waste signs
- Groups of workers whispering
- Individual workers whispering to themselves
- Groups of workers silently praying
- Office layout based on slave ship rather than feng shui
- Carpet stains that could be coffee, could be blood
- If you observe three or more of the above danger signs, you may have discovered a nightmare workplace.

5 Evaluate.

Is this the job for you?

ON THE JOB

How to Survive a Spill in Aisle Seven

1 Stay with the spill.
Monitor the area from the moment you discover it.

2 Examine the spilled item.
A spill will be "dry," "wet," or "wet with glass." Determine which type you are facing.

3 Announce the spill.
Shout, "Wet spill with glass, aisle seven." Ask the employee who responds to remain with the spill while you get cleaning materials.

4 Prepare the cleaning supplies.
Bring a broom, dustpan, and rolling garbage can with bag if the spill is dry. If the spill is wet or wet with glass, also get two Caution signs, rubber gloves, paper towels, a rag mop, and a filled bucket with wringer. Add an all-purpose cleaning agent to the water.

5 Prepare the spill area.
Place a Caution sign on either side of a wet spill. Keep your bucket clear of the spilled material to avoid leaving tracks when you move it.

6 Remove the glass pieces and sweep.
Wearing the rubber gloves, pick up all noticeable glass shards and place them in the garbage bag. (Use paper towels if no gloves are available.) Sweep as much of the spilled item into the dustpan as possible and dump in the garbage can.

7 Mop.
Thoroughly soak the mop head. Mop using short, back-and-forth strokes until no spillage remains. Avoid wide strokes, which will spread the spilled item. Dunk the mop head in the water frequently and wring thoroughly.

8 Check the floor.
Some items (spaghetti sauce, for example) may stain floor surfaces. If you cannot remove the stain by mopping, leave a message for the night cleaning staff to clean and buff the area.

9 Leave the signs in place.

10 Wait 20 minutes, then check the spill area.
Remove the signs when the floor is dry.

Turn off machine; cut the tie or call for help.

How to Remove a Tie Caught in a Document Feeder

1 Determine how quickly you will need to act.
If your breathing is constricted, do not hesitate—cut the tie off quickly (see step 5). You may be able to reduce some of the constriction by getting as close to the feeder as possible.

2 If your breathing is not constricted, try pulling the tie.
Use firm but steady pressure. Do not yank: if the document feeder uses gear-driven rollers, you may strip the gears or tear the tie. If the feeder is particularly powerful, you may be unable to pull the tie out.

3 Turn off the copier.
If you can reach the power switch, turn it off. Alternatively, yank or kick out the power cord.

4 Search the area for a cutting implement.
Copier areas often house scissors, utility knives, paper cutters, and other devices you might use to cut the tie free. Open the copier supply door and look in there. Feel around on nearby tables and inside nearby cabinets for useful items.

5 Make a single fast cut across the tie at its shortest visible point.
Pull the tie taut with your neck or free hand, and slice through it quickly.

6 Call for help if you cannot fix the situation yourself.
Cry out for help. If a phone is within reach, call the receptionist or a coworker.

How to Restore a Shredded Document

1 Determine the identifying characteristics of the document.

Use paper color and weight, distinctive fonts, illustrations, and logos to establish which is the document you are trying to restore. Find an unshredded document or letter from the same sender as a model.

2 Sort the shreds.

Using the identifying characteristics of the stationery and comparing the angle of the edges of each shred, begin to organize the shred strips. Separate and discard shreds from other documents until all remaining shreds are from the target document.

3 Begin pasteup.

Place the first shred vertically on your pasteup board (a whiteboard works well) using clear, removable tape. Using the same orientation, place a second shred alongside the first. Compare it against one side, then the other. If it is a match, tape it down next to the original shred. If it is not, lightly tape it down an inch away, parallel to the first strip.

4 Repeat.

Continue comparing strips. Keep the "raw" (uncompared) strips separate from the "rejected" (compared but non-matching) strips. If you run out of room, use a second pasteup board. Join matching strips as soon as the match is discovered.

5 Copy the reconstituted document.

When the document is reassembled, sandwich taped strips between two sheets of clear overhead projector film or clear contact paper and photocopy.

WARNING!

- A three-page document will have 100 to 200 shred strips, and reassembly will take one to two hours, depending on skill level.
- Cross-cut shredders, which shred documents in both directions, make salvage virtually impossible.

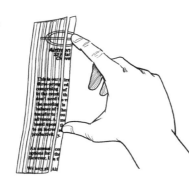

Sort shreds by distinctive color, type, and design. Discard shreds not from target document. Tape each shred in place to reassemble document.

Rock the machine forward and back slightly.

How to Get a Candy Bar Out of the Vending Machine

1 Wait several seconds.

Newer vending machines may be equipped with special technology that senses when an item has not dropped; the machine may return your money or give you another selection.

2 Purchase the item again.

Depending on how severely the snack is stuck and how much money you have, you may be able to jar it loose and get a second one by selecting the same item again.

3 Choose an item from the row above.

If your snack is stuck at an angle toward the glass at the end of the row, an item dropping from above may knock it free.

4 Jostle the machine.

Vending machines are extremely heavy and can cause major injury if they tip over. Carefully bang on the side of the machine. Do not hit glass areas.

5 Rock the machine.

Tip the machine backward very slightly (not side to side), and let it drop back in place to jar the item loose. Do not press on the glass.

AVOID BEING FIRED

How to Survive If You're Caught Slacking

Asleep at Your Desk

○ **Blame work.**
Say, "I'm so exhausted; I was here until midnight last night!" Do not attempt this if your boss works late and you do not.

○ **Blame medication.**
Claim that your new allergy medicine has been making you drowsy. Say, "Those antihistamines just knock me out!"

○ **Blame lunch.**
Say, "Wow, I guess I should not have eaten that turkey sandwich. Tryptophan really makes me sleepy!"

> **WARNING!**
>
> ⚡ When taking a nap, always rest your elbow on your desk and keep your arm perpendicular to the desktop. Your forehead should rest on your four fingers—your thumb, spread apart from the fingers, should support your jaw. This position will keep your head up and aimed at your desk. Face in a direction so that it is not immediately visible to someone approaching your desk that your eyes are closed. Keep an important group of documents in your perceived line of sight so as to appear to be reading intently.

The proper napping position: Forehead on fingertips. Thumb supporting jaw. Arm perpendicular to desk.

Surfing the Web

○ **Blame your search engine.**
Explain that your search engine mistakenly has provided you with an address to an inappropriate site. Alternatively, claim that you made a typing error in the Web address.

○ **Blame your browser.**
Say that someone has set a new home page on your Internet browser. Sounding annoyed, loudly ask, "Who keeps setting my browser to open on this sports page? I'm trying to get those new numbers for my report!" You can also claim that you're having trouble loading certain work-related Web sites and so you are visiting more popular sites to see if the computer is working properly.

○ **Blame the Web site.**
Claim that the window with inappropriate material opened unexpectedly while you were viewing something else. Lament that such "pop-ups" are very common and should be regulated.

○ **Blame an e-mail correspondent.**

Claim that someone sent you the hyperlink, and you clicked it without knowing what it was.

> **WARNING!**
>
> ⚡ When surfing the Web, always keep the corporate intranet site up in a separate browser window. Be ready to click over quickly.
>
> ⚡ Position your monitor at an angle that prevents anyone standing at the entrance to your office or cube from viewing the screen.

How to Enhance Your Stature

Pretend That You Have an Assistant

○ **Alter your outgoing voicemail message.**
Ask a spouse or friend, preferably with an intriguing foreign accent, to record your outgoing message. It should be a version of the following: "You have reached the office of [*your name here*]. S/he is not available to take your call. Please leave a message, and s/he will return your call as soon as possible."

○ **Receive calls on your mobile phone.**

While you are with someone you want to impress, either in an office conference room or at a restaurant, have a friend call you at a prearranged time. Answer the phone and say to the person with whom you are meeting, "Sorry, but I have to take this call. No one but my assistant has this number, and I told him to call me only in emergencies."

○ Tip the host at a restaurant.
Tell the host to come to your table during the meal and say that you have an urgent phone call from your assistant.

○ Attend meetings to which you are not invited.
Ask the receptionist for a conference room reservation schedule.

○ Determine which meetings are worth crashing.

○ Choose meetings carefully.
Do not attend any meeting at which your direct supervisor is present. If your supervisor is out of the office, definitely attend the meeting, and people will think you have been designated as a replacement. If your supervisor is in town, go to other departments' meetings.

○ Invent a reason for attending.
Approach the person running the meeting in advance and explain that you are attending for "professional development." The chairperson will most likely assume that there is some new Human Resources department program. Others attending the meeting will assume that you are supposed to be there.

○ Bring snacks.
People will never question your attendance if you bring food.

Move into an Unoccupied Office

1 Take note of offices that have been vacant for a significant length of time.

2 Slowly take possession of an office.
Begin by working on a project in the office. If questioned, explain that you "needed a little peace and quiet in order to get [project name] done."

3 Occupy the office regularly.
For two weeks, spend at least an hour a day in the space, working on your project.

4 Expand your hours of occupancy.
After two weeks, begin leaving personal items and other files in the office.

5 Log on to the computer in the new office with your password.

6 Forward your phone calls.
Program your phone to send your calls to the extension in the new office.

7 Complain to the IT department.
Tell the information technologies department that your old extension still hasn't been transferred to your new phone.

8 Move your nameplate.
Place your nameplate on the new desk or in the slot outside the door, depending on company practice.

9 Close the door when working.
Look annoyed when anyone knocks or tries to come in. After approximately eight weeks of squatting, the office will be perceived as yours.

Alter Your Business Cards

○ Count the number of characters in your title.
The new title you select needs to occupy roughly the same space on the card so that it doesn't float or appear obviously doctored. For example, "Editorial Assistant" can become "Editorial Director," but not simply "Editor" or "Senior Editor." Suggested replacements:

- "Marketing Manager" with "Marketing Director"
- "Assistant to the President" with "Assistant Vice-President"
- "Executive Secretary" with "Chief Exec. Officer."
- "Customer Service Rep." with "Customer Service Mgr."

Use correction fluid, tape, a razor blade, and modified printer labels to add or subtract words and letters from your business card.

Use Props

○ Carry a briefcase.
Invest in a good-quality leather briefcase or attaché case and carry it at all times. When someone asks you for something, say, "Oh, I have it here in my briefcase." Consider a locking model for added stature.

○ Carry a fountain pen.
Fountain pens denote wealth and good breeding. Do not carry the pen in a pocket protector.

Look Busier Than You Are

○ Purchase a headset and attach it to your phone.
It doesn't matter whether it's actually connected or not—tape it to the bottom of the phone if it won't hook in. Wear it constantly, and talk loudly whenever someone passes by.

○ Keep large piles of paper on your desk at all times.
Rearrange the stacks occasionally.

● Type furiously from time to time.

Position your monitor so that the screen is not visible to anyone passing by or entering your space. Periodically, look intently at the monitor and type as fast as you can. Type nonsense, if you must—but do it at a speed of at least 70 words per minute.

● Show up early and stay late.

You can maintain the same eight-hour day—just run your errands in the middle of the day. Few people will think twice about your absence from your desk in the middle of the day, but everyone will notice how early you get there and how late you leave. Long midday absences, if noticed, will be interpreted as business lunches, a sign of importance.

● Muss your hair and look stressed whenever you pass your supervisor's office.

Start a Helpful Rumor

● Receive messages from headhunters.

Have a friend, posing as a headhunter, make repeated calls to the receptionist. The friend should say, "I'm with [official-sounding name] Headhunting Agency—may I speak with [your name]?" Word will likely get back to your supervisor.

● Plant a reference check with the Human Resources department.

When the office is sure to be closed—late at night, on a weekend, or when you are certain that everyone in the Human Resources department has left for the day—have a friend leave a voicemail message saying he or she is checking references on [your name] and will call back later. The caller should not leave a return phone number or a company name but can leave their own name. The caller should sound casual but busy, as if he or she is checking a list of names with a variety of employers.

● Take the receptionist or your direct supervisor's assistant into your "confidence."

Explain that you are "entertaining" a position at another company but that you "really want to stay." Ask for advice, knowing that word will get back to the boss.

● Talk with people in other departments about forthcoming changes in your department.

Say you are not at liberty to reveal the whole story, but major changes will be coming. Ask if they know anything about future plans for your supervisor's parking place/office.

● Conduct rumor-inducing conversations in public areas.

Spend time conversing at the watercooler, the lunchroom, the bathroom, the lobby, stairwells, elevators, and hallways. A loud whisper is most effective in getting people's

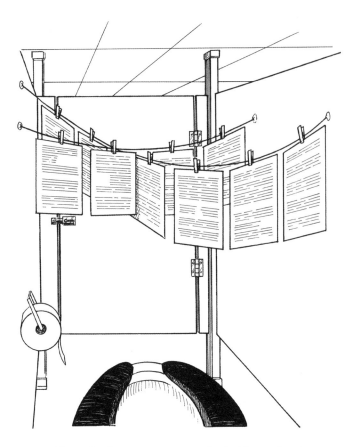

Hang the document to expose both sides to the air.

attention. What you are talking about is not important: the fact that you are engaging in so many hushed conversations is the important factor.

HOW TO SALVAGE A COFFEE-STAINED DOCUMENT

If you are working with a signed contract or a document you cannot replace, you will have to restore the existing pages.

1 Blot the stain immediately.

Use a clean rag or paper towel to remove as much of the coffee as possible before it dries. Blot, do not wipe. The longer the stain sets, the more difficult the removal.

2 Examine the stain.

If the stain caused the ink to run, you are probably dealing with an unsalvageable document. Follow the directions in step 3 to be sure.

3 Determine the printing method.

Wet the end of an cotton swab, and quickly run it across a nonstained word. If the ink transfers to the cotton, the document was printed on an ink-jet printer and salvage is not possible. Use as is.

4 Make a vinegar solution.

For a small stain (one to two inches in diameter), mix 1 tablespoon white vinegar with 1 tablespoon cold water. (Double or triple the amounts based on stain size.) Pour the mixture into a plate or shallow dish.

5 Place the stained document on the edge of the dish.

Using a metal spoon, weigh down the stained portion so it rests in the solution. It is not necessary to immerse the entire sheet.

6 Soak for five minutes.

If the stain is still present, let the document soak for five additional minutes.

7 Remove from the solution and blot.

Blot the wet area using a clean, dry paper towel. Do not rub.

8 Dry.

For best results, clip the paper to a string with a clothespin or paper clip to expose both sides to the air. Drying time is about 30 minutes. If time is of the essence or the document is very wrinkled, use a warm iron to carefully smooth the stained area to speed the drying process.

WARNING!

↗ Do not rub the stained area when the stain is fresh or damp from the vinegar, as you may rip the document.

↗ Depending on the severity and freshness of the stain, blotting repeatedly with a vinegar-soaked paper towel instead of soaking may be more effective for removal. When the stain has faded, blot with a clean, dry paper towel and dry as above.

↗ If the signature page at the end of a contract is the stained page, do not try to remove the stain. Blot dry and leave alone. The signatories may have used a fountain pen or a type of ink that is water soluble.

How to Cover Up Mistakes

Expunge a Nasty E-mail

○ Recall it.

Some e-mail programs allow you to "recall" a message you sent, giving you the option of deleting or replacing it. This feature works only if the recipient is also using the same brand of software and if the recipient is in your local area network. In the Sent Items folder, open the e-mail and click Recall This Message in the Tools menu (or Actions menu, depending on which software you have). Follow the instructions.

○ Retract it.

Several free software programs or add-ins allow you to "retract" (delete) an e-mail before it is read. Instead of sending the actual message, these programs send the recipient a link to a Web site that stores your sent e-mail, enabling you to send a "delete" command before the recipient opens the message. If you tend to get angry and impulsive, consider buying such a program.

○ Delete the message from the recipient's computer.

As soon as you realize your mistake, call the recipient and send him on a fool's errand, or have the recipient paged to another area. Go to his desk. Kneel so that you are not easily visible. Open his e-mail program and delete the message. Check the Trash mailbox to make sure it was fully deleted and not just moved. Delete it permanently.

○ Claim poor spelling or blame the automatic spelling checker.

Insist to the recipient that your message isn't what you meant to say. Explain that the bad language was a typo, or that it was a typo that the automatic spell-checker changed into another, unintended word.

○ Claim that someone else sent the e-mail from your machine.

○ Blame computers generally.

Explain that a moment's frustration was blown way out of proportion because computers make it so easy to vent and send. Claim that before computer technology and e-mail, this never would have happened.

WARNING!

↗ It is best to queue outgoing e-mail in your outbox rather than send it immediately. This gives you the opportunity to pause and reflect on your wording, and then change or delete the message before it is sent.

↗ One e-mail program offers a "Mood Watch" function that monitors your typing and alerts you if a message is approaching "flame" status.

Cultivate realationships.

Workplaces aren't always meritocracies. Employees who are better liked are often kept on, even if they're less competent at their work.

— *Marty Nemko, Columnist*

6

THE NATURAL WORLD

THE DESERT

HOW TO SURVIVE WHEN LOST IN THE DESERT

1 Do not panic, especially if people know where you are and when you are scheduled to return.

If you have a vehicle, stay with it—do not wander!

2 If you are on foot, try to backtrack by retracing your steps.

Always move downstream or down country. Travel along ridges instead of in washes or valleys, where it is harder for you to see and for rescuers to see you.

3 If you have completely lost your bearings, try to get to a high vista and look around.

If you are not absolutely sure you can follow your tracks or prints, stay put.

4 Build smoky fires during daylight hours (tires work well), but keep a bright fire burning at night.

If fuel is limited, keep a small kindling fire burning, and have fuel ready to burn if you spot a person or vehicle.

5 If a car or plane is passing, or if you see other people off in the distance, try to signal them with one of the following methods:

- In a clearing, you can use newspaper or aluminum foil weighed down with rocks to make a large triangle; this is the international distress symbol.
- A large I indicates to rescuers that someone is injured.

How to Prepare for the Desert

Always inform someone of your destination, the duration of the trip, and its intended route. Leaving without alerting anyone and getting lost means no one will look for you.

If traveling by car, make sure your vehicle is in good condition, and make sure you have the following:

- A sound battery
- Good hoses (squeeze them: they should be firm, not soft and mushy)
- A spare tire with the proper inflation
- Spare fan belts
- Tools
- Extra gasoline and oil
- Water (five gallons for a vehicle)

- An X means you are unable to proceed.
- An F indicates you need food and water.
- Three shots from a gun is another recognized distress signal.

6 To avoid heat exhaustion, rest frequently.

Deserts in the United States can reach temperatures upward of 120°F during the day, and shade can be scarce. In the summer, sit at least 12 inches above the ground on a stool or a branch (ground temperatures can be 30 degrees hotter than the surrounding air temperature). When walking during daylight hours:

- Walk slowly to conserve energy, and rest at least 10 minutes every hour.
- Drink water; don't ration it.
- Avoid talking and smoking.
- Breathe through your nose, not your mouth.
- Avoid alcohol, which dehydrates.
- Avoid eating if there is not a sufficient amount of water readily available; digestion consumes water.
- Stay in the shade and wear clothing, including a shirt, hat, and sunglasses. Clothing helps ration sweat by slowing evaporation and prolonging cooling.
- Travel in the evening, at night, or early in the day.
- In cold weather, wear layers of clothing, and make sure you and your clothes are dry.
- Watch for signs of hypothermia, which include intense shivering, muscle tensing, fatigue, poor coordination, stumbling, and blueness of the lips and fingernails. If you see these signs, get dry clothing on immediately and light a fire if possible. If not, huddle close to companions for warmth.

7 Try to find water. The best places to look:

- The base of rock cliffs.
- In the gravel wash from mountain valleys, especially after a recent rain.
- The outside edge of a sharp bend in a dry streambed. Look for wet sand, then dig down three to six feet to find seeping water.
- Near green vegetation. Tree clusters and other shrubbery, such as cottonwood, sycamore, or willow trees, may indicate the presence of water.
- Animal paths and flocks of birds. Following them may lead you to water.

Where to Find Water

At the base of rock cliffs.

In the gravel wash from mountain valleys.

Near green vegetation.

8 Find cactus fruit and flowers.

Split open the base of cactus stalks and chew on the pith, but don't swallow it. Carry chunks of pith to alleviate thirst while walking. Other desert plants are inedible and will make you sick.

How to Drive Safely

⊘ Keep an eye on the sky.

Flash floods can occur in a wash anytime thunderheads are in sight, even though it may not be raining where you are.

⊘ If you get caught in a dust storm while driving, get off the road immediately.

Turn off your driving lights and turn on your emergency flashers. Back into the wind to reduce windshield pitting by sand particles.

⊘ Before driving through washes and sandy areas, test the footing.

One minute on foot may save hours of hard work and prevent a punctured oil pan.

⊘ If your vehicle breaks down, stay near it; your emergency supplies are there.

Raise the hood and trunk lid to denote "help needed." A vehicle can be seen for miles, but a person is very difficult to find.

- Leave a disabled vehicle only if you are positive of the route to help.

- If stalled or lost, set signal fires. Set smoky fires in the daytime, bright ones for the night. Three fires in a triangle denotes "help needed."

- If you find a road, stay on it.

What to Bring

⊘ When Traveling by Foot

- Water (one gallon per person per day is adequate; two or more gallons is smarter and safer)

- A map that shows the nearest populated areas

- Waterproof matches

- A cigarette lighter or flint and steel

- A survival guide

- Strong sunscreen, a hat, warm clothes, and blankets

- A pocketknife

- A metal signaling mirror

- Iodine tablets

- A small pencil and writing materials

- A whistle (three blasts denotes "help needed")

- A canteen cup

- Aluminum foil

- A compass

- A first aid kit

How to Avoid Getting Lost

- When hiking, periodically look back in the direction from where you have come. Taking a mental picture of what it will look like when you return helps in case you become lost.

- Stay on established trails, if possible, and mark the trail route with blazes on trees and brush, or by making *ducques* (pronounced "ducks"), which are piles of three rocks stacked on top of one another.

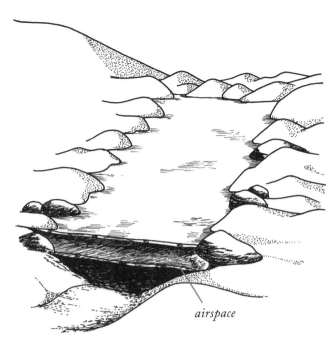

Position your shelter so the opening is downwind of the prevailing breeze.

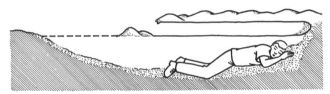

Sleep with your head in the less-exposed part of the shelter.

How to Make an Underground Sand Shelter

1 Choose a location.

A natural depression or the hollow between two dunes offers the best protection from the wind and weather if a sandstorm erupts.

2 Dig.

Use a shovel, a pot, an empty cup, or your hands to excavate enough sand to form a two- to three-foot-deep trench that is long and wide enough to accommodate your body. Pile the sand around the perimeter of the trench on three sides, leaving open the narrow end downwind of the prevailing breeze.

3 Build the roof.

Spread a tarp or a large swath of fabric over the ground, aligning one side of the tarp with the long end of the trench and anchoring it in place with rocks and sand along one side. Fold the remaining half of the tarp over the pile of sand and rocks, and stretch it back over the trench, creating a foot-wide airspace between the two layers. This will create an insulating layer that will keep the trench as cool as possible. Pile more rocks or sand around the edges to anchor the top layer.

4 Cover the shelter with a reflective or light-colored fabric.

Spread a white or reflective fabric over the shelter, creating another airspace between it and the layer of tarp below it. This will block sunlight and may also attract the attention of rescue aircraft.

WARNING!

⚡ An underground shelter can reduce heat significantly, but the effort required to build one can hasten dehydration due to sweating. Work when the sun is just rising or just setting, when the air is cooler but there is still enough light to work by.

How to Survive a Sandstorm

1 Wet a bandanna or other cloth and place it over your nose and mouth.

2 Use a small amount of petroleum jelly to coat your nostrils on the inside.

The lubricant will help to minimize the drying of mucous membranes.

Wear a wet cloth or bandanna over your nose and mouth to avoid inhaling sand particles.

3 Keep your group together.

Link arms or use a rope to avoid becoming separated during the storm and to keep track of group members who might become injured or incapacitated.

4 If driving in a car, pull off the road as far as possible.

Turn off your lights, set the emergency brake, and make sure your taillights are not illuminated. Vehicles approaching from the rear have been known to inadvertently leave the road and collide with the parked car. Keeping your taillights out will help to avert this danger.

5 Try to move to higher ground.

Sand grains travel across the surface of the earth mostly by saltation, or bouncing from place to place. Because grains of sand will not bounce high on grass, dirt, or sand, moving to solid high ground is advisable, even if it's just a few feet higher. However, sandstorms can be accompanied by severe thunderstorms, and there may be a risk of lightning. If you hear thunder or see lightning during a sandstorm, do not move to high ground.

WARNING!

Whenever you are in an area with sandstorm potential (basically, anywhere that there is a lot of sand and wind), wear long pants, socks, and shoes. Because of the way sand moves, your feet and lower legs are more likely to be "burned" by the abrasion of sand than the upper part of your body.

HOW TO FREE A VEHICLE MIRED IN SOFT SAND

1 Determine an escape route.

Examine the sand around you to establish the path on which you will be least likely to get stuck again. Look for sand with a pale yellow hue, indicating a coarse grain, and a rippled surface. Avoid tracts of golden red sand, which consists of fine particles through which traction is difficult to maintain; smooth tracts of sand, which can indicate a fresher, looser makeup; and the hollows between two dunes, which typically collect loose, powdery sand that offers little traction.

2 Dig.

Using a shovel, an empty cup or widemouthed container, or your hands, remove the soft sand from beneath the undercarriage of your vehicle, forming a gradual downward slope toward the direction of escape. Point the front wheels straight ahead.

3 Build a ramp.

Place long lengths of steel, aluminum, or wood under or against the vehicle's wheels, leading down the slope you

Lay cloth, metal, or wood in front of the front wheels to increase traction.

have created. If these materials are not available, use a canvas mat, floor mats, tenting materials, or even a pair of denim pants—anything that will increase traction. If material is limited, place it beneath whichever pair of wheels is powered by the engine.

4 Adjust the tire pressure.

If it is possible to let air out of the tires without lowering the undercarriage into the sand, do so to increase traction.

5 Start moving.

When the wheels gain traction on the metal, wooden, or canvas channels you have created, slowly accelerate to pick up speed.

6 Maintain your speed.

Don't stop. If the car or truck falters before you reach firmer ground, it will get stuck again.

WARNING!

Cars and trucks moving over dunes tend to whip up the top layer of sand, making it less firm. Virgin sand usually affords better traction. If you are traveling in a convoy and there is no known danger of land mines, make your own tracks instead of following behind the other vehicles in single file. Four-wheel drive vehicles are the preferred mode of transport in desert terrain.

MOUNTAINS

HOW TO ESCAPE FROM A MOUNTAIN LION

1 Do not run.

The animal most likely will have seen and smelled you already, and running will simply cause it to pay more attention.

2 Try to make yourself appear bigger by opening your coat wide.

The mountain lion is less likely to attack a larger animal.

3 Do not crouch down.

Hold your ground, wave your hands, and shout. Show it that you are not defenseless.

4 If you have small children with you, pick them up—do all you can to appear larger.

Children, who move quickly and have high-pitched voices, are at higher risk than adults.

5 Back away slowly or wait until the animal moves away.

Report any lion sightings to authorities as soon as possible.

6 If the lion still behaves aggressively, throw stones.

Convince the lion that you are not prey and that you may be dangerous yourself.

7 Fight back if you are attacked.

Most mountain lions are small enough that an average-size human will be able to ward off an attack by fighting back aggressively. Hit the mountain lion in the head, especially around the eyes and mouth. Use sticks, fists, or whatever is at hand. Do not curl up and play dead. Mountain lions generally leap down upon prey from above and deliver a "killing bite" to the back of the neck. Their technique is to break the neck and knock down the prey, and they also will rush and lunge at the neck of prey, dragging the victim down while holding the neck in a crushing grip. Protect your neck and throat at all costs.

How to Avoid an Attack

Mountain lions, also called cougars, have been known to attack people without provocation; aggressive ones have attacked hikers and especially small children, resulting in serious injury. Still, most mountain lions will avoid people. To minimize your contact with cougars in an area inhabited by them, avoid hiking alone and at dusk and dawn, when mountain lions are more active.

Upon sighting a mountain lion, do not run. Do not crouch down. Try to make yourself appear larger by opening your coat wide.

HOW TO SURVIVE A LIGHTNING STORM ON A MOUNTAINSIDE

1 Recognize the signs of an approaching storm.

Typical visual cues like cloud cover and light flashes may be obscured by the terrain, tree cover, or your location. Other signs of electrical storms include the smell of ozone, a buzzing sound in the air, or hair that stands up straight. A halo of light known as St. Elmo's fire may be apparent around trees or people.

2 Break away from the group.

If everyone gets struck at once, no one will be able to help the victims.

3 Remove any jewelry or metal on your body.

If your backpack has a metal frame, take off the backpack.

4 Seek a dry, safe shelter.

If you are surrounded by trees, position yourself among the shortest trees in the vicinity. Stay away from trees scarred by previous lightning strikes. If the mountainside is bare, retreat to a lower position if there is time. Avoid overhangs and ridgelines. Try to find a slight bump in the mountainside that will elevate you—but only slightly—from the path that electricity will likely travel if lightning strikes the ground nearby. A dry cave that is deeper than its mouth is wide is also a good location to wait out the storm.

5 Separate yourself from the ground.

Place insulators like wood, rubber, plastic, or natural (not synthetic) cloth on the ground in your sheltered location.

6 Make yourself as small a target as possible.

Crouch on the balls of your feet on top of the insulation. Put your head down and keep your mouth open to protect your eardrums. Do not put your hands on the ground.

7 After the storm passes, assess whether anyone in your group has been hit.

Common indications that someone has been struck by lightning include temporary hearing loss, dilated pupils, amnesia, paralysis, confusion, weak pulse at the extremities, and irregular heartbeat. If the victim is unconscious, make sure he or she is breathing, and perform CPR if necessary. Seek medical attention as soon as possible.

Avoiding Altitude Sickness

Giving your body time to adjust to the reduced oxygen in the air as you move into higher elevations is the best way to avoid high-altitude illnesses. When hiking at altitudes greater than 10,000 feet, sleep at an altitude of no more than 1,000 feet higher than you slept the night before. For every three consecutive days of 1,000-feet elevation gains, rest an extra day and night before ascending farther. Drinking at least four quarts of fluids a day will help you acclimatize.

How to Survive Being Pinned under a Fallen Rock

Break the wedge and try to shift the rock's weight by digging at its edges with any implement that you can find. Use smaller rocks, sticks, or other available objects to brace the rock away from you. Stay calm; control your breathing; conserve your body heat; ration food, water, and flashlight power; and call out at regular intervals until rescuers arrive.

High-Altitude Illnesses

ILLNESS	SYMPTOMS	TREATMENT
Mild acute mountain sickness	Headache, dizziness, and nausea during first 12 hours in high altitude	Descend 1,500 feet or more and wait for body to acclimate.
Moderate acute mountain sickness	Bad headache, nausea, dizziness, insomnia, fatigue, and fluid retention after 12 hours at high altitude	Descend at least 1,500 feet; take oxygen if possible.
High-altitude cerebral edema	Acute headache, nausea, dizziness, and fatigue for 24 hours; mental confusion; clumsiness and lack of muscle coordination	Take oxygen; descend immediately; evacuate the mountain or use a portable hyperbaric chamber; take dexamethasone and/or acetazolamide.
High-altitude pulmonary edema	Moist cough, shortness of breath, rapid breathing, severe weakness and drowsiness, rapid heartbeat, bluish skin	Take oxygen; descend as soon as possible; use a portable hyperbaric chamber; take nifedipine.
High-altitude retinal hemorrhage (bleeding in retina)	Blind spots; if bleeding is light, may have no symptoms	Descend immediately if blind spots develop. Problem typically resolves itself two to eight weeks after occurrence.

JUNGLE

How to Build a Jungle Shelter

1 Clear the vegetation from a flat, dry area.

The space for your shelter need only be slightly longer than your body and about twice the width. Avoid areas where signs of erosion indicate a danger of flash floods.

2 Drive four posts into the ground, one at each corner of the area.

Collect four logs or branches about as tall as your shoulder and about six inches across. Use a sharpened stick to dig the post holes; then pound a post into each hole to a depth of at least one foot, so the pole stands as tall as your waist.

3 Carve a notch on each pole.

Use a pocketknife or a sharp stick to carve a two-inch notch into the outward face of each pole, at a uniform height just below knee level.

4 Collect materials for the frame of the structure.

Find six straight sapling trunks or sturdy tree branches about four inches in diameter, or thick enough to hold your weight. You'll need two saplings about two feet longer than the width of your shelter area (probably five and seven feet long) and four more saplings about two feet longer than the length of your shelter (about nine feet long).

5 Create the frame at the head and foot of the shelter.

Form a horizontal bar by placing the ends of one of the shorter saplings into the notches in the poles at the head of the shelter. Repeat at the foot of the shelter. Secure both saplings to the poles with ropes or vines. Ideally, the ends of both crossbars should protrude about one foot beyond the posts they're resting on.

6 Create the frame for the sides of the shelter.

Use two of the long remaining saplings to form the crossbars for the sides, laying them on top of the protruding ends of the crossbars at the shelter's top and bottom. Lash them in place with ropes or vines.

7 Make a bed from sturdy, smaller branches.

Gather several dozen straight branches about two inches in diameter and about two feet longer than the width of the shelter frame. Place them so that they span from one side of the frame to the other, and lash them in place with ropes or vines.

8 Collect materials to make the roof.

Find five straight branches or saplings measuring about two inches in diameter: one should be two feet longer than

Sleep about two feet off of the ground to protect yourself from flash floods, insects, fungal infections, hypothermia, and wild animal attacks.

the length of the shelter (this will form the apex), and the other four should be two feet longer than the width of the shelter (these will form the gables).

9 Make the frame for the roof.

Carve a two-inch notch into the outward face of each upright pole an inch or two from the top. Lay the two remaining long and thick saplings gathered in step 4 into the notches to create another pair of lengthwise crossbars at the top of the shelter. Lash a pair of gable branches together at one end, creating a right angle between them; then lash the free ends to the top of the head posts. Repeat with the other gable branches at the foot of the shelter. Finally, lash the long apex sapling into the V shape at the top of each gable, creating a lengthwise crossbar for your roof.

10 Finish the roof.

Fill in the frame by lashing branches that run horizontally from one end of the shelter to the other. These branches should be about an inch thick, or sturdy enough to support heavy leaves. Drape large leaves over the frame, overlapping them from top to bottom to form natural shingles.

WARNING!

An elevated shelter is essential in tropical environments. Sleeping directly on the ground may lead to fungal infections; leech infestation; attacks from wild boars, snakes, and other large animals; hypothermia; or drowning by flash flood.

How to Survive When Lost in the Jungle

How to Find Civilization

1 Locate a river.
Generally, animal trails will lead you to water. Water is the key to jungle navigation and usually the quickest way to travel.

2 Fashion a makeshift raft.

3 Let the current carry you downstream.

4 Travel on the river only during the daylight hours.
Alligators and crocodiles are generally night hunters, so avoid traveling on water at night.

5 Watch closely for signs of villages or settlements.
Many jungle settlements and villages are located along the shores of rivers.

How to Find Food and Water

⊙ If you do not have the means to purify water, cut sections from large water vines, or cut banana trees and capture the water welling out of the stalks.
Only drink water from streams and rivers as a last resort, when dehydration and death are a near certainty. Diarrhea will most likely result, so increase your water intake and keep moving.

⊙ If you cannot peel it or cook it, do not eat it.
Avoid brightly colored plants or plants with a milky sap (many of these are poisonous). Insects, grubs, and raw fish (except those with bristles or spines rather than scales) are safe to eat. Look for grubs and insects beneath rotting logs and vegetation. Pinch the heads off and eat them raw. Peel fruits carefully before eating; the peels may harbor diarrhea-causing bacteria.

How to Travel over Land

- Mark your trail by breaking and turning over fresh vegetation. This will reveal the bright undersides of leaves and will leave a clear trail should you need to backtrack.

- Look for shelter during bad weather. Large, hollow tree buttresses can often be used. Line the ground with palm fronds, and stand several more palm fronds over the opening. Note: Do not build this shelter under a tall tree during a thunderstorm because of lightning danger.

WARNING!

⚡ Before traveling to a remote area, take the time to look at any available maps. Pay attention to topography and any roads or waterways nearby. If you get lost, you will need to know what general direction of travel will intersect a road or waterway and thus, eventually, civilization.

⚡ The jungle canopy can totally occlude the sun, so a compass may be your only means of determining direction. The same heavy canopy will make it impossible for would-be rescuers to find you, or even to locate a downed aircraft. Unlike being lost in a wilderness situation, staying put in the jungle means virtually certain death.

⚡ To make a natural insect repellent, you can use a termite nest. These nests are abundant on the ground and in trees. They resemble irregular-shaped dirt mounds the size of five-gallon barrels. Break up the mounds (they look like dirt but are actually digested wood) and rub the material on your skin.

How to Make a Raft

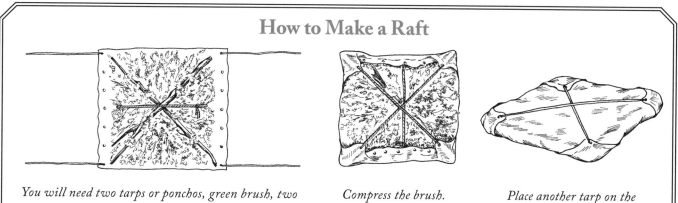

You will need two tarps or ponchos, green brush, two large saplings, and ropes or vines. Tie rope to the corners of one tarp. Pile fresh green brush 18 inches high all around. Place two saplings across the brush in an X. Pile another 18 inches of brush atop the X.

Compress the brush. Pull the sides of the tarp tightly around the pile and tie diagonally.

Place another tarp on the ground. Put the bundle open-side down in the center of the tarp on the ground. Tie tightly as shown. Use the raft rope-side up.

THE FOREST

How to Leave a Trail for Rescuers If Lost in the Wilderness

1 **Walk through "track traps."**

Mud pools, wet sandy areas, snow, and other soft terrain can hold footprints for long periods (days or weeks, between storms). Step in these areas, write "HELP," and draw arrows to signal your direction of travel to potential rescuers. If you reverse course, step in the tracks again on your way out. Your footprints will indicate that the search should not continue past the track trap.

2 **Build campfires.**

Smoke from campfires can be seen for miles, and fires show up well at night. Warm fire rings also indicate to rescuers that you were recently in a particular area. Do not leave fires burning, but make sure coals or dirt is still warm when you leave. (Warm coals can reignite, so leave warm fire rings only in wet areas or under conditions of low fire danger.)

Step in soft terrain to signal rescuers.

Form an arrow to mark your direction.

The Universal Edibility Test

1. Abstain from eating for eight hours before testing a new possible food source.

2. Separate the plant into its basic components: seeds, leaves, stems, flowers, buds, and roots.

3. Test for contact poisoning by placing the plant part in the crook of your elbow for 15 minutes. If no irritation follows, proceed.

4. Place the plant part on your lips for three minutes to make sure it won't cause a burning or itching sensation.

5. Place the plant part on your tongue for 15 minutes to make sure it causes no irritation.

6. If there has been no adverse reaction, chew a small portion and hold it in your mouth for 15 minutes.

7. If no irritation or numbness results, swallow the small plant morsel.

8. Abstain from eating anything else for eight hours. If vomiting or nausea ensues, drink plenty of water to flush out your system. If there are no adverse effects, prepare a small handful of the plant part and eat the whole portion. If another eight hours pass without irritation or vomiting, consider the plant safe to eat.

3 **Follow roads and rivers.**

Rescuers will use natural boundaries to limit their search area. Do not cross roads or rivers. Rather, follow them to more populated areas. Do not climb steep slopes unless you must: your searchers will follow, delaying your rescue.

4 **Leave markers.**

If you abandon marked trails, signal your direction of travel by turning over fresh vegetation or leaving small piles of rocks.

5 **Listen carefully.**

In addition to shouting your name, searchers may use a "call word," an unusual word yelled back and forth to distinguish members of the search party from the victim when not in the line of sight. Listen for odd words ("Hoboken," "spaghetti," "Internet") that sound out of place in the wilderness.

6 Yell loudly and make noises in groups of three.
Three calls is the international distress signal. Use a whistle, if available, to signal your position.

7 Sleep lightly.
A rescue party may continue during the night, so use a flashlight or head lamp. Look for flashlights and listen for searchers between naps.

8 Leave personal items behind.
If you are lost in warm weather and have excess clothing or supplies, leave small items along your path as a signal to rescuers. Traveling light will also make hiking easier.

9 Use a mirror to signal to air searchers.
A mirror or other reflective device will help rescuers in planes or helicopters locate your position. Special "survival" mirrors with a hole in the center are especially effective in focusing sunlight.

How to Escape from a Forest Fire

1 Monitor the horizon.
If you see smoke rising above the trees in the distance, watch to see if it increases in size or strength. If so, move upwind and downslope, away from the fire.

2 Watch for burning embers.
The wind may blow embers more than half a mile from their origin; remain alert to avoid getting burned, and be ready to change course in case a stray ember ignites another area of the forest.

3 Find a firebreak.
Move to a pond, river, road, rocky area, open field, or another area lacking in burnable fuel. Avoid areas thick with brush and dried grasses, as these materials burn quickly and hot. Do not climb uphill, as the fire and superheated air will updraft on even the slightest slope, concentrating the flames and heat most intensely in these chimneys.

4 Seek a gap in the fire line.
A forest fire may advance across a front several miles wide, but it does not always travel at a uniform rate. If you are trapped by a wall of fire, look for a spot where the flames are thin and low to the ground. If possible, cloak your body in natural fibers (synthetic materials may melt and burn your skin) and soak yourself with water. Wrap a wet cloth around your mouth and nose. Cover your face and head with your arms and run through a thin line of fire as fast

as possible. If the moisture in the cloth around your mouth turns into steam, take it off to protect your lungs.

5 If you are trapped on a hillside, move to an outward curve in the trail.
The contour of the land can concentrate intensely hot air currents in protected pockets and indentations on the hillside. The outward rounding bends on the outside of a hill provide a safer location; the heat is more diffuse and travels more slowly. Position yourself as far away from the trail's outer edge as possible to avoid rising heat. Once the fire has burned up the chimneys, you may be able to move to the burnt area before the fire reaches the outside curve.

6 Crawl in a ditch.
If the fire is near and you cannot find another means of escape, lie down in a ditch with your feet facing the direction of the fire. Cover your feet, legs, and body with as much dirt and noncombustible material as possible. Wait for the fire to pass completely before getting back up.

7 Signal passing aircraft to seek their attention.
Wave white or brightly colored clothing, or shine a reflective mirror toward the airplane. If the plane contains fire fighting personnel, they will likely provide you with instructions over their loudspeaker.

WARNING!

↗ A field of grass can produce a fire more than 10 feet tall that moves at a rate of 20 mph. Deciduous trees burn more slowly than grass but can elevate temperatures to preheat the nearby trees, causing them to ignite more quickly. The needles and resin in pine trees are highly combustible and will rapidly spread a very hot fire.

↗ Dangerous wild animals, such as rattlesnakes, bears, and mountain lions, will also be anxious to escape the fire and may cross your path as you seek safety.

↗ If you are surrounded by a forest fire while you're in your vehicle, remain inside rather than attempting to escape on foot—the protection offered by the car outweighs the relatively low risk that your gas tank will explode in the heat. Drive to low, bare ground as free from brush and trees as possible and park facing the oncoming fire. Roll up the windows, shut all the air vents, and turn on your hazards and headlights to make the car more visible to rescuers. Lie on the floor below window level, and cover your head and face with blankets to protect yourself from radiant heat. Smoke will enter the vehicle as the fire surrounds the car, so take shallow breaths close to the floor, breathing through a damp cloth. Stay in the vehicle until the fire passes and the radiant heat has dissipated enough so that the air feels no hotter than the heat felt from bad sunburn. The door handles and interior car parts will be extremely hot; do not touch them with bare skin.

RIVERS AND RAPIDS

How to Cross the Amazon River

If You Are Alone

1 Protect your feet.
Remove your socks and lace up your shoes as tightly as possible to shield your feet from rocks or sticks that could cut them and lead to infection. Shoes with sturdy soles offer the best protection against stingrays that may be found nestling in the river bottom. If you are wearing boots, tuck in your pant legs to reduce your resistance in the water.

2 Assess the depth and speed of the current.
The force of the current will be weakest where the river is at its widest. If the water is moving quickly and filled with stationary or moving obstacles, explore the area to find the widest point you can. Find a long, sturdy branch and probe the water from the bank to gauge the depth and force of the current. Fast-moving water higher than your knees can sweep you off your feet and carry you away.

3 Wear your backpack by the shoulder straps only.
Unfasten the waist strap to enable a quick jettisoning of the backpack in an emergency.

4 If wading is possible, use your branch to help you across.
As you work your way across, face upstream and use the branch to help maintain your balance and to probe for underwater obstacles. Even a smooth, sandy bottom can conceal dangerous stingrays. Take small, incremental steps with the end of the branch leading your way along the bottom.

5 If the water is moving too quickly to wade, swim over the rapids.
In shallow rapids, lie on your back and point your feet downstream. Keep your arms close to your sides and use them like flippers to steer your body in the right direction. In deep rapids, lie on your stomach and swim diagonally across the river facing downstream. Do not attempt to swim while wearing a backpack.

If You Are Traveling in a Group

1 Unfurl a length of rope about three times as long as the river is wide.
Tie the ends together to create a big loop.

2 Station two people about 20 feet apart on the riverbank.
Each person should hold onto the rope with both hands.

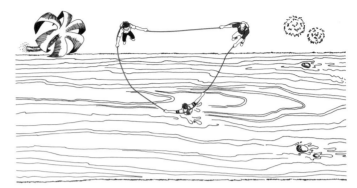

Grasp the rope midway between the two people who will remain on shore, and walk across the river.

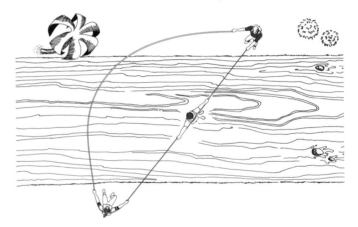

Pull the rope taut across the river so that subsequent people can cross. Allow the slack part of the loop to float downstream.

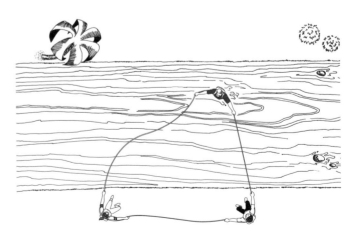

Station two people on the opposite side of the river to hold the rope as the last person crosses.

One part of the rope will now be tight between them, and the other slack.

3 **Send the first crosser through the river.**
Direct the first person crossing to use both hands to grip the slack section of the rope midway between the two handlers and to hold on to the rope as he walks into the water. If the first person gets swept off his feet by the current, the other two should reel him back to shore.

4 **Pull the rope taut across the river.**
When the first person has made it across, he should pull on the looped rope to produce a tense length between him and one of the people on the opposite bank. The slack part of the loop will now be adrift on the river downstream from the taut part of the rope. This way, if subsequent crossers lose hold of the taut rope line, they have a chance to catch on to the slack line as a backup.

5 **Instruct subsequent crossers to hold the taut rope line as they traverse the river.**
Crossers should face upstream as they work their way across; it is easier to maintain balance this way.

6 When the last person is ready to cross, station two people about 20 feet apart on the riverbank's destination side, each holding on to the rope loop.
Bring the last person across the river in the same manner as the first person crossed.

HOW TO CROSS A FROZEN RIVER

1 Anchor a short, thick log to the riverbank.
Find or chop a log measuring approximately two feet long and at least one foot thick. Lay it on the ground parallel to the river, about two feet from the water. Drive several stakes into the ground on either side of the log to hold it in place.

2 Find a log for the bridge.
The log should be long enough to span the river with three feet of clearance on either side.

3 Test the weight-bearing capacity of your log.
Lift one end of the long log onto the log you've anchored next to the river; prop the other end of the long log onto a tree stump or a flat stone tall enough to lift the log off the ground. Step on the middle of the span to test its strength. If it doesn't break, it's safe to use.

Wedge the log in the corner formed by the anchor log and the rock. Pull the log into a vertical position, then lower it across the river.

4 Drag the long log next to the anchor log.
Place the log parallel to the river, between the water and the anchor, so that one end lines up with the end of the anchor.

5 Place a heavy stone next to the anchor at the end of the long log.
Form a solid corner between the stone and the anchor. This will keep the bridge log from sliding as you maneuver them into position.

6 Tie a rope around the far end of the long log.
If you are working alone, leave enough slack in the rope to span the width of the river. If you have help and enough rope, leave twice as much slack.

7 Raise the log to a vertical position.
Using the stone and the anchor to prevent slippage, pull on the rope to stand the long log straight up.

8 Lower the log across the river.
Slowly let out the rope so that the far end of the log ends up on the opposite bank.

9 Elevate the bridge if necessary.
If the riverbank is soggy and the log is touching the cold water, prop the near end of the log on the anchor to provide more space between the river and the bridge.

Point your feet downstream. Assume a sitting position.

How to Run a Canyon River

1 Read the rapids.
Look for a V-shaped pattern of ripples that points downstream into the churning waves. This is usually where the water is deepest and fastest, reducing the potential for collision with an underwater rock. With your boat facing straight ahead, paddle into the current that will naturally lead you to the middle of the V.

2 Paddle furiously.
Hit the white water with as much speed as possible. The bigger the waves, the more important it is to paddle hard and maintain momentum as you pass over them. If the raft is moving too slowly, it may slide backward over a standing wave and get stuck or capsize.

3 Use the weight of the rafters to propel the raft forward.
Roiling water will spin the raft sideways, causing it to lose momentum. Quickly move all the passengers to the side of the raft that has been thrown up into the air by a wave. If the raft loses forward momentum altogether, stay on the high side of the raft and use paddle strokes to pull the boat out of the hole.

4 If you get tossed overboard, attempt to get back in the boat.
Grab for another rafter's forearm with one hand and a rope on the side of the boat with the other.

5 If you can't get back in the boat, point your feet downstream and assume a sitting position.
Bend your knees, and bring your toes above the surface. Watch the boat and maneuver yourself so you don't come between it and a boulder. Resist the urge to stand up, which will likely result in the current's hurling you dangerously forward. Avoid fallen trees, which can force a swimmer beneath the surface. At the end of the rapid, get back onto the nearest boat or swim to the shore as soon as possible.

6 If the boat flips, let your life preserver bring you to the surface.
If you come up beneath the raft, use your hands to move to one side. If there is no serious danger downstream, hold on to the raft on the upstream side, then climb on top of the overturned raft. If there are serious hazards downstream, move away from the raft and swim the rapid on your own, as described above. Once you reach placid water, bring the boat to the shore, turn it over, and assess your losses.

How to Fish in Rapids

1 Find "pocket water."
You want a spot just downstream from many large rocks, where an eddy pool has formed, providing shelter for fish. In this calm spot, the line won't be dragged and spook the fish.

2 Cast directly out across the river.
Keep your rod held high to minimize drag.

3 Let the fly float downstream.

4 Let the fly circle.
When your fly lands in an eddy pool, let it make several cycles before pulling it back into the current; this may not be necessary if the line drags your fly into the current by itself.

BE AWARE!

⚡ A bait fisherman can use basically the same technique; just be sure not to use soft bait, which can be stripped off your hook by swift rapids.

CRITICAL KNOTS

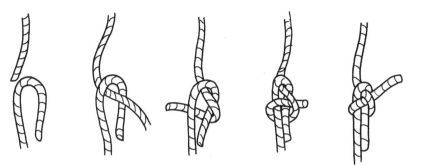

Sheet Bend
Typically used to join two ropes together.

Two Half-Hitches
Used in mooring a boat.

Bowline
Used to make a small, nonslipping loop to secure around an object.

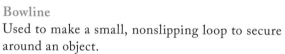

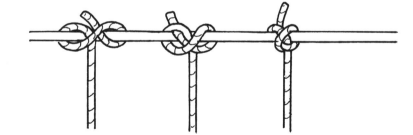

Figure 8
Used to keep the end of a rope from running out, as through a pulley on a boat.

Constrictor
Used for securing a load. May be difficult to untie when pulled tight.

GEOLOGICAL DISASTERS

How to Survive an Earthquake

1 If you are indoors, stay there.
Get under a desk or table and hang on to it, or move into a doorway; the next best place is in a hallway or against an inside wall. Stay clear of windows, fireplaces, and heavy furniture or appliances. Get out of the kitchen, which is a dangerous place. Do not run downstairs or rush outside while the building is shaking or while there is danger of falling and hurting yourself or being hit by falling glass or debris.

2 If you are outside, get into the open, away from buildings, power lines, chimneys, and anything else that might fall on you.

3 If you are driving, stop, but carefully.
Move your car as far out of traffic as possible. Do not stop on or under a bridge or overpass or under trees, light posts, power lines, or signs. Stay inside your car until the shaking stops. When you resume driving, watch for breaks in the pavement, fallen rocks, and bumps in the road at bridge approaches.

4 If you are in a mountainous area, watch out for falling rocks, landslides, trees, and other debris that could be loosened by quakes.

5 After the quake stops, check for injuries and apply the necessary first aid or seek help.
Do not attempt to move seriously injured persons unless they are in further danger of injury. Cover them with blankets and seek medical help for serious injuries.

6 If you can, put on a pair of sturdy thick-soled shoes (in case you step on broken glass, debris, etc.).

7 Check for hazards.
- Put out fires in your home or neighborhood immediately.
- Gas leaks: shut off the main gas valve only if you suspect a leak because of broken pipes or odor. Do not use matches, lighters, camp stoves or barbecues, electrical equipment, or appliances until you are sure there are no gas leaks. They may create a spark that could ignite leaking gas and cause an explosion and fire. Do not turn on the gas again if you turned it off—let the gas company do it.
- Damaged electrical wiring: shut off power at the control box if there is any danger to house wiring.
- Downed or damaged utility lines: do not touch downed power lines or any objects in contact with them.

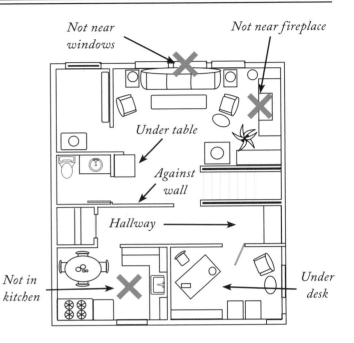

Places to take shelter and to avoid.

- Spills: clean up any spilled medicines, drugs, or other harmful materials such as bleach, lye, or gas.
- Downed or damaged chimneys: approach with caution and do not use a damaged chimney (it could start a fire or let poisonous gases into your house).
- Fallen items: beware of items tumbling off shelves when you open closet and cupboard doors.

8 Check food and water supplies.
Do not eat or drink anything from open containers near shattered glass. If the power is off, plan meals to use up frozen foods or foods that will spoil quickly. Food in the freezer should be good for at least a couple of days. If the water is off, you can drink from water heaters, melted ice cubes, or canned vegetables. Avoid drinking water from swimming pools and spas.

9 Be prepared for aftershocks.
Another quake, larger or smaller, may follow.

WARNING!

- Use your telephone only for a medical or fire emergency—you could tie up the lines needed for emergency response. If the phone doesn't work, send someone for help.

- Do not expect firefighters, police, or paramedics to help you immediately. They may not be available.

*Struggle to stay on top of the snow by using
a freestyle swimming motion.*

How to Survive an Avalanche

1 Stay on top of the snow by using a freestyle swimming motion with your arms.

2 If you are buried, your best chance of survival is if someone saw you get covered.

The snow in an avalanche is like a wet snowball: it is not light and powdery, and once you are buried, it is very difficult to dig your way out.

3 If you are only partially buried, you can dig your way out with your hands or by kicking at the snow.

If you still have a ski pole, poke through the snow in several directions until you see or feel open air, then dig in that direction.

4 If you are completely buried, chances are you will be too injured to help yourself.

However, if you are able, dig a small hole around you and spit in it. The saliva should head downhill, giving you an idea of which direction is up. Dig up, and do it quickly.

WARNING!

⚡ Never go hiking or skiing alone in avalanche territory.

⚡ Carry an avalanche probe—a sturdy, sectional aluminum pole that fits together to create a probe six to eight feet in length. Some ski poles are threaded and can be screwed together to form avalanche probes.

⚡ Avalanches occur in areas with new snow; on the leeward side of mountains (the side facing away from the wind); and in the afternoons of sunny days, when the morning sun may have loosened the snowpack. They occur most often on mountainsides with angles of 30 to 45 degrees—these are often the most popular slopes for skiing.

⚡ Loud noises do not cause avalanches except if they cause significant vibrations in the ground or snow.

⚡ Carry a beacon to broadcast your position to the other beacons in your group.

How to Survive a Volcanic Eruption

1 Watch out for falling rocks, trees, and debris.

If you are caught amid falling debris, roll into a ball to protect your head. If you are trapped near a stream, watch out for mudflows. (Mudflows are mudslides caused by a large volume of melted snow or ice combined with rocks, dirt, and other debris.) Move upslope, especially if you hear the roar of a mudflow.

2 If you are in the path of lava, try to get out of its path in any way possible.

You will not be able to outrun the lava, so do not try to race it downhill. If you are near a depression or valley that might divert the flow from you, try to get to the safe side.

3 Move indoors as soon as possible.

If you are already inside, stay there and move to a higher floor, if possible. Close all doors and windows, and move any cars or machinery indoors, if there is time.

4 Do not sit or lie on the floor or ground.

It is possible to be overcome by volcanic fumes. The most dangerous gas is carbon dioxide: it does not have a strong odor, and it is denser than air, so it collects near the ground.

5 Evacuate the area, but only if authorities tell you to do so.

Your best chance of survival is to use a car to drive to a safer area, but even a car may not be fast enough to outpace a lava flow. Some flows travel at 100 to 200 miles per hour. Since volcanic ash can quickly clog the radiator and engine of your car, avoid driving except to evacuate.

If you are caught amid falling debris, roll into a ball to protect your head.

STORMS

How to Survive a Flash Flood

In a Car

✪ **Watch cars in front of you.**
If you see drivers stalling or notice water reaching halfway up car wheels, do not proceed.

✪ **Estimate the water depth.**
Water may be deeper than it appears. A car will stall (and float) in six inches of water. If you are unsure if a road is safe to drive through, get out of your car and check the water level using a stick.

✪ **Exit the vehicle immediately if the car stalls or begins to float.**
If the door will not open, crawl out the window (you may need to break a power window if the car's electronics become saturated).

✪ **Walk or run to safety.**
Get to higher ground as fast as possible.

✪ **Float.**
If you are knocked off your feet by the rushing water, cover your head with your arms and attempt to float on your back, feetfirst, until you can grab a stationary object and climb to safety.

At Home

✪ **Call for help.**
When you see floodwaters heading toward your house, seek help. Because of the risk of electric shock, avoid using a wired telephone if there is water in the house. Use a cellular phone.

✪ **Observe the water level.**
If the water outside is less than six inches deep, and you are able to walk without falling down, move to higher ground. If walking is impossible, go back inside.

Avoiding Floodwaters

Do not attempt to swim across floodwaters. Deep, quickly moving floodwaters will almost certainly overpower you and sweep you away. You will be unable to see large objects, such as trees, that may be carried by the water, and you may be struck by them.

Exit the vehicle immediately if it stalls or begins to float.

✪ **Move to the highest floor.**
If the house is three or more stories, move to a high floor. If the house is two stories or less, get on the roof.

✪ **Signal rescuers.**
Use a whistle, wave a white T-shirt or another piece of clothing, or shout to make your presence known. Continue to call for help until you are rescued or the waters recede.

WARNING!

⚡ If time permits, quickly gather these supplies and place them in a plastic bag: flashlight with spare batteries; battery-operated radio; first-aid kit; rope; whistle; gallon of water; granola bars, or other nonperishable, high-carbohydrate foodstuffs; essential medications. Take them with you when you leave your house.

⚡ Do not eat or drink any foods that have been touched by floodwaters. The packaging may harbor dangerous germs or chemicals.

⚡ When reentering a flooded building, wear boots and waders, and watch for snakes.

⚡ Pump out flooded basements gradually (approximately one-third of the water per day) to avoid sudden structural damage.

⚡ Have the property checked by a qualified structural engineer before moving back in.

On Foot

○ **Find a flotation device.**

Put on a life jacket, inflate a pool toy, or grab a foam (not down or cotton) sofa cushion. Wood floats, but a large piece of furniture may be unwieldy and difficult to carry.

○ **Run.**

Get to high ground or a high floor of a multistory building immediately. Avoid low-lying areas such as spillways, areas near storm drains, and creeks and riverbanks. Before crossing flooded open areas and streets, watch for floating objects (trees, cars, appliances) that might knock you down.

○ **Check shallow water.**

If the water is less than six inches deep and not moving quickly, you should be able to walk quickly or run. The water level may rise quickly, however, and fast-moving water can knock you down. Prepare to move fast.

○ **Move to the roof.**

If you are trapped by rising, fast-moving water and cannot get to higher ground, get on the roof of a two- or three-story house. Avoid the first and second floors, as these may become inundated quickly.

How to Survive a Tornado

1 Be inside.

Do not go outside during a tornado; if you are outside when the warning is sounded, go indoors as quickly as possible, even if you do not yet see the approaching funnel.

2 Close the windows.

High winds can toss debris in through any open windows or doors in the home.

3 Move away from the window.

After they have been securely closed, stay clear of windows to avoid shattered glass.

4 Go farther into the home's interior.

Stay in a room close to the center of the house, putting as many walls and doors between you and the outside as possible. Stand in a stairway or bathroom.

5 Go below ground.

If the home or building you are in has a basement, tornado shelter, or garage level, head there and stay there till the all clear has been sounded.

6 Walk carefully.

When surveying the damage done during the tornado, watch for post-storm hazards such as flooding, collapsed or collapsing buildings, and downed trees.

Lie down flat in a ditch or ravine if you cannot get inside during a tornado.

WARNING!

⚡ Those living in tornado-prone areas should have a plan.

⚡ If you are outdoors when the tornado strikes and cannot get inside, lie down flat in a ditch or ravine and put your hands over your head.

⚡ When your house is struck by a tornado, turn off the utilities, and if you smell gas or anything burning, leave the house immediately.

⚡ If you are in a vehicle when the tornado strikes, drive at a 90-degree angle away from the storm, and never seek shelter under a highway overpass.

⚡ Never drive in a tornado. If you are in your car when a tornado approaches, exit your car and lie down on your stomach in a ditch or low-lying area, and cover your face and head with your arms.

⚡ Tornados kill between 50 and 60 people in the United States every year.

How to Drive in a Hurricane

○ Roll up the windows.

○ Turn on your high beams.

○ Do not drive next to or behind buses and trucks.

A strong gust of wind can topple a large vehicle over onto your car. Slow down to allow heavy vehicles such as busses and trucks to get ahead and past you. Do not drive behind buses and trucks, as their tires will kick up large amounts of water from the roadway and send it back onto your windshield.

- **Weigh down the car.**
Fill the trunk of your car with heavy objects such as bricks, lumber, appliances, or debris for ballast, to keep the wind from grabbing and flinging the car.

- **Reduce your speed.**
Drive at 10 miles per hour or less, keeping alert for flying debris and other cars that have stopped or stalled and are blocking the roadway.

- **Apply the brakes as little as possible.**
In a heavy downpour, there is a significant chance of hydroplaning as water builds up between your wheels and the road. Slow down by taking your foot off the gas rather than applying the brake, and watch for deep puddles.

- **Note protected and unprotected areas, and adjust your speed accordingly.**
You will be sheltered from the wind when driving in protected areas, such as tunnels. When emerging from the protected area, remember to slow down again.

- **Drive in the middle lane.**
Water will pool more in the outer lanes of the roadway.

- **Be alert for standing water.**
If you cannot see the roadway at the bottom of an area covered by water, do not drive into it. Turn around and find another route. Even if it looks like the water is shallow, there may be hidden pits; water of six inches or higher can cause damage and/or stall your car.

- **Be alert for flash floods.**
Flash floods occur when there is extremely heavy rainfall over a short period of time. They occur most frequently in low-lying areas, such as narrow canyons and valleys. Do not stay in a flooded car; if your car starts to fill up, get out.

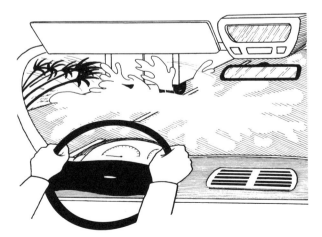

Avoid driving behind buses and trucks, as their tires will kick up large amounts of water.

Never touch a vehicle that has come into contact with a live wire. Even when the wire is removed, it may retain a charge.

How to Deal with a Downed Power Line

1 Assume that all power lines, whether sparking or not, are live.

2 Stay far away from downed lines.
Current can travel through any conductive material, and water on the ground can provide a "channel" from the power line to you. An electrical shock can also occur when one comes in contact with the charged particles near a high-voltage line; direct contact is not necessary for electrocution to occur. Never touch a vehicle that has come in contact with a live wire—it may still retain a charge.

3 Do not assume that a nonsparking wire is safe.
Often, power may be restored by automated equipment, causing a "dead" wire to become dangerous. Stay away from downed lines even if you know they are not electric lines—the line could have come in contact with an electric line when it fell, causing the downed line to be "hot."

4 If a person comes into contact with a live wire, use a nonconductive material to separate the person from the electrical source.
Use a wooden broom handle, a wooden chair, or a dry towel or sheet. Rubber or insulated gloves offer no protection.

5 Avoid direct contact with the skin of the victim or any conducting material touching it until he or she is disconnected; you may be shocked also.

6 Check the pulse and begin rescue breathing and CPR if necessary.

WARNING!

⚡ If you are in a car when a pole or line falls, you are much safer remaining inside a grounded vehicle than being on foot. If the wire falls on the car, do not touch anything—wait for help.

CAMPING

How to Escape from a Bear

1 Lie still and quiet.

Documented attacks show that an attack by a mother black bear often ends when the person stops fighting.

2 Stay where you are, and do not climb a tree to escape a bear.

Black bears can climb trees quickly and easily and will come after you. The odds are that the bear will leave you alone if you stay put.

3 If you are lying still and the bear attacks, strike back with anything you can.

Go for the bear's eyes or its snout.

How to Avoid an Attack

✪ Reduce or eliminate food odors from yourself, your camp, your clothes, and your vehicle.

✪ Do not sleep in the same clothes you cook in.

✪ Store food so that bears cannot smell or reach it.

✪ Do not keep food in your tent—not even a chocolate bar.

✪ Properly store and bring out all garbage.

✪ Handle and store pet food with as much care as your own.

✪ While all bears should be considered dangerous and should be avoided, three types should be regarded as more dangerous than the average bear:

- Females defending cubs
- Bears habituated to human food
- Bears defending a fresh kill

Bears habituated to human food.

Females protecting cubs.

Bears defending a fresh kill.

While all bears are dangerous, these three situations render even more of a threat.

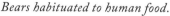

What to Do If You See a Bear

✪ Make your presence known by talking loudly, clapping, singing, or occasionally calling out. (Some people prefer to wear bells.) Whatever you do, be heard—it does not pay to surprise a bear.

✪ Keep children close at hand and within sight.

✪ There is no guaranteed minimum safe distance from a bear: the farther, the better.

✪ If you are in a car, remain in your vehicle. Do not get out, even for a quick photo. Keep your windows up. Do not impede the bear from crossing the road.

How to Go to the
Bathroom in the Woods

1 Find an appropriate location.
Find a location behind a tree or rock for privacy, far from any trail. Stay at least 100 feet from any water source.

2 Dig a ditch.
Use a stick to dig a hole one foot deep and two feet wide.

3 Gather materials.
Find some soft leaves to use as wipes. Some hikers use pinecones, dry pine needles, or even a smooth "wiping stone."

4 Bury the deposit.
When you are done, bury everything, including the leaves or other wiping material.

5 Wash your hands.
Wet your hands with water from a canteen or use hand sanitizer.

How to Rig Up Your Food

1 Tie your food tightly inside plastic bags.
Plastic bags, securely tied, seal in all odors so the food will be less attractive to bears and raccoons.

2 Find the right tree limb.
You want your food to be rigged up at least one foot off the ground and at least one foot horizontally away from the trunk of the tree.

3 Sling a sack over the limb.
Put a small rock in one plastic sack to give it some heft, attach it to a five-foot length of rope or heavy twine, and heave it over the limb.

4 Tie another sack to the other end of the rope.
Now you should have two sacks dangling down from opposite sides of the limb.

5 Fill both sacks with food.
Take the rock from the first sack and fill it instead with half of your food; then fill the other sack with food of equal weight. The two sacks need to be of approximately equal weight in order to counterbalance one another and dangle up out of reach of a bear.

Improvised Outdoor Shelters

TYPE OF SHELTER	BASIC CONSTRUCTION	DRAWBACKS
Dugout shelter	Dig long narrow trench, line with leaves, erect canopy of leaves.	Digging takes a long time with no tools.
Poncho tent or poncho lean-to	String poncho between two trees, anchor with stakes.	Waste of nice poncho.
Three-pole tepee	Lean three sticks together to make frame, drape with canopy or tenting.	Requires ax to fell trees.
One-person tent shelter	String line triangularly from tree to ground, drape with sheet or coat.	Collapsed by even light snow or heavy rain.
Swamp bed	Cut poles to make an elevated bed hung on four trees lifted up over the swamp.	Must be high enough to accommodate shifting mud levels.
Snow cave	Dig at an angle into a large drift, creating separate spaces for sleeping, cooking.	Get extremely wet during construction.

How to Find Your Way Without a Compass

Stick and Shadow Method

What you need:

- An analog watch
- A six-inch stick

Northern Hemisphere

1 Place a small stick vertically in the ground so that it casts a shadow.

2 Place your watch on the ground so that the hour hand is parallel to the shadow of the stick.

3 Find the point on the watch midway between the hour hand and 1:00.

If the watch is on daylight saving time—which is during most of the summer—use the point midway between the hour hand and 1:00.

4 Draw an imaginary line from that point through the center of the watch.

This imaginary line is a north-south line. The sun will be located toward the south.

Southern Hemisphere

✪ Place your watch on the ground so that 1:00 is parallel to the shadow.

Then find the point midway between the hour hand and 1:00. Draw an imaginary line from the point through the center of the watch. This is the north-south line. The sun will be located toward the north.

BE AWARE!

⚡ The closer you are to the equator, the less accurate this method is.

Star Method

Northern Hemisphere

✪ Locate the North Star, Polaris.

The North Star is the last star in the handle of the Little Dipper. Walking toward it means you are walking north. You can use the Big Dipper to find the North Star. A straight imaginary line drawn between the two stars at the end of the Big Dipper's bowl will point to the North Star. The distance to the North Star is about five times the distance between the two "pointer" stars.

In the Northern Hemisphere, place your watch on the ground so that the hour hand is parallel to the shadow. In the Southern Hemisphere, place your watch so that 1:00 is parallel to the shadow.

Southern Hemisphere

✪ Find the Southern Cross.

The Southern Cross is a group of four bright stars in the shape of a cross and tilted to one side. Imagine that the long axis extends in a line five times its actual length. The point where this line ends is south. If you can view the horizon, draw an imaginary line straight down to the ground to create a southern landmark.

Cloud Method

✪ Look at the clouds to determine which direction they are moving in.

Generally, weather moves west to east. While this may not always be true in mountain regions, it is a good rule of thumb and may help orient you.

Moss Method

✪ Locate moss.

Mosses grow in places with lots of shade and water: areas that are cool and moist. On tree trunks, the north sides tend to be more shady and moist than the south sides, and therefore, moss usually grows on the north sides of trees. However, this method is not infallible—in many forests, both sides of a tree can be shady and moist.

MAKING FIRE

HOW TO MAKE A FIRE WITHOUT MATCHES

What You Will Need

- Knife
- Kindling. Several pieces, varying in size from small to large.
- Wood to keep the fire going. Select deadwood from the tree, not off the ground. Good wood should indent with pressure from a fingernail but not break easily.
- Bow. A curved stick about two feet long.
- String. A shoelace, parachute cord, or leather thong. Primitive cordage can be made from yucca, milkweed, or another tough, stringy plant.
- Socket. A horn, bone, piece of hard wood, rock, or seashell that fits in the palm of the hand and will be placed over a stick.
- Lube. You can use earwax, skin oil, a ball of green grass, lip balm, or anything else oily.
- Spindle. A dry, straight ¾- to 1-inch-diameter stick approximately 12 to 18 inches long. Round one end and carve the other end to a point.
- Fire board. Select and shape a second piece of wood into a board approximately ¾ to 1 inch thick, 2 to 3 inches wide, and 10 to 12 inches long. Carve a shallow dish in the center of the flat side approximately ½ inch from the edge. Into the edge of this dish, cut a V-shaped notch.
- Tray. A piece of bark or leaf inserted under the V-shaped notch to catch the ember. The tray should not be made of deadwood.
- Nest. Dry bark, grass, leaves, cattail fuzz, or some other combustible material, formed into a bird's nest shape.

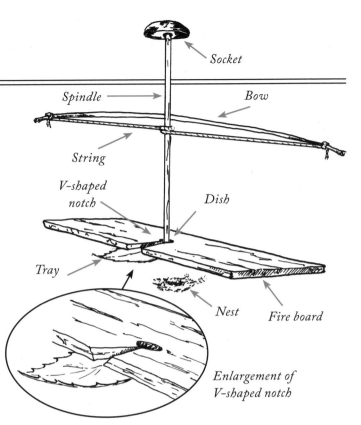

Socket · Spindle · Bow · String · V-shaped notch · Dish · Tray · Nest · Fire board

Enlargement of V-shaped notch

Making a Fire in the Snow

To make a dry bed for your fire in snow-covered terrain, gather green logs about as thick as your forearm. Arrange half of them parallel to one another, forming a square platform, then arrange the other half crosswise across the lower layer. Use dry wood to build your fire on top of the platform.

How to Start the Fire

1 Tie the string tightly to the bow, one end to each end of the stick.

2 Kneel on your right knee, with the ball of your left foot on the fire board, holding it firmly to the ground.

3 Take the bow in your hands.

4 Loop the string near the center of the bow.

5 Insert the spindle in the loop of the bowstring so that the spindle is on the outside of the bow, pointed end up. The bowstring should now be tight—if not, loop the string around the spindle a few more times.

6 Take the hand socket in your left hand, notch side down. Lubricate the notch.
Add pressure to the socket, and speed your bowing motion until an ember is produced.

7 Place the rounded end of the spindle into the dish of the fire board and the pointed end of the spindle into the hand socket.

8 Pressing down lightly on the socket, draw the bow back and forth, rotating the spindle slowly.

9 Add pressure to the socket and speed to your bowing until you begin to produce smoke and ash.
When there is a lot of smoke, you have created an ember.

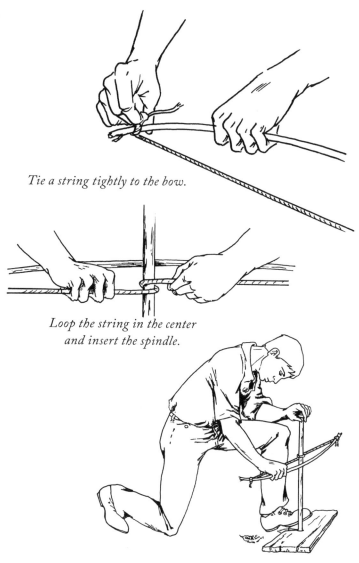

Tie a string tightly to the bow.

Loop the string in the center and insert the spindle.

Press down lightly on the socket. Draw bow back and forth, rotating spindle.

10 Immediately stop your bowing motion and tap the spindle on the fire board to knock the ember into the tray.

11 Remove the tray and transfer the ember into your "nest."

12 Hold the nest tightly and blow steadily onto the ember. Eventually, the nest will catch fire.

13 Add kindling onto the nest. When the kindling catches, gradually add larger pieces of fuel.

HOW TO MAKE A FIRE WITH A SINGLE STALK OF BAMBOO

1 Split a piece of dry bamboo down the middle.
A dry bamboo stalk will be brown or tan and may have brown leaves near the top. Use a machete or sharp stone to crack it down the center. The grain of the bamboo makes it easy to split.

2 Anchor one piece of the bamboo to the ground.
Lay half of the split bamboo horizontally on the ground, with the hollow side facing up. Use several wooden stakes to secure it in place.

3 Make a notch halfway down the other piece of bamboo.
Use a pocketknife to make a wedge-shaped notch that is about an inch wide on the outside of the bamboo and a narrow slit on the inside.

4 Gather several sticks of various sizes.
You will use these to feed the fire once it's started.

5 Shave thin filaments from the notched piece of bamboo.
Scrape your machete or a sharp stone back and forth over the split edges. The fine grain will peel off, forming a soft tuft of dry tinder.

6 Place the clump of tinder inside the carved notch.
Settle the wide part of the notch on the edges of the anchored bamboo, forming an X. Rapidly drag the top piece of bamboo back and forth to create friction against the anchored stalk. After a while, the tinder will begin to smoke and burn.

7 Nurse the small flame into a full-blown fire.
Place several small, dry sticks on top of the burning tinder, gradually adding larger pieces of fuel until the fire is of the desired size.

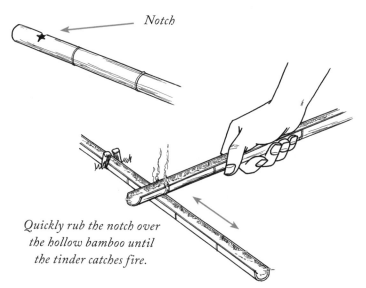

Notch

Quickly rub the notch over the hollow bamboo until the tinder catches fire.

WATER

How to Find Water on a Deserted Island

1 Collect rainwater in whatever container is handy.
A bowl, plate, or helmet will work—so will a life raft and stretched clothing. In very dry environments, condensation forms on surfaces overnight. Use a tarp or other fabric—shaped as a bowl—to collect water.

2 Collect dew.
Tie rags or tufts of fine grass to your ankles and walk in grass or foliage at sunrise. The dew will gather on the material, which can then be wrung out into a container.

3 Head for the mountains.
An island that appears barren on the coast may have a green, mountainous interior, which is an indication of freshwater streams and creeks. Find these by following trails of vegetation. Do not waste too much energy hiking or moving long distances unless you are relatively certain you will find water (meaning that the lush greenery is not far away).

4 Catch fish.
The area around a fish's eyes contains drinkable liquid, as do fish spines (except shark spines). Suck the eyes, and break the vertebrae of the spine apart and suck the liquid from them. Fish flesh also contains drinkable water—but fish are high in protein, and protein digestion requires additional water, so you are better off squeezing raw fish in clothing or a tarp to extract water.

5 Look for bird droppings.
In arid climates, bird droppings around a crack in a rock may indicate a water source. (Birds often congregate around cracks where water collects.) Stuff a cloth into the crack, then wring it out into a container or your mouth.

6 Locate banana and plantain trees.
Cut down the tree, leaving a stump about one foot high. Scoop out the center of the stump, so that the hollow is bowl shaped. The roots will continually refill the stump with water for about four days. The first three fillings will be bitter, but subsequent fillings will be less so. Cover the stump to keep out insects.

WARNING!

⚡ Seawater is generally not safe to drink; its high salt content can cause kidney failure. Moreover, two quarts of body fluid are required to rid the body of the waste in one quart of seawater. As a last resort, you can drink less than three ounces of seawater per day; while not healthy, it may keep you alive.

⚡ Rainwater collected in a container is generally safe to drink, provided the container is clean and the water does not stand; any standing water is capable of breeding bacteria.

Tie rags to your ankles to collect dew.

How to Purify Water

Filtration

Filter water from all sources in the wild—mountain stream, spring, river, lake, or pond.

1 Find or make your filter.
Coffee filters, paper towels, ordinary typing paper, or even your clothing can serve as filters (the more tightly woven, the better). You can also make an effective filter by filling a sock with alternating layers of crushed charcoal, small crushed rocks, and sand.

2 Pour the water through a filter.
Do this several times to clean out impurities.

WARNING!

Filtration will only remove some of the water's impurities. It will not kill bacteria or other microorganisms. The best procedure is to filter water first, then treat it with chemicals or boil it.

Chemical Treatment

1 Add two drops of household bleach for each quart of water.
Use three drops if the water is extremely cold or cloudy.

OR

Use one iodine tablet or five drops of drugstore iodine (2 percent) per quart of water.

2 Mix the water and bleach or iodine, and let it sit for at least one hour.
The chemicals will kill microorganisms; the longer the water sits, the purer it will be. Leaving the water overnight is the safest course of action.

Distillation

1 Dig a hole about a foot deep, and wide enough to hold your container.

2 Place a clean container at the center of the hole.

3 Cover the hole with a piece of plastic.
A tarp or a section of a garbage bag works well as a cover.

4 Place sticks or stones around the edges of the plastic so that it is flush with the ground and air cannot escape.

5 Poke a ¼- to ½-inch hole in the center of the tarp, and place a small stone next to the hole, so that the tarp looks like a funnel.
Make sure the hole is above, but not touching, the top of the container.

6 Wait.
The heat from the sun will cause water in the ground to evaporate, condense on the plastic, and drip into the container. While your solar still will not produce much liquid (less than one cup), the water is safe to drink immediately. The process can take anywhere from several hours to a full day to produce water, depending on the water in the ground and the strength of the sun.

Boiling

Boil water for at least one minute, plus one minute of boiling time for each 1,000 feet above sea level.
If fuel is abundant, boil water for 10 minutes before drinking it. The longer the water boils, the more microorganisms that are killed. Beyond 10 minutes, however, no further purification occurs. Be sure to let the water cool before drinking it.

MAROONED

How to Survive When Marooned

⊕ Find drinkable water.

- Gather rainwater by hollowing out the stumps of trees, but do not let the water sit for more than a day before drinking it.

- Tie rags around your ankles and walk through the grass at dawn, then squeeze the dew from the rags into your mouth.

- Drink the water in coconuts, though excessive consumption may cause diarrhea and dehydration.

- Move to higher ground to survey as much of the terrain as possible. An island that appears to be dry may have a wet, mountainous interior.

- In arctic environments, search for blue ice with round corners that splinters easily—this is old sea ice and is nearly free of salt. Icebergs are also made of freshwater.

- If you are desperate, drink the water found in the eyes and spines of large fish.

⊕ Take care of your body.

- Stay in the shade to protect yourself from the sun as well as from the reflection of the sun on the water.

- If you are in a tropical environment, dampen your clothes during the hottest part of the day to cool yourself and to avoid losing water through perspiration.

- If freshwater is readily available, use this water to moisten your clothes to avoid boils and sores caused by salt water.

- If you are in an arctic environment, find a cave or dig yourself a shelter in the snow to keep your body temperature up.

- Relax and sleep when possible.

⊕ Find food.

- Make a fishnet by placing your shirt over a forked tree branch and tying off both ends. Pull fish out of shallow water as they swim over the net. Fish without spiny scales may be eaten raw or cooked.

- Kill seabirds by throwing rocks at them, as long as you have fire to cook them. You may be able to attract birds by flashing metal into the sky.

- Do not eat anything if you feel nauseated; drink only water and wait to eat until your stomach is calm.

⊕ Signal.

- Make a signal fire by quickly rotating a small stick back and forth between your palms while one end is pressed against a piece of flat wood on the ground. The friction will create heat, which will ignite dry grass.

- Keep a small fire burning at all times, with plenty of fuel ready in case you spot a passing ship. Do not let the fire get out of control. Be prepared to douse it when help arrives.

⊕ Keep a good lookout.

- Chances are your ship was sailing on a known trade route, and other ships are likely to sail within several miles of your island. Move to high ground so you can see the horizon in every direction.

How to Open Coconuts

Drive the end of a stick into the ground and sharpen the top end. Slam the nut down on the point of the stick, using both hands to crack the outer fibrous covering. Smash the inner shell against a rock or tree.

HOW TO FISH
WITHOUT A ROD

1 Determine the best location for your fishing.
Fish usually congregate in shadow, near the edges of lakes, rivers, and streams.

2 Find a forked sapling approximately two feet long.
Cut it down or break it off. The forked ends should be around one foot long.

3 Bend the two ends toward each other and tie them together.
The tied ends will form the circular frame of a net.

4 Remove your shirt or T-shirt.

5 Tie a knot in the shirt just below the arm and neck holes.

6 Slip the sapling into the shirt.

7 Pin or tie the shirt securely to all sides of the frame.

8 Scoop up the fish.

Alternative

Large fish can be speared with a pole sharpened to a point at one end. This method works best at night, when fish come to the surface.

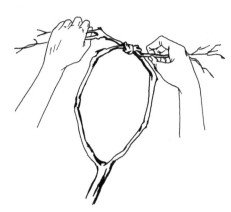

Find a forked branch.
Tie the ends together.

Tie a shirt into a knot.

Slip the branch into the shirt.
Secure the shirt to the frame.

Scoop fish from
underneath to catch.

HOW TO MAKE A FRIEND FROM
MATERIALS ON THE ISLAND

○ Examine the debris.
Examine the flotsam and jetsam, or debris from your vessel or plane's wreckage, looking for beach balls, soccer balls, bowling balls, or other spherical objects upon which faces and hair can be drawn.

○ Make seashell friends.
Gather largish seashells and glue them together with tree sap into humanoid shapes.

○ Make tree friends.
Carve smiling faces into the bark of palm trees.

○ Make wild pig and lizard friends.
Follow around the indigenous species of the island, assigning each of them a distinct personality. When it becomes necessary, eat them.

○ Draw a face on your hand.

○ Draw a friend in the sand.
Use a fallen branch to trace a stick figure in the wet sand of the beach. Each morning, grieve that the tide has taken away your friend, and trace a new one.

○ Make friends with yourself.
Find a body of still water that reflects your appearance. Smile. Compliment yourself, and ask yourself about the details of your day.

SIGNALS

How to Signal with a Mirror

1 Make your fingers into a sight.
Extend your arm and spread two fingers to form a **V**.

2 Position your mirror under one eye.
Use your other hand to position your mirror just under one eye, facing away from you.

3 View the airplane between your fingers.
When you see the rescue plane or helicopter approaching, frame it between your two raised fingers.

4 Swivel the mirror back and forth.
Let the reflected light jump from one finger to another. As you do, the light will hit the plane in the middle.

BE AWARE!

- You can use a handheld mirror, as from a compact, or a wristwatch dial to signal passing aircraft.

- Mirror signals can be seen for up to 100 miles in the desert, and rescue pilots are trained to look for them and trace them to their source.

Position the mirror under your eye and sight the airplane between the fingers on your other hand. Swivel the mirror so the reflected light moves from one finger to the other, hitting the plane in between.

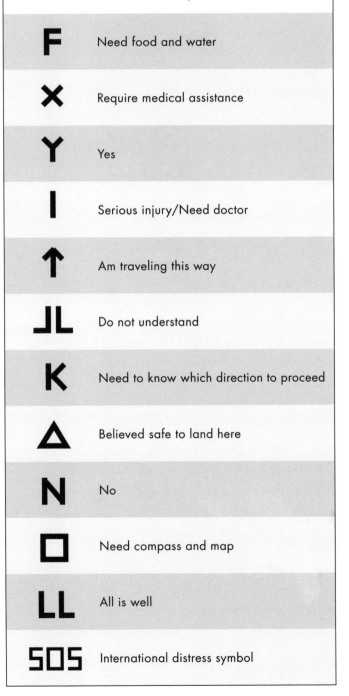

Ground Signals for Passing Aircraft

Pilots can read these symbols and help accordingly. Find a clearing or hilltop, and make your signals with twigs, clothes, or footprints, keeping them far enough from one another to avoid overlap and confusion.

F	Need food and water
X	Require medical assistance
Y	Yes
I	Serious injury/Need doctor
↑	Am traveling this way
⌐L	Do not understand
K	Need to know which direction to proceed
△	Believed safe to land here
N	No
□	Need compass and map
LL	All is well
SOS	International distress symbol

How to Create a Signal Fire

1 Seek the highest ground.

The fire and smoke will have the greatest visibility from a high, unobscured spot. Take branches with you if you go above the tree line.

2 Make a tripod.

Put three long branches together in a tripod formation, tying them at the top with cord, rope, or vines.

3 Make horizontal ties.

About three-quarters of the way down the boughs, tie smaller branches horizontally between them. Lay sticks across the smaller branches to create a platform. Elevating your kindling on a platform like this ensures that it stays dry.

4 Lay tinder.

On the platform you've created, add a thick layer of dry tinder (e.g., dry grass and leaves, wood chips, birch bark, twigs, paper) and use it to build your fire. Keep adding branches to fuel the fire further.

5 Add leafy green vegetation and living brush to the fire.

This healthy vegetation will create white smoke, best seen when the sky is very blue or at night.

6 Add oil.

If it is a foggy or overcast day, add an oily substance (e.g., motor oil, tire rubber, brake fluid, cooking oil) to create black smoke.

7 Put it out.

Once help arrives, fully extinguish your fire before leaving.

WARNING!

↗ Observe which way the wind is blowing and how much dry vegetation is surrounding you to avoid starting a brush fire. You may need to create a clearing or find an area by a stream.

↗ Even white smoke can be hard to see at night. Once it is dark, focus on creating high flames that can be seen unobstructed from far away.

↗ If you have limited branches and other fuel available, wait until you see or hear signs of a search and rescue team before lighting your signal fire.

↗ Never create a fire so big that you won't be able to control it and eventually put it out with the resources at hand.

Make a tripod of three long branches, tied at the top. Three-quarters of the way down, tie smaller branches between them making a platform.

On the kindling platform, add dry grass, leaves, and twigs and leafy green vegetation.

CAN I EAT IT?

How to Set Animal Traps

Holding Traps

Use a holding trap (or snare) to trap small ground animals. Holding traps capture animals but do not kill them.

1 Procure a two-foot-long wire and a small stick.
Wire is essential—animals can bite through string and twine.

2 Wrap one end of the wire around the stick.
Twist the stick while holding the wire on both sides of the stick with your thumb and forefinger. You will create a small loop around the stick while wrapping the wire around itself.

3 Remove the stick by breaking it near the wire.
Slide the ends out. You will be left with a small loop at one end of the wire.

4 Take the other end of the wire and pass it through the loop.
This will make a snare loop, which becomes a snare that will tighten as the animal struggles. The snare loop should be about five inches in diameter.

5 Twist and tie the end of the wire to a one-foot stake.

6 Place the snare in an animal track or at the entrance to an animal burrow or hole.
You can also use two snares, one behind the other, to increase your odds of catching something. The struggling animal that escapes one snare will likely become caught in the other.

7 Anchor the stake in the ground.
Position the stake in an area where the animal won't see it. Mark it so that you can find it later.

Machine trap

8 Check the trap only once or twice daily.
Checking the trap too often may frighten away the animals. When an animal heading for its home becomes caught in the snare, it will struggle to get away, which will tighten the wire trap.

Machine Traps

Machine traps use gravity, activated by a trigger, to trap or kill animals. The easiest machine trap to build is a deadfall, where a trigger releases a rock or heavy piece of wood to trap or kill an animal.

1 Look for a well-worn animal path on which to place the trap.

2 Find three straight sticks or pieces of wood that are approximately the same length and diameter, and a large, heavy stone or log.
The length and thickness of the sticks you need will depend upon the weight of the stone or log you intend to prop up—use your judgment.

3 Cut a squared notch in the middle of one stick.
Cut the point of the stick to look like the tip of a flathead screwdriver—thin and flat. This is your upright support bar.

4 Cut a squared notch (to fit into the first squared notch like Lincoln Logs) in the middle of another stick.
On this stick, cut a triangular notch a couple of inches from one end, and whittle the other end of the stick to a point. This is your bait bar.

5 Cut a triangular notch into the middle of the last stick.
This notch should fit on the top of your support stick. Cut one point of this stick to look like the tip of a flathead screwdriver (to fit into the triangular notch of your bait bar), and cut the other end flat. This is your locking bar.

Holding trap (or snare)

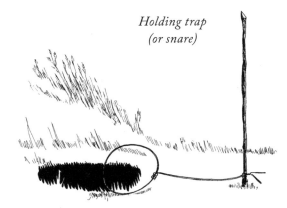

6 Anchor your support stick in the ground, perpendicular to the ground.

7 Attach a piece of meat or food to the end of your bait bar, and insert the bait bar into the notch of your support stick, parallel to the ground.

8 Place your locking bar on top of your bait and support bar, forming a 45-degree angle with your bait bar.

The screwdriver tip of your locking bar should fit into the notch at the end of your bait bar, and the tip of the support bar should fit into the triangular notch of your locking bar.

9 Lean the stone or log so that the top end rests on the top of your locking bar.

When an animal comes along the trail, it will take the bait, causing the locking bar to dislodge and trigger the deadfall, trapping or crushing your prey.

WARNING!

- To increase the odds of trapping an animal, always set multiple traps, preferably 8 to 10.
- Set the traps where animals live or in areas they frequent, near water and feeding areas. Watch animal patterns to see where they come and go regularly. Dung piles indicate nesting areas.
- Check traps once or twice daily. Dead animals will quickly rot or become food for other animals.
- Do not build the trap where you intend to place it. Build the trap components in camp, then bring them to the place you have chosen. This way, you will not frighten away animals by spending too much time in their habitats. Try to de-scent your traps using leaves or bark to remove your smell.
- Set traps in the narrow parts of animal trails, such as between rocks or in areas with thick brush on either side. Animals will generally only approach traps if there is no easy way around them. Like humans, animals tend to take the path of least resistance.
- Be careful around traps. Animal traps can injure you and can trap bigger animals than you expect.
- Be alert when approaching any trapped animal. It may not be dead, and it may attack you.
- Do not leave traps or trap elements behind when you leave an area.

How to Clean and Cook a Squirrel

1 Place the dead squirrel on the ground, belly up.

2 Pull the end of the squirrel's tail up slightly toward you.

3 Cut.

Using a very sharp knife, make a small incision across the base of the tail, where it meets the body. Do not cut the tail completely off: the cut should be deep enough to sever the tail but should leave the skin on top of the squirrel intact.

4 Split the hide.

Make an incision through the hide down the inside of one hind leg so it connects to the cut at the tail. Repeat for the other hind leg. You should have one continuous incision from the tip of one hind leg to the tail, then back up the other hind leg.

5 Place your foot on the squirrel's tail.

6 Pull.

Pull up sharply on the squirrel's hind legs. The skin should peel off from the bottom of the squirrel to the head. Squirrels have tough skin that is difficult to remove, so it will take some time.

7 Remove the head and feet.

Cut the squirrel's head off at the neck; then cut off the feet.

8 Field dress.

Slice the belly from stem to stern and remove all entrails. Discard. Rinse off excess blood with clean water.

9 Cook.

A smaller, younger squirrel will be tender and may be roasted, while an older squirrel will have tough meat that is better stewed, if a pot is available.

- **To roast.** For a youngster, sharpen a green stick (sapling) and impale the squirrel from stem to stern. Lay the sapling horizontally between two upright, forked branches positioned on either side of a fire. Slowly cook the squirrel, rotating the sapling periodically for even cooking. The meat is done when it is slightly pink inside the thickest part of the thigh. Cut with your knife to check.

- **To stew.** Cut an older squirrel into serving pieces: legs, back, and rib sections. Place the sections in a pot of boiling water. Add fuel to the fire to return the pot to a boil, then remove fuel as necessary to maintain a simmer. The squirrel is done when the meat falls off the bone easily. Remove from the heat and remove bones before eating.

Eating Lizards

Virtually all lizards are edible, but some have glands that contain toxins. Before cooking a lizard, cut it from shoulder to shoulder and discard the head and neck, where poisonous glands are located.

Edible Plants of the Ocean

NAME		CHARACTERISTICS	EDIBLE PART	HOW TO EAT
Sea lettuce (Ulva)		Light green leaves with ruffled edges	Whole plant	Wash and boil.
Dulse		Red or purple foot-long fronds attached to rocks	Whole plant	Raw, fresh, or dried.
Kelp		Olive green or brown fronds as long as 10 feet	Leaves	Discard leaf's dark membrane; boil middle section.
Irish moss		Bushy, anchored to rocks, color varies widely	Leaves	Boil; dry fronds in sun for storage.

Edible Plants of the Desert

NAME		CHARACTERISTICS	EDIBLE PART	HOW TO EAT
Acacia		Short tree; gray-white bark; small, alternating leaves; yellow ball-shaped flowers	Dark brown pods, flowers, young leaves	Raw.
Agave		Cluster of long, fleshy green leaves radiating from a central stalk	Flowers, flower buds	Boil flowers and buds before eating.
Amaranth		Tall, with alternating leaves; green flowers at top; brown/black seeds	Seeds, leaves	Seeds and leaves: raw; seeds: pound into flour.
Date palm		Tall tree with no branches; huge compound leaves at crown; yellow fruits	Fruits	Fresh or sun-dried.
Prickly pear cactus		Thick stem; clustered pads covered with needles; red or yellow flowers; punctured pads seep non-milky juice	Fruits at the top of the stalks; the pads themselves	Fruit: raw; pads: remove thorns and nodes, peel, and boil or grill.

THE OCEAN

Keep your regulator in your mouth. Keep your airway as straight as possible by looking toward the surface. Swim at a slow to moderate rate, exhaling continuously.

How to Get to the Surface If Your Scuba Tank Runs Out of Air

1 Do not panic.

2 Signal to your fellow divers that you are having a problem—point to your tank or regulator.

3 If someone comes to your aid, share their regulator, passing it back and forth while swimming slowly to the surface.

Take two breaths, then pass it back to the other diver. Ascend together, exhaling as you go. Then take another two breaths, alternating, until you reach the surface. Nearly all divers carry an extra regulator connected to their tank.

4 If no one can help you, keep your regulator in your mouth; air may expand in the tank as you ascend, giving you additional breaths.

5 Look straight up so that your airway is as straight as possible.

6 Swim to the surface at a slow to moderate rate.

Exhale continuously as you swim up. It is very important that you exhale the entire way up, but the rate at which you exhale is also important. Exhale slowly—do not exhaust all your air in the first few seconds of your ascent. As long as you are even slightly exhaling, your passageway will be open and air can vent from your lungs.

WARNING!

⚠ Never dive alone.

⚠ Watch your pressure and depth gauges closely.

⚠ Make sure your fellow divers are within easy signaling/swimming distance.

⚠ Share a regulator in an emergency. It is much safer to use your partner's regulator than to try to make a quick swim to the surface. This is especially true the deeper you are, where you need to surface gradually.

⚠ Always use an alternate air source instead of swimming up unless you are less than 30 feet below the surface.

How to Survive a Tsunami

1 If you are near the ocean, be aware of the warning signs of an approaching tsunami:

- Rise or fall in sea level
- Shaking ground
- Loud, sustained roar

2 If you are on a boat in a small harbor and you have sufficient warning of an approaching tsunami, move it quickly. Your first choice should be to dock and reach high ground. Your second choice is to take your boat far into open water, away from shore where it might be thrown into the dock or the land. Tsunamis cause damage when they move from deeper to shallower waters; the waves back up against one another at the shallow shelf. Often tsunamis are not even felt in deep water.

3 If you are on land, seek higher ground immediately. Tsunamis can move faster than a person can run. Get away from the coastline as quickly as possible.

4 If you are in a high-rise hotel or apartment building on the coastline and you do not have enough time to get to higher ground away from the shore, move to a high floor of the building.

The upper floors of a high-rise building can provide safe refuge.

How to Survive Adrift at Sea

1 Stay aboard your boat as long as possible before you get into a life raft.

In a maritime emergency, the rule of thumb is that you should step up into your raft, meaning you should be up to your waist in water before you get into the raft. Your best chance of survival is on a boat—even a disabled one—not on a life raft. But if the boat is sinking, know how to use a life raft.

2 Get in the life raft, and take whatever supplies you can carry.

Most important, if you have water in jugs, take it with you. Do not drink seawater. A person can last for several days without food at sea, but without clean water to drink, death is a virtual certainty within several days. If worse comes to worst, throw the jugs of water overboard so that you can get them later—they will float. Many canned foods, particularly vegetables, are packed in water, so take those with you if you can. Do not ration water; drink it as needed, but don't drink more than necessary—½ gallon a day should be sufficient if you limit your activity.

3 Remain in the vicinity of the ship you've abandoned.

Rescuers answering an SOS message have the best chance of finding you if you stay close to your starting coordinates. Construct a makeshift sea anchor by tying a rope around the handle of a bucket or a roll of expendable clothing, and secure the other end of the rope to the raft. Put the anchor in the water on the windward side to keep the front of the boat facing into the wind, making the raft less likely to capsize and minimizing the amount of drift caused by wind.

4 If you are in a cold water/weather environment, get warm.

You are more likely to die of exposure or hypothermia than of anything else. Put on dry clothes and stay out of the water; prolonged exposure to salt water can damage your skin and cause lesions, which are prone to infection. Stay covered. Modern life rafts have canopies, which protect passengers from sun, wind, and rain. If the canopy is missing or damaged, wear a hat, long sleeves, and pants to protect yourself from the sun.

5 Find food, if you can.

Life rafts include fishing hooks in their survival kits. If your raft is floating for several weeks, seaweed will form on its underside and fish will naturally congregate in the shade under you. You can catch them with the hook and eat the flesh raw. If no hook is available, you can fashion one using wire or even shards of aluminum from an empty can.

6 Use the wind to your advantage.

If you were not able to issue a distress call before you abandoned ship and you do not believe that help is on the way, improvise a sail. Tie two paddles securely to opposite sides of the raft. Stretch a sheet or poncho between the upright paddles. Use a third paddle as a rudder.

7 Read the clouds for signs of land.

Dense, puffy clouds with a flat bottom (cumulus clouds) in an otherwise clear sky usually form over land. White, fluffy clouds indicate good weather. A darker color spells rain. A greenish tint is known as "lagoon glare," which results from sunlight reflecting off shallow water, where it may be easiest to catch fish.

8 Let animals be your guides.

Seals in water are a guarantee than land is nearby, since they rarely venture far from shore. Single seabirds often leave land far behind, but flocks of birds are almost never more than six miles from the shore. They fly out to sea in the morning and return in the late afternoon to roost. Base your direction of travel on the time of day, heading in the opposite direction of the birds' flight in the morning and following them to shore in the evening.

9 Try to get to land, if you know where it is.

Most rafts include small paddles, but life rafts are not very maneuverable, especially in any wind above three knots. Do not exhaust yourself—you will not be able to move any significant distance without great effort.

10 If you see a plane or boat nearby, try to signal them.

Use a VHF radio or a handheld flare kit to get their attention. A small mirror can also be used for signaling.

WARNING!

↗ Any craft that sails in open water should have at least one life raft. Smaller boats may have only life jackets, so these vessels should stay within easy swimming distance of land.

↗ Do not drink salt water directly from the ocean. Spread a tarp for collecting rainwater and dew. If the tarp is coated with dried salt, wash it off in seawater before spreading it; there will not be enough salt introduced by rinsing the tarp in seawater to harm you. Drink as much rainwater as you can to remain hydrated, especially when your freshwater supply is limited.

↗ Sunburn is a serious concern while afloat at sea. If your life raft does not already have a roof, rig one using whatever material you have available and cover all exposed skin. Your face and neck are especially vulnerable and in need of protection.

↗ If you see sharks in the water near you, remain still and quiet. Do not put any body parts or equipment in the water. If you have a fish on the line when you spot a shark, let the fish go. Do not gut the fish into the water when sharks are near.

How to Eat at Sea If You're Allergic to Fish

⊙ Test possible food sources for poison.
There is a wide variety of non-fish animal and plant life in the ocean, including sea cucumbers, sea urchins, and many varieties of snails. To analyze any potential food, place it on your tongue. If it stings your mouth or tastes revolting, spit it out. If the taste is acceptable, swallow a thimble-sized portion and wait one hour. Since most poisons produce symptoms in a short time, if you still feel fine, eat a small serving. If no symptoms occur within the next 12 hours, the food can be considered edible.

⊙ Eat seaweed.
Red, brown, and green seaweed are all excellent sources of protein, carbohydrates, iodine, and vitamin C. Dry thin leaves in the sun until they are crisp; then use them to flavor soups or broths. Thick varieties are best if they are washed in freshwater and boiled before they are consumed.

⊙ Make a bird trap.
Tie a loose noose knot with a piece of thin twine. Place fish entrails or another bait in the middle of the circle, then hold one end of the twine in your dominant hand. When the bird lands in the circle, cinch the line around its legs. Eat all of its meat and save the feathers, which can be used for insulation and fishing lures to catch more bait.

⊙ Collect plankton.
Plankton is the foundation of the food web for a good reason: it contains protein, fat, and carbohydrates. If you are unable to find any other edible plants or animals, tie a cotton shirt or another piece of permeable fabric to a sea anchor to collect and strain a remarkable amount of plankton from the sea. Remove all spiny material and stinging tentacles before eating. Exhaust all other food options first—it is easy to consume too much salt water along with plankton, and depending on your location, there is a danger of ingesting poisonous dinoflagellates.

WARNING!

🗡 Shoe leather and other items of clothing are not viable sources of energy, even when you are starving. The human digestive tract is not built to process leather, and the nutritional value of fabrics such as cotton or wool is insignificant. However, the taste of leather bears enough similarity to overcooked meat that chewing on it may deliver a psychological benefit in truly desperate situations.

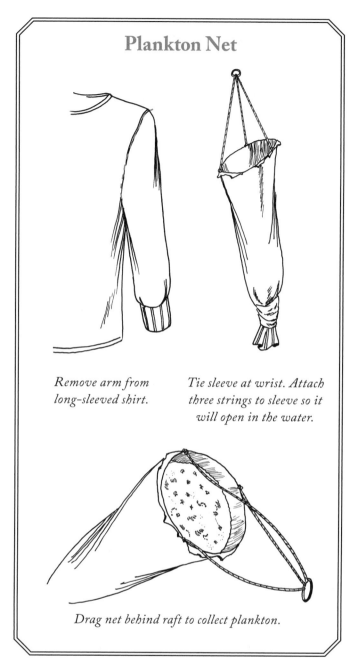

Plankton Net

Remove arm from long-sleeved shirt.

Tie sleeve at wrist. Attach three strings to sleeve so it will open in the water.

Drag net behind raft to collect plankton.

Rip Currents

- A long line of sandy or muddy water and debris heading out to sea, perpendicular to the shore, are signs of a rip current.

- If you are caught in a rip current, swim parallel to the shore until you are free of the water's pull—a typical rip current is less than 10 feet across.

- Never attempt to swim directly to shore in a rip current; you will quickly tire and will not be able to fight the power of the current.

COLD WEATHER

How to Survive Being Stranded in Snow

1 Get as far off the road as possible.
Drive or push your vehicle fully clear of the roadway, but be sure that your car is still visible to any vehicles that may pass by and be able to offer assistance.

2 Make your car visible to potential rescuers.
Turn on your emergency flashers. When the snow stops falling, raise the car's hood to signal distress; when snow begins to fall again, close the hood. Set up flares along the roadside between your car and the road. Hang a brightly colored cloth such as a red scarf or a torn-off piece of blanket from the antenna.

3 Spell out HELP in the snow.
Use rocks and sticks to spell the word HELP in six-foot-long block letters next to the car so your position is visible from the air.

4 Stay near the car.
Do not leave the vicinity of your vehicle unless help is visible within 10 yards. Blowing and drifting snow can be extremely disorienting, causing you to wander away from your car deeper into the snow and become lost. Shelter is your most important priority in inclement weather.

5 Put on all available clothing.
If traveling with clothes, put them on in layers. Wrap yourself in blankets stored in the trunk. Strip the leather or vinyl from your seats and wrap yourself in them.

6 Run the engine for 10 minutes once an hour.
Clear snow from the exhaust pipe, and crack one upwind window to keep carbon monoxide from building up in the car. While the engine is running, turn on the heater to keep body temperature above 90°F, warding off hypothermia and frostbite.

7 Remain active.
While sitting in the car, periodically rotate your torso from side to side, move your torso from side to side, and move your arms and legs to keep blood flow moving.

8 Huddle for warmth.
If traveling with others, sit in a row in the backseat, wrapping your arms and legs together to stay warm. Take turns sleeping.

Spell out "HELP" in the snow with rocks and sticks.

9 Forage.
If the snow stops, walk along the shoulder of the road in either direction of your car in search of water, cast-off fast-food containers, edible plants, or roadkill. Never let your vehicle out of sight.

10 Eat snow.
Keep hydrated by eating chunks of the cleanest snow you can find.

11 Build a signal fire with a tire.
Remove the spare tire from the trunk, or remove one tire from the car using a tire jack. Set the tire on the roadway or on the ground near the road that's cleared of snow. Fill up the center of the tire with dry sticks and paper products from your car, and ignite it with the car's cigarette lighter or any other means of ignition. Keep the fire burning until it achieves the 400°F necessary to ignite the tire itself. Once lit, a tire will produce a thick black smoke. Do not inhale the smoke, as it contains carbon monoxide, sulfur dioxide, and numerous other toxic chemicals.

How to Fish on Ice

1 Find bait or fashion a lure.
Small fish sometimes congregate near the surface in shallow waters. If the ice is thin enough to see through, drop a heavy rock and gather the fish that have been stunned. If finding live bait is impractical, make a lure by tying feathers from a bird or a down sleeping bag to the base of a fishing hook, camouflaging its barb.

2 Identify the best spot for catching big fish.
Large fish tend to favor deep pools. Investigate your surroundings to determine where the deep water is likely to be, such as on the outer banks of a bay. Remember that ice fishing is like all fishing: some spots will be more productive than others for reasons that are difficult to parse.

3 Read the ice to minimize your danger of falling through.
Dirty ice tends to be weaker than thick ice. Snow-covered ice tends to be thinner than bare ice. Always avoid rocks or other objects that protrude from the surface of the ice; underlying currents and eddies can have a warming effect. When walking on river ice, stick to the inside portion of any bends; the faster-moving water on the outside of bends makes for weaker ice.

4 Cut a hole in the thick ice.
Use a saw or a long knife to carve out a hole in the ice. Never use a naturally occurring hole, which is likely to be surrounded by dangerously thin ice. If your tools are insufficient, build a small fire to melt a hole in the ice.

5 Bait your hook.
If you are using live bait, insert the hook below the dorsal fin, making a hole beneath the backbone.

6 Lower your line as deep as possible.

7 Slowly pull the line toward the surface.
Jiggle it up and down as you raise it.

8 If your hole is productive, keep it from freezing over when not in use.
Cover the hole with branches and snow. Check it routinely, and chop through any new layer of ice that has formed.

BE AWARE!

⚔ Make hooks of various sizes to maximize your potential catch. The sturdiest hooks are made from strips of metal or carved bone. Carved wood can also be used; season it over a flame to harden it first.

⚔ When you catch a fish, investigate the contents of its stomach. If it contains freshly swallowed fish, save them as bait. Use partially digested food as chum, tossing it through your hole to attract more fish. Learn what the fish like to eat and try to bait your hook with similar food.

Warm the pole with your hands until your tongue comes loose.

How to Treat a Tongue Stuck on a Pole

1 Do not panic.

2 Do not pull the tongue from the pole.
Pulling sharply will be very painful.

3 Move closer to the pole.
Get as close as possible without letting more of the tongue's surface area touch the pole.

4 Warm the pole with your hands.
A tongue will stick when the surface of the pole is very cold. The top few layers of the tongue will freeze when the tongue touches the pole, causing bonding. Place your gloved hands on the area of the pole closest to the tongue. Hold them there for several minutes.

5 Take a test pull.
As the pole warms, the frozen area around the tongue should begin to thaw. Gently pull the tongue away from the pole. You may leave a layer or two of skin on the pole, which will be painful, but the tongue will quickly heal.

Alternative Method

⊙ Use warm water.
Pour water from a water bottle over the tongue and the pole. Do not use water that is cold, or it may freeze and exacerbate the problem.

WARNING!

⚔ Do not try to loosen your tongue with your own saliva: Although saliva is relatively warm, the small amount you will be able to generate is likely to freeze on your tongue.

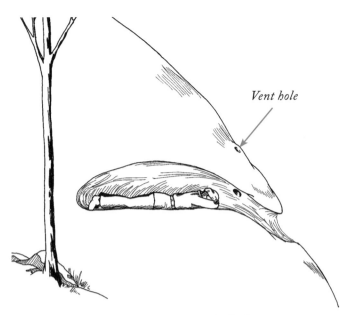

Dig your snow cave into the drift, at a right angle to the prevailing wind.

Vent hole

How to Build a Shelter in the Snow

Building a Snow Trench

1 Map out a trench so that the opening is at a right angle to the prevailing wind.

You need to find a space large enough so that the width and length are just a bit longer and taller than your body when lying down. You need only a minimal depth to maintain a cozy space for body heat conservation.

2 Dig the trench with a wider, flatter opening on one end for your head, using whatever tools you have or can create.

A cooking pan or long, flat piece of wood works well as an entrenching tool.

3 Cover the top of the trench with layers of branches; then a tarp, plastic sheeting, or whatever is available; then a thin layer of snow.

A "door" can be made using a backpack, blocks of snow, or whatever materials provide some ventilation and yet block the heat-robbing effects of the wind.

Building a Snow Cave

1 Find a large snowdrift or snowbank on a slope.

Plan your cave with the opening at a right angle to the prevailing wind.

2 Dig a narrow tunnel into the slope (toward the back of the slope) and slightly upward.

Create a cavern big enough to lie in without touching the sides, roof, or ends.

3 Make the ceiling slightly dome-shaped.

A flat ceiling has no strength and will in most cases collapse before you are finished digging. The roof should be at least 12 inches thick. If you can see blue-green light (from filtered sunlight) through the top, the roof is too thin.

4 Put a small vent hole in the roof.

The hole will provide fresh air and a vent for a candle, if you are going to use one. Do not add any heat source larger than a small candle. Excessive heat will cause the ceiling to soften, drip, and weaken.

Building a Quin-Zhee

If snow depth is minimal and you have a lot of time and energy, build a quin-zhee. A quin-zhee is a snow shelter that was developed by the Athabascan Indians, who lived mainly in Canada and Alaska.

1 Pile up a very large mound of packed snow.

The pile needs to be big enough for you to sit or lie down comfortably inside when it is hollowed out.

2 Wait an hour for the snow to consolidate.

3 Dig in and build a snow cave.

BE AWARE!

🗡 A preferable alternative to building a snow shelter is a man-made structure or vehicle. If none is available, search for anything that will help protect your body from heat loss. Caves, downed timber, or rock outcroppings can help protect you from the elements.

🗡 If you cannot stay dry in the process of building a snow shelter, or you cannot get dry after you have built it, do not build it! Moving enough snow to create a shelter big enough for even just one person is hard work, and any contact of your skin or clothing with snow while digging will amplify your body's heat losses.

🗡 When building a shelter, the oldest snow will be the easiest to work with, since it consolidates over time.

🗡 Snow is an excellent insulating and sound-absorbing material. From within a snow shelter, you will be unlikely to hear a search party or aircraft. You may want to make a signal aboveground that can be noticed by a search party (a tarp, the word "HELP" or "SOS" spelled out in wood).

🗡 In any shelter, use whatever you can find to keep yourself off the ground or snow. If pine boughs or similar soft, natural materials can be found, layer them a foot or more high, since the weight of your body will compress them considerably.

🗡 When you are inside, the warmth from your body and your exhaled warm air will keep your shelter somewhat comfortable.

How to Treat Frostbite

1 Remove wet clothing and dress the area with warm, dry clothing.

2 Immerse frozen areas in warm water (100°F–105°F) or apply warm compresses for 10 to 30 minutes.

3 If warm water is not available, wrap gently in warm blankets.

4 Avoid direct heat, including electric or gas fires, heating pads, and hot water bottles.

5 Never thaw the area if it is at risk of refreezing; this can cause severe tissue damage.

6 Do not rub frostbitten skin or rub snow on it.

7 Take a pain reliever such as aspirin or ibuprofen during rewarming to lessen the pain.

Rewarming will be accompanied by a severe burning sensation. There may be skin blistering and soft tissue swelling, and the skin may turn red, blue, or purple in color. When skin is pink and no longer numb, the area is thawed.

8 Apply sterile dressings to the affected areas.

Place the dressing between fingers or toes if they have been affected. Try not to disturb any blisters, wrap rewarmed areas to prevent refreezing, and have the patient keep thawed areas as still as possible.

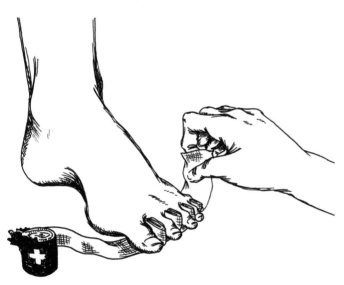

After thawing the skin in warm water, sensation will return and it may be painful. Apply sterile dressings to the affected areas, placing it between toes or fingers if they have been frostbitten. Severe frostbite may cause the skin to blister or swell. Wrap area to prevent refreezing, and seek medical treatment.

9 Get medical treatment as soon as possible.

WARNING!

⚡ Frostbite is a condition caused by the freezing of water molecules in skin cells and occurs in very cold temperatures. It is characterized by white, waxy skin that feels numb and hard. More severe cases result in a bluish-black skin color, and the most severe cases result in gangrene, which may lead to amputation. Affected areas are generally fingertips and toes, and the nose, ears, and cheeks. Frostbite should be treated by a medical professional.

How to Build a Trail in Waist-Deep Snow

⊙ Read the terrain before choosing a route.

In the mountains, perfectly flat expanses of snow can indicate a body of water underneath. Where possible, follow a path made up of slight inclines next to steeper slopes, to minimize the possibility of traversing incompletely frozen ponds or lakes. Never walk within five feet of a precipice, as snow can drift to form unstable cornices that overhang solid ground by several feet.

⊙ Favor hard snow.

Hard snow tends to be shiny, with light reflecting off its upper crust. It will bear your weight better than soft, powdery snow.

⊙ Make your footprint bigger to minimize sinking.

Wear snowshoes, or wrap rags and bundles of sticks around your legs. If you don't have snowshoes and cannot locate natural materials to make your own, wrap your legs in extra clothes, a torn tarp, or another material that will help prevent your pants from becoming waterlogged, which would increase the potential for frostbite and hypothermia.

⊙ Use walking poles or a stick to probe the ground in front of you.

If the tips break through the ice, walk backward several paces, retracing your footsteps. Survey your surroundings, then choose another route.

⊙ Take small steps.

As you progress, tamp down the snow forcefully with your feet and knees to make the trail more permanent.

⊙ When in a group, walk in a single-file line.

Because breaking trail requires far more energy than walking over a firm path, share the effort by rotating the leader to the back of the line every 15 minutes. Switching frequently will minimize water lost through perspiration by any one member of the group, ultimately conserving fluids for all and preventing unwanted sweat from cooling the body too rapidly.

ARCTIC

How to Survive on Ice until the Rescue Party Arrives

✪ **Wear several layers of loose clothing.**
While exposure is the obvious danger in an arctic environment, you must also avoid overheating, which can lead to sweat that may freeze and cause hypothermia.

✪ **Breathe slowly, through one or more layers of clothing.**
Very cold air inhaled too rapidly can damage the lungs and chill the entire body.

✪ **Keep all of your skin covered at all times.**
Frostbite can kill human tissue in minutes under extreme conditions.

✪ **Protect your eyes with UV-blocking goggles.**
Snow and ice amplify the effects of solar radiation, making snow blindness a real possibility. Keep your eyes covered at all times, even in cloudy conditions; just because the sun isn't visible doesn't mean that it isn't emitting harmful UV rays.

✪ **Melt snow and ice thoroughly before drinking.**
Heating snow or ice in your mouth consumes valuable calories stored in your body and may elevate the risk of hypothermia. If you can't make a fire, use your body heat: place the snow or ice in a bag and insert it between layers of clothing. If you have the option, melt ice, which yields more water than a similar volume of snow.

✪ **Carry a long, sturdy pole while walking over ice.**
Position the pole across your body, at belt level, as you move. Should the ice break beneath you, the pole may save you from falling all the way through into the frigid water below.

✪ **Remain constantly aware of the conditions of the ice and snow beneath you.**
Dirty ice is weaker than clean ice of the same thickness because its dark color absorbs more heat from the sun. Snow-covered ice tends to be thinner than bare ice. In areas where there is a danger of avalanche, travel early in the morning, before the sun warms any of the snow and increases the chance of a slide. In mountainous terrain, snow often forms cornices that extend several feet from the lee side of ridges; these can easily break off when stepped on.

✪ **When crossing thin ice, crawl on all fours to distribute your weight.**

When walking across ice, hold a long pole parallel to the ice at waist level.

✪ **Dig in during whiteout conditions.**
Never travel during a severe storm, as you will quickly lose your way and expose yourself to dangers in the terrain that could be avoided if you were able to be more alert.

✪ **Build small, well-ventilated shelters.**
Ice caves and snow trenches should be as small as possible to take advantage of your body heat, with holes for air to prevent suffocation. Never build a shelter out of metal, such as airplane wreckage, as it will whisk away whatever heat you generate. Don't sleep directly on the ground; create a layer of bedding made of fabric or grass to insulate your body.

Techniques for Staying Warm in Subzero Temperatures

- Wear a foundation garment of synthetic material.
- Eat a lot, twice as much as you would in warm weather.
- Eat carbohydrates in the beginning and middle of the day.
- Constantly perform small exercises.
- If you begin sweating, slow down or pause exercise, to avoid cold/freezing sweat.

How to Build an Igloo

1 Trace a circle on a flat stretch of hardened snow.
Make the circle about 12 feet in diameter.

2 Cut bricks of dry, densely compacted snow.
Using a saw or knife, carve about 50 bricks from the snow, each about three feet long, one foot high, and eight inches thick. Cut some of them from one half of the area within your circle and the rest from a rectangular trench extending six feet from the near edge. The wall of your igloo will pass between these two pits, which you will later connect to create an entrance.

3 Arrange a layer of bricks around the edge of the circle.
Allow the bricks to lean slightly inward. Press the edges together firmly, and pack snow into crevices and cracks.

4 Shave a diagonal cut from the top of the layer of bricks.
Use a snow saw to cut the bricks at an angle toward the center of the circle to enable you to stack the rest of the bricks in a spiral.

5 Stack bricks on the first layer to form the walls.
Stop building when the dome is halfway complete. Use snow to seal cracks and cement each new brick in place. Take your time; building an igloo is a slow process.

6 Dig a tunnel through (or beneath) the foundation bricks.
When the dome is about halfway complete, create a crawl space that will serve as an entryway to the igloo. Connect the tunnel to the trench from which you cut your bricks to serve as a cold sink—cold air will fall to the bottom of the finished igloo, allowing you to sleep in comparatively warm air.

7 Build an elevated bed inside the unfinished dome.
Pile insulating materials atop the ledge where you did not cut any bricks.

8 Complete the dome.
Continue adding bricks until you reach the top. The last brick must be larger than the final hole at the top. Standing inside the igloo, shape it with your knife or saw until it nestles into the space.

9 Cut airholes in the walls of the igloo.
Carve one hole near the top and another near the entrance. Insufficient ventilation may lead to suffocation or carbon monoxide poisoning (if you build a fire inside the igloo). Check the holes regularly for blockage from ice and snow.

10 Build a roof over the entrance trench.
Use the remaining bricks to cover the entry, which will prevent snow from blowing into the igloo.

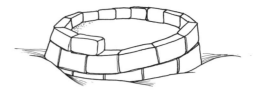

Shave a diagonal cut from the first layer of bricks.

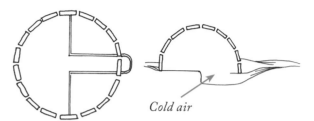

Cold air

Stack bricks on top to form walls.

Cold air will sink into the lower level of the igloo.

The final square must be larger than the hole at the top.

WARNING!

⚡ Igloos are hard to construct but offer a warmer, sturdier home than a snow cave. If there is good reason to believe that help will arrive in a day or two, consider saving your energy and building a more primitive shelter. If you will be on the ice for several days or longer, however, an igloo will repay your efforts with unbeatable protection from sun, wind, and cold exposure.

⚡ The ideal snow for building an igloo is sturdy enough that you can stand on it without sinking but soft enough that you can insert a stick into it without difficulty.

⚡ Even with a multitiered shelter and a fire, you will not be able to heat the air in the igloo warmer than a few degrees above freezing. However, the temperature inside will not drop below 0°F, no matter how cold it is outside the shelter.

⚡ Keep plenty of food, fuel, and a shovel inside the igloo; if a storm blows in, you may be trapped inside for days and have to dig yourself out of the newly fallen snow.

⚡ Stop drips in the walls of the igloo by packing new snow over the source.

⚡ Knock loose snow off your boots and clothing before entering the igloo.

7

Getting Around

UNSAFE AT ANY SPEED

BOATS

How to Make an Emergency Flotation Device Out of Your Pants

1 Remove your pants.
Slip out of your pants one leg at a time, treading water with the opposite leg and arm to stay afloat until the pants are off.

2 Knot the legs.
Take the bottom hole of each leg and tie it off like a trash bag.

3 Button the fly.

4 Flip the pants over your head.
Grasp the waistband on one side and swing the pants over your head from back to front, bringing the waist opening down hard on the surface of the water. This traps air in each leg.

5 Pull the waist down under the surface of the water so the inflated legs are poking up in a V formation.

6 Lean into the V of inflated pant legs.
Kick your legs to propel yourself to safety.

How to Sail Through a Typhoon

1 Reduce speed.

2 Determine your position.
Plot your position on your chart relative to the position of the storm, wind direction and speed, and estimated time to your destination.

3 Adjust your course.
Navigate toward the closest shoreline.

4 Instruct all passengers to put on their personal flotation devices immediately.
Put on your life jacket as well.

5 Assign specific duties to each passenger.
Instruct one crew member to look out for danger areas, debris, or other boats, and another to turn on all bilge pumps.

6 Close hatches, ports, and windows.

7 Secure loose items.
Move loose items below deck. Tie down anything that cannot be moved below deck.

Remove your pants, knot the legs, close the fly, and flip the pants over your head so they fill with air.

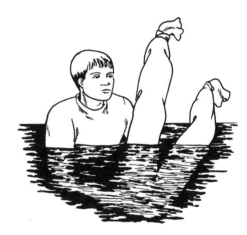

Holding the waist, pull the pants straight down into the water.

Lean into the V of the inflated pant legs and kick.

8 Lower the sails or change to storm sails.

9 Prepare the lifeboat.
Equip with emergency food, water, and first aid kit.

10 Unplug any electrical equipment.
Turn off circuit breakers and disconnect antennas. Instruct passengers and crew to avoid contact with metal objects.

11 Direct the bow into winds.
Approach waves at a 40- to 45-degree angle.

12 Keep passengers low and to the center of the boat.
Rig jack lines, lifelines, and safety harnesses to anyone who needs to be on deck.

WARNING!

🗲 Clouds are the best indicators of weather. Watch for stratus clouds that lower or cumulus clouds that rise up and turn into cumulonimbus clouds, both indicators of approaching storms.

🗲 When you first realize that you are facing inclement weather, radio in to the Coast Guard, as well as other boats. Inform them of your location and float plan.

HOW TO FLIP AN OVERTURNED KAYAK

1 Bend forward at the waist.
Being upside down in a kayak puts your entire torso underwater, making it impossible to breathe. Do not thrash about in the water, which is only likely to empty your lungs of air and make your situation worse. When your kayak overturns, curl at the waist and count to three to help you regain your calm as the kayak naturally aligns in a stable position in the turbulent water. Keep a tight grip on your paddle.

2 Lean toward the left side of the boat.
Flex at the hip to hold yourself in position.

3 Line up your paddle parallel to the kayak.
Hold the paddle firmly in both hands.

4 Sweep the paddle blade away from the boat.
With your right hand, which will be closest to the bow (front) of the kayak, move the paddle outward, keeping it just beneath the surface of the water.

5 Lean upward.
Move your head and torso as close to the surface as possible, resisting the urge to pull your head completely out of the water.

6 Snap your hips to flip the kayak.
As your sweeping paddle motion is midway to completion, quickly snap your hips in one fluid motion so that instead of leaning your torso all the way toward your left side, you will be leaning all the way to the right as the kayak comes underneath your center of gravity. The friction of your paddle in the water will combine with the hip snap to create enough momentum to flip the boat partially onto its keel. Your head and torso will still be touching the water's surface.

7 Recover your stability.
In a fluid continuation of the flip, bend your torso out of the water, using your legs and abdominal muscles to bring the kayak closer to your head. As the kayak begins to sit upright in the water, whip your head from the water surface and sit up straight.

WARNING!

🗲 Kayaks flip easily in turbulent water. If you are not confident in your kayaking skills, or if you lack experience in fast-moving water, practice flipping the kayak over in still water.

Sweep the paddle away from the boat, moving your head and torso closer to the surface.

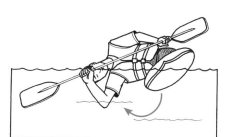

Rotate your hips so that you are leaning all the way to the right.

As the kayak rights itself, pull your shoulders and head back into an upright position.

HOW TO SURVIVE GOING DOWN WITH A SINKING SHIP

1 Dress in your warmest clothes.

When the abandon-ship signal is given, or if you suspect it is about to be given, put on multiple layers of clothes, preferably made of wool. Wear a hat and gloves, and wrap a scarf or towel around your neck. Clothes offer the best protection against hypothermia.

2 Put on your life vest.

Cabins are equipped with life vests for each passenger. Pull one over your head and securely fasten the straps.

3 Gather portable, high-calorie foods.

Stuff chocolates and candy in your pockets.

4 Move to the top deck.

Quickly make your way to the uppermost deck of the ship, to put as much distance as possible between yourself and the water.

5 Get in a lifeboat.

Women and children will be taken into the boats first.

6 If you cannot get into a lifeboat, jump at the last possible moment.

A human can expect to live only 30 to 90 minutes in water that is 32°F to 40°F. Remain on the ship until you see crew members jumping. Swim toward the lifeboats and as far away from the ship as you can get, so that you won't be pulled under when the ship goes down. Swim no farther than you have to, since movement in cold water increases the rate of heat loss.

7 Make a life raft.

If you are unable to get on a lifeboat, grab a piece of floating debris to use as a raft. An overturned boat, a door, and a large piece of wood are all good alternatives. You want something larger than you are so that you can completely climb out of the water, as cold water saps your body heat 25 times faster than air of the same temperature.

8 Wring out your wet clothes.

Once on a raft or improvised flotation device, squeeze the water out of your clothes so that they will provide better insulation.

9 Assume the "heat escape lessening posture" (HELP).

If you are still in the water, cross your ankles, draw your knees to your chest, and cross your arms over your chest. Keep your hands high on your chest or neck to keep them warm. Remain still.

10 Look for signs of hypothermia.

Once you are rescued, watch for slurred speech and a lack of shivering, both signs of severe body-temperature loss.

11 Warm up.

Remove wet clothing and wrap your body in several layers of warm, dry clothing. Drink warm beverages, but avoid coffee, tea, and alcohol, which will lead to dehydration.

WARNING!

↯ Cardiac arrest can occur immediately upon exposure of the head and chest to cold water, due to the sudden increase in blood pressure. Another danger is respiratory shock, when cold water causes the trachea to close, making it impossible to breathe.

↯ A sinking ocean liner creates a column of air bubbles above it, so people who get pulled under are falling through air rather than water. This decreases the chance to resurface and survive.

Survival Time in Water

WATER TEMPERATURE	LOSS OF DEXTERITY	EXHAUSTION/UNCONSCIOUSNESS	ESTIMATED SURVIVAL TIME
32.5°F	Less than 2 minutes	Less than 15 minutes	15–45 minutes
32.5°F–40°F	Less than 3 minutes	15–30 minutes	15–90 minutes
40°F–50°F	Less than 5 minutes	30–60 minutes	30 minutes–3 hours
50°F–60°F	10–15 minutes	1–2 hours	1–6 hours
60°F–70°F	30–40 minutes	2–7 hours	2–40 hours
70°F–80 °F	1–2 hours	2–12 hours	3-plus hours
Above 80°F	2–12 hours	Unlikely	Indefinite

TRAINS

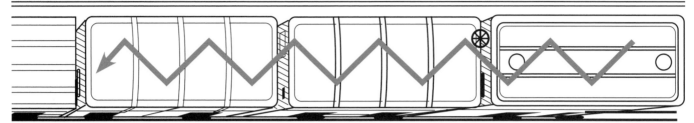

Crouch low and move slowly forward, swaying with the side-to-side motion of the train. Look for a ladder between cars.

HOW TO MANEUVER ON TOP OF A MOVING TRAIN AND GET INSIDE

1 Do not try to stand up straight (you probably will not be able to anyway).

Stay bent slightly forward, leaning into the wind. If the train is moving faster than 30 mph, it will be difficult to maintain your balance and resist the wind, so crawling on all fours may be the best method until you can get down.

2 If the train is approaching a turn, lie flat; do not try to keep your footing.

The car may have guide rails along the edge to direct water. If it does, grab them and hold on.

3 If the train is approaching a tunnel entrance, lie flat, and quickly.

There is actually quite a bit of clearance between the top of the train and the top of the tunnel—about three feet—but not nearly enough room to stand. Do not assume that you can walk or crawl to the end of the car to get down and inside before you reach the tunnel—you probably can't.

4 Move your body with the rhythm of the train—from side to side and forward.

Do not proceed in a straight line. Spread your feet apart about 36 inches, and wobble from side to side as you move forward.

5 Find the ladder at the end of the car (between two cars) and climb down.

It is very unlikely that there will be a ladder on the side of the car—they usually appear only in the movies, to make the stunts more exciting.

WARNING!

↗ The sizes and shapes of the cars on a freight train may vary widely. This can make it either easier or significantly more difficult to cross from one car to another. A 12-foot-high boxcar may be next to a flatbed or a rounded chem car.

HOW TO ESCAPE FROM A STALLED SUBWAY CAR

1 Alert the authorities about the situation.

Locate the two-way radios at the front or rear of the car. Depress the call button to speak. Release the button to listen.

2 Move forward to the next car.

Walk to the front of the train (in the direction in which the train had been traveling) if the danger is in your car. Open the door at the front of the car, and step carefully over the coupling between cars to the door of the next car. If you cannot see in the darkness of the tunnel, use a cell phone or other mobile device to cast illumination on the tracks.

3 Remain on the train.

Do not get off the train unless you are in immediate danger and have no other option.

4 If you must leave the train, pull the emergency brake.

Pull the emergency brake before leaving the train car. This will make it impossible for the train to move, so it cannot run you over once you are down on the tracks.

5 Exit the train car and climb down from the coupling between cars.

Take off any backpacks or other encumbrances. Step down onto the track bed and step over the tracks to the platform wall. Avoid stepping on the "third rail," which runs alongside the subway tracks and carries more than 600 volts of electricity. Climb up onto the platform.

6 If you cannot reach the platform, walk alongside the tracks until you reach a benchwall.

Hug the platform edge and move as quickly as possible in the direction the train was traveling. Locate the benchwall, a small passageway leading off the main tunnel. Enter the benchwall and await help.

7 If the train begins moving behind you, lie down.

Find the depression in the concrete between the rails and lie down. There will be enough room for the train to pass over you.

How to Stop a Runaway Passenger Train

1 Locate the emergency brake.
There is an emergency brake valve just inside each end of every passenger car. These valves are generally red and should be clearly marked.

2 Pull the handle.
This opens a valve that vents brake-pipe air pressure to the atmosphere, applying the brakes for an emergency stop. There is a possibility of derailment, depending upon track curvature and grade, train weight, and the number of coaches.

If the Brake Does Not Work

1 Call for help.
Locate a crew member's radio. Depress the Talk button between the earpiece and the microphone. Do not change the channel, even if you do not hear an answer. Transmit an emergency distress call: give any information that may help the listener understand the location of the train (for example, train number and destination). The train dispatcher should hear you and may clear traffic without responding. If you cannot find anyone on the radio, you will have to attempt to stop the train yourself.

2 Make your way to the front of the train.
Pull all emergency brake valves as you proceed, or instruct other passengers to apply hand brakes. These brakes are different from the red valves described earlier and are located at each end of the passenger coach, inside the vestibule. They are applied by turning a wheel or pumping a lever. Tighten these valves as much as possible, and leave them applied.

3 Enter the locomotive.
The locomotive is usually right after the baggage car, just in front of the passenger coaches. Exercise extreme caution when stepping over and across the car couplers that connect the locomotive and baggage car. There may be several locomotives on the train—not just one. Repeat the following steps in each locomotive. However, there is a chance that the trailing locomotive cab will be reversed, and that you will not be able to proceed any farther forward. If this is the case, retreat to the last car of the train and follow the instructions for "If the Train Is Not Slowing or a Crash Is Imminent" (facing page).

4 Open all emergency valves located in the engine room on or near the dash (at the left side of the cab).
The emergency valves will be clearly marked. Place the handles in the farthest position forward.

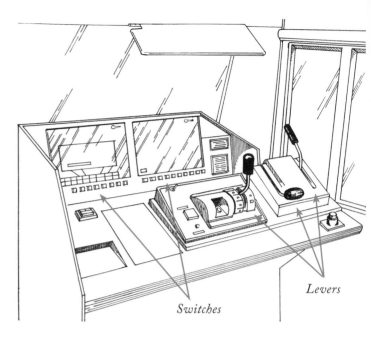

Move all levers and handles forward, toward the windshield. Push all white switches down.

5 Move all levers and handles forward, toward the windshield.
Be certain to move the brake valves forward (they will have the word "Brake" at the base of the handles). Quickly push or move down all white sliding switches on and around the control stand to shut off electricity to the engine(s).

6 If the train is still not slowing down, enter the engine room, which will be behind you to your right.
A very loud engine room will indicate that the locomotive is "under load," or still operating.

7 Move rapidly through the engine room, along the engine block.
The engine block stands about four or five feet tall and looks like a large automobile engine.

8 Shut down the engine by pulling the layshaft lever.
This is a two-foot-long handle at shoulder height near the end of the engine block. It may be difficult to find, as it is not painted a different color from the engine itself. Push the handle all the way in, and the engine will run too fast and shut down. This lever is mechanical and will shut down the engine without fail.

9 Return to the cab and sound the whistle to warn others of your approach—it may take several miles to stop the train completely.
The whistle is either a handle the size of your hand that points upward, or a button located on the control panel marked Horn.

How to Jump from a Moving Train

1 Move to the rear of the last car.

If this is not an option, you can jump from the space between cars, or from the door if you can get it open.

2 If you have time, wait for the train to slow as it rounds a bend in the tracks.

If you jump and land correctly, you will probably survive even at high speeds (70 mph or more), but you increase your chances of survival if the train is moving slowly.

3 Stuff blankets, clothing, or seat cushions underneath your clothes.

Wear a thick or rugged jacket if possible. Use a belt to secure some padding around your head, but make certain that you can see clearly. Pad your knees, elbows, and hips.

4 Pick your landing spot before you jump.

The ideal spot will be relatively soft and free of obstructions. Avoid trees, bushes, and, of course, rocks.

5 Get as low to the floor as possible, bending your knees so you can leap away from the train car.

6 Jump perpendicular to the train, leaping as far away from the train as you can.

Even if you jump from the last car, leap at right angles to the direction of the train. This way, your momentum will not carry you toward the wheels and tracks.

7 Cover and protect your head with your hands and arms, and roll like a log when you land.

Do not try to land on your feet. Keep your body straight and try to land so that all parts of your body hit the ground at the same time—you will absorb the impact over a wider area. If you land on your feet, you will most likely break your ankles or legs. Do NOT roll head over heels as if doing a forward somersault.

If the Train Is Not Slowing or a Crash Is Imminent

1 Proceed as calmly and quietly as possible to the rear of the train.

This is the safest place to be in the event of a crash. Instruct the other passengers to move to the back of the train with you.

2 Prepare for a crash.

Sleeping cars are usually placed on the tail end of the train and have mattresses and pillows that can be used for protection. Sit or lay against a wall that is toward the leading end of the train, so you will not fly forward in the event of a crash. The farther you are from the locomotive the better.

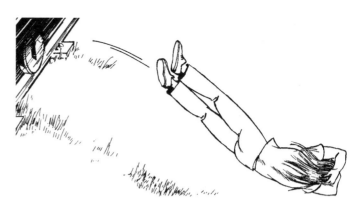

Pick your landing spot, and jump as far away from the train as you can. Protect your head.

Try to land so that all parts of your body hit the ground at the same time.

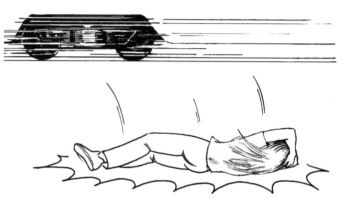

Roll like a log, keeping your head protected.

CARS

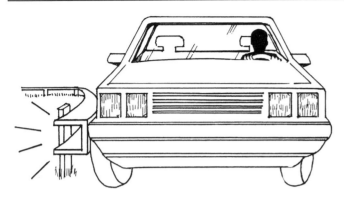

Sideswiping guardrails or rocks may help slow you down. Do this only at lower speeds.

How to Stop a Car with No Brakes

1 Begin pumping the brake pedal, and keep pumping it. You may be able to build up enough pressure in the braking system to slow down a bit or even stop completely. If you have antilock brakes, you do not normally pump them—but if your brakes have failed, this may work.

2 Do not panic—relax and steer the car smoothly.
Cars will often safely corner at speeds much higher than you realize or are used to driving. The rear of the car may slip; steer evenly, being careful not to overcorrect.

3 Shift the car into the lowest gear possible, and let the engine and transmission slow you down.

4 Pull the emergency brake—but not too hard.
Pulling too hard on the brake will cause the rear wheels to lock and the car to spin. Use even, constant pressure. In most cars, the emergency brake (also known as the hand brake or parking brake) is cable operated and serves as a fail-safe mechanism that should still work even when the rest of the braking system has failed.

5 If you are running out of room, try a "bootlegger's turn." Yank the emergency brake hard while turning the wheel a quarter turn in either direction—whichever is safer. This will make the car spin 180 degrees. If you were heading downhill, this spin will head you back uphill, allowing you to slow down.

6 If you have room, swerve the car back and forth across the road.
Making hard turns at each side of the road will decrease your speed even more.

7 If you come up behind another car, use it to help you stop.
Blow your horn, flash your lights, and try to get the driver's attention. If you hit the car, be sure to hit it square, bumper to bumper, so you do not knock the other car off the road. This works best if the vehicle in front of you is larger than yours and if both vehicles are traveling at similar speeds.

8 Look for something to help stop you.
A flat or uphill road that intersects with the road you are on, a field, or a fence will slow you further but not stop you suddenly. Scraping the side of your car against a guardrail is another option. Avoid trees and wooden telephone poles.

9 Do not attempt to sideswipe oncoming cars.

How to Escape from a Car Hanging Over the Edge of a Cliff

1 Do not shift your weight or make any sudden movements.

2 Determine how much time you have.
If the car is like the majority of cars, it is front-wheel drive with the engine in front. This means the bulk of its weight is over the front axle. If the rear, rather than the front, is hanging over the edge of the cliff, you probably have more time to climb out. If the front of the car is over the edge, assess your situation. What is the angle of the car? Is it teetering? Does it sway when you shift your weight? If the car is shifting, you must act quickly.

3 If the front doors are still over land, use these doors to make your escape, regardless of which way your car is facing.
Open the door gradually, move slowly, and get out.

4 If the front doors are over the edge, move to the rear of the car.
Proceed slowly and deliberately; do not jump or lurch. If you have a steering wheel lock or a screwdriver, take it with you—you may need it to get out.

5 Reassess your situation.
Will opening the rear doors cause the car to slide? If not, open them slowly and get out quickly.

6 If you think that opening the rear doors will cause the car to slide over the edge, you must break the window.

*If the front doors are over the edge of the cliff,
move slowly to the rear of the car and get out.*

Without shifting your weight or rocking the car, use the steering wheel lock or screwdriver to shatter the rear door window (this is safer than breaking the back window because it will require less movement as you climb out). Punch it in the center—the window is made of safety glass and will not injure you.

7 Get out as quickly as possible.

WARNING!

⚡ In situations involving several people, everyone in the front (or everyone in the back) should execute each step simultaneously.

⚡ If driver and passengers are in both front and rear seats, the people who are closest to the edge of the cliff should attempt to get out of the car first.

How to Brace for Impact

1 Stay in control until the last possible moment.
Keep your hands on the wheel and continue efforts to steer and avoid the obstacle until all options are exhausted.

2 Perform a seat belt check.
Tug quickly on the lap and shoulder of your belt to make sure you are clicked in and the belt is fully tightened.

3 Lean back.
Move your body fully back in your seat and lay your head against the headrest.

4 Release the wheel.
Take your hands off of the steering wheel. At the moment

of impact, the wheel may jerk violently, transmitting the shock to your body and breaking your fingers and thumbs.

5 Hang on to your seat belt.
Clutch the seat belt with both hands near the place where the lap belt clicks into the shoulder belt, so that both hands are secure and out of the way of the deploying front and side air bags.

6 Lift your feet off the pedals.
Remove your feet from both the brake and accelerator pedals to avoid having your ankles and shins crushed on impact.

7 Close your eyes.
Protect your vision by closing your eyes tightly. Most cars have shatter-resistant glass, but it may not hold together in certain impacts.

How to Bail Out of a Car at High Speeds

1 Look for the best place to bail out.
Try to bail out into a body of water or into foliage. Failing that, drive as close to the curbside as possible to avoid leaping into traffic.

2 Unbuckle your seat belt.
Steer the car with one hand as you unbuckle the seat belt with the other. Bring the lap and chest belts fully clear of your body to avoid entanglement.

3 Tuck your chin.
Close your mouth tightly and angle your neck down until your chin rests on your breastbone.

4 Brace your feet.
Remove both feet from the pedals and place them squarely on the floorboards of the vehicle, in front of the pedals.

5 Open the door.
In one swift movement, grasp the door handle and fling open the door of the vehicle.

6 Spring out of the car.
As soon as the door is completely open, push against the floor of the car with both feet to throw your body upward and outward from the car.

7 Cross your arms.
With each hand, grab the opposite shoulder tightly, keeping your arms across your chest.

8 Land and roll.
As you hit the ground, roll as far from the car as possible, to avoid your rear wheels and other cars.

How to Survive a Rollover

1 Pull your feet off the pedals.
As the car starts to roll, lift your feet from the brake and accelerator pedals and tuck them under the seat to keep your ankles from breaking against the floor of the vehicle.

2 Let go of the wheel.
If you are hanging on to the wheel when the car slams into the ground again, the impact will be transmitted through your entire body. Once the car has begun to roll, turning the wheel will not have any effect.

3 Cross your arms over your chest.
Keep your arms and hands as far as possible from the windows of the car as the window side slams into the ground.

4 Brace yourself with your feet.
Once the car is upside down, find purchase somewhere with both feet, either on the windshield, the driver's side window, or the ceiling of the car.

5 Count to 60.
Remain still and suspended from your seat belt until you are certain that your vehicle has stopped moving, and that any other vehicles involved in the accident have stopped moving and are not sliding across the roadway into yours.

6 Check yourself for injuries.
While hanging on to the seat belt with one hand, pat your body with the other hand to check for injuries. Run your hand through your hair and over your scalp. In case of any injury, do not move.

7 If you appear to be uninjured, reach up and stabilize yourself.
As you are dangling from the seat belt, slowly bring one hand up and lay it firmly against the ceiling of the car.

8 Unfasten your seat belt.
When you are certain that your weight is fully supported by your hands and feet, undo your seat belt and drop down onto the ceiling.

9 Get out of the car.
Check for oncoming traffic. Open the door and exit the vehicle. Get clear of the roadway and await emergency personnel.

Support your weight against the ceiling of the car and unfasten your seat belt.

WARNING!

- Rollovers occur when a driver loses control of the vehicle and it slides sideways and hits a "trip," such as a curb or guardrail. A second common cause is when a driver takes a turn or curve too quickly.

- Rollovers account for only 3 percent of total accidents but cause about a quarter of fatal crashes. More than half of the people killed in single-vehicle crashes die in rollovers.

- Many rollover injuries occur after the accident itself, when the victim unbuckles her seat belt and falls to the roof of the car.

- Rollovers are more common in pickup trucks than cars—mostly in SUVs, defined as passenger vehicles with high ground clearance (generally eight inches or higher) and with the same platform as a truck.

- Always wear your seat belt.

CAR MANEUVERING

How to Ram a Car/Barricade

1 Disable your air bag, if you can.
It will deploy on impact and will obstruct your view after it deploys.

2 Wear a seat belt.

3 Accelerate to at least 25 mph.
Do not go too fast—keeping the car at a slow speed will allow you to maintain control without slowing down. Then, just before impact, increase your speed to greater than 30 mph to deliver a disabling crunch to the rear wheel of the obstacle car.

4 Ram the front passenger side of your car into the obstacle car at its rear wheel, at a 90-degree angle (the cars should be perpendicular).

5 If you are unable to hit a car in the rear, go for the front-right corner.
Avoid hitting the car squarely in the side; this will not move it out of your way.

6 The car should spin out of your way—hit the gas, and keep moving.

> ### WARNING!
>
> ✏ Ramming a car to move it out of your way is not easy or safe, but there are some methods that work better than others and some that will minimize the damage to your vehicle. The best way to hit a car blocking your path is to clip the very rear of it, about one foot from the rear bumper. The rear is the lightest part of a car, and it will move relatively easily. Hitting it in the rear can also disable the car—with the rear wheel crushed, you have time to get away without being pursued.

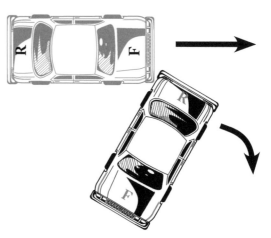

Ram the obstacle car with the passenger side of your car, and deliver a disabling crunch to its rear wheel.

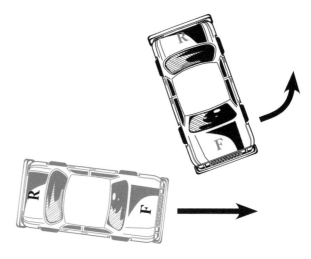

If you are unable to hit the car in the rear, go for the front-right corner.

How to Drive Down a Flight of Stairs

1 Aim.
Set your eyes on a spot dead center over the horizon of the staircase. Steer the car toward that spot.

2 Floor it.
When you are 20 feet from the stairs, slam your foot down on the accelerator to get a burst of speed approaching the lip.

3 Shut your mouth.
Pull your tongue back in your mouth and grit your teeth to keep them from knocking together as the car bounces down the stairs.

4 Grip the wheel.
Hold on to the wheel tightly, and steer to counterbalance each time the car jerks one way or the other as it bounces forward.

5 Lift your foot from the accelerator.
As the front bumper crosses the lip of the top stair, lift up your feet. Further acceleration is unnecessary as gravity pulls your vehicle forward, and leaving your feet on the pedals will cause your shins to absorb the shock as the car bangs down the steps.

6 Floor it again.

When you feel the back wheel hit the bottom stair, bring your right foot back down on the pedal and give another burst of speed to keep your back bumper from catching on the lip of the bottom step.

7 Even out.

Hold tightly to the wheel, and steer to regain control of the vehicle.

How to Perform a Fast 180-Degree Turn

From Reverse

1 Put the car in reverse.

2 Select a spot straight ahead. Keep your eyes on it, and begin backing up.

3 Jam on the gas.

4 Cut the wheel sharply 90 degrees around (a quarter turn) as you simultaneously drop the transmission into drive.

Make sure you have enough speed to use the momentum of the car to swing it around, but remember that going too fast (greater than 45 mph) can be dangerous and may flip the car (and strip your gears). Turning the wheel left will swing the rear of the car left; turning it right will swing the car right.

5 When the car has completed the turn, step on the gas and head off.

From Drive

1 While in drive, or a forward gear, accelerate to a moderate rate of speed (anything faster than 45 mph risks flipping the car).

2 Slip the car into neutral to prevent the front wheels from spinning.

3 Take your foot off the gas, and turn the wheel 90 degrees (a quarter turn) while pulling hard on the emergency brake.

4 As the rear swings around, return the wheel to its original position and put the car back into drive.

5 Step on the gas to start moving in the direction from which you came.

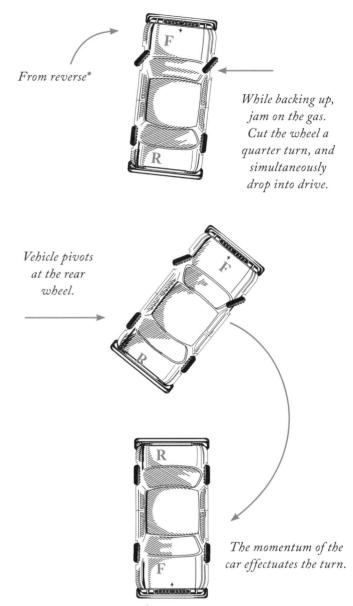

From reverse*

While backing up, jam on the gas. Cut the wheel a quarter turn, and simultaneously drop into drive.

Vehicle pivots at the rear wheel.

The momentum of the car effectuates the turn.

*At speeds no greater than 45 mph.

WARNING!

⚡ The 180-degree turn while moving forward is more difficult for the following reasons:

- It is easier to swing the front of the car around, because it is heavier and it will move faster with momentum.

- It is harder to maintain control of the rear of the car—it is lighter and will slip more easily than the front. Spinning out of control or flipping the car is a potential danger.

- Road conditions can play a significant role in the success—and safety—of this maneuver. Any surface without sufficient traction (dirt, mud, ice, gravel) will make quick turns harder and collisions more likely.

HOW TO EVADE A PURSUING CAR

Escape Method

1 Identify the pursuer.
Note the make, the model, the color, and any other distinguishing features (including the number of passengers) of the pursuing vehicle to help keep track of it in your escape, especially if it is a common vehicle type.

2 Drive to a high-traffic environment.

3 Drive fast.
Stay ahead of the flow of traffic.

4 Weave in and out of lanes.
Look for gaps between cars, and suddenly speed up to shift into the gaps. Do not signal your lane changes.

5 Turn frequently and unexpectedly.
When possible, turn right out of the far left lane, or left out of the far right lane.

6 Seek cover near large vehicles.
Get as many large, eye-line-blocking vehicles as possible between you and your pursuer. Ride with one truck or bus in front of you and another behind, and then follow the front vehicle into a turn.

7 Accelerate through yellow lights.
When you see a traffic light turn yellow, slow until just before it will turn red, then accelerate through the intersection at the last moment. Watch for oncoming traffic.

8 Pitch your pursuer through a yellow light.
When you see a traffic light turn yellow, and your pursuer is slightly behind you but not in your lane, speed up to the light as if you intend to speed through it. At the last second, slam on your brakes and let your pursuer speed through the light. Check for oncoming traffic, and then turn.

Disabling Method

1 Drive normally.
Do not let on that you know you are being followed.

2 Situate your car so that your pursuer is directly behind you.
If your pursuer is trying to maintain his distance, slow down sufficiently so that the traffic between your cars will accelerate to pass you.

3 Accelerate gently.
Once your car is directly in front of your pursuer, accelerate gently to put 20 or 30 feet of road between your vehicles.

4 Slam on the brakes and throw the car in reverse.

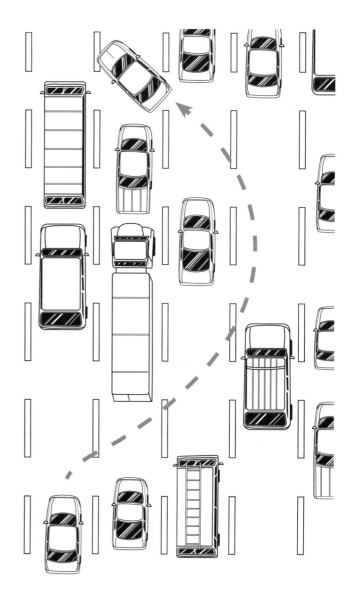

Weave in and out of lanes. Do not signal your lane changes.

5 Accelerate backward into your pursuer's car.
Striking your pursuer's front bumper going at least 15 mph will cause his air bag to deploy, locking the starter of his vehicle.

6 Put the car in drive and accelerate forward.
Drive away quickly.

TRAPPED IN THE CAR

As soon as you hit the water, open your window. Otherwise, the pressure of the water will make it very difficult to escape.

If you were unable to exit before hitting the water, attempt to break a window with your foot or heavy object.

How to Escape from a Sinking Car

1 As soon as you hit the water, open your window.
This is your best chance of escape, because opening the door will be very difficult given the outside water pressure. Opening the windows allows water to come in and equalize the pressure. Once the water pressure inside and outside the car is equal, you'll be able to open the door.

2 If your power windows won't work or you cannot roll your windows down all the way, attempt to break the glass with your foot or shoulder or a heavy object such as an anti-theft steering wheel lock.

3 Get out.
Do not worry about leaving anything behind unless it is another person. Vehicles with the engine in front will sink at a steep angle. If the water is 15 feet or deeper, the vehicle may end up on its roof, upside down. For this reason, you must get out as soon as possible, while the car is still afloat. Depending on the vehicle, floating time will range from a few seconds to a few minutes. The more airtight the car, the longer it floats. Air in the car will quickly be forced out through the trunk and cab, and an air bubble is unlikely to remain once the car hits bottom. Get out as early as possible.

4 If you are unable to open the window or break it, you have one final option.
Remain calm and do not panic. Wait until the car begins filling with water. When the water reaches your head, take a deep breath and hold it. Now the pressure should be equalized inside and outside, and you should be able to open the door and swim to the surface.

BE AWARE!

✔ You can purchase and keep in your car a purpose-built window-breaking hammer or a spring-loaded center punch, either of which will be much quicker and more reliable than your foot or a random blunt object.

✔ Drive with the windows slightly open and the doors unlocked whenever you are near water or are driving on ice.

Recommended Items Always to Have in the Trunk

- Local map, atlas, or GPS system
- Crank or battery-powered radio and batteries
- Large flashlight and batteries
- Matches or lighter
- Basic automotive tool kit
- First aid kit

- Emergency flares
- Spare tire
- Jack
- Jumper cables
- Three days' worth of non-perishable food
- Six quarts of water per adult passenger
- Duct tape

- Pepper spray, emergency whistle
- Collapsible shovel
- Ice scraper, rock salt (for cold weather)
- Insulated sleeping bag
- Two two-by-fours
- Rain poncho and boots

- License and registration
- Phone charger
- Emergency road-side assistance phone number
- Car owner's manual

How to Escape from the Trunk of the Car

1 If you are in a trunk that has no wall separating the backseats and the trunk, try to get the seats down.
Although the release for most seats is inside the passenger compartment, you may be able to fold or force them down from the trunk side. (If not, continue to step 2.)

2 Check for a trunk cable underneath the carpet or upholstery.
Many new cars have a trunk release lever on the floor below the driver's seat. These cars should have a cable that runs from the release lever to the trunk. Look for the cable beneath carpeting or upholstery, or behind a panel of sheet metal. If you locate the cable, pull on it to release the trunk latch. (If not, continue to step 3.)

3 Look for a tool in the trunk.
Many cars have emergency kits inside the trunk, underneath or with the spare tire. These kits may contain a screwdriver, flashlight, or pry bar. Use a screwdriver or pry bar to pry the latch open. You can also pry the corner of the trunk lid up and wave and yell to signal passersby. (If there is no tool, continue to step 4.)

4 Dismantle the car's brake lights by yanking wires and pushing or kicking the lights out.
Then wave and yell to signal passersby or other cars. This method is also recommended if the car is moving and you need to signal cars behind you.

WARNING!

No car trunk is airtight, so the danger of suffocation in a car trunk is low. Breathe regularly and do not panic—panic increases the danger of your hyperventilating and passing out. Keep in mind, however, that on a hot day the interior temperature of a car trunk can reach 140°F. Work quickly but calmly.

If there is a trunk cable beneath carpeting or upholstery, pull it to release the lock. If not, look under the spare tire for tools to pry the latch.

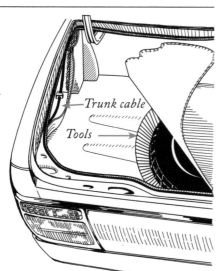

Trunk cable

Tools

Bring only what you really need.

How to Survive a Family Car Trip

1 Line the seats with a large bath towel or sheet.
The cover will protect the backseat and expedite cleanup later.

2 Leave early.
Start a long trip early—before dawn—to ensure that kids will be sleepy and will nap for the first few hours of the ride. If they awaken at or near rush hour, pull over to avoid traffic and get a break from driving.

3 Bring along a few key items, but only what you really need.
Essential items include snacks, games, open-ended creative toys, and passive entertainment devices (such as music players and portable DVD players).

4 Make frequent stops.
Do not expect small children to sit still for more than an hour or two at a time. Make frequent rest stops to switch drivers, stretch, throw a ball, run around, and use the bathroom. These stops also serve to fend off carsickness and keep the driver alert.

BICYCLES

How to Steer Your Bike Down a Rock Face

1 Choose a line to follow.
The instant you feel the bike pitching forward downslope, look ahead of you and choose the line that you will follow down the rock face. The line should be as free of large boulders, drop-offs, and deep ruts as possible. Follow this line.

2 Adjust your seating position.
Move slightly "out of saddle," above the seat with your knees bent, similar to a jockey on a horse running down the stretch. Keep your weight shifted toward the back of the saddle, or behind it, to counteract the pull of gravity.

3 Move the pedals to the 3 and 9 o'clock positions.
Keep your feet on the pedals, with the pedals positioned across from one another. Do not put your feet straight up (12 o'clock) and down (6 o'clock), where the risk of making contact with rocks or the ground is greater. It is also more difficult to maintain a level position with the pedals straight up and down.

4 Heavily apply the rear brake.
On most bikes, squeezing the brake lever by your right hand will apply the rear brake. Do so as you ride downslope to maintain control of the bike. If you do not brake sufficiently, you risk "bombing," or speeding out of control down the rock face. Apply the brakes enough to maintain a speed that enables you to see oncoming obstacles in your path.

5 Feather the front brake.
Using your left hand (on most bikes), gently apply the front brake as you climb obstacles, and release it to maintain momentum as you overcome them. This gentle apply-and-release action is called "feathering." Avoid applying the front brake suddenly and with full force, or the bike will stop short and you will pitch over the handlebars.

6 Keep the bike in the middle-to-low gear range.
Low gears are easier to pedal; high gears are harder. The gear should be low enough that you can pedal easily over an obstacle, but not so low that you don't have any traction. It should not be so high that surmounting an obstacle becomes difficult or impossible.

7 Shift your weight.
As you approach large rocks and boulders, shift your body back to take the weight off the front wheel. This shift will

Choose a line to follow down the rock face.

allow the front wheel to more easily ride up and over the obstruction.

8 Keep your knees and elbows bent.
Bend your knees and elbows to absorb shocks and to make fast, fluid position changes easier.

9 Bail if you lose control.
If you feel yourself gaining sudden momentum and you begin to lose control, do not attempt to stay with the bike: you do not want to crash while riding at high speed. Let the bike drop out from beneath you, guiding it so it lands on the non-derailleur side to minimize damage that might make the bike unrideable. Tuck your elbows and knees in as you roll to safety.

WARNING!

A wrong turn can send your mountain bike down a sheer rock face.

How to Slow or Stop with No Brakes

1 Lean forward.
Angle your body forward on the seat, taking as much weight as you can off your rear tire.

2 Lock your legs and push your feet in the opposite direction of that in which the pedals are turning.

This will take a lot of strength. Push firmly against the forward momentum.

3 Make an abrupt turn to stop forward motion.
Lean into the turn and throw out one foot to prevent yourself from tipping over.

4 Whip the back end of the bike out to skid to a stop.

5 Jump forward off the seat.
Throw your legs down and drag yourself to a stop "Fred Flintstone style" with your feet.

6 Leap backward off the seat into a run.
If all efforts have failed and you're about to ride into dangerous territory (e.g., into traffic or a tree), hurl yourself off the bike and roll up into a run.

BE AWARE!

↗ Rubbing your foot firmly against the rear tire may also help slow it down.

↗ If you are deliberately riding a bike without brakes, attach foot straps to your pedals to make stopping easier.

How to Treat Road Rash

1 Remove any clothing from around the wound.
Skidding when you fall off your bike will partially tear your clothing. Cut away or remove the rest.

2 Clean out debris.
Using sterile gauze, carefully brush away any debris, such as cloth, glass, gravel, leaves, or dirt that has gotten in the abrasion. Avoid scrubbing or rubbing, which can further irritate the wound.

3 Trim away dead skin.
Use sterile medical scissors to cut away any loose skin.

4 Irrigate with saline.
Flush out the wound with soap and warm water or a mild saline solution.

5 Apply a topical antibiotic ointment.
Cover the wound. Choose a dressing that won't stick to the abrasion, such as gauze with petroleum jelly. Avoid plain gauze. Secure with medical tape.

6 Lift bandage daily.
Allow the wound to breathe and fluids to drain.

7 Change dressing often.
Clean wound daily with soap and water. Reapply ointment and cover with new gauze.

8 Watch for signs of infection.
Redness, pus, fever, or a foul smell can all be signs of infection.

Car-Doored

Throw your weight backward. Stand on the pedals and above the seat. Apply only the rear brakes. Turn slightly to the side to disperse the impact as you hit the door. If you land in the street, move immediately toward the curb to get out of the way of traffic.

WARNING!

↗ Bike accidents are the most common cause of road rash. Wear protective clothing, especially if you are traveling at high speeds, and leathers if you're on a motorcycle.

↗ Avoid undiluted antiseptics, which can actually harm the tissue under the skin, delaying the healing process.

↗ Verify when you had your last tetanus shot. Road rash can make you susceptible to tetanus, an infectious disease that can develop in burnlike abrasions.

↗ Once healed, the area will be susceptible to sunburn. Apply a high-SPF sunscreen and keep covered when outside.

AIRPLANES

Airspeed indicator

Altimeter

Heading

Yoke

Throttle

Fuel guage

Landing gear

How to Land a Plane

1 If the plane has only one set of controls, push, pull, carry, or drag the pilot out of the pilot's seat.

2 Take your place at the controls.

3 Put on the radio headset (if there is one).
Use the radio to call for help—there will be a control button on the yoke (the plane's steering wheel) or a CB-like microphone on the instrument panel. Depress the button to talk; release it to listen. Say "Mayday! Mayday!" and give your situation, destination, and plane call numbers, which should be printed on the top of the instrument panel.

4 If you get no response, try again on the emergency channel—tune the radio to 1215.
All radios are different, but tuning is standard. The person on the other end should be able to talk you through the proper landing procedures. Follow their instructions carefully. If you cannot reach someone to talk you through the landing process, you will have to do it alone.

5 Get your bearings and identify the instruments.
Look around you. Is the plane level? Unless you have just taken off or are about to land, it should be flying relatively straight.

Yoke. This is the steering wheel and should be in front of you. It turns the plane and controls its pitch. Pull back on the column to bring the nose up, push forward to point it down. Turn left to turn the plane left, turn right to turn it right. The yoke is very sensitive—move it only an inch or

two in either direction to turn the plane in flight. While cruising, the nose of the plane should be about three inches below the horizon.

Altimeter. This is the most important instrument, at least initially. It is a red dial in the middle of the instrument panel that indicates altitude: the small hand indicates feet above sea level in thousand-foot increments, the large hand in hundreds.

Heading. This is a compass and will be the only instrument with a small image of a plane in the center. The nose will point in the direction in which the plane is headed.

Airspeed. This dial is on the top of the instrument panel and will be on the left. It is usually calibrated in knots, though it may also have miles per hour. A small plane travels at about 120 knots while cruising. Anything under 70 knots in the air is dangerously close to stall speed. (A knot is 1¼ miles per hour.)

Throttle. This controls airspeed (power) and also the nose attitude, or its relation to the horizon. It is a lever between the seats and is always black. Pull it toward you to slow the plane and cause it to descend, push it away to speed up the plane and cause it to ascend. The engine will get more or less quiet depending on the direction the throttle is moved.

Fuel. The fuel gauges will be on the lower portion of the instrument panel. If the pilot has followed FAA regulations, the plane should have enough fuel for the amount of flying time to your intended destination plus at least an additional half hour in reserve. Some planes have a reserve fuel tank in addition to the primary one, but do not worry about changing tanks.

Flaps. Due to their complexity, wing flaps can make the plane harder to control. To control the airspeed, use the throttle, not the flaps.

6 Begin the descent.
Pull back on the throttle to slow down. Reduce power by about one-quarter of cruising speed. As the plane slows, the nose will drop. For descent, the nose should be about four inches below the horizon.

7 Deploy the landing gear.
Determine if the plane has fixed or retractable landing gear. Fixed landing gear is always down, so you need do nothing. If it is retractable, there will be another lever between the seats near the throttle, with a handle that is shaped like a tire. For a water landing, leave the landing gear up (retracted).

8 Look for a suitable landing site.
If you cannot find an airport, find a flat field on which to land. A mile-long field is ideal, but finding a field of this length will be difficult unless you are in the Midwest. The plane can land on a much shorter strip of earth, so do not bother to look for the "perfect" landing site—there is no such thing. Bumpy terrain will also do if your options are limited.

9 Line up the landing strip so that when the altimeter reads 1,000 feet, the field is off the right-wing tip.
In an ideal situation, you should take a single pass over the field to look for obstructions; with plenty of fuel, you may want to do so. Fly over the field, make a big rectangle, and approach a second time.

10 When approaching the landing strip, reduce power by pulling back on the throttle.
Do not let the nose drop more than six inches below the horizon.

11 The plane should be 100 feet off the ground when you are just above the landing strip, and the rear wheels should touch first.
The plane will stall at 55 to 65 miles per hour, and you want the plane to be at just about stall speed when the wheels touch the ground.

12 Pull all the way back on the throttle, and make sure the nose of the plane does not dip too steeply.
Gently pull back on the yoke as the plane slowly touches the ground.

13 Using the pedals on the floor, steer and brake the plane as needed.
The yoke has very little effect on the ground. The upper pedals are the brakes, and the lower pedals control the direction of the nose wheel. Concentrate first on the lower pedals. Press the right pedal to move the plane right, press the left pedal to move it left. Upon landing, be aware of your speed. A modest reduction in speed will increase your chances of survival exponentially. By reducing your ground-speed from 120 to 70 miles per hour, you increase your chance of survival threefold.

WARNING!

⚠ These instructions cover small passenger planes and jets, not commercial airliners.

⚠ A well-executed emergency landing in bad terrain can be less hazardous than an uncontrolled landing on an established field.

⚠ If the plane is headed toward trees, steer it between them so the wings absorb the impact if you hit.

⚠ When the plane comes to a stop, get out as soon as possible and get away—and take the pilot with you.

HOW TO LAND A PLANE ON WATER

1 Once you have determined your landing location, turn the autopilot off and reduce power by moving the throttle toward you.
Slowly move the throttle enough to cause the nose to drop and the plane to descend slightly. You will need to be at approximately 2,000 feet to be able to clearly see the water below you.

2 When the altimeter reads 2,000 feet, level the nose with the horizon using the yoke.
Increase power slightly by moving the throttle away from you if pulling back on the yoke does not work.

3 Assess the water ahead of you.
It is imperative that you land in calm water and that you avoid landing the plane in the face of swells, where there is a significant risk of waves breaking over the aircraft. The plane should be heading into the wind (called a headwind), so that you land on the back side of any waves.

4 Reduce power by moving the throttle toward you.
Do not use your flaps or your landing gear, which might

Jet Lag

To beat jet lag, drink a lot of water before, during, and after the flight. Exercise, eat, and sleep well immediately before the trip. Avoid drinking alcohol, and eat lightly in the air. Purchase a small self-inflating pillow to make your onboard sleep more comfortable.

catch on the water. Bring the plane to an altitude of 100 to 200 feet.

5 Continue to reduce power until the tachometer reads 1,500 to 1,700 rpm or 15 to 17 inches of mercury.

6 Move the nose of the plane up at least 5 to 10 degrees above the horizon by pulling the yoke toward you slightly. You must exercise a nose-up landing to keep the propeller out of the water and prevent the plane from flipping end-over-end. The angle of the nose should be such that the horizon is almost completely obscured.

7 Just before touchdown, make sure the throttle is in its farthest position toward you.
The plane should be no more than 10 feet above the water at this point.

8 Pull the red fuel mixture control knob toward you to cut fuel to the engine when the plane is about five feet above the water.
Use the surface of the water, not the altimeter, to judge your altitude at this low level.

9 Keep the nose up by pulling back gently on the yoke.
The plane should fall gently onto the water. Concentrate on making sure the rear of the plane hits the water first. If the plane has nonretractable landing gear, it will most likely flip over because the landing gear will catch on the water.

10 Open the door or window as soon as you hit the water, and quickly get out of the plane.
It may be difficult to open the door or window once you begin to sink. If you are unable to open the cabin door, kick out the windshield.

11 If the plane has life vests or a raft, inflate them outside of the plane.
The plane's emergency location transmitter (ELT) should continue broadcasting your location to rescue personnel.

How to Survive an Airplane Crash

To Decrease the Odds of a Crash

1 Take a nonstop flight, if possible.
Most accidents happen in the takeoff and landing phases of flight; the fewer stops you make, the less chance of an accident.

2 Watch the skies.
Many accidents involve severe weather. As takeoff time approaches, check the weather along the route, particularly in places where you will land. Consider delaying your flight if the weather could be severe.

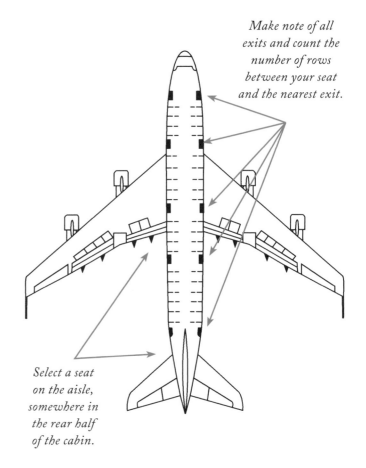

Make note of all exits and count the number of rows between your seat and the nearest exit.

Select a seat on the aisle, somewhere in the rear half of the cabin.

3 Wear a long-sleeved shirt and long pants made of natural fibers.
Radiant heat and flash burns can be avoided if you put a barrier between you and the heat. Avoid easy-care polyester or nylon: most synthetic materials that aren't specifically treated to be fire-resistant will melt at relatively low temperatures (300°F to 400°F). Synthetic fabrics will usually shrink before they melt, and if they are in contact with skin when this happens, they will make the burn—and its treatment—much more serious. Wear closed-toe, hard-soled shoes; you might have to walk through twisted, torn metal or flames. In many cases, people survive the crash but are killed or injured by post-impact fire and its by-products, like smoke and toxic gases.

4 Select a seat on the aisle, somewhere in the rear half of the cabin.
The odds of surviving a crash are higher in the middle-to-rear section compared with the middle-to-front section of the cabin. An aisle seat offers the easiest escape route access, unless you are sitting right next to an emergency exit: if you can get a window seat right next to the emergency exit, this is a better choice.

5 Listen to the safety briefing and locate your nearest exits.

Most airplane accident survivors had listened to the briefing and knew how to get out of the plane. Pick an exit to use in an emergency and an alternate in case the first one is not available.

6 Count the seats between you and the exits in case smoke fills the plane and you cannot see them.

Make sure you understand how the exit doors work and how to operate them.

7 Practice opening your seat belt a few times.

Many people mistakenly try to push the center of the buckle rather than pull up on it.

To Prepare for a Crash

1 Make sure that your seat belt is tightly fastened and that your chair back is fully upright.

2 Bend forward with one arm across your knees.

Place your pillow in your lap and hold your head against the pillow with your free arm.

3 Push your legs forward and brace for impact by placing your feet or knees against the chair in front of you.

If you are over water, loosen your shirt (and tie) so that your movement is not restricted when you attempt to swim. Be ready for two jolts: when the plane first hits water and when the nose hits water again.

4 Stay calm and be ready to help yourself.

The vast majority of crash survivors were able to get out either under their own power or with the help of someone already on the plane. Fire and rescue personnel are unlikely to enter the airplane to pull you out.

5 Do not take anything with you.

If you have something you absolutely cannot part with, you should keep it in your pocket and not in your carry-on baggage.

6 Stay low if the plane is on fire.

Follow the exit procedures described in the safety briefing. Illuminated floor lights should indicate the exits: the lights are red where exit rows exist.

How to Deal with a Canceled Flight

◐ Do not stand in line.

When a flight is canceled, for any reason, hundreds of people line up at the ticket counter for rebooking. Ignore them and find a telephone.

◐ Go to the airline's Web site.

Find another flight online. If you do not have access to the Internet, call the airline or your travel agent to find a seat on the next flight going to your destination.

◐ Book a new flight.

Carry a list of all airlines that fly to your destination. The airline on which you are ticketed may not be able to rebook you on a later flight or might not be the airline with the next available flight. Go to the Web sites of other airlines, or call them to book a seat on a convenient flight. Depending on the ticket you originally purchased and its restrictions, it might be simpler and faster to purchase a new ticket on a different airline and not use your original ticket. If you purchase a new ticket, proceed directly to the new airline's gate.

◐ Have your ticket endorsed.

If you have made a reservation on a different airline but have not purchased a new ticket, you will need to get your existing ticket endorsed over to the new carrier. You will have to stand in line at the counter of the airline that canceled the flight, but you, unlike others in line, will already have another flight arranged.

◐ Save unused ticket information.

Unused reservations, one-way or round-trip, may be credited toward another flight on the same airline or, in some cases, refunded.

WARNING!

✗ When flying within the United States, know Rule 240, which covers what an airline will do for you in the event of a flight delay or cancellation. Legally, airlines must compensate only ticketed passengers who arrive on time but are denied a seat. In the event of a lengthy flight delay or cancellation, airlines as a matter of good public relations generally will provide passengers a hotel, a meal, a free phone call, and other amenities (be sure to ask if they're not offered) or arrange flights on another airline. Check each airline's Web site for its delay/cancellation policies.

✗ If you know you will be traveling on a busy holiday weekend to a very busy airport, and especially if there is the possibility of severe weather, book a room in an airport hotel; you will be ready if your flight is canceled. Check the hotel's cancellation policy, so that you are not charged for an unused room, and be sure to cancel the room if you don't need it.

✗ Do not use electronic tickets if there is a chance of bad weather, labor problems, or security delays. The computer systems of different airlines cannot communicate with one another, so e-tickets cannot be endorsed from one airline to another. A paper ticket must first be issued, extending the amount of time you will have to spend at the ticket counter.

✗ Carry on your bags whenever possible. If your luggage has been checked through to your final destination but you encounter delays, you may not be able to switch your luggage's flights and airlines as easily as your own.

8

Oh S#&%t!

EXTREME EMERGENCIES

FALLING FROM GREAT HEIGHTS

How to Survive a Fall Down a Flight of Stairs

1 Lower your center of gravity.
When you sense yourself falling, crouch low to the floor.

2 Do not attempt to break your fall.
Avoid using your hands to try to break your initial fall. The weight of your body, in conjunction with the gravitational forces of the fall, may break your wrists.

3 Move to the inside wall.
As you fall, keep your body close to the wall of the stairway, if there is one. You are more likely to catch an arm or a leg in the banister (or fall through or over it) than to injure yourself on the wall.

4 Tuck.
Move your arms, legs, hands, and knees in close to your body. Tuck your chin to your chest. With your elbows tucked in, place your hands on the sides of your head.

5 Roll in a zigzag pattern.
Concentrate on rolling on your major muscle groups: lats (back), deltoids (shoulders), quads (thighs), and gluteus maximus (rear end). Avoid rolling head over heels, straight down: your increasing momentum may cause injury, even with your body positioned correctly. Instead, roll in toward the wall on one shoulder, then out toward the banister on the other. Repeat the pattern until you reach the bottom. A zigzag roll will help you reduce speed and maintain control. Do not attempt the zigzag roll on a stairway with an old, rickety banister, an open railing, or no banister at all.

6 Check for injury.
Do not get up immediately. Slowly move each limb in turn to make sure nothing is broken. If you are in extreme pain, yell.

How to Survive If Your Parachute Doesn't Open

1 As soon as you realize that your chute is bad, signal to a jumping companion whose chute has not yet opened that you are having a malfunction.
Wave your arms and point to your chute.

2 When your companion (and new best friend) gets to you, hook arms.

Roll in toward the wall on one shoulder, then out toward the banister on the other.

3 Once you are hooked together, the two of you will still be falling at terminal velocity, or about 130 miles per hour. When your friend opens his chute, there will be no way either of you will be able to hold on to one another normally, because the G-forces will triple or quadruple your body weight. To prepare for this problem, hook your arms into his chest strap, or through the two sides of the front of his harness, all the way up to your elbows, and grab hold of your own strap.

Hook arms with your companion. Then hook your arms into his chest strap, up to the elbows, and grab hold of your own.

4 Open the chute.

The chute-opening shock will be severe, probably enough to dislocate or break your arms.

5 Steer the canopy.

Your friend must now hold on to you with one arm while steering his canopy (the part of the chute that controls direction and speed). If your friend's canopy is slow and big, you may hit the grass or dirt slowly enough to break only a leg, and your chances of survival are high. If his canopy is a fast one, however, your friend will have to steer to avoid hitting the ground too fast. You must also avoid power lines and other obstructions at all costs.

6 If there is a body of water nearby, head for that.

Of course, once you hit the water, you will have to tread with just your legs and hope that your partner is able to pull you out before your chute takes in water.

How to Prepare

Check your chute before you jump. The good news is that today's parachutes are built to open, so even if you make big mistakes packing them, they tend to sort themselves out. The reserve chute, however, must be packed by a certified rigger and must be perfect, as it is your last resort. Make sure of the following:

- The parachute is folded in straight lines—that there are no twists.

- The slider is positioned correctly to keep the parachute from opening too fast.

HOW TO SURVIVE IN A PLUMMETING ELEVATOR

1 Flatten your body against the car floor.

While there is disagreement among the experts, most recommend this method. This should distribute the force of impact, rather than concentrate it on one area of your body. (Standing may be difficult anyway.) Lie in the center of the car.

2 Cover your face and head to protect them from ceiling parts that may break loose.

WARNING!

⚡ Hydraulic elevators are more likely than cable elevators to fall. These elevators are pushed from the bottom by a giant piston, similar to car jacks at service stations. Because the jack is subject to ground corrosion, it can rot, which could eventually cause the car to fall. The height of hydraulic elevators is limited to about 70 feet, so a free fall would probably result in injury—but not death.

⚡ Elevators have numerous safety features. There have been very few recorded incidents involving death from plummeting elevators. In general, it is highly unlikely for a cable (also called traction) elevator to fall all the way to the bottom of the shaft. Moreover, the compressed air column in the elevator hoistway and the car buffers at the bottom of the hoistway may keep the forces of the impact survivable.

⚡ Jumping just before the elevator hits the bottom is not a viable alternative. The chances that you will time your jump exactly right are infinitesimally small. Besides, the elevator will not remain completely intact when it hits—it will likely collapse around you and crush you if you are in the middle of your jump, or even if you are still standing.

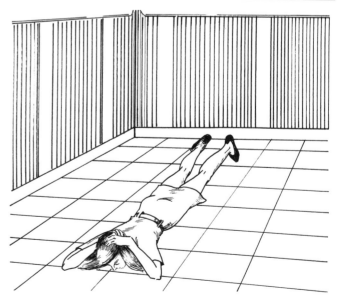

Lie flat on the floor in the center of the elevator, covering your head for protection.

CHEMICALS

How to Deal with a Suspicious White Powder

○ **Hold your breath.**
As soon as you see suspicious white powder, stop inhaling. Anthrax spores are generally fatal only when inhaled in large numbers.

○ **Do not crouch on the floor.**
Unless aerosolized as a bioweapon, anthrax spores fall to the ground and stay there when released. Stand on a table or chair when handling the envelope or other container of the spores to reduce the chance of inhalation—when the spores fall to the floor, you'll be farther from them.

○ **Stay upwind of the letter or parcel.**
Anthrax spores travel on wind gusts. Hold the envelope or container away from you and downwind of any air vents or room fans. If outside, leave the envelope in place and get inside. Close all windows and doors.

○ **Cover your nose and mouth.**
For the best protection, wear a gas mask capable of filtering particles of one to five microns in size. If no gas mask is available, use a surgical mask or bandanna to cover your nose and mouth.

○ **Do not wash clothes or disinfect surfaces.**
Detergents may increase the virulence of anthrax spores.

○ **Call the authorities to report the incident.**

WARNING!

⚡ Anthrax cannot be transmitted from person to person, so it is safe to warn people around you of the danger.

⚡ Anthrax spores may cause localized infection if they enter the body through the skin, especially through a cut. Wear rubber gloves when handling a suspect letter or parcel.

How to Survive Acid Rain

○ **Stay covered**
When walking in rain or fog in a heavily industrial area, wear several layers of clothing, as well as a poncho and face mask. Carry an umbrella.

○ **Cover your car.**
Keep your car under a tarp or other protective coating anytime you are not driving it, to prevent acid etching the paint. Wash and hand-dry the car immediately after you drive it and after every rainstorm.

Hold breath

Stay above and upwind of a suspicious white powder.

○ **Eliminate fish from your diet.**
Lake-dwelling species such as bass, perch, and crayfish are directly affected by the lowered pH balance and increased aluminum in their habitats created by acid rain, and this toxicity is passed on to the humans who eat them.

○ **Add limestone to the soil.**
Human food crops such as corn and wheat can be severely damaged when acid rain lowers the pH balance of the soil. To counter these effects, add lime and fertilizers to your fields to restore nutrients leached out by acid rain.

○ **Get an inhaler.**
A high incidence of acid rain has been correlated with high incidences of respiratory ailments such as bronchitis and asthma.

- ✪ Wear night-vision goggles.

Areas with a lot of acid rain are also hazier, due to high concentrations of particulate matter in the atmosphere. To see long distances through the haze, use an infrared viewing device.

- ✪ Switch to wind power, and tell your neighbors to do likewise.

The burning of fossil fuels for heat and energy releases sulfur dioxide and nitrogen oxide into the atmosphere, creating acid rain. Mass shifting to alternative forms of energy, such as wind and solar power, would drastically alleviate the problem of acid rain.

WARNING!

- ⚠ Acid rain is the result of elevated levels of nitric acid and sulfuric acid in the atmosphere, almost always as a result of pollution from the burning of fossil fuels. There is no strict chemical definition of "acid rain," but a pH balance of less than 5.7 is generally considered acidic.

- ⚠ Regions of the world heavily affected by acid rain include the northeastern United States, Central Europe, and eastern China.

- ⚠ Acid rain cannot directly impact human health. The presence of acid rain, however, signals the presence of particulate matter in the air, which causes a raft of respiratory problems in humans.

HOW TO DRIVE THROUGH A CHEMICAL SPILL

1 Extinguish any cigarettes.

Many hazardous chemicals are highly combustible. If you are smoking, stub out the cigarette completely in your ashtray. Make sure all embers are fully extinguished. Do not throw a lit cigarette out the window.

2 Turn off the air circulation systems.

Make sure the heat, air-conditioning, and all blower fans are off and vents are closed. These systems will bring contaminated outside air into the car.

3 Shut the windows.

Make sure all windows (and the sunroof, if you have one) are fully closed.

4 Cover your mouth.

Tie a handkerchief, cloth napkin, or bandanna around your head so the fabric covers your nose and mouth. Do not wet the fabric beforehand: some gases and vapors are attracted to water and may combine with it to form dangerous and/or unstable compounds.

5 Monitor your speed.

In most cases, you should drive though chemical hazards at a moderate speed. However, when driving through a dry chemical spill, move extremely slowly (less than 15 mph) to avoid kicking up plumes of toxic dust.

6 Drive uphill and upwind of the spill site.

Once through the spill, continue driving away from it. Many dangerous gases are heavier than air and will tend to settle in low-lying areas. Get to a higher elevation immediately.

7 Abandon your car.

When you are uphill and upwind of the spill, at least half a mile away and in an unpopulated and low-traffic area, leave your car, which is now contaminated. Use caution when getting out, and do not touch any external surface.

8 Run.

Proceed uphill and upwind of your car as quickly as possible. Do not crawl.

9 Inform authorities that your vehicle and possibly your person are contaminated.

WARNING!

- ⚠ It is always safer to turn around and drive away from a spill rather than through it. Do not drive through a spill unless you are instructed to do so or have no other choice.

- ⚠ HEPA and other microfilters used in the air circulation systems of some cars are not effective protection from toxic substances.

Household Chemical Poisons

SUBSTANCE	RECOMMENDED TREATMENT
Ammonia	Administration of humidified oxygen; dilute with milk and water.
Rat poison	Injection of vitamin K.
Sodium hypochlorite (common in household cleansers, bleach) on skin or eyes	Flush with water for minimum of 15 minutes.
Sodium hypochlorite swallowed	Water or milk, unless person is choking.
Chemical burns	Remove clothing; flush with cold running water.
Rubbing alcohol	Keep upright until stomach can be pumped.

Never give ipecac syrup or otherwise induce vomiting, regardless of what has been consumed.

EXPLOSIVES

As soon as you realize you are in danger, do not proceed. Back up slowly in your own footsteps.

How to Navigate a Minefield

1 Keep your eyes on your feet.

2 Freeze—do not move any farther.

3 Look for spikes, detonators, wires, bumps, or discoloration in the ground around you.

4 Avoid spikes, detonators, wires, bumps, or discoloration in the ground, and back up slowly in your own footsteps. Do not turn around. Walk backward.

5 Stop when you are certain you are safe.

How to Identify and Avoid Minefields

✪ Ask locals.
Explosive Ordnance Disposal (EOD) technicians, and local women and children are the best sources of information (in that order) for where danger zones are located.

✪ Observe animals.
Field animals are considered de facto minesweepers. Fields with large quantities of mutilated animals, untouched by people, may indicate a minefield.

✪ Watch the movements of locals.
Locals who avoid perfectly good trails are probably avoiding a mined area. Observe which routes they will not travel on and avoid them. Never travel alone in a suspected mined area.

✪ Look for dirt that has been disturbed.
Transference of dirt or discoloration of fields may indicate hasty placement of mines.

✪ Look for wires across trails.
Trip wires strung across trails indicate mines or other explosives.

✪ Look for newly destroyed vehicles on or just off the road.
Evidence of recent mine detonations includes burning or smoking vehicles and craters. Never assume that because a mine has already detonated the path is clear.

✪ Avoid brush and overgrown fields and trails.
These will not be clearly marked with mine clearance signs, and they are more difficult to navigate on your own.

How to Detect a Letter Bomb

1 If a carrier delivers an unexpected bulky letter or parcel, inspect it for lumps, bulges, or protrusions, without applying pressure.

Check for unevenly balanced parcels.

2 Handwritten addresses or labels from companies are unusual.

Check to see if the company exists and if they sent a package or letter.

3 Be suspicious of packages wrapped in string—modern packaging materials have eliminated the need for twine or string.

4 Watch out for excess postage on small packages or letters—this indicates that the object was not weighed by the post office.

It is no longer legal to mail stamped parcels weighing more than 16 ounces at mailboxes in the United States—they must be taken to a post office.

5 Watch out for leaks, stains (especially oily stains), protruding wires, and excessive tape.

6 Watch out for articles with no return address or a nonsensical return address.

WARNING!

⚡ Letter and package bombs can be very dangerous and destructive. However, unlike a bomb that goes off suddenly and with no warning, they can be identified.

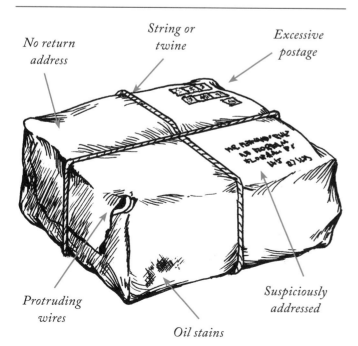

No return address · *String or twine* · *Excessive postage* · *Protruding wires* · *Oil stains* · *Suspiciously addressed*

Pressure-sensitive pad

Typical direct-pressure land mine

Types of Mines

Trip wire mines. Stepping across a wire attached to the detonator will cause the mine to explode.

Direct-pressure mines. Stepping down on a pressure-sensitive pad will activate the detonator.

Timer mines. A timer can be an electrical clock, an electronic digital clock, a dripping/mixing chemical, or a simple mechanical timer that will detonate the mine.

Remote mines. A remote mine can be detonated via an electrical charge across a wire (a "clacker"), via a radio signal, or from a heat or sound sensor.

How to Search for a Bomb

Government agencies use well-defined search procedures for bombs and explosive devices. After a bomb threat, the following can be used as a guide for searching a room, using a two-person search team.

1 Divide the area and select a search height.

The first searching sweep should cover all items resting on the floor up to the height of furniture; subsequent sweeps should move up from there.

2 Start back-to-back and work around the room, in opposite directions, moving toward each other.

3 Search around the walls and proceed inward in concentric circles toward the center of the room.

4 If you find a suspicious parcel or device, do not touch it—call the bomb squad.

GREAT ESCAPES

Familiarize yourself with the trap. Press to compress the springs and relieve pressure on the jaws.

How to Free Your Leg from a Bear Trap

1 Move your foot and wiggle your toes.
Bear traps are designed to catch and hold the leg of a bear, not cut it off. Your leg may be badly bruised, but it should not be severely injured or amputated. Attempt to move your foot and toes to determine if you still have circulation and to check for tendon and muscle damage. In general, the steel "jaws" of the trap are not sharp. Each side of the jaw should have "teeth" that are designed to allow circulation. If you cannot feel your foot or do not have range of movement, you will have to work quickly.

2 Sit with the trap in front of you.
Sit on the ground and move the trapped leg so it is in front of you, bent slightly. The trap may be anchored to the ground with a short chain, or the chain may be attached to a loose hook. (When the caught animal runs away, the hook leaves a trail that is easy to track.)

3 Familiarize yourself with the trap.
The trap will have one piece of bent steel (a "spring") to the

left and another piece to the right of the jaws. The center of the trap will have a flat steel plate called a "pan." Your leg will be between the jaws, your foot on the pan.

4 Place one hand on the top of each spring.

5 Close the springs.
With as much force as possible, press down hard on the springs to compress them. As the springs compress, they will lower and relieve pressure on the jaws.

6 Once the jaws are loose, slip your foot out of the trap.

7 Release the springs.
Take pressure off the springs slowly to avoid snapping the jaws closed suddenly.

8 Check your leg for damage.
Look for broken skin and tissue damage. Seek medical attention if you are injured. Be sure to request a tetanus booster if metal has pierced the skin.

How to Escape from a Bad Date

Slip Away Unnoticed

1 Identify your escape route.
Observe your surroundings. Take note of the exits, especially the back doors. Look for the best way out and an alternative.

2 Plan to alter your appearance.
Think about your most distinctive features, and figure out how to hide or disguise them. The person you are trying to leave is going to see a figure moving past and away at a distance and will be focusing on the first impression. If you are not familiar to him and are uninteresting, you will not get a second look.

3 Excuse yourself from the table.
Move to the restroom or any private area with a mirror to begin your transformation. Your date will probably wait only two or three minutes before expecting you to return, so act quickly, before he begins looking for you.

4 Add or remove clothing.
Layering garments will change your body shape and even suggest a different gender. A long coat will obscure your body type. Hats are especially useful because they conceal your hair and facial features. Eyeglasses, whether added or removed, work wonders. A shopping bag is a handy prop and can be used to hold your belongings.

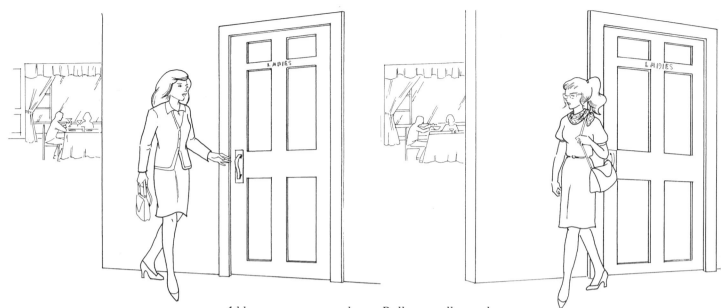

Add—or remove—eyeglasses. Roll or unroll your sleeves;
tuck in or untuck your blouse. Modify your hairstyle.

5 Change your walk and posture.

If you usually walk quickly, move slowly. If you stand up straight, hunch over. To alter your gait, slip a pebble in one shoe or bind one of your knees with a piece of string or cloth.

6 Use or remove cosmetics.

Lipstick can change the shape of your mouth, heighten the color in your cheeks and nose, and even give you tired eyes if dabbed and blended on your eyelids. An eyebrow pencil can be used to add age lines, change the shape of your eyes and brows, or create facial hair.

7 Change your hairstyle or color.

A rubber band, hair spray, water, or any gooey substance can be useful for changing a hairstyle, darkening your hair, or altering a hairline. Borrow flour from the kitchen to lighten or gray your hair color.

8 Adopt a cover role.

A waiter in the restaurant may have an apron and be carrying a tray. If you can manage to procure these items, add or subtract a pair of eyeglasses, and alter your hairline or hairstyle, you can become invisible as you are moving out of the restaurant, into the kitchen, and out the rear door. Or you can take on the role of a maintenance worker; carry a convenient potted plant out the front door, and no one will think twice.

9 Make your move.

Do not look at your date.

Slip Out the Window

If you do not think you will be able to change your appearance enough to slip past your date, you may have to find another way to depart. Back doors are the simplest; they are often located near the restrooms or are marked as fire exits. Do not open an emergency exit door if it is alarmed unless absolutely necessary; an alarm will only draw attention. If there are no accessible alternate doors, you will need to find a window.

1 Locate a usable window.

Avoid windows with chicken wire or large plate glass. Bathroom windows often work best. If you are not on the ground floor, be sure there is a fire escape.

2 Attempt to open the window.

Do not immediately break the window, no matter how dire your need to get out.

3 Prepare to break the window if you cannot open it.

Make sure that no one is around. If you can, lock the bathroom door.

4 Find an implement to break the window.

Try to avoid using your elbow, fist, or foot. Suitable implements:

- Wastebasket
- Toilet plunger
- Handbag or briefcase
- Paper towel dispenser

5 Strike the center of the glass with the implement.

If the hand holding the implement will come within a foot of the window as you break it, wrap it with a jacket or sweater before attempting to break the glass. If no implement is available, use your heavily wrapped hand; be sure you wrap your arm as well, beyond the elbow.

6 Punch out any remaining shards of glass.

Cover your fist with a jacket or sweater before removing the glass.

7 Make your escape.

Do not worry about any minor nicks and cuts. Run.

Fake an Emergency

1 Excuse yourself from the table.

Tell your date that you are going to the restroom to "wash up." Take your cell phone with you. If you do not have one, locate a restaurant phone that's out of your date's line of vision. Bring a restaurant matchbook or a business card that includes the restaurant's phone number.

2 Call a friend or relative for help.

Tell him to call you (either on your cell phone or on the restaurant's phone) and pretend that there has been an emergency. Some believable emergencies are:

- Personal crisis: "My friend just broke up with her husband—she's having a breakdown. I have to go."

- Business crisis: "My boss just called—she's in Seattle for a major presentation and has lost all her files. I have to e-mail them to her immediately."

- Health crisis: "My sister just called—our grandmother is alone and ill."

3 Leave quickly before your date can protest.

Apologize, but refuse any attempt your date makes to accompany you. If you leave swiftly and without hesitation, your date won't have time to understand what's happening or to object.

How to Escape From Quicksand

1 Carry a stout pole when walking in quicksand country.

2 As soon as you start to sink, lay the pole on the surface of the quicksand.

3 Flop onto your back on top of the pole.

After a minute or two, equilibrium in the quicksand will be achieved, and you will no longer sink.

4 Work the pole to a new position: under your hips and at right angles to your spine.

When in an area with quicksand, bring a stout pole and use it to put your back into a floating position.

Place the pole at a right angle from your spine to keep your hips afloat.

The pole will keep your hips from sinking, as you (slowly) pull out first one leg and then the other.

5 Take the shortest route to firmer ground, moving slowly.

How to Avoid Sinking

Quicksand is just ordinary sand mixed with upwelling water, which makes it behave like a liquid. However, quicksand—unlike water—does not easily let go. If you try to pull a limb out of quicksand, you have to work against the vacuum left behind. Here are a few tips:

- The viscosity of quicksand increases with shearing—move slowly so the viscosity is as low as possible.

- Floating on quicksand is relatively easy and is the best way to avoid its clutches. You are more buoyant in quicksand than you are in water. Humans are less dense than freshwater, and salt water is slightly more dense. Floating is easier in salt water than freshwater and much easier in quicksand. Spread your arms and legs far apart and try to float on your back.

FIREARMS

How to Survive If You Are in the Line of Gunfire

If You Are the Primary Target

1 Get as far away as possible.
An untrained shooter isn't likely to be accurate at any distance greater than 60 feet.

2 Run fast, but do not move in a straight line—weave back and forth to make it more difficult for the shooter to draw a bead on you.
The average shooter will not have the training necessary to hit a moving target at any real distance.

3 Do not bother to count shots.
You will have no idea if the shooter has more ammunition. Counting is only for the movies.

4 Turn a corner as quickly as you can, particularly if your pursuer has a rifle or assault weapon.
Rifles have much greater accuracy and range, and the person may be more likely to either aim or spray bullets in your direction.

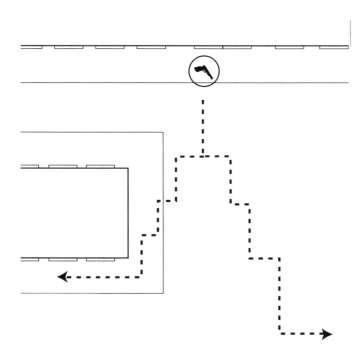

Run in a zigzag pattern to make yourself more difficult to hit. Try to turn a corner if possible.

If You Are Not the Primary Target

1 Get down, and stay down.
If the intended target is near you or if the shooter is firing at random, get as low as possible. Do not crouch down; get flat on your stomach and stay there.

2 If you are outside and can get to a car, run to it and lie behind a tire on the opposite side of the car from the shooter.
If no cars are present, lie in the gutter next to the curb. A car will stop or deflect a small-caliber bullet fired toward you. However, higher caliber bullets—such as those from an assault rifle or bullets that are designed to pierce armor—can easily penetrate a car and hit someone on the opposite side.

3 If you are inside a building and the shooter is inside, get to another room and lie flat.
If you cannot get to another room, move behind any heavy, thick objects (a solid desk, filing cabinets, tables, a couch) for protection.

4 If you are face-to-face with the shooter, do anything you can to make yourself less of a target.
Turn sideways, and stay low—stray bullets are likely to be at least a few feet above the ground. If the shooter is outside, stay inside, and stay away from doors and windows.

5 Stay down until the shooting stops or until authorities arrive and give the all clear.

Attempt to keep large objects between you and the shooter.

How to Take a Bullet

1 Face the shooter.
You do not want to take the bullet in your back or the base of your skull.

2 Get low.
In addition to making yourself a smaller target, by keeping a low profile you will be better able to protect your head, neck, and midline—all areas where a bullet wound is most likely to cause fatal injury or permanent disability.

3 Sit.
Sit with your rear end on the ground. Bend your knees and keep your legs in front of you, protecting your midline with your shins and thighs.

4 Move your elbows into the center of your body.
Place both forearms in front of you, covering your face.

5 Place your hands over your head.
Hold your fingers together, with your palms toward you. Keep your hands an inch or two in front of you to absorb the impact of the bullet.

6 Wait for the impact.
You may notice little more than a "punch" sensation, or you may feel nothing at all.

7 Determine the site of the injury.
Bullet wounds in the hands and feet, lower legs, and forearms are rarely fatal, provided blood loss is controlled.

8 Control the bleeding.
Place firm, direct pressure on the wound to slow blood loss. If the bullet entered an appendage and pressure does not stop the bleeding, use a belt or narrow strip of cloth as a tourniquet. Place the tourniquet on the affected limb, several inches above the injury site. It should be tight enough to stop heavy blood flow. A tourniquet may cause permanent damage to the affected limb and should be used only as a last resort. Never leave a tourniquet in place for more than a few minutes.

9 Get help.
Seek medical attention as soon as possible.

WARNING!

⚡ If you are crouching next to a wall, stay a foot or more away from the surface. Bullets will skid along the wall after impact.

⚡ Gunshot wounds to the neck are almost always fatal.

⚡ Most interior walls and doors (including car doors) will not stop a bullet larger than .22 or .25 caliber.

How to Treat a Bullet or Knife Wound

1 Do not immediately pull out any impaled objects.
Bullets, arrows, knives, sticks, and the like cause penetrating injuries. When these objects lodge in the vital areas of the body (the trunk or near nerves or arteries), removing them may cause more severe bleeding that cannot be controlled. The object may be pressed against an artery or other vital internal structure and may actually be helping to reduce the bleeding.

2 Control the bleeding by using a combination of direct pressure, limb elevation, pressure points, and tourniquets (in that order).
Direct pressure. You can control most bleeding by placing

Attempt to apply pressure directly to bleeding surfaces. Using fingertips rather than the palm is more effective for scalp wounds. Attempt to promote clotting. Press on bleeding arterioles (small squirting vessels). If injury is in a limb, use pressure to control bleeding and elevate the limb. Dress the wound to prevent spread of infection.

Means of Bulletproofing

WHAT'S IT CALLED	WHAT'S IT MADE OF	HOW MUCH OF YOUR BODY IS COVERED
Brewster Body Shield	chrome, steel	upper torso and head
bulletproof vest	Kevlar, a strong synthetic fiber	torso
combat helmet	Kevlar	scalp, upper part of the neck
bulletproof glass	laminated glass over polycarbonate thermoplastic	everything, if you're behind it
armored car	galvanized, chromium-reinforced steel plating	everything, if you're inside it
riot shield	Kevlar	top of head to knees
force field	telekinesis, Green Lantern's ring	everything

direct pressure on the wound. Attempt to apply pressure directly to bleeding surfaces. The scalp, for instance, bleeds profusely. Using your fingertips to press the edges of a scalp wound against the underlying bone is more effective than using the palm of your hand to apply pressure over a wider area. Use the tips of your fingers to control bleeding arterioles (small squirting vessels).

Limb elevation. When a wound is in an extremity, elevation of the extremity above the heart, in addition to direct pressure, may reduce the bleeding further. Never make people who are in shock sit up simply to elevate a bleeding wound.

Pressure points. To reduce blood flow, you usually have to compress an artery (where you can feel the pulse) near the wound against an underlying bone. Just pressing into the soft belly of a muscle does not reduce blood flow by this mechanism.

Tourniquets. A tourniquet is a wide band of cloth or a belt that is placed around an extremity and tightened (usually using a windlass) until the blood flow is cut off. The blood supply must be compressed against a long bone (the upper arm or upper leg), since vessels between the double bones in the lower arm and lower leg will continue to bleed despite a tourniquet. The amount of pressure necessary typically causes additional vascular and nerve trauma that is permanent. A tourniquet should be used only as a last resort—to save a life at the expense of sacrificing a limb.

3 Immobilize the injured area.
Using splints and dressings to immobilize an injured area helps protect it from further injury and maintain clots that have begun to form. Even if an injury to a bone or joint is not suspected, immobilization will promote clotting and help healing begin.

4 Dress the wound, and strive to prevent infection.
Use sterile (or at least clean) dressings as much as possible. Penetrating injuries may allow anaerobic (air-hating) bacteria to get deep into the tissue. This is why penetrating wounds are typically irrigated with sterile or antibiotic solutions in surgery. While this is rarely practical outside of the hospital, it is important to remember that smaller penetrating wounds (nail holes in the foot and the like) should be encouraged to bleed for a short period to help "wash out" foreign material. Soaking an extremity in hydrogen peroxide may help kill anaerobic bacteria as well. Do not apply ointments or goo to penetrating wounds, as these may actually promote infection.

Emergency Tip

Some data indicate that pure granulated sugar poured into a penetrating wound can decrease bleeding, promote clotting, and discourage bacteria. You are not likely to see it used in your local emergency department, but it might be worth consideration if your circumstances are dire.

5 Get medical attention as soon as possible.

WARNING!

Tourniquets are rarely helpful—it is uncommon to have life-threatening bleeding in an extremity that cannot be controlled by the methods described above. The areas that cause fatal bleeding (like the femoral arteries or intra-abdominal bleeding) do not lend themselves to the use of a tourniquet. Even most complete amputations do not bleed all that much and are controlled by direct pressure. Arteries that are severed only part of the way through tend to bleed more profusely than those that are completely severed.

POLITICAL UNREST

How to Drive a Tank

1 Survey the area.

Evaluate the immediate surrounding area before entering the tank, since your field of vision is limited once inside. Note obstacles or unstable ground and steep slopes or banks, which can cause the vehicle to roll.

2 Board the tank.

Use the skirt step on the left front of most tanks to climb onto the front of the tank. Locate the driver's hatch, below the turret. Lift and swing the hatch to the side, locking it in the open position. Climb inside. Close and lock the hatch behind you.

3 Sit down.

The driver's seat, located in the center of the space, is tilted back like a dentist's chair to accommodate the driving area's low ceiling. Adjust the angle and height of the seat until you are comfortable and can see through the periscopes directly in front of your seat and can reach the controls.

4 Identify the gauges and instruments.

Your driver's master control panel sits to your right and instrument panel to your left. The instrument panel features your fuel level indicator and other gauges; the control panel holds the switches and knobs necessary to turn on the tank's engines, fans, and other systems. The controls and gauges are clearly marked. The gearshift is located atop the steering handle in front of you.

5 Check the fuel gauge.

Examine the fuel gauge on the instrument panel to your left to determine whether you have enough fuel to start the tank and reach your destination. Tank fuel consumption is measured in gallons per mile. You will need 10 gallons just to start the engine and about 2 gallons per mile once you get going. You can travel about 300 miles on a full tank of fuel.

6 Start the tank.

Flip up the silver ignition switch at the bottom left-center of your control panel to the On position. The engine will need about three to five minutes to warm up. You can help speed the process by revving the engine, twisting back the throttle on the right steering grip as you would on a motorcycle grip.

7 Test the periscopes.

The driver's visual system consists of three periscopes that look like windshields. The two on either side of you allow you to view in front of the tank and to its left and right

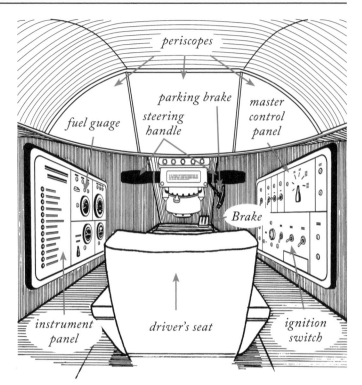

Adjust the angle and height of your seat until you can see through the periscopes and can reach the controls.

for about a 120-degree visual field. In between those two periscopes, you will find a central image-intensifying periscope, which looks straight ahead, for use in driving at night or in smoky or dusty situations.

8 Release the parking brake.

The parking brake control is to the right of your steering handle. Pull on its black, T-shaped handle, and then twist and ease it downward to release it.

9 Put the tank into gear.

Pull the silver transmission selector knob above the steering handle and ease it into the D (Drive) slot, second from the right.

10 Start slowly.

Some tanks can accelerate from 0 to 45 mph in less than 10 seconds. Ease the throttle back to move ahead, slowly at first, twisting back farther as you feel more comfortable with handling the tank at higher speeds.

11 Steer.

Guide the tank as you would a bicycle, snowmobile, or motorcycle by rotating the steering handlebar to the left and right.

12 Listen for tread buildup.

The tank's treads can become disabled with debris. If the tank is not responding quickly to your steering, you may have mud, sand, or some other substance built up on your tracks, which can cause the treads to come off the wheels, leaving the tank essentially immobilized. This buildup is usually accompanied by a popping sound. Drive the tank forward in a straight line over level ground until the popping stops, indicating that the tracks have cleared themselves.

13 Brake.

Once you have arrived at your destination, come to a stop by easing your foot all the way down on the service brake, located on the floor beneath your steering handle. Before exiting the tank, reapply the parking brake by pulling the black T-shaped handle to your right.

WARNING!

* Put on protective headgear before entering the tank. Tank interiors are full of levers, knobs, and other protruding objects that can cut, burn, or daze.

* Never try to get onto and into a tank while it is in motion, no matter how slowly it is moving.

* Wear earplugs or noise-canceling headphones. Tank engines are loud.

* Run the exhaust fan for at least five minutes for every hour onboard to replenish the tank's limited oxygen supply.

* Tank interiors can be claustrophobic and nauseating, as they tend to fill with overpowering odors from their huge engines. Skip your previous meal before your tank ride.

How to Survive a Hostage Situation

1 Stay calm.

Help others around you to do the same—remember that the hostage takers are extremely nervous and scared. Do not do anything to make them more so. Do not speak to them unless they speak to you.

2 If shots are fired, keep your head down and drop to the floor.

If you can, get behind something, but do not move far—your captors may think that you are attempting to make an escape or an attack.

3 Do not make any sudden or suspicious movements.

Do not attempt to hide your wallet, passport, ticket, or belongings.

4 Comply with all demands.

Hesitation on your part may get you killed instantly, or may mark you for later retribution or execution. Remain alert, and do not try to escape or be a hero. If you are told to put your hands over your head, to keep your head down, or to get into another body position, do it. It may be uncomfortable, but do not change your position on your own. Talk yourself into relaxing into the position—you may need to stay that way for some time. Prepare yourself both mentally and emotionally for a long ordeal.

5 Never look at a terrorist directly or raise your head until you are directed to speak to him or her.

Always raise your hand and address the hostage takers respectfully. When answering questions, be respectful but not submissive. Speak in a regulated tone of voice.

6 Never challenge a hostage taker.

They often look for potential execution victims, and if you act contrary in any way, they may select you.

7 Carefully observe the characteristics and behavior of the terrorists.

Give them nicknames in your mind so that you can identify them. Be prepared to describe them by remembering attire, accents, facial characteristics, or height—any aspect that might later help authorities.

8 If you are the victim of a skyjacking, know where the plane's closest emergency exits are located.

Count the rows between you and the exit. In the event of an emergency rescue, smoke may obscure visibility, and you must know the fastest path out of the aircraft. Do not attempt escape unless it is clear that a massacre is imminent.

9 If a rescue team enters, get down and stay still.

Shots may be fired, and any sudden movements may draw terrorist or friendly fire.

10 Upon resolution, be prepared to identify yourself and terrorists to the rescuers.

Some terrorists may try to exit with you, posing as hostages.

WARNING!

* To avoid making yourself attractive to terrorists, try not to take out your passport in public places.

* Be especially alert in airports, train stations, bus stations, lobbies of expensive hotels, and stores that cater to affluent tourists. While civil strife and guerrilla activity usually focus on nationals—thus tourists are relatively safe—terrorists often choose targets that will get them the most attention.

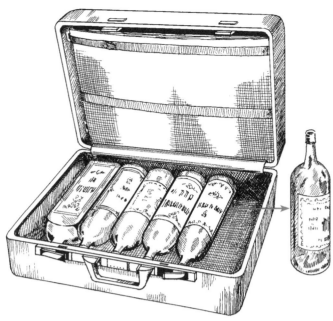

To resolve a customs dispute, offer the official a "sample" of the goods in question–for example, a bottle of liquor.

How to Pass a Bribe

1 If you are hassled by an official, be friendly but aloof.
Do not show concern or act surly. Remain calm and good-natured. Try to determine if there is an actual problem or if the official is seeking some additional, unofficial compensation.

2 Never blatantly offer a bribe.
If you have misinterpreted the official's intentions, you may get yourself in additional trouble by overtly offering a bribe.

3 If you are accused of an infraction, ask to pay a fine on the spot.
Say that you would rather not deal with the mail or go to another location, citing your fear that the payment will get lost. Mention that you want to make sure the money gets to the proper person.

4 Try to speak to and deal with only one official.
Speak to the person who acts as though he or she is in charge. If you offer money to a junior officer while a superior is present, the superior may demand more.

5 Offer to make a "donation" to the official's organization.
Say that you would like to pay for gas, uniforms, car repairs, expenses, or other needs.

6 If you do not have cash, be prepared to offer goods instead.
Watches, cameras, and other electronics are often accepted as bribes. You might consider offering goods instead of cash

even if you have the money, particularly if the "problem" concerns these goods. If, for example, a customs official tells you that you are transporting too many bottles of liquor, you might speed your trip and lighten your load by offering some of the items in dispute to the official.

WARNING!

⚡ Carry only a small amount of money in your wallet and hide the rest. This will prevent an unscrupulous official from seeing your entire wad.

How to Survive a Coup

1 Remain indoors if you learn about any nearby rioting or civil unrest.
Avoid the windows. Listen for reports on radio or television. If you hear gunfire, try to find out where the shooting is located. Use the telephone if it is still functioning, or ask an official or your hotel manager for information.

2 If you believe the crisis is unresolvable or seriously threatens your life, plan to leave the country quickly.

3 Determine the best route to the airport or embassy, and leave the building through any safe exit.
Make sure that the airport is operating before you travel there. If you cannot make it to your own country's embassy, plan to head for the embassy of an allied nation.

4 Wear clothing in muted tones.
Put on a long-sleeved shirt, a jacket, jeans, a hat, socks, and lightweight boots. (Although you may be in a tropical or warm part of the world, it gets quite cold on planes, and you may have to sleep in an airport or connect to a flight landing in a colder region.)

5 Exit away from gunfire or mobs.
Select a way out that is not easily observed. Exits include windows, vents, or even the roof.

6 Leave as a group.
Especially if you have to dash across an open area, such as the front of a building, a wide street, or a plaza, you are safer with company. Snipers or enemies will have multiple objects to focus on, not just one, and will not be as likely to make a move.

7 Do not run.
Unless your life is in imminent danger, walk. Walking is harder for the eye to detect: the human eye can quickly sight someone running. Running can also generate excitement—people may chase you.

8 If you must travel by car, be prepared for evasive maneuvers.

Drive on back streets, not main roads, and be prepared to abandon your car if necessary. Get to an airport or friendly embassy.

Drive on backstreets, not main roads, and be prepared to abandon the car if the situation becomes critical. Watch out for checkpoints, roundabouts, major intersections, and military/police barracks. Do not stop for anything—remember the car can be a useful 2,000-pound weapon that even a mob cannot stop. If you cannot drive forward, drive in reverse. A reliable driver who knows the area will be able to navigate much better than you. If no driver or taxi is available, hire a local to drive your car for you. (You may need to promise to give your car in exchange.) Abandon the car outside the embassy or airport. If a Molotov cocktail (flammable liquid in a glass container with a lighted wick) hits your car, speed up—it may burn out as you gain speed.

9 **If you encounter unavoidable roadblocks, be prepared to bargain your way to safety.**
You might need to give up everything you are carrying in order to get away. Offer cash first, equipment (watches, cameras, jewelry) second.

10 **Get to an embassy or to the airport as soon as possible.**

WARNING!

✈ If you are in a volatile region where there is a likelihood of civil disorder, be prepared for a rapid evacuation. Each person and family member should have an escape pack set aside near the front door. A good, small backpack is preferable to any type of luggage. It should contain the following:

- **Flashlight.** Pack a mini-flashlight with extra batteries. Affix a red or blue lens if you have one; red or blue light is difficult for observers (snipers, mobs) to see at night.

- **Small compass and a detailed map of the city.** Be sure to mark the embassy and helicopter landing zones on the map.

- **Knife.** Include a small pocketknife.

- **Fire-starting tool.** Carry storm-safe matches or a lighter in a waterproof bag. Pack small baggies of dryer lint, which is light and highly flammable.

- **Black garbage bags.** Use these for emergency shelter and camouflage.

- **Water and food.** Carry at least two quarts of water per person. Bring only high-energy or instant foods. Do not eat unless you have water.

✈ Conceal on your person, in a multipocket neck pouch, the following items:

- **Money.** Take $25 in single U.S. dollars and all of your local currency, and divide it among your pouch and pockets. This will serve as bribe money for checkpoints. Dole it out in heaps until it appears you have no more. Do not offer your papers. Carry more money in your neck pouch, but keep the bulk of your cash in your socks, crotch, or ankle pouch.

- **Passport.** Place a full photocopy of your passport in the main section of the pouch for easy access. Keep your original passport in a separate section. Show the copy to locals who demand it. Never give up the original.

- **Official documents.** Visas, phone numbers, proof of citizenship, birth certificates, and so on should be kept with your original passport.

- **Soft earplugs.** Helicopters are very noisy, and earplugs are useful when you want to sleep in a battle zone.

NUCLEAR EVENT

How to Survive Nuclear Fallout

1 Put distance between yourself and the blast site.
Radioactivity diminishes significantly with physical protection, time, and distance from the epicenter of the explosion. For a five-megaton weapon detonated at 2,000 feet (an average weapon yield and detonation altitude), move at least 20 miles away for safety. Travel in a crosswind direction (not with or against the wind) as quickly as possible. Drive a car with the windows rolled up. If no car is available, ride a bike or run.

2 Find shelter.
Any material will at least partially block radioactive particles. However, dense materials like lead, concrete, and steel are more effective than porous materials like wood, tile, drywall, and insulation of equal thickness. If you cannot get into a designated fallout shelter, move to the basement of a building made of stone or concrete, preferably with few windows. The deeper the basement, the more protection you'll have from radioactive particles.

3 Gather water.
The existing water in a basement water tank should be safe to drink, as is water in pipes. However, if dams and water treatment plants become contaminated, new water entering the system may be dangerous. Stored bottled water is safe, provided the water does not come into contact with the outside of the bottle, which may be covered with radioactive particles.

4 Gather food.
Packaged foods and those that can be peeled or shelled—and that are already in the house—are safe to eat, provided that the packages, peels, or shells are rinsed thoroughly with clean water to eliminate radioactive alpha and beta particles. Canned goods are also safe, as long as the cans are washed with clean water and food does not come into contact with the can's exterior. Avoid foods from opened packages, even if the packages have been resealed with tape or clips.

5 Wash your hands before eating and drinking.
Using soap and clean water, wash your hands (and under your fingernails) thoroughly before handling food. Radioactive particles traveling on dust can be transferred to food easily. Once ingested, these may settle in bone marrow and internal organs, causing long-term illness.

6 Stay in your shelter.
Without a radiation rate meter, you will not know when it is safe to leave your shelter. If you have access to a battery-powered radio, listen for news and monitor emergency announcements regarding the safety of your location. Cellular and wired telephones may not work, and even satellite phones may suffer from severe interference. If available, use a CB or shortwave radio to communicate with others until telephone service is restored.

Radiation Exposure Risks

EVENT	RADIATION DOSE (IN MILLIREMS)
sleeping beside another person for eight hours	2
five-hour transatlantic flight	3
chest X-ray	3.2
full-body airport scan	8
barium enema	54
radon in the home	200 a year
bone scan	440
whole body CT scan	1,000

- *The average person receives about 360 millirems a year just from natural background radiation.*
- *A dose of 1,250 millirems is required to raise one's risk for contracting cancer by a factor of 1 in 1,000.*
- *A lethal dose is in the area of 450,000 to 600,000 millirems, when the entire body is exposed.*

WARNING!

A radiation suit will prevent you from tracking radioactive particles into the shelter (as long as you remove the suit upon entering) but will not offer protection from fallout.

How to Improvise a Nuclear Fallout Shelter

1 Move a large, sturdy table or workbench into a windowless corner of the basement.

The table or bench must have enough room under it to shelter you and your family. If you are sheltering more than a couple of family members, or if you do not have a strong table or workbench, take a thick solid door or doors off their hinges and place on top of dressers, bookcases, trunks, etc.

2 Pile shielding materials on and around table.

The denser the shielding materials, the more protection they will provide. Use books, magazines, boxes filled with soil or sand, stacks of firewood or lumber, appliances, concrete blocks, bricks, full water containers, and boxes and pillowcases full of anything that has mass and can absorb and deflect gamma particles. Leave gaps for air.

3 Stock up on water.

Gather sufficient liquid to allow each person one quart each day for two weeks. Store in containers with tight-fitting lids.

10 Things to Know About Radiation

- People who live at higher elevations are exposed to higher levels of cosmic radiation.

- As many as 8,000 people died in the April 26, 1986, Chernobyl accident and its cleanup; an estimated 4.9 million people, however, were exposed to radiation.

- The March 28, 1979, Three Mile Island nuclear disaster in the United States has never been found to have any negative effects on public health.

- A car or building will provide some level of radiation protection.

- Radioactive alpha particles can be blocked with a sheet of paper.

- Radioactive neutrons can travel long distances in the air but can be blocked with water or concrete.

- Half of all people with cancer are treated with radiation.

- There is no effective treatment for radiation sickness.

- The most radioactive foodstuff in the world is Brazil nuts, which have radium concentrations 1,000 times higher than that of most foods.

- The Capitol building in Washington, D.C., has an extremely high level of background radiation, because of the uranium content in its granite walls.

Nail pieces of wood across basement windows, then pile dirt outside to cover the glass.

4 Gather food.

Canned foods or foods in sealed packages that do not require refrigeration are best. Make sure to bring a can opener and a pair of sturdy scissors for opening cans and packages.

5 Put a radio in the shelter.

In case of disaster, listen to the radio to find out when it is safe to move around. Also take extra batteries into the shelter.

6 Cover basement windows.

Nail pieces of wood across windows to prevent breakage, then pile sandbags or shovel earth outside any basement windows and entrances.

7 Seal yourself in.

Climb under the table, pull shielding material around the open space you crawled through, and turn on the radio to await further instructions.

ZOMBIES

How to Survive a Zombie Attack

First 24 Hours

1 **Evaluate means of escape.**
Access to a vehicle, and the type of vehicle available, will dictate the amount of survival supplies you will be able to bring. If you do not have access to a car or truck, pack lightly so that you will be able to move quickly until you can locate an operating vehicle. Look for humans in operating vehicles or a car in which the human occupants have been killed but the keys are still inside.

2 **Gather immediately available survival materials.**

- **Food:** Gather nonperishable foodstuffs as well as perishable food that you will be able to eat before spoilage sets in.
- **Communication:** Take radios, mobile phones, laptop computers, and batteries.
- **Clothing:** Pack layers sufficient for sleeping in cold weather, at least one extra pair of shoes or boots, and items that may offer physical protection, such as sports pads or helmets.
- **First aid supplies:** Empty the contents of your medicine cabinet into a bag and take it with you.
- **Weapons:** Gun use may be limited by your supply of ammunition, but don't leave these deadly weapons behind. Include long-handled bladed tools or weapons, such as axes or shovels, that may be used to kill zombies while affording you distance of reach. Bludgeoning items, such as baseball bats, will also come in handy. Power tools are useful only if they have a battery charge or fuel; they also tend to be heavy, and the weight may not be worth carrying.
- **Fuel:** Kerosene, gasoline, lighter fluid, lighters, and matches will all be valuable for light and heat; they are also indispensable as additional weapons against zombies, which are flammable and fearful of fire.
- **Water:** A heavy but vital survival supply; bring as much as you can manage without slowing yourself down, especially if you're traveling on foot.

3 **Gather more supplies.**
The days immediately following zombie infection will be when supplies are most plentiful—before further infestation complicates access, other human survivors obtain the goods, or they are destroyed (by uncontrolled fires, for

Cover your face to avoid internalizing any zombie gore.

example). Obtain more or improved supplies in the above categories from stores or abandoned residences close to your immediate location.

4 **Consider including others in your survival plans.**
Incorporating other uninfected humans can offer increased security in numbers, but these additional people will also increase the rate at which you consume supplies. Unless their own supplies supplement yours, or their zombie-fighting abilities seem dynamic, ask yourself this question: Are they slowing me down?

5 **Trust no one.**
Watch for signs of infection when encountering human survivors: open wounds, bite marks, aggressive confusion, inability to articulate thoughts, and spastic movements are all warning signs of zombification. Flee from or destroy the infected individual by removing its head or critically damaging the brain with a blade, bullet, or blunt trauma. Uninfected human survivors may in fact be seeking to obtain your survival supplies for themselves.

6 **Avoid splatter.**
Do not internalize any matter—blood, flesh, or brains—from a zombie. When destroying zombies, be certain that no gore comes into contact with your eyes, nose, mouth, inner ears, or open wounds. Such contact will result in zombification.

7 **Get out of town.**
Opt for less-populated routes out of the city to minimize contact with zombie hordes. Do not stop to comfort any weeping children or helpless wounded, since such isolated figures bear a high chance of being zombies trying to trick you.

8 Seek out less densely inhabited areas.

Drive as far as possible, as quickly as possible.

First Week

1 Find a safe haven.

Seek out a place to make a secure camp. A city setting is less than ideal; it is easy to be trapped by a horde in an apartment building or in a maze of city streets. A rural area is safer but may take you too far from contact with other survivors. Drive to a suburb, where you can find a single-family home on about a quarter acre of land. This allows the benefit of an enclosed structure with room to maneuver, as well as a wide vista from which you can spot approaching zombie hordes.

2 Make your haven habitable.

Perform a meticulous sweep, with a gun leveled in front of you, to ensure that your new home is free of zombies. Wearing heavy gloves and a mask, remove rotting corpses, being sure to dispose of them far from water sources. If the water taps are working, collect as much water as possible in clean containers, in case the water source later malfunctions. Raid the kitchen, storeroom, and garage for useful supplies. Carefully catalog what you now own.

3 Secure the perimeter.

Nail wood paneling around all windows, lock all doors, and push heavy furniture behind those that swing in. Push a refrigerator or other extremely heavy object over the trapdoor to the basement, and set a trap of protruding spikes beneath the door from the attic. Outside, use your ax to chop down any trees that could obscure your view of oncoming hordes. Working as quickly as possible to minimize your time outdoors, dig a system of deep trenches across the lawn. Light a fire in the fireplace so that anyone or anything entering via the chimney will fall into the open flame.

4 Set traps.

Zombies are not sophisticated hunters and can be duped into their own destruction with simple traps. Make a recording of talking human voices, and bury it in the bushes to draw the zombies into your field of vision; then open fire on them from a second-story window. Use department store mannequins as decoys to draw the zombies into the trench system you dig in the lawn. Sever the chain of the automatic garage door and rig it to crash down onto zombies entering the garage. Hang a net full of bowling balls over the front door so that a zombie forcing its way in will trigger the balls to rain down and crush its head.

5 Remain vigilant.

Perform daily perimeter checks, peeking out of windows and emerging onto the roof to check for oncoming hordes. Rig walkie-talkies or an old baby safety monitor to alert you to an onslaught. Place a gun under your pillow or clutch it in your hand while sleeping. Do not drink alcohol or become otherwise impaired in any way. Do not relax for even one second.

6 Consume carefully.

Limit food and drink consumption to only the bare caloric minimum so that supplies hold out as long as possible.

7 Remain clued-in.

Build a ham radio to maintain communication with other survivors. Monitor the progress of the infestation, waiting to see if it is improving or worsening and whether the putrefying hordes are approaching your sanctum.

8 Add to supplies.

When absolutely necessary, venture forth to find more food, water, and first aid supplies. When traveling in zombie-infested countryside, keep off main routes of transportation, and always travel with several weapons on your person and at the ready. Be prepared to use your weapons against zombies or other noninfected humans who challenge you for your food.

9 Be ready to go.

Keep your essential equipment packed and ready, in a room just off the garage, so that it can be thrown in the trunk at a moment's notice. Leave the car facing out toward the driveway, with the keys in the ignition. The moment it seems you are in danger of being overrun by the horde, floor the accelerator, smash through the garage door, and mow through the pack of zombies, all the while firing your gun through the windshield.

Long Term

1 Put down roots.

Slowly transform your improvised safe haven into a home. Pin up tattered photographs of deceased or zombified friends and loved ones; build permanent structures, such as a gravel driveway, reinforced well, and sanitary outdoor toilet.

2 Teach yourself skills.

Raid abandoned libraries and bookstores to study rainwater filtration, carpentry, car repair, waterborne illness prevention, and other skills you will need to survive long term in a postapocalyptic nightmarescape. Practice martial arts, riflery, horseback riding, and wilderness survival. Learn how to hunt and field-butcher animals and to cook over an open flame.

3 Seek out fellow survivors.

Broadcast your location on a ham radio or over wireless networks. Over time, the survival equation will tip in favor of groups of humans, rather than individuals, as long as the group is vigilant about protecting the perimeter of its location. Share responsibilities, such as cooking, wound dressing, and zombie killing.

4 Ruthlessly purge infected members of the community.

Make solemn agreements with every member of the group to kill them should they become infected and for them to do the same to you. Doing so will ease everyone's conscience and ensure that there will be no fatal hesitation when the crucial moment comes.

5 Destroy corpses.

If fellow survivors are bitten and must be killed, quickly destroy their bodies before they can return to life. Wearing a mask and gloves, douse each corpse in kerosene and set it on fire.

6 Plant crops.

Most animal life will have disappeared in the zombie plague, but the soil will still yield fruit-bearing trees and vegetables. Defend the perimeter of your fields from zombie invasion until harvest season, and send out harvesters in well-armed teams of two: one to bring in crops, the other to defend against attack. Focus on planting turnips, potatoes, and other root vegetables that can stored for a long time, should a crop have to be destroyed or abandoned. Make fruits into preserves so they will last longer.

7 Record your travails.

Create a record of anything you learn about the zombies, rates of infection, survival tips, and the names of humans known to have succumbed to the infection. Make multiple digital and hard copies of this record to ensure its availability to future generations or to other surviving groups, should your own copy perish during the plague.

8 Wait out the zombies.

Zombies cannot survive without feeding on human brains for more than a few weeks, but that countdown does not begin until they have consumed all available humans. Remain in your secure encampment until your wireless communication networks indicate that no zombies have been seen or heard for at least three months.

9 Reestablish civilization.

Begin the long process of reconstructing cities, creating a workable government, and developing an economy.

Weapons for Killing Zombies

WEAPON	ADVANTAGES	DISADVANTAGES
Chain saw	Does a lot of damage very quickly.	Can jam with gore; fuel is limited.
Dishwasher	Satisfying sound of drowning zombies.	Hard to get zombies into dishwasher.
Rocks	Endless supply.	Not much damage.
Sword or ax	Can dismember zombies even when they are not killed.	Unwieldy, gets stuck in zombie.
Fire or flame	Zombies are highly flammable.	May create a larger conflagration.
Automobile	Kills several zombies at once.	Can damage car.
Pistol	Kills zombie with single shot to head.	Requires good aim; ammunition in limited supply.
Bow and arrow	Can fashion own arrows.	Requires excellent aim.
Machine gun	Kills many zombies at once.	Rapidly uses up limited stores of ammunition.
Hand grenade	Kills many, many zombies at once.	Danger to thrower, other nearby survivors.
Shovel	Broad side to whack, sharp side to hack.	Requires hand-to-hand encounter.
Fists	None; last-resort option.	Maximizes chances of deadly gore splatter.
Baseball bat	Satisfying crunch.	Requires powerful upper-arm strength.
Steamroller	Extremely effective.	Where are you going to get a steamroller?

How to Outrun a Pack of Zombies

Depending on the type of plague, the zombies you face will be either "fast" zombies, with roughly human running speed, or "slow" zombies, with impeded speed and motion.

Fast Zombies

1 Get a vehicle.
Escaping the zombies in a car allows you to bring supplies, to vastly outpace your pursuers, and to use the vehicle as a weapon when necessary.

2 Leave morsels.
If you are fleeing fast zombies and encounter other survivors, outpace them and keep the survivors between you and the zombies. Attacking the other survivors will slow the zombies' pace.

3 Trick the zombies.
Travel in circles, double back, and follow no definite pattern as you flee. The zombies are persistent but not particularly intelligent.

4 Pace yourself.
Expend only as much energy as necessary to get yourself to safety, then rest. You may escape a particular group of zombies, but you must be ready to avoid others. Remember, there will always be more zombies.

Slow Zombies

1 Make a lot of turns.
Zombie hordes, lacking both leaders and functioning brains, tend to move forward as a ragged clump along a straight line. Simply backtracking and making frequent turns can shake loose your followers.

2 Cross water.
Forge a small creek or row across a lake or stream. Slow zombies are terrible swimmers.

3 Set obstacle fires.
Like humans, zombies will avoid fire. Setting a strategic fire line can afford time for escape as the zombies work their way around the line.

4 Climb stairs.
Slow zombies are not good at climbing stairs. If you are absolutely sure there is another means of exit above, climb stairs and, on arriving at a higher story, leap out a window, landing as silently as possible, and sprint away.

Do not attempt to flee zombies by climbing a tree, as they can wait you out.

All Zombies

1 Stick with the familiar.
Seek escape along routes you know well to avoid becoming disoriented and stumbling into the horde.

2 Do not go up.
Do not climb trees or enter high buildings without any definite path of escape, else you risk becoming entrapped; the zombies will swarm below and simply wait you out. They have nothing better to do.

3 Do not go underground.
For similar reasons, resist the urge to escape into sewers or hide in an abandoned well or swimming pool.

4 Avoid hospitals.
Hospitals are gathering points for sick and dying people, which means that they will also now be full of zombies.

5 Do not enter tunnels.
Zombies may enter from the other side, sealing off any possible escape.

HISTORICAL EMERGENCIES

How to Survive Being Thrown to the Lions

1 Remove your animal skin clothing.
Your captors will have covered you in animal blood or dressed you in the skins of prey animals; such garments may arouse the lions and cause them to attack. Use the skins to wipe off the blood and immediately move as far from the discarded skins as possible.

2 Do not provoke the lions.
If the lions appear sick, sedate, distracted, or disinterested, do not approach them, or you risk inciting an attack that is not forthcoming. Though the lions will have been starved in preparation for your confrontation, there is no certainty that the beasts in the arena will attack you. If the animals don't become aggressive, your fight may be rescheduled for another day's circus games, sparing your life at least until the following day.

3 Fight an animal handler to secure a weapon.
If the lions appear agitated, use your bare hands to attack the smallest, weakest-looking animal handler (*bestiarii*) in the arena. Procure his whip, sword, shield, and/or other protective gear.

4 Watch for mock charges.
A lion may make several mock charges before actually attacking. It will run forward suddenly, then stop. It may back away before charging again. Mock-charging is an indication that a real attack is imminent. Stand your ground and be ready.

5 Yell.
Shout as loud as you can. Lions are sensitive to loud noises, and yelling may discourage one from further charges. Yelling will also act as an impressive display of strength for the crowd in the arena.

6 If you are unable to prevent an attack, use the sword to fight the animal.
Push the lion's paws and head away from you, thrusting the sword into its abdomen.

7 Behave courageously.
Though the animals are typically the victors in cases of *damnatio ad bestias* ("condemnation to the beasts"), the outcome is not always certain. A particularly brave fight leading to victory in the arena may grant you a temporary reprieve or, possibly, a pardon.

Remove any animal skins. Yell to discourage lion from charging.

BE AWARE!

↗ There are wooden doors set into the dirt floor; these doors may lead to passageways or empty animal cages that can provide some measure of protection from lions already in the arena. Do not open the doors in an attempt to escape. The cages may still have vicious, live animals in them, and even an empty cage is only a temporary refuge. You will be pulled out and forced to continue the fight, but since you attempted to hide rather than facing your challenge head-on, it will be impossible to receive a pardon or reprieve even if you are victorious against the animals in the arena.

↗ You may be able to keep the animals at bay by cracking a whip stolen from a *bestiarii*. Circle the whip as far above your head as you can while still allowing for smooth movement. Keep your back straight and your elbow slightly bent to ensure a smooth motion, with your opposite arm out to the side to give you balance. Make one large circle overhead and then a quick upright S approximately two feet in front of you, keeping your wrist at a 45-degree angle to your body as you bring the whip down and complete the motion. Wherever you follow through with your wrist is where the tip—the most dangerous part of the whip—will go.

How to Survive a Joust

1 Don your armor.

The ideal armor for a joust is curved and smooth to help deflect your opponent's lance, with extra protection on your left side, which will be closest to your opponent and the most likely place for him to strike.

2 Mount your steed.

Sit hard in the saddle. Place your feet into the stirrups and use your knees to steady yourself on your horse in preparation for collision with your opponent's lance.

3 At the signal, spur your horse forward.

Hold your lance in your right hand, perpendicular to the ground, and guide your horse ahead, on the left side of the tilt barrier. Lean forward slightly to increase your visibility; the narrow eye slot in your helmet will impair your vision.

4 At the last possible moment, lower your lance toward your opponent.

Extend the lance over your horse's left shoulder at a 35-degree angle across your body.

5 Aim your lance low on your opponent's breastplate.

Though your ultimate goal is to knock your opponent off his horse to win the match, you can also score points by striking your opponent on his helmet (two points) or on his breastplate or shield (one point).

6 Hold your *ecranche* directly facing the impending impact to disperse the force of your opponent's lance.

Your shield, or *ecranche*, will be attached to your chest or your left shoulder. Hold your rein hand just ahead of the front of the saddle, and rest your knuckles on or just above the ridge between the horse's shoulder bones. Do not allow the *ecranche* to sit so high that it scoops upward, or your opponent's lance will slide up to hit your helmet. Note that defensive moves, such as ducking or weaving, are not allowed and will result in a loss of points.

7 Lean backward on impact.

Use your legs like a vise around your horse to remain in your saddle. Meeting force with force, at a slight angle, will diffuse the power of the strike (equal to the force of a blow from a blacksmith's hammer). If you are knocked from your steed, immediately tuck and roll. If possible, angle your fall so that you land on your shoulder and roll with—don't resist—your forward momentum once you strike the ground. The weight of your armor will stop you quickly enough.

8 Repeat steps 3 through 7 until either you or your opponent is knocked from the saddle.

Aim for your opponent's helmet or breastplate to score points.

WARNING!

The rules for each joust differ from tournament to tournament, though typically each match consists of several warm-up runs, called "measuring passes," followed by three to six contacting passes.

Hegel remarks somewhere that history tends to repeat itself. He forgot to add: the first time as tragedy, the second time as farce.

—Karl Marx

Weep

Cry

Sink

How to Prove You're Not a Witch

1 Get rid of any pets.

Witches use animals as agents to carry out the devil's commands, so any animals in your charge, including any insects that enter the courtroom during your trial, may be interpreted as your "familiars" and offered by prosecutors as further proof of your status as a witch.

2 Weep.

Witches are unable to shed tears, so cry when you are arrested.

3 React to pain during the needle ordeal.

All witches have a devil's mark somewhere on their bodies to show that they have made a pact with Satan. During the needle test, any blemish, wart, scar, mole, or other imperfection will be poked to test your reaction. It is believed

that the devil's mark is immune to pain and cannot bleed, so wince and cry out as each blemish is pricked.

4 Sink during the water ordeal.

Witches float in water because they weigh less than ordinary people. During the water ordeal, you will be tied at the hands and feet and thrown into a body of water in the presence of the court and members of the public. When your body hits the water, tense all of your muscles and imagine that you are made of lead or another heavy substance. Take short, shallow breaths before going under rather than filling your lungs with air. The guards will judge your ability to float, and if you sink to the bottom, they will probably pull you up before you drown.

WARNING!

↯ You are a witch if you have
- made a pact with the devil
- had sex with the devil
- practiced harmful magic
- flown through the air
- communicated with "familiar spirits" in the form of animals
- murdered children to eat them or to make ointment from their rendered fat
- met with other witches

↯ Because witchcraft is a *crimen exceptum*—an exceptional crime, on the same level as treason, conspiracy, forgery, and robbery with murder—the courts suspend normal rules of evidence to ease conviction.

↯ Unless you are a child or pregnant, any circumstantial evidence will lead to your torture in order to force a confession. Such evidence can include the following:
- being named a witch by another witch testifying under torture
- being a relative of someone executed for witchcraft
- being homeless
- committing adultery
- learning too quickly
- making threats against another person that have come true
- being in the fields shortly before a hail shower
- making a sick person well
- attending church services sporadically
- attending church services regularly
- showing fear during arrest
- remaining calm during arrest

↯ If you are found guilty of witchcraft, you will be burned alive or hanged. In some regions, you will be strangled before your body is burned as an act of mercy.

How to Fight with Bayonets

⊕ **Maintain eye contact with opponent.**
Watch his weapon and body using peripheral vision. Size up each moment of the fight, pursuing all openings and weaknesses your opponent reveals.

⊕ **Make constant, unpredictable movements.**
Do not allow your opponent to take a clean shot or to anticipate your next move.

⊕ **Growl.**
Make aggressive, threatening noises to frighten your opponent and instill confidence in your own abilities to finish the fight.

⊕ **Start in the attack position.**
Stand with your feet a comfortable distance apart, with your body bent slightly forward at the waist, knees slightly bent, and weight balanced on the balls of your feet. Hold the musket firmly, with your dominant hand on the butt or just behind the trigger guard and your other hand on the grip below the barrel. Position the musket diagonally across and slightly away from your body at about nose level.

⊕ **Thrust the bayonet.**
Grasp the musket tightly and pull the butt in close to your hip; partially extend your nondominant arm, guiding the point of the bayonet toward your opponent's face, throat, abdomen, or groin. Step forward with one leg and push with the full power of your body's movement, using your back heel, waist, and hips rather than relying solely on upper-body strength. Upon penetration, twist the bayonet. To withdraw, shift your weight back, and pull out along the line of penetration. Resume the attack position to continue with the fight.

⊕ **Strike with the musket butt.**
Step forward with the leg opposite your dominant hand and raise the musket in an arc, using your dominant hand to force the butt of the musket underneath your opponent's weapon or onto a vulnerable area of his body (anywhere from his face to his thighs). If delivered with enough force, a strike from the butt of the musket to a bony area can disable your opponent and possibly kill him. Resume the attack position.

⊕ **Smash with the musket butt.**
Push the butt of the rifle upward until it is horizontal, with the muzzle just above your nondominant shoulder and the bayonet pointing behind you. Step forward with the leg opposite your dominant hand and forcefully push with both arms, slamming the butt into your opponent's face. This move is often effective after striking with the musket butt.

Step forward with your leading foot. Strike your opponent's musket. Deflect your opponent's musket to your right.

⊕ **Parry your opponent's attacks.**
Counter the movements of your opponent by quickly raising your bayonet and striking the opponent's musket with your own. If the butt of his musket is at his left hip, deflect his thrust to your right; if the butt of his musket is at his right hip, deflect to your left. This will throw your opponent off balance and enable you to follow up with a thrust, strike, or smash.

⊕ **Block surprise attacks.**
To stop an opponent from striking your groin with the butt of his musket, extend your arms downward and slightly out from your body, catching his weapon at the center part of your musket. To stop a butt stroke to your upper body or head, hold your musket vertical so your opponent's weapon will hit at the center of your musket. Counterattack immediately.

⊕ **Be relentless.**
Quick action is imperative in a bayonet fight. You are fighting for your life.

WARNING!

⚡ In the majority of bayonet charges, the defensive side flees before any contact is made. Bayonet charges are often more of a symbolic coup de grâce meant to finish off the morale of the opposition than an order to actually engage in hand-to-hand combat. Because soldiers running toward a line with bayonets drawn present such an intimidating sight, the commander with the field advantage often delivers the order to stop the battle by chasing the remaining enemy troops from the field. If you hear your field commander give the order for a bayonet charge, you can assume that you are on the winning side of an almost-finished fight.

⚡ Most actual bayonet fights occur not on a battlefield but in close combat situations in villages, woods, or gardens or on highly irregular, broken terrain.

⚡ Aiming at an opponent's breast may lead to impalement of the breastbone, making removal of the bayonet very difficult.

How to Survive Being Buried Alive

1 Conserve your air supply.

If you are buried in a typical coffin, you will have enough air to survive for an hour or two at most. Take deep breaths, then hold for as long as possible before exhaling. Do not breathe and then swallow, which will lead to hyperventilation. Do not light a match or lighter. Combustion will quickly use your available oxygen. It is safe to use a flashlight if you have one. Do not yell. Yelling will lead to panic, which will increase your heart rate and lead to fast breathing that will rapidly consume your air supply.

2 Press up on the coffin lid with your hands.

An inexpensive "pine box" (chipboard coffin) or a recycled paperboard coffin will have some give to it, so it will be relatively easy to break through. If you feel flex in the coffin lid, continue to step 3. A metal-clad or hardwood coffin will be impossible to pierce. In this case, your only hope is to signal for rescue. Use a metal object (ring, belt buckle, coin, flask, pen) to signal that you are alive. Tap SOS, the international distress signal, on the coffin lid: three quick taps, followed by three slower taps, followed by three quick taps. Continue to repeat the distress call until someone hears you.

3 Remove your shirt.

Cross your arms over your chest, then uncross your arms so that your elbows are bent and your hands are at your shoulders. Pull your shirt up and off your head from the shoulders, do a partial sit-up (as much as you can in the space available), then pull your shirt over your head and off.

4 Tie the bottom of the shirt in a knot.

The shirt should have only one large opening, at the neck, as does a bag.

5 Place your head through the neck hole.

The knot should be on the top of your head. The shirt will prevent you from suffocating on loose earth.

6 Break through the coffin.

Using your feet, begin kicking the coffin lid. A cheap coffin may have already split from the weight of the earth above, making your job easier. Break apart the lid with your hands and feet, and let the loose dirt rush in.

7 Use your hands to push the dirt toward your feet.

There should be some space at the bottom end of the coffin, below your feet. As the dirt rushes in, work quickly but

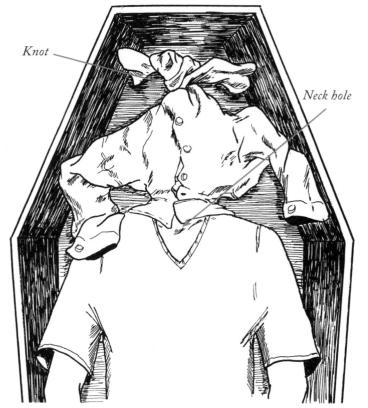

Knot

Neck hole

Your shirt will prevent you from suffocating on loose earth.

calmly to fill the space at your feet. When this space fills up, push dirt to your sides. Breathe slowly and regularly.

8 Sit up.

As you move to a seated position, the loose earth above will move to fill the space you just occupied. As the dirt falls, continue to push it into the coffin until you can stand up.

9 Stand.

Once you are standing, you should be able to push the dirt above you up and out of the grave. When you have cleared all the dirt above you, climb out.

WARNING!

⚐ A recently interred coffin will be covered with loose earth that is relatively easy to dig through.

⚐ Escaping from a coffin interred during a rainstorm will be difficult. The compacted weight of the wet earth will make digging almost impossible.

⚐ The higher the clay content of the soil, the more difficult your escape will be.

HOW TO MAKE A DEAL WITH DEATH

1 State your proposal up front.

Let Death know from the outset how much time you'd like and how you'd like to go.

2 Don't accept Death's first offer.

Death is obligated to take a hard line. Don't let yourself be shaken by Death's insistence on a "right here, right now" stance.

3 Make Death a counteroffer.

Find a realistic middle ground between your offer and the one Death proposes. For example, if he says, "Tomorrow, wolves," respond with, "Five years from now, skiing accident."

4 Don't appear too enthusiastic.

Make it seem like continued life isn't that big a deal to you.

5 Keep it professional.

Death will not respond to pleading, crying, or complaining about unfairness. Death has heard it all before.

6 Look Death in the eye.

Or if Death has come in his traditional guise, look into the black vortex beneath Death's cowl.

7 Ask to speak to Death's supervisor.

Tell him you cannot agree to die without speaking directly to God about the matter.

8 Finalize.

Put the final agreement in writing, and sign it in blood.

9 Use the "nibbling" negotiation technique.

At the last possible moment, demand more concessions. As Death reaches forward to sign the contract, say, "Oh, this does include reincarnation, right?"

Is Your Pet Really Dead?

Cats often sleep without moving for hours, dogs can be lazy, reptiles are cold-blooded and still, fish with parasites sometimes float upside down at the surface, and opossums are well known for feigning. Observe the pet's chest: if it rises and falls, even very slowly, the animal is still alive. Hold a mirror to the pet's nose. If no condensation appears, the animal is probably dead. Pick up the animal. If it does not move and its body is stiff and cold, it has passed away. As a last resort, check the involuntary blinking reflex: lightly touch the pet's cornea. Any animal that is alive will blink reflexively.

HOW TO BEAT DEATH AT CHESS

✪ Distract Death.

Point over Death's shoulder and ask, "Hey, is that Elvis?" When he looks, quickly and quietly move one of your pieces to a more advantageous position.

✪ Question Death.

Ask Death if he's sure that's his next move. If he says yes, raise your eyebrows and say, "Okay, that's cool." If Death then says, "Wait, hold on a second," sigh heavily and say, "Fine."

✪ Go to the bathroom.

While in the restroom, consult a strategy book or miniature board.

✪ Use accomplices.

Many people hold a grudge against Death and may be enlisted to distract him or surreptitiously feed you moves.

✪ Demand a rematch.

Complain loudly about every aspect of the game. Appeal to Death's vanity by saying, "If you really want to win that way, fine. Whatever. Kill me."

✪ Ask to play Scrabble instead.

Death is terrible at Scrabble.

Distract Death and improve your game position while he's not looking.

How to Survive an Accident in Which You Were Meant to Die

⊕ Avoid public transportation.
Do not ride or go near buses, trains, shuttles, trams, trolleys, pedicabs, or horse-drawn carriages.

⊕ Avoid private transportation.
Do not ride or go near cars, vans, trucks, minivans, bicycles, tricycles, motorcycles, or motorcycle sidecars.

⊕ Take baths.
Do not take showers. Before running the water for your bath, unplug all electric devices and lock the bathroom door; while running the water, check the temperature constantly. Stay in the bath only long enough to clean yourself and never more than four minutes.

⊕ Avoid gigantic neon signs.

⊕ Do not swim.
Don't go in the ocean, do laps at the gym, or go to your friend's backyard pool, especially if it is equipped with a suctioning drain.

⊕ Do not go near guns.
Avoid pistols, rifles, handguns, shotguns, BB guns, and nail guns.

⊕ Avoid rickety fire-escape ladders.

⊕ Avoid trucks with cherry pickers.

⊕ Avoid fire.
Do not touch matches, gasoline, downed electric cables, ovens, stoves, or torches. Do not smoke, and do not be friends with or go near people who smoke.

⊕ Do not walk by rickety scaffolding.

⊕ Do not attempt to rescue other people from death.

⊕ Do not go near chain-link fencing.
Be wary of large objects, such as carbon dioxide tanks, that can smash your body into the fencing, thereby dicing it into small pieces.

⊕ Do not take elevators.

⊕ Do not ride roller coasters.

⊕ Do not go near horses.
In fact, avoid animals of all kinds.

WARNING!

⟋ The only way to permanently remove Death's attention, after you have survived an accident in which you were meant to die, is to purposefully put yourself in a near-fatal situation and then survive.

Means of Communicating with the Dead

MEANS OF COMMUNICATION	THE BASICS	PROS	CONS
Séance	Small group chants in dark, invites the dead.	Dramatic.	May take many tries to work.
Ouija board	Board game contacts the other side.	Fun for parties.	May accidentally invite demons.
Waking dream	Spirit met in supernatural desert of the soul.	Subject feels like rock star or guru.	Subject always wakes up before the really good part.
Hire a medium	Professional dead-whisperer delivers your message.	Can hand off messy personal issues.	Medium gets all the credit if things go well.
Channeling	Invite dead person to take over your body.	Extremely intimate.	Will they ever leave?
Visiting the underworld	Journey to hell in company of Virgil.	Can ask the damned anything you want.	May get extremely hot.
Skype	Internet video link.	Picture-in-picture spiritual communication.	Service spotty in lowest levels of hell.

How to Tell If You're Dead

It is a rare but not unheard-of phenomenon that a person will die and become a ghost while remaining unaware of this change in status.

○ **The "grammar check."**
When people speak about you, note whether they do so in the present or past tense.

○ **The "appropriateness check."**
Listen for the sorts of statements people avoid in the presence of a living person, such as "I never told her I loved her" or "I never liked that guy."

○ **The "interaction check."**
Note whether other individuals respond when you speak directly to them. Eliminate other reasons for ignoring you, such as inappropriate behavior or poor hygiene.

○ **Consult an expert.**
Find someone who speaks to dead people professionally, such as a medium or creepy psychic child, and ask them whether you are a ghost.

○ **Judge your ability to have a physical affect.**
You may be able to lift and hold certain objects, but these may be spirit-objects that only you can see. Try performing an action with the object, such as hitting a baseball or another person.

○ **The "fork check."**
Poke yourself in the forearm with a fork, the point of a pencil, or another sharp object. Does it hurt?

Poke yourself with a fork to test for solidity and pain response.

○ **Attempt to fly.**
Squeeze your eyes shut tightly and imagine yourself soaring across the air, ducking in and out of moonbeams. Open your eyes and note whether or not you are actually doing so.

○ **Try to speak to other dead people.**
Speak to people who you know have passed away, and see if you receive a response.

○ **Look at yourself in the mirror.**
Are you there?

WARNING!

⚡ Having a conversation with a seemingly living person does not always mean you are alive; it is possible that the speaker is also dead, and neither one of you is aware of it.

How to Get the Dead to Leave You Alone

1 Be firm.
Once a ghost is aware that it can reach you, it may not have a sense of personal boundaries and will try to talk your ear off. When the ghost appears, use a firm, calm voice (both inner and audible) to compel it to depart. Be consistent; even if the ghost returns in a more compelling form, repeat your desire for it to stop talking to you.

2 Block inner channels.
If you have been hosting séances or other reaching-out activities, cease them immediately. Imagine a happy, soothing "place of peace," and think of it anytime thoughts of death or spirits begin to well up in your mind.

3 Stay busy.
Ghosts in search of human connection may glom onto those with excessive spare time. Spend more time at work and develop a more active social life.

4 Move.
Many ghosts are moored to a particular location. Relocate to a new place, ensuring first that it is not built over the site of an old burial ground or abandoned mental hospital.

5 Satisfy their requests.
Perform whatever action the ghost is asking you specifically to do, such as returning the gold you stole and thought no one knew about or reburying his improperly interred body.

ALIENS

How to Survive an Alien Abduction

1 Remain calm.

Aliens who abduct human beings rarely exert permanent physical harm on their victims. The best strategy is to remain calm and endure the experience without resistance.

2 Cover your eyes.

Press the inside of your elbow tightly over your face to shield your eyes from the painfully bright white lights that accompany abduction.

3 Focus on remaining conscious.

Nearly all abductees are rendered insensible during the period of abduction and only recover the memory later. Maintain active awareness by pinching yourself or digging your nails into your thighs. Chant, "I am awake, I am alive, I am awake, I am alive," as you are tractor-beamed or ushered up the staircase of light that leads onto the ship.

4 Be observant.

Noting every aspect of the ship's interior, including the color and shape of the aliens themselves, will distract your mind from its terror and increase your ability to later communicate the details of your experience.

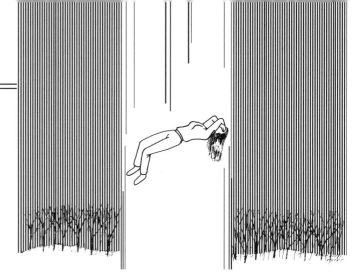

Remember to shield your eyes from the blinding lights of alien technology.

5 Be cooperative.

Obey the aliens' instructions, which may range from removing your false teeth to learning an alien language or even making love to an alien.

6 Call someone.

When the aliens deposit you back on Earth, immediately contact a friend or law-enforcement official to report your experience. The longer you wait, the less likely you are to be believed.

7 Spread the message.

Tell as many people as possible any warnings the aliens have asked you to communicate.

Close Encounters by Kind

ENCOUNTER NUMBER	DESCRIPTION	HOW YOU KNOW YOU'VE HAD ONE
Close Encounter of the First Kind (CE1)	Sighting of UFO.	You see strange lights or a flying saucer.
Close Encounter of the Second Kind (CE2)	UFO has effect on environment.	In presence of UFO, your car stalls or becomes superheated; you are paralyzed.
Close Encounter of the Third Kind (CE3)	Aliens emerge from UFO.	You see an alien being.
Close Encounter of the Fourth Kind (CE4)	Abduction.	You are brought aboard an alien ship, or you experience a gap in memory and wake with physical scars and painful and confusing memories.
Close Encounter of the Fifth Kind (CE5)	Human-initiated contact.	Using communication devices or telepathy, you send/receive messages with aliens.
Close Encounter of the Sixth Kind (CE6)	Alien attack.	After a CE2 or CE3, you have a major, life-threatening injury or are dead.
Close Encounter of the Seventh Kind (CE7)	Human-alien hybridization.	Following a CE4, you discover yourself pregnant with an alien baby.

How to Thwart an Alien Abduction

1 Hide your fear.
The extraterrestrial biological entity (EBE) may sense your fear and act rashly.

2 Control your thoughts.
Think of nothing violent or upsetting—the EBE may have the ability to read your mind. Try to avoid mental images of abduction (boarding the saucer, anal probes); such images may encourage them to take you.

3 Resist verbally.
Firmly tell the EBE to leave you alone.

4 Resist mentally.
Picture yourself enveloped in a protective shield of white light or in a safe place. Telepathic EBEs may get the message.

5 Resist physically.
Physical resistance should be used only as a last resort. Attack the EBE's eyes (if they have any)—you will not know what its other, more sensitive areas are.

BE AWARE!

- Abduction experiences generally follow a seven-step model: capture, examination, conference, tour, journey, return, and aftermath.

- People most likely to be abducted include those with a history of terrestrial abduction in their family, those living in wealthy Western countries, and those who have already been abducted by aliens.

- Some ufologists argue that UFOs come not from outer space but from another dimension, from the future, or from the center of the Earth.

Remain calm in the face of an alien presence. Use physical resistance only as a last resort.

How to Make a Tinfoil Hat

1 Measure your head.
Gather the dimensions of your scalp using a soft tape measure, measuring from the middle of your forehead to the base of your skull.

2 Unroll tinfoil.
Using clean, premium-brand foil that has not been used to wrap food, measure double the length from your forehead to skull, plus four inches. Detach the foil using the serrated edge of the box and fold the foil in half, shiny side facing out.

3 Mold the hat to your head.
Carefully place the sheet of foil over your head and scrunch it down to follow the shape of your skull, as would a shower cap or helmet. If any exposed scalp remains, attach additional pieces of foil to cover; adhere using clear tape.

4 At each temple, poke a quarter-inch hole on either side of the foil.

5 Create a chin strap.
Unroll an additional three-inch strip of foil and fold it over twice, creating a durable, double-folded chin strap.

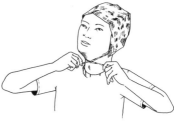

6 Thread the chin strap through the holes and attach with clear tape.

7 Don your hat.
Wear your hat anyplace and anytime you wish to screen your thoughts from extraterrestrial-alien, governmental, or other types of surveillance.

WARNING!

- Tinfoil hats are based on science: a layer of aluminum protects whatever lies beneath it from radio-frequency electromagnetic radiation.

- For maximum protection, wrap foil around not just the head, but the entire face and skull.

ACKNOWLEDGMENTS

David Borgenicht would like to thank his longtime editors, Jay Schaefer and Steve Mockus, for their tireless work on this book, as well as his talented co-authors Joshua Piven and Ben Winters, in addition to Victoria De Silverio, James Grace, Sarah Jordan, Piers Marchant, Dan and Judy Ramsey, Sam Stall, and Jennifer Worick. He would like to thank Mary Ellen Wilson, Jane Morely, John McGurk, and the rest of the team at Quirk for helping to pull this together. Finally, David would like to thank his grandfather, A. Wally Sandack, for his timeless survival advice: "You have to laugh, or you're f*cked."

ABOUT THE AUTHORS

David Borgenicht is a writer and publisher who lives with his family in Philadelphia. He is the coauthor of all the books in the *Worst-Case Scenario Survival Handbook* series.

Brenda Brown is an illustrator and cartoonist whose work has been published in many books and publications, including the *Worst-Case Scenario* series, *Esquire, Reader's Digest, USA Weekend, 21st Century Science & Technology*, the *Saturday Evening Post*, and the *National Enquirer*. Her Web site is www.webtoon.com

James Grace is coauthor of *The Worst-Case Scenario Survival Handbook: Golf*.

Sarah Jordan is coauthor of *The Worst-Case Scenario Survival Handbook: Parenting* and *The Worst-Case Scenario Survival Handbook: Weddings*.

Piers Marchant is coauthor of *The Worst-Case Scenario Survival Handbook: Life* and *The Worst-Case Scenario Almanac: History*.

Joshua Piven is the coauthor, along with David Borgenicht, of all the *Worst-Case Scenario Survival Handbooks*. He lives in Philadelphia with his family.

Dan and Judy Ramsey are coauthors of *The Worst-Case Scenario Pocket Guide: Retirement*.

Victoria De Silverio is coauthor of *The Worst-Case Scenario Pocket Guide: Breakups*.

Sam Stall is coauthor of *The Worst-Case Scenario Pocket Guide: Dogs*.

Ben H. Winters is coauthor of *The Worst-Case Scenario Pocket Guides* for *Cars, Cats, Meetings, New York City*, and *San Francisco*.

Jennifer Worick is coauthor of *The Worst-Case Scenario Survival Handbook: College* and *The Worst-Case Scenario Survival Handbook: Dating & Sex*.